HIDEOUS DREAM

A Soldier's Memoir of the US Invasion of Haiti

STAN GOFF

HIDEOUS DREAM

A Soldier's Memoir of the US Invasion of Haiti

STAN GOFF
Master Sergeant, U.S. Army,
Special Forces (Retired)

Soft Skull Press
2000

HIDEOUS DREAM
© 2000 Stan Goff
ISBN: 1887128-63-8

First Edition: December 2000

Cover Photograph: Robert Nickelsburg / Liaison Agency
Author Photograph: Nick Zlonis
Editorial: Nick Mamatas, Spencer Sunshine
Design: David Janik, Sander Hicks

PRINTED IN CANADA
by Kromar Printing Ltd., Winnipeg, Manitoba

For interactive information on this title and others of similar high
quality and daring, please see our situation on the world wide web:
www.softskull.com

SOFT SKULL

Radically Intelligent Aesthetics

CONTENTS

INTRODUCTION

I have only seen one book so far about the United States 1994 military invasion of Haiti. I've plodded on with my own description of the intervention, having banged out the first 400 pages or so of the initial draft while I was still seething from the experience, then taking months at a time when I couldn't stand the thought of writing about it again. The other book I have seen is *The Immaculate Invasion*.

I put off reading *The Immaculate Invasion*, Bob Shacochis's account of the 1994 mission in Haiti, for the same reasons I avoid reading books about Vietnam. I don't like stirring up past and painful emotions. I was also afraid it would color my own account—this account—or somehow distract me from completing it.

But Katherine Kean, a documentary film-maker, finally cornered me on the plane when we were headed back to Port-au-Prince, in 1999, and she gave me the damn thing. I ended up with a lot of dead time and nothing else to read, so I opened it.

The book jacket synopsis reads: *Based on eighteen months in the field in Haiti—where he bunked, ate, and dodged bullets as a non-combatant with a team of Special Forces commandos—Shacochis's book brings us the stories of the 'new military.' Here are the most highly trained and sophisticated warriors in history, deployed in a surreal war zone 'where there are no friends and no enemies, no front or rear, no victories and, likewise, no defeats, and no true end-*

*ings.' With the eye of a novelist, Shacochis captures the exploits and frustra-
tions, the inner lives, and the heroic deeds of young Americans as they struggle
to bring democracy to a country ravaged by tyranny. This is what it is like to be
a soldier in a military environment in which 'acceptable losses' has evolved to
mean 'no losses whatsoever.'*

I was one of those soldiers, the operations chief for a Special
Forces[1] team. I had an "on the ground" view of the "immaculate" invasion, but my movements were limited. Shacochis, however, was able
to move around freely, in and between the moving parts of the operations. Thus, his narrative and anecdotes felt like a complement to and
expansion of my own experience, and it resolved several mysteries for
me about just what in the hell was going on at headquarters. I appre-
ciated that aspect of the book.

But in other areas I was disappointed. Shacochis almost gets Haiti
right. He almost gets U.S. foreign policy. And he almost gets the military. The problem—as we used to say in the Army—is that "close"
only counts in horseshoes and hand grenades. It's what he misses or
avoids, or denies, that most needs to be said. And in not saying it, he
collaborates in Haiti's isolation and oppression. He collaborates in the
deeply racist characterization of Haiti as deviant and incapable of self-
governance. And finally he collaborates in justifying U.S. foreign policy and in perpetuating the pathological U.S. ideology of militarism.

"In a country as fucked up as Haiti," he begins on the first page,
"you had to wrap your hands around the throat of everything—the
language, the music, especially the songs and potent rhythms of the
songs, because in the people's centuries-old war against the tyrants,
drums were weapons, words were deadly ammunition."

At other points in the book, I felt that the heavies were not just
Haitian tyrants, but the Haitian people themselves. The masses of
Haitian townspeople and peasants become the exotic backdrop for
Shacochis' adventure. What's on display is the intrepid journalist and
his facility with the English language. What's not on display is the
dominant U.S. role in Haitian economic, political, and social life since

---

[1] A subset of the United States Special Operations Command and the United States
Army Special Operations Command, active duty Special Forces is a Regiment divided
into five "Groups," each Group consisting of three Battalions, each Battalion consisting
of three line companies and a Headquarters Company, each company divided into a
Headquarters team (B Team) and six 12-man Operational Detachments (A Teams).
Each Groups has responsibility to operate in a particular Theater (3rd Group, for
instance, has Sub-Saharan Africa and the Caribbean). The missions of Special Forces,
by doctrine, are Special Reconnaissance, Direct Action, Foreign Internal Defense, and
Unconventional Warfare. The A Detachment is designed and trained specifically to
work directly with "indigenous" forces, military, partisan, or civilian. Special Forces is
often incorrectly referred to as the Green Berets because of its distinctive headgear.

the turn of the century. The U.S. is absolved.

I will grant that Shacochis catches the cadence and the idiom of Creole and culture. He also took the trouble to learn something about military organization, protocol, procedure, and policy—something that the vast majority of journalists get way wrong. He gives wonderful descriptions of the markets, the slums, the countryside, the roads, the music, the bourgeois bars. His scenes are detailed and amplified by his poetry to the point of being almost rococo. But in all his devoted attention to the trees, he fails to see the forest. Furthermore, by emphasizing all that is dramatic in Haiti, he obscures the more pedestrian evidence—economic and historical evidence—that renders Haiti and its people more like us, his North American readers, more comprehensible, less exotic, less "the Other."

"In a country as fucked up as Haiti. . . ", "How the Haitians seemed to accept fucked-upness as an essential condition." The theme is repeated again and again. Haitians as exotic. Haitians as perverse. Haitians as incompetent. On leaving Haiti, Shacochis writes that "the nation was in a shambles, and what was there to hope for now? People were beginning to say, Maybe the price of democracy is too high. Haiti had no jobs to give its sons and daughters." In other words, Haitians don't seem ready for "democracy" or to feed themselves. The reality, which Shacochis misses, is that the U.S. mission was never to "restore democracy" nor economic development but only to stabilize existing class relations, with a co-opted Aristide to provide a nationalist-democratic facade. He never understood that the US was calling the shots before, during, and after the invasion.

"The government had proved incapable of either reforming or privatizing its corrupt monopolies." First, the state "monopolies" are not inherently corrupt, as the first 7 months of Lavalas administration[1] demonstrated. Secondly, it wasn't that the government was "incapable" of "reforming or privatizing" them. It was that the Haitian masses have fought tooth and nail the "improvements" Shacochis touts.

---

[2] A popular movement of peasants, workers, and some sectors of small business in Haiti. Began in the "ti egliz," or little church, as the network of Catholic parishes advocating for the poor, are called. Combined elements of liberation theology with Haitian nationalism, and opposed the autocratic system left behind by the 1915-1934 United States Marine occupation of Haiti, of which Francois "Papa Doc" Duvalier was an emblem though only one in a series of autocrats. The word "lavalas" means flood. It was popularized by Father Jean-Bertrand Arisitde, who emerged as the national leader of the Lavalas Movement, was elected President of Haiti in its first open election in 1990, took office in 1991, and was deposed in a violent coup d'etat eight months later. Each person, said Aristide, is like a mere drop of rain, and therefore insignificant by herself. But the combination of many drops of rain can be unified into a cleansing flood--lavalas.

"Lavalas has divided like an amoeba, each cell at the other's throat." A colorful metaphor, but hardly enlightening about a complex and unpredictable political struggle.

And then there is Shacochis, the agnostic. "[A]n epidemic of assassinations had been orchestrated by—depending on who was raking through the evidence—Aristide, the oligarchic families on the mountaintop, or the CIA." You see, Shacochis is really not sure who is the aggressor and who is the victim. He shrugs when asked to decide who is behind Haiti's current "insecurity": Aristide or the CIA. This is how he cleverly defends the U.S. low intensity war against Haiti. While posturing as a critic, in reality he defends the empire.

Shacochis was taken in by a Special Forces (SF) detachment, literally and figuratively. He was "saved" from the angry masses (when he was unwisely hanging out inside a hated FAd'H (*The Force Armee d'Haiti*) caserne with *de facto* criminals) by ODA 311 (the SF team), so he repaid them—and all of SF—by papering over their ugly side and accentuating their perceived "professionalism and courage."

ODA 311 allowed him to encamp with them at the Limbé caserne. They obviously sensed his profound paranoia about Haitian crowds and his inexperience with combat. They fed his paranoia with dramatics I could spot even in a second-hand account. They were both playing with him and doing the Special Forces macho-narcissistic strut. He bought it, and the book became an apology for SF. This latent Tom Clancy tendency contaminates the entire read. It becomes an awful nod to militarism and chauvinism, the flip side of his irrational fear of and contempt for the Haitians, for whom he simultaneously declares his compassion.

His portrait of ODA 311 is not without value. His humanization of the team members is important. People who oppose the military, for whatever reason, tend to stereotype military life and service members, and this polemical bent hurts their credibility and their ability to understand how things actually work. Military apologists are quick to dehumanize soldiers by stripping them of anything that is sinister. Military opponents dehumanize them by simplifying soldiers into mindless robots or monsters. Either distortion gives us—the soldiers—a degree of separation from what is recognizable in the lives of non-soldiers. It reduces us to an Other, as Shacochis did the Haitians, which opens the door to shortcut thinking.

Shacochis gives a very true picture of the fundamental incompetence of General David Meade, the conventional commander who was placed at our head to torment us during Operation Uphold Democracy; of the ersatz brilliance and idiosyncratic millenarianism of Colonel Mark Boyatt, the Special Forces commander; and of the collective personality of an A-Detachment. But he never asks the question, why SF?

Special Forces are designed for deployment into "politically sensitive" environments. They are older than regular troops. They hold higher security clearances. They are accustomed to working in concert with agencies like the State Department and their CIA-controlled political sections. You can put them at the end of a rope, then jerk the rope around, and they keep to themselves. They don't freak out and shoot people as readily as young soldiers, so they are less apt to create "incidents."

His love for the men of Special Forces and his apologetic tendency on their behalf lead Shacochis to conclusions that are spookily reminiscent of right-wing critiques of the Vietnam invasion. The military, he seems to say, was being hobbled on a righteous mission by the infighting and maneuvering of politicians. Historical myopia, I suppose.

The people in the military need their rationalizations, too. It's the only way they can continue to do what they do—which has never in U.S. history had anything to do with guaranteeing democracy or human rights, and has always had to do with the business of business. The uniform I wore and that Shacochis's friends wore is imbued with an outrageous and unearned prestige to keep people in it. Sometimes we are asked to murder. Sometimes we are asked to die. My own troops whined pitifully when they understood the Haiti mission would not net them a merit badge that is sewn over the left breast pocket, a piece of embroidered cloth, one by three inches. They would risk death for it, but not for other human beings. Our minds are that colonized, but the real role of the military as an institution is to enforce the will of the dominant class in the U.S. and to continue bankrolling the bloated trade in military hardware. Military Capitalism.

He ascribes the apparent stasis of the operation to competing tensions, to the unrelenting impasse of competitive politics, civil and military. But the truth is, the operation went exactly as it was supposed to. It was a tightrope walk to re-install a co-opted, defanged Aristide. We were pawns, and our mission—the one truly consistent mission—was not democracy, but stability.

To his credit, Shacochis did recognize the hypocrisy of the U.S.

mission with regard to FRAPH[3], and he did make the connections. He was rightly enraged by Task Force Commander Admiral Miller's minimizing the September 30th attack by FRAPH on a crowd of pro-Aristide demonstrators in Port-au-Prince. Shacochis spotted the dissembling of the U.S. Embassy. He was bowled over by the official military policy—which was handed down to me and with which I never complied, leading in part to my expulsion—that FRAPH was to be treated as the "legitimate political opposition."

Shacochis can't see that this directive made perfect sense. The mission was never to restore popular power. It was to put Aristide's face on a neoliberal fraud. Lavalas was a movement with real potential to be mobilized, and the U.S. could not provide the counter-balance even with its monstrous military forces. Bad publicity. Huge political minefield. But by rehabilitating the FRAPH and giving them a little slack in their leash, the U.S. could blunt the power of Lavalas. . . and eventually split it.

The author seemed surprised when he learned that the directive to define FRAPH as a "political party" came to Special Forces directly from Clinton's staff at an embassy briefing. If he'd have drifted past Fort Liberté for a chat, I would have told him that straight up. My own men protested when I began telling Haitians in our sector that this was clearly a ploy by the U.S. government and that it stank of CIA. But I had worked out of embassies before—in Guatemala in '83 and El Salvador in '85—and this was not some new maneuver. My own warnings to the Haitians were characterized during the investigation the Army launched against me as "seditious."

The teams were in on it, too. Bob Shacochis so fell in love with his team that he began omitting and ignoring things about them that would portray them as less heroic. I have seen copies of letters from team sergeants, contacting the local FRAPH, soliciting and offering assistance in identifying and rooting out the "Lavalas communists." Here were some team sergeants and team leaders who really understood their mission, who had read between the lines.

The description of ODA 311 dumping a mentally ill man in the

---

[3] An acronym for the Allied Front for Progress in Haiti, FRAPH is phonetically the same as the French word for a blow. Composed of military, former military, and members of the former Tonton Macoutes, FRAPH was a network of right-wing death squads that was strengthened in the wake of the 1991 coup d'etat against Aristide. FRAPH's principle purpose, which it pursued with determination, was to annihilate the Lavalas Movement. It functioned as a kind of secret police on behalf of the Cedras regime. It was headed by Emmanuel "Toto" Constant, who also worked as an agent for the United States Central Intelligence Agency.

country just to be rid of him in town is harrowing. Shacochis inadvertently exposes his heroes here. Did he realize the team would not have done the same thing to a white man? The essential colonial cruelty of several SF members comes through starkly, but Shacochis whitewashes it with pro-American pathos.

His own presence and the fairly unusual presence of an African-American team member served to drive the racism of the white team members underground. But it's there. Racism is the dirty little secret of Special Operations. Special Forces members often see themselves as the last bastion of white male supremacy. He de-racialized the SF contempt for Haitians as a mass—sadly, I think—as he does with his own contempt for Haitians. He actually repeats the epithet "boukie" in his narrative, never understanding that this is how it begins. We have to dehumanize "them." It was "gooks" in Korea and Vietnam. It was "ragheads" in Iraq. It was "the skinnies" in Somalia.

After reviewing an incident when I'd gone off one of my team members for using the term "nigger-rigged," Army's investigators looking into my activity in Haiti, asked if I really thought SF was a racist organization. I did. I still do. My own experience leads me to believe that two-thirds of the organization's members harbor clearly white supremacist beliefs.

But Shacochis seems oblivious. He gives a very sympathetic account of ODA 344, Master Sergeant Frank Norbury's team. I knew Norbury and his team. Our team rooms in Bragg were 25 feet apart. We were both Military Free Fall parachute teams, and we jumped together. Back in Fort Bragg, ODA 344 had its own T-shirts. The "344" was written with the two 4's as SS lightening bolts. Shacochis probably never saw the T-shirts, but if he went to the team house in St. Marc, as he said he did, then he couldn't help but notice the same Nazi "344" carved prominently in the wooden support column at the front of the house. Given Shacochis's keen eye for detail, his failure to mention this in his narrative is very curious. Was it an oversight, or did this fascist graffiti not "fit" into his portrait?

I was back in Haiti in December 1995, on leave, and dropped by 344's team house in St. Marc. Frank had taken to entertaining himself by shooting neighbors' cats, dogs, and chickens with a pellet pistol. Their team had been the first to train Haiti's new Palace Guard, and they all agreed proudly that their "boys" would be in charge of the next coup. But I guess they talk and act differently toward one of their own than they do with a reporter. My own expulsion had been buried, and the word wasn't out yet that I had become politically unreliable.

"Fuckin' boukies!" I'd hear time and again from 344. Again, they were stripping the Haitians of their humanity. The population had to be redefined as animals. Shacochis should be made to understand, because in my opinion, he erected the same barrier, albeit with a compassionate facade.

He took an emotional nose dive when ODA 311, at the behest of commanders, eagerly initiated an operation that rousted the entire population of Limbé as retribution for the murder of a FAd'H lieutenant. His dismay, combined with his blind allegiance to the standard lines—about democracy, about SF, and about Haiti—threw him into a funk. His liberal moral universe broke down. Sometimes reconciliation and justice just can't co-exist. Sometimes the only solution left to people is revolutionary violence. And revolutionary solutions cannot be attained within the convenient and fundamentally anti-revolutionary boundaries of existing orders.

This is the fundamental point Shacochis never gets. Our mission in Haiti was to stop a revolution, not a coup d'état. *The Immaculate Invasion* obscures this, and that is my main problem with the book. We were deployed to Haiti not to protect or restore democracy, but to protect class privilege and to prevent the inevitable popular uprising that would have come in the invasion's stead. Bill Clinton and the global economic elite he represents wanted to fold Haiti into the New Economic World Order. So far they have failed, not due to Haitian exoticism, fucked-upness, ignorance of democracy, emotionalism, nor government incompetence. It is due to popular resistance. . . democratic resistance.

This account—which may be seen after this introduction as a counter-account—can not aspire to the stylistic beauty of Shacochis. I am an old soldier, but a novitiate writer. So I give it to him now. His book is better art. But on Haiti, we don't need a lot more art. This is written on its own merits with its own flaws. The only thing that may counter-pose it to the other book about the invasion is this introduction. *The Immaculate Invasion* stirred a lot in me, and it gave me a point of departure to begin to introduce this offering.

I shall be glad to be rid of it, this book, to give it to you, whomever you are. It's yours now. You take this tangle of impressions and shocks and connections, and you do with it what you need to do with it. I'm tired of wading around in these aging emotions, so you freshen them up. I've got to move on.

Before I turn this narrative over to you, however, I have to say a few thank-you's. That seems to be what people do in introductions, and the people I have to thank deserve it. The first is Mike Gallante. You'll find out who he is in the narrative, but without the copies of his little journal, I could have never untangled the dates nor remembered some of the details. And Mike stuck. He never rolled over. Then there are Katherine Kean, and Kim Ives, and Dan Coughlin, and the folks with the PPN—you know who you are—who encouraged me when I hid behind my excuses. There's Nick Mamatas, too, who decided to be a booster for this, who was willing to take the chance that a former Green Beret might write something worthwhile, and who labored mightily to discipline my slipshod prose. Then there's the person who covered for me when I was wrapped up in it, who defends me unconditionally every time I am right, who forced me to maintain a connection to the real world, and who saved me more than she'll ever know with the words, "Are you all right?" That would be Sherry Long-Goff, who some would describe as my wife, but who I describe as my lover, my friend, and my comrade.

Of course, there are millions more. They toil and wait and resist. They are the granddaughters and grandsons of rebel slaves. I thank the heroic Haitian people.

Stan Goff
May, 2000

Since Cassius first did whet me against Caesar
I have not slept.
Between the acting of a dreadful thing
And the first motion, all the interim is
Like a phantasma or hideous dream.
The Genius and the mortal instruments
Are then in council; and the state of a man,
Like to a little kingdom, suffers then
The nature of an insurrection.

—Brutus

—William Shakespeare
Julius Caesar
II.i, 63-69

1 :The Emotional Attachment

I was arrested on the tenth of December. It was a very kind arrest, as arrests go. There were no handcuffs. My face wasn't jammed into a wall or the quarter panel of a car. No cop took a cheap shot at my nuts while he conducted a cursory search. It was a stealth arrest, one might say, because I wasn't ever told I was under arrest, but the situation was clear. I was being detained and transported back to Port-au-Prince. So was my detachment commander.

Don't expect exciting combat tales. Definitely don't expect any Tom Clancy. Clancy, the darling of closet fascists everywhere, always has been and always will be full of shit. This is just the account of a journey that took a misplaced man to the oxymoronically named town of Fort Liberte, in the most misunderstood nation in the Western Hemisphere.

I could back up and make more sense of this account. I should. I should begin where we were the best team in 3rd Special Forces by some reckoning, though all that is subjective. Nonetheless, it would add to the overwhelming sense of paradox. Layers of paradox that you could peel off like an onion, and if you are the sensitive type, each layer might bring tears to your eyes. You could start on the outside, with the paradox of the most powerful army in the world for the

1

nation with the least legitimate need for one. From there, you could look at the contradiction of Special Forces, the last artisan class in the army, a kind of guild, resisting the Taylorization that has reduced every other job in the army to a list of identifiable tasks plugged into a list of algorithms. Beneath that, there is the mission—a force sent to reintroduce a democracy where their own countrymen had been intimately involved in erasing it three years earlier, with the aim of nullifying the replacement with what it had replaced, in order to legitimize erasing it again, to make way for new replacements.

Then there was 3rd Special Forces, a tool in the hands of a slightly inspired, slightly mad, mercurial, quietly egomaniacal commander, who himself never understood the roots of the situation. Neither did I, of course, and there I was two layers in, leading a team with a commander who grew up on the streets of Philly, a half-Iranian, half-German, quintilingual Elvis impressionist, two Puerto Ricans, one chickenshit Dominican (no disrespect to all other Dominicans intended), one third generation Hungarian who fantasized about a race war, a Mexican who had just sent his wife to Texas so he could move in with his girlfriend, a Cajun, and a redneck who was waiting to be chaptered out of the army for failing the weight standard. All the way in the middle was me. Forty-three, a dinosaur by Special Forces standards. In my eighth official conflict area, though I had seen active combat in only three. A raw nerve in what passed for my conscience extended back through Vietnam and past. I already thought of myself as a kind of generic socialist, though I really had no clear idea what that meant. Believe me, any kind of a red at all is a paradox in Special Forces. And I really don't put myself in the center because I'm in love with myself or anything. It's just to point out that this account is from that singular point of view, so the reader will be traveling out through all that onion.

Back to the arrest. Mike Gallante, my captain and the nominal commander of Detachment 354, and I were met at our house in Fort Liberte by two army Majors. They'd driven out from Company Headquarters in Cap Haitien. We knew Major Fox. He was our next in command for this mission. The other guy was a total stranger. They told us to be quiet and read us our rights. That got our attention, I can tell you. We probably blanched for an instant. Getting your rights read to you will stimulate a fight or flight response every time. Then they read off a list of accusations, while Mike and I stood stock-still and expressionless. Most of them were either silly or pure bullshit, but a couple of them were quite true. . . though neither of us had ever thought of them as charges before. We were searched, politely but sternly. Our quarters were searched. Once they had scattered our belongings on the floor to go through our foot lockers and our duffel bags and the wicker hampers we had bought from the locals, they told us to pack up everything and put it on their Humvee. They prohibited us from talking with any of our men. We were relieved, they told us, pending the results of an Article 15-6 investigation. And off they whisked us to Cap Haitien.

News of the investigation spread like wildfire, and rumors proliferated like mushrooms after a four-day rain. Many people had considered us to be the most competent, the most together team in 3rd Special Forces. We had invented ourselves out of disarray, made local legends of ourselves through streamlined planning and the most brutal regimen of training over the preceding six months that anyone had seen in years. We were always tired, always dirty, always integrating task after mastered task into a cumulative goal, always pushing the envelope of physical risk. We had a reputation. Motivated soldiers on other teams tried to gain transfers to our team.

Lieutenant Colonel Gary Jones, our Battalion Commander, told me, even as he was reviewing our charges before we were ejected from Haiti, that we had demonstrated the greatest combat focus of any team he had ever seen.

I was a budding ideologue when they sent me to Haiti. It would be dishonest for me to say that I developed a radical's point of view after I worked there. It makes a nice story, ingenuous soldier is confronted with contradictions, experiences epiphany, but it's not true. I was already deeply into a radicalization process, a long, slow one that had started in Vietnam. I am a very slow learner. I was a budding ideologue, and I acted on my own political understanding, flawed and incomplete as it was, often in the face of clear intent to the contrary from the Task Force commanders.

We did, nonetheless, make a difference, in a small way, for a short time, before my team rebelled against me and my rebellions against the Task Force reached their inevitable conclusion. I ignored one of my own favorite maxims in the execution of my duties as the senior enlisted supervisor of my own team: One only rules by the consent of the governed. Not only did I openly declare my sympathy for Lavalas and the stated goals of the Aristide government. . . not only did I openly declare my antipathy for the direction of US foreign policy past and present. . . I ruled the team with an iron fist, and tried to bend them to the task of supporting a genuine change in Haiti, (creatively) within the policies and parameters laid down by our commanders.

Based on an information vacuum with regard to Haiti, my understanding of its history and its role vis a vis the United States was very sketchy. I therefore developed a naive emotional attachment to the idea that I was to be involved in a liberation. A liberation. It's almost a perfect word, liberation. Musical and intoxicating. That naiveté and that intoxicated attachment were combined with a stunning ignorance of Haitians. So I made a lot of mistakes. . . not with regard to the official mission—I knew from early on that I was in a state of sin on that account—but with regard to my own agenda, ill defined as it was. Captain Mike Gallante supported me, and I can honestly say that I never deceived him about my intentions or political leanings. The fact of the matter was, we worked well together. I had brought the team a long way, and he trusted me. So Mike allowed me to have my head, and it cost him his. Mike was not political, but he enjoyed seeing results, and during the initial phases of the operation, even given all the mistakes we made, we were astoundingly effective. In many ways, we charted the crazy course for this mission ourselves and took several other teams with us. I know for a fact that our actions were responsible for the role of jailers some teams adopted over the Haitian Armed Forces, which gave us immense credibility and rapport with the masses of poor Haitians. Mike Gallante's only "mistake" was listening to me. He trusted me, and it cost him his job and his career, and he never thought of making me a patsy, which he could have. He's an FBI agent somewhere in Tuscon now. And I'm a red. And even though I haven't seen Mike in several years, in my head, he is my friend. He trusted me, and he suffered for it, and he never held it against me. He behaved like an adult. . . even if he is now in a childishly wicked profession. I harp on this, because without Mike the mission to Fort Liberte could not have happened, and without many of the notes he kept on the mission, I could not have picked through the litter of my memory to get the story straight.

In all of it, we managed to have some very good days. Not many people can say they started the roundup and disarmament of the *chefs du seccion,* or that they once arrested the former Ambassador to France.

It was a hell of a ride.

2: RUMORS AND PROMOTIONS

Interview pursuant to Article 15-6 investigation of the action of Master Sergeant Stanley A. Goff, 500-58-5666, ODA 354, Company B, 2nd Battalion, 3rd Special Forces Group (Airborne) for actions taken during Operation Restore Democracy, September-December, 1994, in the Republic of Haiti. Investigating Officer: Major Robert McCoart. Interviewee: Master Sergeant Goff.

Are you anti-FRAPH?
Yes.
Why?
They're a death squad network.
According to the task force command, they are to be treated as the legitimate political opposition.
They're still death squads. Were we ordered to work with them, too?
No, you weren't ordered to work with them. But it sounds like you harassed them.

I first heard of the military plan to invade Haiti when I returned from the debacle in Somalia. That was October, 1993. The Governor's Island accord had established a deadline for the departure of the

Cedras de facto regime in Haiti. That deadline was 30 October.

George Bush had committed US troops to the task of "fixing" Somalia shortly before he was unelected. Some speculate that it was a sick practical joke he played on Bill Clinton. His fate was being read on the wall. The polls in late 1992 showed Mr. Bush to be about as popular as febrile diarrhea.

Most people remember how combat was avoided in the initial phases of the operation in Somalia, how a very successful "humanitarian" action was being executed. Eventually, of course, there had to be a reckoning with the warlords who had scavenged the food reserves of the population in order to feed the warriors. . . or that was the hype. I've never actually seen the military used for any higher moral purpose. There is always the bottom line, somewhere, somehow.

One of the most powerful militias was controlled by Mohammed Farah Aidid of South Mogadishu. This militia was held responsible for an ambush that killed 23 Pakistanis in 1993. The UN response, headed by the 10th Mountain Division, of the United States Army, was to attack a building in the middle of town where they suspected Mr. Aidid of hiding. The attack was executed with helicopter gunships, and dozens of civilians were killed. So the Pakistanis were embittered toward Aidid forces, and the Aidid forces as well as many relatives of the dead civilians in South Mogadishu were embittered toward Americans.

Aidid's well-armed militia then took to shooting mortars and rockets at American positions. Mr. Aidid was declared Public Enemy No. 1. It was time to call on Special Operations, specifically the components of the Joint Special Operations Command (JSOC), which included Army Counter-Terrorist teams (Delta), Rangers, Air Force paramedic search and rescue teams, and the specially trained aviators, crews and support troops of the 160th Special Operations Aviation Regiment.

In August, 1993, the Special Operations Task Force was ordered to Somalia with the mission of capturing Aidid. I was part of that task force, until a conflict with an obtuse captain culminated in my redeployment to the United States in September. Perhaps it was a blessing in disguise.

On the 3rd of October, the Special Operations Task Force conducted a raid, using a plan that had been executed repeatedly in former raids (violating the dictum against setting patterns), in broad daylight (violating the dictum to use our technology to its best advantage), sliding down ropes onto (as in directly on top of) a militia armed on a par with any of the old players from Beirut (thanks to weapons infusions from the US and Soviet Union). The "ignorant bush negroes", as I had heard them referred to (violating the dictum to never underestimate your enemy), failed to throw up their hands and surrender to the well fed, well supplied, well muscled, high-tech task force. Instead they shot down two helicopters with rocket propelled grenades, a bold and elementary act that was the first in an armed drama that lasted over ten hours.

Eighteen Americans were killed, forty more wounded. In turn, they killed and wounded an unconfirmed number of Somali militiamen (estimates from 100-400), and hundreds of civilians.

American bodies were dragged through the streets in front of news cameras, and an American prisoner (one of the aforementioned specially trained pilots) was trotted out for the media by Aidid forces.

The Clinton administration was blamed, in particular the Secretary of Defense, Les Aspin. Bob Dole, who had been holding his tongue in case the mission turned out to be a success, began making demands for the immediate withdrawal of American forces. He conveniently ignored the fact that it had been his party's man, Curious George Bush, who had committed us to the Strategic Horn of Africa in the first place. Here was the fire-breathing Republican hawk demanding that we run away in the face of determined resistance. It was the most startling sort of demagogy.

Between the shock of seeing American corpses being desecrated and the hypocritical pronouncements of the politicos, the immediate business of American foreign policy became a withdrawal from Somalia. Thousands of lives were lost in Somalia to war and famine. Hundreds of civilians had been killed and maimed in the great firefight of October 3rd. They weren't American lives, so they had no value in the final account.

The invasion of Haiti was tabled. Temporarily.

I had some initial doubts that we'd have the political will to stage an operation into Haiti after the Somalia episode. Moreover, it seemed too simply a decent thing to do. The anti-African sentiment of white America would not permit it. There was no petroleum to liberate from states run by former clients. There were no significant American business interests to protect from wild-eyed, revolutionary, anti-colonial peasants. There was no nation whose sovereignty we needed to violate to arrest an alleged drug dealer. Just a country that had elected a government which was ousted by the military. My thinking was simpler then.

Word of the operation leaked, as it always does. The Haiti Option became general knowledge in the Regiment. There were misgivings.

"I'm not touchin' 'em. They all got the AIDS."

"They worship the devil."

"Let's invade with a neutron bomb and turn that motherfucker into a parking lot."

"Where is Haiti? Ain't that in South America?"

I supported the idea of "liberating" Haiti. This made me the tiniest minority in the "Special Ops" community. One of the most exalted statesmen for the Special Operations community is Senator Jessie Helms. Helms, the man who referred to the University of North Carolina at Chapel Hill as the "University of Niggers and Communists," who staunchly supported Salvadoran death squad chieftain, Roberto D'Abuisson, who associated with Cuban gusano terrorists, was, in 1993 and 1994, participating in the character assassination of Jean-Bertrand Aristide. His partners in this effort were members of the Central Intelligence Agency and the Haitian military. Aristide was being portrayed as a foaming, homicidal lunatic. More than a few journalists were ready, willing, and able to act as Aristide slanderers, parroting every unexamined rumor generated by the Haitian military. His economic pronouncements ran counter to the "end of history" thesis popular among capitalist triumphalists. Aristide, for his part, had the audacity to repeatedly call attention to the fact that the US government had historically aligned itself with the most undemocratic forces in Haiti for the last two centuries. The wiry little cleric seemed doomed to continue his exile. That was fine with most of the Special Operations community. Based on my own experience with diplomats and journalists, both of whom I had learned to generally abhor, I found Aristide to be an immensely attractive character.

In spite of my initial doubts, my personal assessment, which I will repeat here because my prognostications are so seldom correct, was that the administration would finally have no choice but to settle the Haiti question by force. Clinton was forced into his first reversal on a foreign policy pronouncement on the question of Haitian immigrants/refugees. Haitians were bailing off the island in ever increasing numbers. We found ourselves in a position where we had to quarter, contain, and nourish the refugees. It was increasingly difficult to justify every Cuban who washed ashore as a political exile, and every Haitian as an opportunist looking for a good job driving a taxi in Miami. Cedras and company were defiantly and gleefully intimidating, beating, jailing and murdering political opponents and bystanders in ways that even our press could hardly ignore. The de facto regime thumbed its nose at the Governor's Island Accord, and showed no inclination to cave into anything less than an invasion. When we floated a contingent of so-called monitors on the USS Harlan County, they were run off by a group of lightly armed FRAPH thugs talking shit on the docks. As it turned out, FRAPH's leader, Emmanuel "Toto" Constant, was a paid employee of the United States Central Intelligence Agency, and the Chief Spook from the US Embassy—John Kamborian—was overseeing this whole charade. And the Congressional Black Caucus had correctly pointed to the racist assumptions underpinning the peculiarities of immigration policy directed at Haitians. The easiest solution, for Clinton, I thought, the one that could demonstrate presidential will, was to simply throw out Cedras, Inc. and reinstate the elected government. Voila! No "political" refugee questions. No disparity in immigration policy. No Florida politicians whining about a flood of "undesirables." No threats from an essentially anti-Republican black electorate who was growing restive in the face of one spineless capitulation after another. No more intangible, draft-dodging, wimp factor. Invasion was not so much a decision as an inevitability.

I just didn't want to go myself.

Somalia had scared the shit out of my wife of less than a year. My body was rebelling, with a different twinge and tweak every day, against over two decades of rucksacks, runs, parachute landing falls, falls into holes and creek beds in the middle of the night, abusive physical training habits, selection through torture courses, vehicle accidents, fights (in and out of combat), exposure to every pathogen known to humankind, et cetera, et cetera. . . and I wanted an easy job. I wanted to go to school. I wanted to feather my nest for my upcoming retirement. I wanted to spend time with my wife and three stepchildren. I wanted to coast through the two years remaining on my current enlistment in my comfortable family housing in Ft. Benning, where I was within a mile and a half of any conceivable necessity, and ten minutes away from the boat ramp at Uchee Creek on the Chatahootchee River. My wife was happily enrolled in college. The kids had acquired a smorgasbord of friends in the neighborhood. The dog, a black mutt perversely named Whitey by my stepdaughter, had successfully insinuated himself into the house on a semi-permanent basis. I had arranged for a job in a training unit to escape the pressure cooker of the Regiment and the possibility of deployment to hostile fire areas.

I had received a promotion from Sergeant First Class to Master Sergeant. This was a raise, and a welcome event in my household. My wife, Sherry, helped pin on the stripes and kissed me soundly in front of the soon to be estranged Rangers. We were in a very good mood. Life was looking up. I received my orders to go to the School of the Americas (where a procession of business friendly despots have received their training in suppression of the democratic impulse) only a few days later. No more stupid "high and tight" haircut, mandatory with the Rangers. No more conflicts. I was to become a faceless cog, cheerfully sabotaging the doctrinal understanding of a parade of Latin American gangsters, as the calendar pages dropped away.

When I reported in to the School, however, another Master Sergeant, the acting sergeant major of the training branch, promptly and coldly informed me that I had no job. He had no place for an E-8 (the pay grade of a master sergeant) in his organization. I had applied for the job, so to speak, when I was still an E-7. So, in a nutshell, my promotion disqualified me for the SOA job. I was now overqualified to pseudo-train the henchmen of Latin American despots. Master sergeants were not needed to refine our Southern Allies' ability to deal with dangerous elements, like peasants' cooperatives, literacy programs, labor organizers, student unions, and (most feared of all) the demonic Maryknoll Order of nuns.

Being a Master Sergeant did one other thing to me. It changed my job description within the Special Forces career management field. I was no longer considered a medic by the bean counting computers in Alexandria, Virginia. I was an Operations Sergeant. I spoke to my branch representatives at the Pentagon on the phone. My options were to terminate Special Forces status, and be sent post-haste to Korea for 13 months, or to return to Ft. Bragg, North Carolina to be a team sergeant on a Special Forces A Team.

I struggled with these options for a while, and eventually accepted the team sergeant destiny. I would return to 7th Special Forces, go back to work on missions in Latin America and make some travel money. It would give Sherry, the kids, and me a little nest egg to start our civilian lives together.

7th Special Forces was full on E-8s. 3rd Special Forces is where I would be going.

I begged my branch representative in Alexandria. I offered sexual favors. I pleaded. I lied.

Third Special Forces had the reputation as the stingiest, most ill equipped, ill managed, regulation-bound group in Special Forces. Third Group had more requests for reassignment processed every year than any other two groups combined. I had never spoken with a single member of Third Special Forces who expressed satisfaction at being assigned there. Moreover, Third's areas of operations were Sub-Saharan Africa and the Caribbean. Haiti.

In March, 1994, I signed into 3rd Special Forces Group (Airborne), Fort Bragg, North Carolina. I had spent from January until then running, rucksacking, lifting weights, reviewing doctrinal literature for SF, compiling information on counseling and evaluating subordinates, and reading up on Africa. Since the die was cast, I wanted to be a good team sergeant (unlike many I had seen), and I was hoping for a chance to go to an Africa-based battalion.

Sherry and the kids, Jessie, Jayme and Jeremy, were moved into a comfortable, roomy house a mile from post, in Fayetteville, North Carolina. Sherry was waiting for the summer semester to start at Fayetteville State University. The kids entered a school that was a mere four blocks away. The dog trotted through and through the house until it was inoculated with his scent to his satisfaction. I had my uniforms appropriately altered, new flashes sewn on two new green berets, and my field gear assembled and altered to suit my own idiosyncrasies.

Less than seven months later, my team entered Haiti.

While we were there, we took the first prisoners in Gonaives, found the first restaurant there, responded to food riots, played Robin Hood, chased crooks with machetes through the rabbit warrens of the neighborhoods, pied pipered thousands of people out of town one night, conducted a successful murder investigation, fired and appointed a mayor, arrested the Northeast department FRAPH president and the former Haitian Ambassador to France, had a Karaoke night with neighbors and children, tore down a FAdH outpost, repaired a street, interviewed hundreds of Haitians, handed out soccer balls, opened the courts, stimulated community watches, turned on electricity and running water, made speeches, arranged political meetings, responded to mass hysteria, and four wheeled, motorcycled or walked all over almost 1000 square kilometers.

I carried in a 110-pound rucksack and emotional baggage from as far back as Vietnam. Haiti was an opportunity for me to make amends. My passion to walk away from this mission with a clear conscience and a sense of having genuinely helped Haiti turned me into a kind of high strung bull terrier, growling and snapping at anything and anyone who threatened the integrity of our actions or the "desired-end-state": My desired end state. Those threats came from every quarter, it seemed. . . from the Haitian military, from the paramilitary forces, from the American military hierarchy in country, from the power vacuum created by our arrival, and finally from the apathy and hostility toward Haitians and the mission that my own people developed when the adrenaline wore off and the clock began to linger.

First, I had to go to work. Here's the story.

3: THE PROBLEM CHILDREN

An operations sergeant is typically referred to as the "team sergeant" or "team daddy." His personal appellation is "Top." He is the senior Non-Commissioned Officer (NCO) on a detachment (or Team, or A Team, or A Detachment. . . the terms are interchangeable), as well as the operations chief. As an NCO, he is held responsible for standard soldier stuff; discipline, accountability, individual training and morale. As the operations chief, he provides the plans for training and operations that support command directives and goals. He is primarily responsible to the detachment commander, a captain in most cases. He is perceived, in the best of all possible worlds, as the most sage and experienced member of the team, and the power behind the Detachment Commander's throne.

I was advised at the Group level, the Battalion level, and at the Company level, before I took the team, that my job was to "straighten out" this team. The perception was that the team had serious problems, and that a forty-two year old Master Sergeant with combat experience and a diverse background in "Special Ops" was just what was needed to do the job.

I was assigned to Operational Detachment Alpha—Three Five Four (ODA-354).

In the spirit of amor fati, I had resolved to invest my last drop of soldierly energy in this venture, and to get as much as possible out of my final assignment on active duty. I was in 3rd Group, the least popular of all Special Forces Groups, and I was back "on the line," leading now. I had made up my mind to be the best team sergeant I could, and to see the detachment through the best training I could plan and coordinate, and the Haiti mission, which I believed more each day to be inevitable. My participation was also now inevitable. Second Battalion's Area of Operational Responsibility (AOR) was the Caribbean. My new Detachment's AOR was the Dominican Republic, which shares the island with Haiti.

When I was assigned, the majority of the team was on leave, having just returned from a training mission in the Dominican Republic. The Battalion was planning an elaborate combat training exercise in Camp Mackall, a training post adjacent to Fort Bragg, used primarily for training Special Forces units. Captain Mike Gallante, the detachment commander, was walking around thoroughly deflated, having been recently reprimanded for the poor accountability of Communications Sergeant Ali Tehrani, who had lost some expensive solar battery chargers, and further reprimanded for "loss of control" at a live fire, where Fortino "Gonzo" Gonzales, the medic on the detachment, had executed a short rush with his M16 selector switch on automatic, his finger on the trigger, and his muzzle wandering, all egregious violations of the most fundamental firearms safety rules. He shot two people with ricochets. One of those people was Ali, who had a bullet fragment in the back of his leg. The other was Mike himself, the commander, who, according to the medical notes on his CAT Scan, had a "conical, cylindrical, metallic object" lodged in his head, above and behind the left eye.

Not only was Mike depressed by the general impression left with his commanders by irresponsible team members, but he felt he had lost control of the team. His eye was full of blood. His vision was impaired, and the doctors had told him to refrain from any strenuous activity to prevent breaking loose possible masses of clotted blood inside the globe of his left eye and causing permanent damage. This was a serious constraint on a former gymnast and varsity boxer at West Point, raised in South Philadelphia, and accustomed all his life to high levels of physical activity.

This was the happy circumstance of my arrival. The commander was under a cloud and physically impaired. The team members had recently demonstrated poor accountability and failure to apply the most rudimentary rules of firearms handling. The actual events on the live fire had been covered up by the team, even to the extent of destroying a videotape that showed Gonzo ripping off the uncontrolled burst while running with his finger on the trigger. A major evaluation exercise was looming. The team had only six people assigned who were available to conduct that training mission. One of them was assigned only days before me. . . a very nice guy, about 40 years old, a medic, with his own medical files thick as a rump roast, just coming off a three year stint as an instructor, and self-admittedly way out of shape. All in all, a delightful situation.

When I met what was available of the team, a mere two days before the mission (called an external evaluation, or EXTEV), I gave them a down and dirty introductory pitch: A synopsis of my professional autobiography; infantryman in Vietnam with a parachute brigade, squad leader in the 82nd Airborne Division, break in service to study English in college, cavalry scout with a tank battalion, Ranger squad leader, patrolling instructor at the Jungle School in Panama, assaulter-then sniper-with the army's counter-terrorist unit Delta, Military Science instructor at West Point, another break in service working for the Department of Energy training SWAT type units, Ranger platoon sergeant, then Special Forces Medic on an A detachment in 7th Group, and finally the short tour at the Ranger Regiment as the Regimental SF Medic. This list always seemed to impress, though it really just involved being caught in some kind of inexorable macho rut early in life. I was not, however, above using this resume as a trump card to establish dominance over both subordinate and supervisor.

I covered professional goals for the detachment. I told them they were going to Haiti, and that we were going to prepare for it. All of them looked a bit askance at this one. So I reassured them that preparing for this mission was identical to preparing for any mission. I re-emphasized that the team's primary operational focus was to be Special Reconnaissance (SR). For that, I explained, we would learn all the component skills to execute this mission. We would train on those skills until we were proficient at each one, then we would test the application of those skills in an actual exercise. The exercise we would systematically approach would be special reconnaissance (SR) launched with a Free Fall infiltration at night, followed by a rollover (when the mission is changed while the unit is still on the ground) into a Direct Action (DA).

It was a nice speech. Two days later I was in isolation with the team, planning for a full-blown exercise. I was still trying to remember everyone's name.

To make a long story short, I led the mission to the field. It was half-assed by Ranger standards, which are very high, but we overcame obstacles that the exercise directors set up for us with some aplomb. We also sent more information back than any other team in the Battalion. I found that by 3rd Group standards, we had performed superlatively. I kept the harsh critiques I had for my own performance and that of the team internal, and regarded it as a worthwhile learning experience.

During the exercise, I operated on the margins, as I have been wont to do. I antagonized an officer from the staff, "killed" an enemy squad as a method of breaking contact, was accused of "stealing" a helicopter (a charge that was a misunderstanding), and called a one kilometer (as opposed to 100 meter) square in as our location (believing, correctly as it turned out, that opposing forces were being given our locations in order to compromise us). The Battalion Commander sent out a team with the express purpose of eliminating us. That was the team we "killed."

All in all, the company commander lived in terror through the whole exercise that I was about to get him into trouble. Some of the Battalion Staff thought I was a smart-ass—a valid judgment. The Battalion Commander started referring to us as his "Killer Team," and detachment members throughout the Battalion were congratulating us for what was perceived to be a refreshing buccaneer spirit. The team was pleased. Ultimately, the company commander was pleased, because the Battalion Commander was pleased. Mike, who stayed behind on account of his eye, was pleased and upset he hadn't gone along.

Given our liabilities, it was a fairly auspicious start.

4: Race Odyssey

There is no way to discuss the issue of Haiti without discussing the issue of race. If the story of Haiti requires I write about Haiti's history from time to time, and some hints of my own history with race are likewise necessary. That experience continues to become richer with each passing day, but I had received a literal baptism by fire in the question of race in the former Republic of Vietnam.

It was March, 1994. The quorum was assembled in the team room, and I was holding court. Mike sat on the sidelines, almost as interested as the subordinates. He knew my general training philosophy, but he was becoming aware that I sometimes ad-libbed into gray areas without warning. As my ostensible supervisor, he could adopt the role of observer. . . watching my technique with a critical eye.

The subject was counseling, evaluation, and awards. I gave them a fairly standard pitch, promising to be brutally honest in counseling, but sufficiently generous on evaluations to make team members competitive on promotion boards provided they performed well in their jobs. Pretty standard stuff, actually. The boss takes charge firmly with assurances to subordinates that their interests will be looked out for.

Everyone understood the implications, with regard to training pace, of the ambitious plan I outlined. In the comfort and lethargy of the team room, they nodded easy agreement and believed that kind of demanding, strenuous work was what they'd wanted all along, after all.

"The next subject," I said, as they glanced at their watches, "is racism."

Not a single head jerked up with surprise, but they quit looking at their watches. The general reaction was subdued, like when someone passes gas in mixed company. A telepathic *Whathefuck?* crackled through the room. Eyes shifted ever so casually, betraying not a flutter of emotion. Mike was no longer merely observing. I had entered the "gray zone." I had the undivided attention of everyone in the room.

Racism is a word seldom used by Special Operations officialdom. I was about to discuss "the dirty little secret."

The policy had become a personal standard. I had repeatedly in my career found it necessary to state my prohibitions. I would not tolerate racism on the team, even if it was limited to racial epithets for people not represented in present company. Looks were exchanged when I spelled it out. I personalized it by stating that my family is multi-ethnic. With this declaration the policy seemed less a mere political position rammed down the throat of the unwilling. A cop-out, but that's what I did.

Race was an issue because in every assignment I have had in Special Operations, racism has been as much a part of the social bond as football and fast cars. I never cared for either of them either, but this was special.

I entered the army with a headful of Ayn Rand's smug, circular logic, and a flaccid, indolent, adolescent body. I rationalized the army and internalized the popular culture's masculine ideal (minus football and cars—I had trapped fur since I was twelve, though). I enlisted, intent on becoming a "Green Beret."

In basic training, I was summarily reduced to a slobbering, faint-hearted idiot by a plague of sadistic drill sergeants. How I recoiled from the practical reality of hard work, when my skinny limbs and tar-speckled lungs encountered true fatigue! Within one day, I wanted nothing more than to retreat to my home town, where I could fritter away the hours, bargaining with girls who had bad reputations, drinking beer, and trying to one-up my acquaintances in debates on topics we had no experience of.

With time, however, my body hardened, my bluster returned, I grew accustomed to being named Dickhead, and I recognized the ever clean, ever starched Drills as the embodiment of power.

When terrorism researchers named the Stockholm Syndrome, they patted themselves on the back for discovering that captives will eventually identify with their captors. Abusive husbands and Drill Sergeants have known this forever. So have battered wives and basic trainees. We even came to admire certain of our oppressors. Over half of my Drill Sergeants were black.

Now my ambivalence on race was mixing with my ignorance of the dynamics of power.

Like many white people, I equated racism with hatred. If I did not hate anyone simply because they were black (or any other shade), then I was not a racist. Actually, "racist" had not yet entered the popular lexicon. "Prejudiced" was the word. My limited intellectual constructions were so lashed to the dogma of Ayn Rand that racism, as a personal or institutional set of expectations—and especially as an economic construction—was a concept completely out of my reach. It was 1970, with the Civil Rights struggle still raging, with the anti-war movement taking off, and I completely missed what was going on around me.

Since black was the color of power in my new world, I accommodated myself to black. On the surface. But that's just a parcel of the truth. I was still a bigot about race, and everything else. Every door in my mind had been safely closed.

I quickly developed an affinity for one particular Drill, an African-American named Smith. He was immaculately pressed in the worst of conditions. He almost whispered when he chewed your ass. He was tall and slender, with chiseled features. His head was made for the campaign hat. He wore it with the brim fore and aft almost imperceptibly turned up. On his right shoulder, he wore a patch. A blue background, with a white wing carrying a red bayonet. Above the combat patch was a blue and white airborne tab. The color pierced the pre-dawn halftones ahead of anything else, a bit of brilliance, as Smith's silhouette strode before the morning formation. The patch defeated darkness.

The patch identified a unit that was created for, deployed to, and would be stood down in Vietnam. The 173rd Airborne Brigade.

Trainees seize bits of combat lore quickly, and The Herd (as the brigade was known) emerged as a kind of Infantry Myth. The Herd was known for hard battles, long stays in the field, clannishness, ferocity. You could almost see it like an aura around Smith. It was there in the opacity of his black eyes.

I coveted that patch.

Smith had something unnamable that I wanted. It wasn't confidence, and it wasn't contempt, and it wasn't sorrow. There was an element of each in his deportment, something Sisyphean that was attractive to us, the youngest ones. Everyone agreed that Smith was somehow. . . cool.

I knew I could be like him, if I had that patch.

I was eighteen.

I got my wish. I went to Vietnam.

The worst thing that ever happened to me, in terms of my development, worse than the drugs, far worse than religion, infinitely worse than the dysfunctions in my family, was my early exposure to the works of Ayn Rand. No adolescent should ever be permitted to read anything written by her. Her ideas are too superficially logical (justice-mercy, independence-unity, reason-faith, wealth-need, happiness-duty. . . opposites according to Rand, one having to be sacrificed for the other), too internally consistent (A is A; reality is that which exists), too glib in the embrace of self-centeredness.

"I am done with this creed of corruption.

"I am done with the monster of 'We,' the word of serfdom, of misery, falsehood and shame.

"And now I see the face of god, and I raise this god over the earth, this god whom men have sought since men came into being, this god who will grant them joy and peace and pride.

"This god, this one word: I" (Rand, *Anthem*, 1946)

The more thoughtful and sensitive the child, the more dangerously seductive the Ayn Rand preposterousness, and the more emotionally damaging the exposure. Her so-called philosophy gives the white, socially retarded, working class intellectual neophyte just enough acumen to make him or her cocksure and brutally narrow-minded. The ease of articulation of this shallow philosophy is matched only by the impossibility of its standard for human behavior, and the result is an unhappy apostle for whom the neither the world nor the people in it will ever measure up. The acolyte, along with tolerance, loses curiosity, sensitivity and humility. Worse, one loses the capacity for community.

One of the subjects most easily dispensed with by the budding Objectivist (what Rand disciples called themselves, because she told them to) is race. It simply doesn't matter. This is a particularly tough position to hold if the devotee is accidentally exposed to real history or social research, or to reality. True believers limit themselves to intellectual intake supportive of, or information vulnerable to, one of the tactics in the Objectivist Playbook.

I entered the army believing that I was "color-blind." I had a philosophical yardstick with which to measure every person. I had nothing against any group. There were simply very few people I could admire and remain true to my "credo." Martin Luther King, for instance, was easily catalogued and dispensed with as a collectivist, the same as Jesus of Nazareth or Joe Stalin. Color was irrelevant. What people could not see, out of a contrary blindness, was that Ayn Rand and I were right about everything.

Problems did impose themselves on my borrowed ideas and imagined actions. There was the pesky, innate desire I had for human company, those aberrant and irresistible hormones, and a rapidly expanding dependence on chemicals (be they airplane glue, diet pills or alcohol). Objectivism touts heroes who have strangely little need for human companionship.

I managed to get through Infantry AIT, then Airborne School, but Special Forces was a dream of the past. It took too long, and I was going to Vietnam as quickly as possible. There were rumors that the war would wind down, and I didn't want to miss it. I was going to join the 173rd Airborne Brigade, and help defeat Communism—the vilest form of collectivism (Ain't life funny?).

And I did get to Vietnam. Little did I know that the turnover rate of soldiers in the 173rd Airborne Brigade was so high that nearly every newly trained infantryman who graduated from Airborne School would be assigned to the 173rd.

On my 19th birthday, I lost four hours by crossing the International Dateline en route to the Republic of Vietnam. I was about to get my patch.

At Camrahn Bay, I was in-processed by a phalanx of faceless staff workers and introduced to high quality marijuana by an acquaintance from AIT. At Charang Valley, where we received the Brigade's indoctrination before being forwarded to our units, I learned how to stir shit in the "burnout" latrines and shoot CS gas at civilians in the garbage dumps for entertainment.

The latter was my first glimpse of how the rules had loosened. 40mm gas grenades could be launched into the middle of groups of men, women and children as casually and thoughtlessly as one might skip a stone. The risk that the grenade body might score a direct hit and kill someone was not even taken into account. In the States, even livestock was given more deference.

Block the question about why they were in the trash dump.

We were in a lethal Disney World, where Laotian cannabis soaked with opium was the ride, and the world was our arcade.

I could almost grow a mustache.

At Tam Quan District, when I joined my platoon, I offered a piece of C-Ration gum to a teenage girl. We were on my first walking patrol, and she seemed frightened and reluctant to take it. Butler, a black kid from DC, turned to Hamby, our squad leader, and pointed out my action. They both laughed. Butler called me a fucking missionary.

"You don't treat gooks like people, mufuckah. You treat 'em like pigs. You get ripped off, you cop that do-goodah attitude. You wanna marry that dink bitch?"" Ripped off did not mean robbed. In Vietnam, it was slang for killed.

Less than two weeks after I joined the platoon, I had repelled a night attack that turned out to be a dog in the trip flares. I had been shot at by snipers (damn poor ones) while buying a Coca-Cola. I had watched the laser light show of the Stag Teams being hit in the low ground at night.

The medic told me that the platoon was going to kill a dink. I was loaded on opium-joints (before Anita Bryant, before the great trial of 1995, OJ had a special meaning for grunts. Opium joints were a product as cheap as they were ubiquitous). Doc was a man bursting with the excitement of a secret. He had told me enough to relieve his smoldering agitation, and not a whit more information was forthcoming. They were going to kill a gook.

I was not allowed to go on the patrol that went out of the wire.

Within minutes of the patrol leaving, an unbelievable eruption of automatic weapons fire erupted, punctuated by a grenade. Cowboy, a platoon communicator, came running out of the commo bunker, hollering that the patrol was in contact. Moments later he emerged again, declaring no friendly KIAs (Killed In Action) or WIAs (Wounded In Action), and one enemy KIA.

I was on guard in the overwatching bunker, when the patrol came struggling up the hill. They dragged what appeared to be a long, heavy sack. First two guys would drag. Then two others would spell them. Then two more.

When they approached the wire, I finally made out the details of an old woman, lifeless, covered like a doughnut with fine, light orange dust, being towed up the hill by her blouse, now tied around her ankles. Her head, dragging behind her, bounced loosely over the pot-holes and stones. Spots of blood were struggling to emerge through the dust coating all over her. The dust was thick and wet on her mouth, especially where it stuck to her teeth. Her fixed, half-open eyes were muddy with dust as well. Her hair was long and, having come undone, was wildly tangled in an anarchy of dry twigs.

After catching his breath, Hamby told the Platoon Leader that the old woman had thrown a grenade at them. He uttered a short laugh, still out of breath, to punctuate the story. So they shot her. The Platoon Leader accepted the story without question. He instructed them to get the body out of the perimeter.

The corpse was placed on a flat area outside the wire, where we received helicopters. A rope was affixed to the feet. The rope led back to the bunker overwatching the Landing Zone (LZ). This was a pre-caution taken, because the Viet Cong were reputed to steal the bodies of their dead back, after dark.

She had thrown a grenade. Everything was on the up and up. I commiserated with the patrol members. You had to do it. She threw a grenade.

Hamby just gave me a blank look. Ski started laughing. Hawk fixed a sad, stony look on me for a moment, then walked back to his bunker. Doc eyes shifted back and forth. His hands were still shaking and covered with blood, where he'd stuck his fingers into the bullet holes in her head and chest before declaring she was dead. Rat changed the subject and asked me if I still had the shits. He was concerned, you see, because he had elected to be my "cherry dad." Mac stalked away angrily and disappeared into the bunker.

Suddenly I had no easy answers. Something vast and empty entered me, and it would never go away.

The next day, the body had started to bloat and draw flies. We had to move it out of the way, so the Battalion Commander could land in his helicopter. He was rotating out of his command, and he smiled benignly, like a gentle father. He told us how proud he was to have worked with us. He congratulated us on our kill. I stood there without a sound or a motion and raged that no one had prepared me for this—not my Mom, not my Dad, not Walt Disney, and not fucking Ayn Rand. Everyone had been in on it, except me, the short kid who read books, smoked pot and ate chocolate bars until his bowels turned to warm jello.

Two days after the kill, some guys from LZ English, our Headquarters location, flew in with a distraught young South Vietnamese lieutenant. They showed the lieutenant the body, which by now had been wrapped in a poncho because of the smell and the flies. The young lieutenant flipped open the poncho and studied the remains for a moment. He saw something that triggered recognition and collapsed next to the corpse. He wailed and cried and beat the ground with his fists inconsolably. He glared at us and screamed in protest. They must have told him the story about the grenade. The guys from LZ English led him off.

The woman had been his mother.

With the progression of hours, then days, as is the case with young men, the discussion became more emboldened. Each retelling was another blow to my shattered innocence.

A booby trap had killed JoJo last month. As payment, it was okay to blow away an old woman who was hoeing her potato patch. To kill a dink for JoJo. This was Vietnam, my introduction to the possibilities of human action.

I was in the company of my peers. I needed their acceptance. They looked like me. They liked the same music. We got high together. They became misty eyed over letters from home. Many claimed they wanted to get out of the army to become hippies. In the extremity of our circumstance, lines between black and white were erased and redrawn between Us, the GIs, and Them, the dinks. It was a brotherhood of youth, engaged, voluntarily or not, in a race war.

The first time I tossed a burning heat tab onto the thatched roof of a barn, it was like pledging a fraternity. I was accepted more thoroughly than I ever had been by peers in my life, into a fraternity that was untouchable by anything but Death.

You don't just set the building on fire. You giggle when the weeping, wailing family tries to put it out. Then you are crazy enough to be safe.

Months later, I was a relative old timer. I was accustomed to the steep, slippery trails we hacked out a yard at a time with machetes. The M60 machinegun was no more bothersome to carry than a briefcase. I had a skull mounted atop my rucksack, tied on with an embroidered headband, through two bulletholes on the occiput (helicopter gunship got 'im), with the mandible secured to the bottom by medical adhesive tape grown dark gray with exposure. My ear was pierced. I had a gold chain around my neck, with a tiny gold lobster hanging on it. My boots were scuffed tan with wear, my second set. I looked crazy. I walked crazy. I was high whenever I could be. I didn't even use the tablets in my water anymore. I could sleep in a mudhole between two rocks. I could put one foot in front of the other indefinitely.

I was angry all of the time, even when I smiled, even when I lay in the frame of the ruck with the wind blowing the sweat off of me, smoking and talking about what I might want to do when I got back to the world.

We were taking a break alongside a road, an unusual circumstance, since we seldom saw roads or villages anymore. We had been in the free fire zones, where anything that didn't wear OG-107 fatigues was killed—by bullets, by Phugas, by Napalm—where you walked and walked, up and down, for days without seeing a trail, or a house, or people beside yourselves. The left toe then the right toe just advanced mindlessly into the crush of mud and cut vegetation.

A young Vietnamese man pedaled past with a bicycle, carrying two saddle baskets full of sugarcane. He looked at me and smiled.

"Keep movin', you fuckin' gook!"

The bicyclist stopped and seemed suddenly very sad. I leapt to my feet at his impertinence. He pushed the bicycle over to me. He spoke some English.

"This my home. I Vietnamese. You and me, why can't we be friend?"

He said that while looking me directly in the face, with a disconcerting sadness and an absolute absence of fear. He then withdrew a length of cane from one of the baskets, cracked off a section on his knee, and handed it to me.

I found myself taking it, but I had some difficulty maintaining my hateful look. I had spent months cultivating it, and it felt foolish when it wasn't scaring anyone. I certainly wasn't going to shoot him here in broad daylight before a hundred witnesses. Unexpectedly, I didn't even want to.

He rode on.

I had never eaten sugarcane before. After day upon endless day of C-Rations and an occasional cold, Mermite meal, the watery, melon-like sweetness of the cane juice surprised me.

For the rest of that day, I fought hard against the hole he had driven in my dam with the simplest act of courage and hospitality. That night the dam ruptured in the darkness, and I cried quietly through a whole guard shift, wanting more than anything to just go home.

I was stunned at how effortless and cunning my transformation had been.

I know plenty about racism.

After leaving the army, studying literature, embracing anarchism in college, trapping myself in a dreadful marriage that nullified politics or any other outside interest, further cultivating my dependence on drugs and alcohol, then re-joining the army in 1977, I went to the United States Army Ranger School in 1979. Upon graduation, I was assigned to 2nd Battalion (Ranger), 75th Infantry, in Fort Lewis, Washington.

Ranger Battalions were the infantry elite, shock infantry some call them, of the United States Army, and it was the most non-African unit I had seen in the army. Predominantly white, the unit had significant numbers of Hispanics and Pacific Islanders, but not even one percent of the unit was black, if you exclude the kitchen and supply room. In the regular army, black participation was higher than the percentage of African-Americans in the general population.

Non-Ranger units were widely referred to as "Leg" units, as they were in the 82nd Airborne, where I had served after the war, but in 2nd Ranger Battalion, "Leg" was often synonymous with black or (the other popular appellation) "boofer." I had never seen such open anti-

Africanism in the military. People recruited for and joined the Klan there. A black soldier coming into the unit had to pass muster at RIP (the Ranger Indoctrination Program), his squad (where the leader had the support of the company commander for summary relief of soldiers for failure to meet "standards"), Pre-Ranger (where candidates for Ranger School learned the basics for attendance), and Ranger School. At each of these weigh stations, there were a number of gatekeepers, willing to use their power as the subjective evaluator of performance "to keep the Tab (Ranger Tab worn by graduates of Ranger School) clean and the Battalions pure."

There are all kinds of speculations and rationalizations about why Special Units employ so few blacks as "operators." One reason is that those units employ so many people who deliberately cull blacks during the selection process. Another reason is that few black soldiers are interested. Gaining entry in Special Operations as an operator generally involves some test, wherein the candidate is exposed to hardship and humiliation. For the average white kid, this is a novelty—a rite of passage. For most black soldiers, there's nothing novel about it. Hardship and humiliation are just more of the same bullshit, especially at the hands of the mostly lily-white cadre at these initiation courses.

When I was in Vietnam, over half my unit was black, and a kind of aggressive racial unity was the code in the field, contrary to all the racial problems the "flatdicks" experienced in the rear, and in contrast to the racial suspicion and hatred most of the boony rats developed toward Vietnamese. But when I went to Second Ranger Battalion in 1979, black faces were hard to find. Members openly expressed their desire to remain in the Battalion so they would not have to work with black soldiers. Some talked of using their military expertise in the conduct of an expected future race war. Nazi regalia could be found in some rooms. One Ranger in my platoon stenciled SS lightening bolts onto the fronts of his T-shirts. This was very perturbing, and I told the squad to refrain from open racism. They looked at me like I was from the moon, but being disciplined soldiers, they complied in my presence.

Hate groups, survivalism and mercenary lore are a mainstay of the young Ranger diet. The prestige associated with the black beret, the genuinely tough adherence to the male code via light infantry craft and brutal physical conditioning, the sense of community engendered in the execution of challenging collective tasks, and the technical/tactical education, are access passes to the pedestals of the rarified, dramatic, war-worshipping subculture. It is the world of weapons as icons. It is the sphere of survival through deadly competition. Adherents need enemies, and enemies need to be easily identified.

I decided to simply outlaw open racism (by my still superficial definition) in my own sphere of influence, and hope that my credibility as a leader and a combat veteran might give others permission to recant their hatreds and their shortcut thinking. The idea was, in a word, naive.

Discipline being what it was in the Rangers, I received complete, unquestioning compliance with my stated prohibition against displays and expressions of racism, first within the squad, and later in the platoon, at least in my presence. They were fine little storm troopers. In this way I was comfortably insulated from both conflict and responsibility.

I left the Rangers to work as an instructor in the Jungle School, named pretentiously the Jungle Operations Training Center, in Fort Sherman, Panama, and for a while was in the real army again. But in less than a year, my desire to run away from reality, particularly the reality of my marriage, and into the rarified, over-traveled, promiscuous, closer-to-combat world of elites seduced me again.

I went to Camp Dawson, West Virginia for Delta tryouts, in the Spring of 1982. Delta is the short name for 1st Special Forces Operational Detachment—Delta, popularly referred to as Delta Force. I was thirty years old, accustomed to spending around four days a week walking in the rugged jungle terrain of Atlantic Side Panama with a rucksack, and determined not to quit. Nonetheless, I was surprised when I was selected. Over sixty had come to try. Fourteen of us proceeded to assignment.

Within a month, I was undergoing my basic counter-terrorist training at Delta, and I became quickly aware that racism was even more overt and thoroughgoing than it had been with the Rangers. There I was not in charge of anything. I was, in fact, so impressed with the sophistication and independence of their operation and with my own membership, that I merely overlooked it.

Delta operators (operator is a term reserved in special operations for trigger pullers, as opposed to administrative and support personnel), by in large, displayed an unblushing animosity toward African-Americans, indeed Africans of any nationality. I gave only token resistance to the phenomenon in the way of arguing against it, in otherwise friendly discussions. There was a lot of prestige associated with that job, not to mention extra money, so the pressure to conform was fierce. Cowardice comes easier with the carrot of self-interest. And the only one who recognized my cowardice was me. I had graduated from my obtrusive racism in Vietnam to a mere collaborator in my failure to confront.

There were only two black operators at Delta. It would be a violation of law and a number of oaths I have taken to specify numbers assigned to the unit, but two black operators was well below the demographic average of both the general population and the army. One of them was Captain Earl Atkinson.

Earl and I were sitting at The Million Dollar Cowboy Bar in Jackson Hole, Wyoming, one night, and I ventured the question, "What is it like to be a black operator?"

Hard, he admitted frankly. He illustrated his complaint by telling me about a hairdo.

In Delta, one of the alleged operational necessities, as well as a perk, is the relaxation of military grooming standards. Even beards are tolerated from time to time, and hair out of military standards is almost universal. Earl decided to grow his hair too. For a few weeks he had sported what most would consider a short Afro. . . no more than two inches out from the scalp. This was in 1983. He began hearing the jokes as soon as the hair began extending past his ears. You're looking pretty militant there, sir. Hey, Earl. Gettin' kinda militant, aren't we?

Delta operators are indoctrinated against being thin-skinned by their peers. "Don't be thin-skinned" is the unwritten law, along with, "Selection is an ongoing process."

Captain Atkinson was compelled by the norm to smile and accept the gentle ribbing graciously. The problem was the ribbing consistently included the word "militant." It became a perpetual drumbeat, a little piece of peer pressure that refused to fade. Earl rightly concluded that there was more to it than mere kidding. He was getting too "ethnic," and even his raters let him know without coming right out and saying it. It did not take Captain Earl Atkinson long to figure out that different rules applied for him, and that his continued ascension up the professional ladder could hinge heavily on the completion of a successful tour with the highest priority unit in the Army. So Earl got rid of the hairdo, but neither the resentment nor the reality.

I ran into Earl again several years later, when he was commanding a battalion of Special Forces in 7th Group. He had put on weight, and he had lines in his face that matched my own. He seemed more contented as he approached the latter portion of his career, and he offered me a job. The job offer was overruled by the Group Headquarters. My impression was that we had changed, and that the army had changed, and I am sure that no one was any longer herding Earl Atkinson into a special conformity. The troops, however, when I talked to them, were applying a more stringent standard to his performance as a commander than to other, white, commanders.

"Colonel Atkinson is okay, but he doesn't really understand our mission."

"Atkinson is a micro-manager."

"He lets the officers have too much power."

Having known Earl Atkinson, most of these comments bordered on idiotic.

1st Ranger Battalion was the same way. So was Special Forces. One of the first conversations I walked into at a team room in 7th Special Forces was a series of "Nigger Jokes," followed by the departing comment of one member to the rest of the guys in the room, "The great thing about fuckin' niggers is you never run out of shit you can say about 'em." This was met with raucous, appreciative laughter.

The man making the comment was Sergeant First Class Frank Kelly, the team sergeant for a detachment across the hall. On his team wall, he posted a city map. It was called the "Murc Map," after the local diminutive for Murchison Road, where a high concentration of the black citizens of Fayetteville lived. Frank scanned the paper for crime stories, and when he found crimes committed in black neighborhoods, he pushed a colored map pin into the site. This was Frank's way, with the help of his team, of demonstrating his stated belief that blacks are innately criminal. No team member ever objected to this display, nor did any officer who worked there. It's just the boys. It's just our dirty little secret.

I later occupied that room, when a different team was organized, and eventually given to a team sergeant named Master Sergeant J. D. Doyle. Doyle turned out to be an old friend of Frank MacKenna, whom I had known from Delta. Doyle was quick to point out that much of his affinity for Frank MacKenna was based on their shared hatred of blacks. MacKenna, I remembered, refused to eat fried chicken or barbecued ribs, because they were "nigger food." I know he worked for the Idaho Falls Department of Energy facility for a while, heading up their SWAT program. Later, rumor had it he went to Coca-Cola, then Westinghouse. Big security man. I'm sure Texaco would love him.

Doyle proceeded to organize a series of training exercises on the land of a rich white supremacist, adjacent to Fort Stewart, Georgia.

A conflict developed between Doyle and me, when I questioned our repeated use of this area, even to prepare for missions in Colombia, especially when I discovered that Doyle was planning to settle down next to his rich racist buddy and get involved in some mysterious joint ventures. That conflict degenerated into shouting matches in Tolemaida, Colombia, and I asked to be released from the team when we returned. It wasn't long after that, that I went to Fort Benning, to be the SF Medic for the Ranger Regiment.

I had begun to confront.

I was at an SF picnic, upon returning to take my team in 3rd Group, when I noticed that a sister team in A Company, had T-shirts made, with SF Crests, HALO jump wings, and their team number, 344. The 44 portion of the team designation was written as SS lightening bolts. No commander or NCO in that unit's chain of command ever lifted a finger to stop the team from wearing them. Just the boys.

Ali Tehrani, my junior communicator, had a best friend, a former member of 354, a fellow named Frank Harris (seems like a lot of Franks doesn't it?), a self proclaimed Nazi, who stencilled Kampfgruppe Harris on his wall locker. Ali, a half Persian-half German, raised in

Luxembourg and the States, assured me that he considered Frank his best friend, but did not share in his theories about race.

I was unspeakably naive to think I could control any of these proclivities. I was extremely credulous to presume I could take my team to Haiti and put myself between the powerful and thoroughly entrenched racial assumptions of the members of my team and the mission.

In the world of Military Special Operations, I have seen Anti-Africanism function as the litmus test for assimilation of non-WASP soldiers. Asians, Europeans, Jews, American Indians, Polynesians, Latinos, all can be legitimized in the eyes of their peers by sharing in the Special Ops contempt for African-Americans. This is my experience. Black people have a special place in special operations—the bottom.

My personal convictions have evolved, from the credulity and illiteracy of my youthful denial, to a belief that the struggle with questions of race and gender are central to any analysis of power and politics. The personal chronology of the traumas and toils that guided that evolution is too convoluted and lengthy for this narrative. Suffice it to say, this conviction was to have consequences.

Nowadays, I've lost my taste for white people. Don't get defensive. I'm white. My kids (I'm in my second marriage) are a mix of African, European, and Native American. But they take what society gives them, and if asked will tell you they are Black. When you raise Black children, you can't be white any more.

All whites are not bigots, but most are, even though they'd never admit it. Many of them will engage you in a conversation, and just assume they can say hateful racist things to you, like you're in their goddamn club or something. So it got personal, they were talking about my kids, now, and every time they did that, I began to show my ass. I really can't handle that kind of confrontation as a constant thing in my life, so I find myself avoiding white folks altogether, unless I know them. I understand now that I shouldn't have needed things to be "personal", that I should have been showing my ass all along. But I was born into a white supremacist family, surrounded by white supremacy all my life, and exempted from the grinding, daily special oppression of race that Black folk take for granted as part of their lives.

So here I am, a white man telling Black children to not give white people the benefit of the doubt. It's not prejudice I'm giving them, it's survival. Don't talk to strangers. Don't trust white folk you don't know. Don't trust cops. The basics. When Black folk don't want to walk right up and be my friend, I don't take it personally, and I don't get defensive. And I'll tell other thin-skinned white people the same thing. It's not personal. It's survival. Get used to it, and quit whining. Start showing your ass with white bigots, and quit putting your unrealistic expectations on Black folk.

Haiti was really going to call the question. It would cut the cord for me on the race thing. Near the end of my time in Haiti, I was asked if I had "become a Haitian." I was really being asked if I had turned Black.

5: THE 51ST STATE

Training from March through September 1994 became very intense for ODA 354. I became very intense.

Mike went from depressed to seemingly very satisfied with the direction the team was taking. The company commander, Major David Fox, seemed satisfied. The Battalion Commander, Lieutenant Colonel Gary Jones, seemed to be impressed.

We ran for maximum intensity, four to six miles four days a week, some of us kicking out six-minute miles. We carried 85 pounds of weight for our training marches, five miles in one hour and fifteen minutes over sandy logging roads every Monday morning. We lifted weights before lunch. We quit wearing jumpsuits and skydiving, electing instead to jump in battle fatigues and combat equipment, mostly at night; a significant increase in discomfort, risk and training value. We re-trained virtually every battle drill, using nothing but tried and true, simple and rugged, light infantry tactics. We trained in stalking skills, photography, marksmanship. We established real Standing Operating Procedures (SOP) for uniform, equipment and deployment procedures. We conducted field layouts, almost unheard of at the team level in a Special Forces Group. Our training tempo was the highest we saw anywhere in the Group, and the focus of that training was Back-To-Basics through repetition. We went home bone weary at the end of every training day.

Mike and I, at the end of each training event, would say, "We're better today than we were yesterday." And it was true.

My humility went to sleep in the back seat.

I was making some terrible errors.

I was preaching that we needed to transition from soldier skills to staff skills in what we taught our foreign nationals on the training missions to the Dominican Republic. But I was concentrating on explaining tactical concepts to my team, when I should have been addressing the fundamental philosophical questions with which I felt the greatest discomfort. I was trying to be a democratic leader on a team that I knew in my gut needed a strong dose of pure autocracy. They had, after all, committed accidental shootings, lost expensive high-tech hardware, suffered an administrative reduction by blowing off advice to work to meet Army weight standards, and repeatedly forced me to repeat instructions to comply with simple safety procedures.

I engaged in off-the-record, bullshit sessions on political subjects. I openly expressed my own political opinions among the group, lefty as they were and moving ever left-er. Those opinions were at variance with virtually every member of the team. I had every right to do it. But it was poor judgment. My pronouncements would ultimately be used to discredit my motives about later decisions.

The team members had complaints. Rod, the senior weapons man, complained that we were not being conservative enough, trying to do too much. Vern, the intelligence sergeant, complained about the physical training. Ali, the junior communicator, complained that we should do fun stuff once in a while, like swimming, and constantly complained about not going to the Dominican Republic, our area of operations for non-combat missions (and also where Ali enjoyed chasing young Dominican women). Kyle, the senior engineer, complained that we were acting too conventional (a buzzword for being held accountable to basic light infantry standards in the field). Skye, the junior weapons man, wanted to use Kung-Fu for physical training. Brad, the junior engineer, had one wazoo idea after another, none of which had anything to do with Special Reconnaissance, Free Fall infiltration, or Direct Action. Pedro, the senior communicator, did not complain, making him exceptional not just on the team but in the army, seeming very pleased at the team having taken the training bull by the horns. Dave

Grau, the warrant officer who arrived in May, also voiced complaints about the tempo (Dave was a shiftless type, full of energy behind a laptop, but indolent in the field), and had to be warned off trying to do my job.

When each strenuous and exacting training session was complete, however, the boys invariably expressed satisfaction at having done it. They bragged to other teams, gloating over the envy of others. We were considered the team that "did things."

In June, LTC Jones called Mike and me into the company commander's office. We were quietly informed that we were to keep this conversation to ourselves, not even to share it with the team. We had been selected to prepare for a mission into Haiti. It was a probable Special Reconnaissance, with a possible Free Fall infiltration. We would likely be required, upon the commencement of hostilities, to direct close air support, specifically the fire from an AC-130 gunship. Our infiltration would occur prior to the commencement of hostilities, and based on the team's experience in the Dominican Republic and our Spanish proficiency, our target would be somewhere near the Dominican border. We assured the Battalion Commander that we were already on track with our training.

Mike and I were intensely gratified by the implication of trust, and by the acknowledgment, from a Battalion Commander whom we both respected, of our hard work.

Our training focus changed not a bit, but the news did precipitate two decisions. We would discretely begin the intelligence preparation for the mission, assembling maps, and reading area studies. For myself, I went to the library and found everything I could get my hands on about Haiti, which wasn't much. The other decision, which I did not like making or executing, was to remove Vern Brown from the team.

Vern was very much overweight, smoked two packs of cigarettes a day, and could not keep up with a single event during our physical training. He had been advised at my assumption of duty to work on his own to rectify his physical status, and had not taken the least initiative to do so. Vern was a personally gregarious fellow, and very effective at getting things done through back channels, but I was not prepared, in the light of this potentially dangerous, strenuous and isolated mission, to permit him to endanger himself or the other team members because he could not keep up. This decision, once implemented, put Rod in the intelligence sergeant's slot.

It was an unpleasant bit of work, securing the blessing of the Company Commander, finding a place to relegate him, then telling Vern that he was fired.

I explained the situation to Vern outside, in front of the Company. He began to rail against the officers, and ask what I could do to reverse the decision. Mike stood silently alongside me. One word from Mike would have at least shared the responsibility. It never came. I told Vern that the decision had originated with me, and that it was final.

Mike's willingness to let me take the role of heavy on this indicated that Mike had lost control of the team through fraternization a long time ago. He knew his doctrine, and he wanted to dig out of the hot water he's fallen into, but he needed me—the guy with no history on the team, no compromises—to get the job done. I was pissed that he stood silent on the Vern firing, but I also realized that I was not the team sergeant. I was the team leader. As long as I put my face on every decision, Mike was going to acquiesce. I was in charge.

Vern was never friendly to me again.

Brad Longerbeam was also transferred that month, to a job at Battalion. Mike Wideman had been moved to Battalion as well. This left us with Mike, Dave, Rod, Kyle, Gonzo, Ali, Skye, Pedro and myself.

As we continued trying to refine our skills, the mission—as we were to hear through the rumor mill—began to mutate. In July, the battalion headquarters moved planning cells into RFABs, semi rigid tent systems that were erected inside the battalion classrooms where prying eyes could not see them. We were told our mission was on, then it was off, then it was on, as the planners teased and tortured the mission in their nylon cloisters. We heard that the only parachute infiltrations were now being reserved for command elements, a sore point when that rumor escaped, because it rang so true. In Grenada and Panama, the hunt for badges, medals and glory, overwhelmed the mission focus. Senior officers not only lack immunity to these preposterous impulses, they are often the very worst about giving in to them.

The combat star on a paratrooper's badge is a highly coveted award. That is why, during Operation Just Cause (the most costly and murderous drug bust in history), when Rangers had secured Tocumen and Torrijos airfields, and they called to the 82nd Airborne Division commander who was flying in to jump onto the airfield, "The airfield is secure. Air land. Air land," the 82nd commander called back and said, "This is the 82nd airBORNE Division, not the 82nd airLAND Division." The Brigade of paratroopers then proceeded to leap into the night, drop troops clear past the airfields, generate dozens of unnecessary injuries, initiate firefights in the dark with Ranger elements, and spend countless hours getting assembled and accounted for. It was not a decision to do the most tactically sound thing, but a decision to get a General and his troops a tiny bronze star on the two inch wide parachutist's badge they wear on their uniforms.

During our team's pre-designated ("block") leave in July, Rod and I were left behind (he had taken his leave a bit earlier to coincide with his daughter's schedule, whom he wanted to spend some time with in Puerto Rico). He and I started to do some intelligence preparation of our own. We collected 1/250,000 (the ratio of map distance to ground distance) maps of Haiti, and 1/50,000 maps of the Northeast region. We cut and taped them into a comprehensive mosaic. We selected the Northeast region, because we had been told we would be deployed near the Dominican Republic. We still believed that the strong Spanish capability on the team would be a factor.

Analysis of the area told us that our target would be one of two places; Ouanaminthe, located on the Riviere Massacre, the shared Haitian-Dominican border, where a Battalion-sized garrison of Haitian military was reported to be; or Fort Liberte, a port town twenty kilometers from Ouanaminthe, with a company garrison and close proximity to the Phaeton airfield, which the map indicated was serviceable and in use. We gave much more weight to the Ouanaminthe option, because LTC Jones had hinted that we would jump in, and an undetected parachute infiltration would be far easier, flying the aircraft through friendly airspace, i.e., the Dominican Republic.

We then began looking for decent drop zones, which was difficult, given the diffuse population distribution through every nook and cranny of the countryside. And we struggled in perplexity with the question of where to go and remain undetected while we watched the Ouanaminthe garrison. We postulated that this would be the mission. This wargaming was a good mental exercise, but like all speculation it was vaporized by reality.

We expected to go in July, then Rwanda loomed. That took us

through August, by which time many of the guys on the team, as well as the company headquarters started saying it would never happen.

"No one's gonna invade fucking Haiti. We'd have to make it the 51st state." This is a quote from Company Commander David Fox. "The chance that we'll invade Haiti is slim to none," said the Company Sergeant Major.

6: Oxymorons: "Sweet Sorrow," "Jumbo Shrimp" and "Military Intelligence"

Have you read the intelligence reports on the activities of Lavalas?
Sure.
Have you seen how much violence they are responsible for?
I dismissed the intelligence reports.
You did what?
I dismissed them. They were never accurate when I had anything to test them against.
Don't you think that endangered your team?
No. The intelligence reports read more like anti-Aristide propaganda than they do as information summaries.
Do you think your government is engaging in propaganda?
Certainly. They always have. You know they do.
Did you take sides with Haitians against your own team?
That's absurd. How could I do that?
Did you take the word of Haitians ahead of your team?
If something had to do with our sector or with the business of Haitians, of

course I relied on the Haitians before my team. They don't know any more about Haiti than I do.

In August we received the one and only pre-deployment intelligence briefing on the nation of Haiti. The Battalion Intelligence Officer, referred to in military-speak as the S-2, had carefully avoided using any of the former Haitian nationals that worked and lived in Fayetteville, North Carolina. These included a professor of Physics at the University and his wife, the Creole instructor for Special Warfare Center Schools in Fort Bragg. It also included various Haitian-American soldiers who were available. To ensure we had a reliable source for the one pre-deployment intelligence briefing we received, our "Intelligence" guru selected an expatriate, white, American, fundamentalist preacher, who had been busy for the last eleven years in a community outside of Cap Haitian saving the heathen souls of some 300 Haitians who constituted his congregation.

He was an emaciated looking fellow, in an austere Calvinist kind of way, with thinning black hair, hairy white wrists exposed at the ends of his suitcoat sleeves, and a set of black framed glasses, behind which set two small, blepharitic eyes burning with years of besieged righteousness.

He began with a personal introduction, followed by a brief historical account of the nation of Haiti. This account was perfectly interesting so long as it confined itself to events, personalities and dates. As soon as the factual synopsis was delivered, however, he calmly explained that Dessalines' revolution (no mention of Toussaint L'Overture) was won in a deal with Satan himself, disguised as a voodoo deity, in which a pig was sacrificed, closing a deal to lend the government of the first independent black nation in the Western hemisphere to the purposes of said devil for a period of 200 years. He said this as if it were an incontrovertible fact. I thought for a moment he was going to produce the signed contract for us. Mike was sitting next to me, and told me to close my gaping mouth.

He proceeded to explain to an alarmingly spellbound audience of Special Forces soldiers (most of whom knew not shit from Shinola about Haiti) that Haitians were totally in the thrall of "Voodoo", which he characterized not as a religion (which it is), but as the worship of demons. They were morally and spiritually lost children, desperately in need of guidance—from people like himself—to snatch them out of the slippery gutter of heathen-African damnation.

He believed in the efficacy of Voodoo "spells and powders," claiming no one could safely open their windows at night, or the demon worshippers would blow "powders" at the unsuspecting victims as they lie abed. I was expecting zombie stories next, having just read *Tell My Horse*, by Zora Neale Hurston, but he transitioned nicely into a discussion of voodoo priests (Houngans) and priestesses (Mambos). Voodoo, he assured us, still practiced human sacrifice. Its adherents even practiced cannibalism. I was aghast to look about the room and see sensible looking adult soldiers in the United States Army paying quiet, rapt attention to this man's bullshit, without so much as batting an eye. Some were even nodding assent. Yup, I knew it all along, the goddamn savages!

Priests and priestesses of this horror, he explained, had accompanied Jean-Bertrand Aristide on all his public journeys, conclusively proving that he was not a Christian at all, but a closeted Satanist.

Mike now looked as if he might have to do a Heimlich maneuver on me.

Aristide, explained our missionary (to an audience who largely enjoyed the fascist diatribes of the likes of Jesse Helms and Rush Limbaugh), was not really a priest at all. He had been defrocked, a sidelong reference to Aristide's expulsion from the Silesean order for daring to take sides with the poor. This was an understandable fumble on the pastor's part, since his own church had warned him about the aberration of Liberation Theology, and since this fundamentalist fellow didn't waste much time keeping up with useless minutiae regarding the idolatrous Papists anyway.

Aristide, also a closet Communist according to our preacher, had personally ordered riots and murders of countless people during his brutal three year regime, which in fact only lasted eight months. Cedras and Francois showed up just in time to save the country, and any intervention would be a terrible mistake. . . not to mention the dangers, he hastened to add, to young Christian GIs, of working with HIV–riddled demon-worshippers.

When he was finished, I was near apoplectic. I could contain myself no more. So I raised my hand. The spotlight was mine.

"I have a real problem with the characterization of Aristide as a demon and Cedras as the savior of Haiti, given the reports coming out of Haiti about this regime. Doesn't it seem a bit arrogant for an American to judge the decision of almost 70 percent of the Haitian people who elected Mr. Aristide. After all, that would be an overwhelming landslide in American politics."

He replied that the election was a fraud perpetrated by Lavalas (the political coalition that supported Aristide), that the reports of violence by the Cedras regime were over-reported. Furthermore, he intimated, the childlike support of many Haitians for Aristide demonstrated that they were not yet ready for self-governance.

The meeting broke up, and the preacher singled me out to shake my hand as if we had conducted a formal debate. Taking his hand, I felt as if I'd retrieved a stiff, cold catfish from a bucket.

The briefing was only partly inexplicable to me. Many of the mindless prejudices of the briefing would resurface later as official documents, from Intelligence, Psychological Operations, and Civil Affairs. It was part of the attempt to minimize American contact with Haitian realities. It went on throughout the mission whenever possible, and it was largely effective.

During the mission, the bullshit was being disseminated by the United States Embassy. The press lapped it up and regurgitates it for us uncritically, awed as usual to be so near the powerful, Scotch-sucking, backbiting, bourgeois bureaucrats known as the Foreign Service.

I had to work out of embassies a couple of times. I was impressed. Does it show?

7 : GREEN LIGHT

In August, ODA 354, our team, received a directive to provide two communicators to the Dominican Republic. They were to conduct a survey for a course of training on tons of new American communications equipment. That equipment had recently arrived in the Dominican Republic as an official bribe to secure their cooperation on Haiti.

Pedro and Ali went, returning a week and a half later. Mike and I refused to send them both back together to conduct the actual training in September because it would have left us with no communicators, and by Special Forces policy, therefore, non-deployable. So we sent Pedro by himself. Ali had tantrums for a couple of days over that, because he wanted to make the per diem money—a rare occurrence in the stingiest Group in SF—and because he had an abiding and acute itch for pubescent, dark-skinned, Dominican female flesh. And he had bought completely into the collective consensus around the company that we would never go to Haiti.

Mike tried to explain to him patiently and diplomatically that we needed him so long as this mission was leaning forward, that the team's needs superseded the desire of an individual. Ali remained pugnacious and disrespectful. I lost all desire to placate him at this point, and became short.

"What would you do if you were us, Ali?" I asked.

"I'd look at how little chance there is of this mission going, and let my guys make a little fucking money for a change," was the petulant response.

"That's why you're not in charge," I replied. "The fucking discussion is closed."

Ali could be humorous and charming at times, but other times he would get on your last tiny fraction of a nerve with his whining, noisy grievances. It was particularly frustrating that he could display such occasional insight, such apparent dedication to mission, then revert without warning to the behavior of a selfish adolescent. He was a classic case of a soldier who "let his dick do his thinking." And I was convinced that it wasn't the money that concerned him. Money was a smokescreen for old sarge, an issue no respectable team sergeant can ignore. . . one of the three M's. . . meals, mail, money. Ali wasn't wound up about the money. Ali was interested in feeding his vanity with worshipful, naive, juvenile, Third World girls. This compulsion of Ali's would resurface as a conflict between us again. And his delicate ego would finally cast him in the role of my own personal Brutus.

September 9, 1994

Pedro was still on the mission in the Dominican Republic.

We were training on reverse cycle. Rest in the day, train at night. The team was trying to get completely caught up on our Level 1 requirements for HALO.

HALO is an acronym for High Altitude Low Opening, which is an unofficial term for Military Free Fall Parachuting. ODA 354 is a "specialty team," that specialty being HALO. To be deployable by free fall parachute into an operational area, by policy, our detachment had to be Level 1 qualified. That meant that within the last ninety days the team had to have performed at least three night combat equipment jumps. It sounds easy, but the coordination of aircraft, drop zones, equipment, external support and weather was a full time hassle. And to perform the night equipment jumps, you had to have conducted so many night non-equipment jumps, and to conduct the night jumps you had to have conducted day equipment jumps, and for them day non-equipment jumps. . . ad nauseum. The point is that to do the qualifying jumps, the team had a lot of other jumps to complete.

We had two night jumps to make. We were scheduled on Normandy Drop Zone to have a Casa 212 aircraft between 0100-0500 (that's between one and five in the morning in English).

We were working on our assembly procedures.

Assembly procedures are no piece of cake. They are the hardest thing to do at the end of a series of hard things to do on any HALO operation.

The idea is to fall more or less together, in the dark, without banging into each other in free fall, and without airing your parachute out into someone's face. If it sounds dangerous, that's because it is.

The free faller tries to relax while his rucksack makes him rock and wobble like a three hundred pound potato chip. He pulls his ripcord at a prescribed altitude, indicated by the altimeter (hope it works) on his wrist, and waits for the pilot chute to slither off his back. He frequently gets his socks rolled down (figuratively, of course) by the opening shock.

Upon completion of this pitching and swaying at 120 miles an hour and being cracked like a whip, in the dark, the jumper is supposed to try to find his companions in the air by looking for the tiny strobe lights taped to their helmets.

The next step is to line up hundreds of feet away from one another in the air and under canopy, low man in the front and high man in the rear, in what we called a stack. The low man becomes the base. Where he lands, everyone else is supposed to glide in behind him on a precise angle and land all within a 50 meter radius. The idea is for the team to be able to count heads quickly, hide the excess gear, and proceed with a mission as a complete unit. Failure to assemble obligates the befuddled team members to spend the next two or three years scouring the countryside for one another instead of performing the assigned mission. Failure to assemble turns the mission into what we referred to in the Rangers as a "goat fuck."

This type of training is stressful and fatiguing.

So we talked our SOP (Standing Operating Procedure) over. Strobes on at the "stand by" command. Out of the plane in a straight line at one second intervals. Keep track of the man you follow out at all times during freefall. Fifty meter interval in the air. No "relative work." High pulls. Base man airs our at 4,500 feet, all others at 5,000. Base man pulls two long, right hand "flat turns" to identify himself, while all others execute one slow, right hand "flat turn" to assess relative altitudes and spot the base man. Low to high, in sequence, turn one tight, right hand corkscrew, then get into the stack. Everyone follows the base man, even if he heads for Tennessee. Land. De-rig weapons. Stay low. Collapse and stow the parachute and air items. Assemble on the base man. Move to a *cache* point.

We rigged up, parachute, load carrying equipment, (those suspenders and belts with all the war gear clipped on) (LCE), rucksack, weapon, helmet. In the dark, we looked like a tribe of Sasquatches.

Rod, the jumpmaster on this drop, coordinated with the aircraft. We didn't want to go to the normal 12,000 feet AGL (Above Ground Level). We wanted out at 8,000. It cut down on the amount of time one spent buffeting around one's equipment in freefall like the tail on a kite, with your ass so tight you couldn't drive a straight pin up it with a five pound sledgehammer.

We conducted two jumps that night. The first one we somehow split into two groups in free fall—someone did not maintain contact with the jumper to his front. The low men for the two groups were so far apart that we ended up in two groups on the ground, around 200 yards apart. On the second grouping, we did well in the air, but got strung out on our final approach, so the landing line would have covered around 100 yards. Nonetheless, we could have assembled off that one.

Mike and I were comparatively satisfied with the last jump.

It was five in the morning when we returned to the team room. We were dead tired. Just breathing seemed like an effort, and we still had to put away our gear and submit a closing report.

Major Fox, the company commander, had left a message compelling us to attend a formation at eight o'clock that morning. We groaned. We were utterly sapped.

0800. Formation. It was Haiti. The green light was on.

Our ultimate target would be Fort Liberte, the political center in the Northeast, located half an hour from the Dominican border.

The concept we were briefed on was different than anything we anticipated. We were to follow the initial assault forces, Rangers and 82nd Airborne types, into Port-au-Prince, from where we would be pushed out into "Hubs." A hub would consist of several teams under the direction of a company headquarters, called an Advanced

Operational Base (AOB). From those AOB hubs, we would be subsequently pushed out into our team Areas of Operational Responsibility (AORs), which were the spokes emanating from the hubs, whereupon we would seize control of our team targets.

Once we had established local security, we were to begin "stability operations." Stability efforts were to be "pushed out," or systematically expanded, as the mission progressed, until we had the whole country under control. Estimated time: Six months. The Force Armee d'Haiti (FAd'H: Haitian armed forces) was to be dismantled and/or destroyed. We were to take our area of operation, an area we estimated between 500 and 1000 square kilometers, and politically reconstruct it with members of the legitimate government.

Mike, electrified as he was, admitted to being a little baffled. This mission was not like anything we'd ever been trained for or conceived of doing.

I suggested that we look at the problem to be solved as a bit like establishing a post-revolutionary local government, and that we prioritize our tasks looking simultaneously at our security needs and at basic problem of reversing the current civil-military relationship. This was a relationship that Mike had studied, and that I had taught, in Military Science courses at West Point.

We entered into an excited conversation about what we would need to do. As we gamed through the options and possibilities, both of us became increasingly enthusiastic. Mike quickly grasped the implications of our autonomy and the scope of our responsibility on this mission. We were going to have our own vastly challenging team sector, and we would have to start from scratch.

"We'll need to contact the most influential people in the community," I speculated.

"Like who?"

"Like the mayor or whatever they have. Like the local priest. Like the voodoo priest or priestess, if they're the ones who have influence. Like educators. Like the Lavalas leaders."

"Lavalas? Why them?" Mike, like everyone, had the media fed misgivings about Lavalas.

"It's their guy. They're in power when he comes back. They are already organized. They have popular support. We'll need them to get things done." This was my initial move in the long struggle to influence the operation.

"I don't know. They're supposed to be pretty radical."

"They'll need us, and we'll need them. They can make things happen."

"Maybe so. We'll look at that. But what do we do when we get there? How do you get control? This is a big fucking area for a team."

"Dunno. Maybe we'll get follow on conventionals to work the security. Maybe not. Definitely, though, we have to eradicate the power of the Haitian armed forces absolutely. We have to gain total control at the outset. Maybe even go to curfews. They briefed 30,000 people in Fort Liberte." (another Military Intelligence coup. . .the actual population of FL was around 6-7,000 folks.)

"Holy Shit!" Mike exclaimed.

"We'll come up with a tactical plan. Don't worry. You and I are strong on planning."

"I'm not worried about the tactical plan. That's the easy part."

"It's a question of what we do afterward really. How do we put the place together? That's why we need to get in touch with the local who's who—to use them to get stuff done. To facilitate their efforts to organize a new political structure." I will reiterate that I did not have the big picture. The fix was already in.

"Political structure?"

"You know. Locally. Set up a system of representation. Look for revenues. Prioritize community needs for attention."

"Yeah. This is like DA and Civic Action all rolled up into one. We have the people. Best French speaker. Best construction engineer."

We went on like this for a while.

We started preparing the team for deployment. We rechecked our packing lists, started organizing team boxes, tracked down every piece of equipment we might conceivably need for every contingency.

The team had high spirits. There was talk of how to react to combat, scenarios constructed in which we killed the wicked Tonton Macoutes, combat patches and Combat Infantryman Badges awarded, all in the military theater of the mind.

The day wore on, and we were nickel-dimed with preparation minutiae until it was past nine at night. Notes at the end of the day included instructions to tell everyone that our cover story was preparation for an EDRE (Emergency Deployment Readiness Exercise) and that we had a 0700 formation to start our POM (Preparation for Overseas Movement). An EDRE. Right! That's gonna fool those ignorant civilians.

"When do you guys go to Haiti?" asked Sherry that night, as we lay in bed.

8: My Guys Have Been There

10 September, 1994

POM (Preparation for Overseas Movement) is an activity to ensure that everyone is legally, financially and medically prepared to deploy on a military adventure overseas.

We stood in lines, reviewed the status of our wills and powers of attorney, re-initialed our life insurance, confirmed addresses and phone numbers, and caught everyone up on their shots. As a Salvadoran poet once said, we were "inoculated against everything except death."

The word about 354, the "killer team" reputation, had leaked into our new Company Headquarters, under the command of Major Mark O'Neill. We were physically imposing, stout fellows with big LCE (load carrying equipment—the war belts soldiers wear for ammo pouches, canteens, first aid dressings, compasses, and other stuff) and big rucks, cocky as only a team fresh from six months of intensive training and twice over Level 1 in the last ninety days can be. Mike and I shamelessly pimped the team's language proficiency.

So, that morning, when the original plan to take Gonaives was briefed to the seven teams under our AOB, Detachment 354 (us) had the mission to enter the breach at the caserne and secure the foothold in the compound.

This is what would be considered by some folks "the sexy mission." I told Mike we'd be better off without it. He understood immediately what I meant. If a portion of a mission goes bad on someone's overall plan, then those responsible for that portion will be held accountable. It's an old military maneuver called "you get to be my sacrificial lamb." It was great that we were thought so highly of that we got this "sexy" sub-unit mission, but we were not comfortable with the overall plan, which seemed not to be developed around planning principles, but slapped together in an incredibly amateurish way.

Military planning doctrine is actually quite sound. When it is applied properly, it works, provided the unit is capable of executing certain fundamental tactics, and the commander has the capability of flexible application of combat principles based on his reading of a dynamic tactical situation. The mission is analyzed to determine exactly what the context of the operation is, and to determine exactly what the commander who assigned the mission wants the end-state to be on the ground at the completion of that mission.

Once the executing commander determines what that desired end state is, he then carefully assesses the intelligence available to determine the enemy's capability, strength, disposition, morale and doctrine (if any), to make an educated guess about that enemy's probable courses of action. The terrain for the operation is carefully analyzed, because sound use of terrain is the linchpin of tactical success, and failure to analyze and properly utilize terrain is a sure recipe for military disaster. Then the commander looks at his own assets, personnel, equipment, training, and develops two, three or four apparently viable courses of action of his own, which he war games against the probable course of action of the enemy.

With careful, objective appraisal of the war-gaming probabilities, one course of action shall always emerge as superior. That course of action is then analyzed to determine what the main effort of that action is to be, in order to prioritize available resources to that effort. And that main effort is analyzed to determine what is the key event that must succeed to ensure the satisfactory completion of that effort. That event is called the decisive point. Again, specific plans have to be generated to absolutely guarantee success at the decisive point. Mike and I understood this process well, and Mike is as proficient at this process as any captain I have ever known in the Army.

None of that was being addressed in the briefing of our "plan" to take Gonaives. We were developing a plan like a board game with no rules. There seemed to be more a concern with getting every element its own little mission. Can't be leaving anyone out, can we? No mention was ever made of what the probable course of enemy action would be. No team or combination of teams was told, you are the main effort. No one had identified what could be called a decisive point. Setting up a roadblock two blocks away was given the same weight as entering the compound.

Mike and I were not appropriately ecstatic about being honored with the entry mission, because we weren't happy with the overall development of the plan, and because we had no control over the other moving parts adjacent to us, all of whom were armed. Their level of training was unknown, and therefore suspect, to us.

The other thing that bothered us, and would continue to bother us, was the double whammy of no specific guidance for what to do after we seized the garrisons, a task everyone was absolutely sure could be accomplished, and the absence of emphasis on the part of planners for what tasks needed to be accomplished immediately after seizure. What would be the priority of work for establishing a security plan, setting up and maintaining communications, establishing a system to ensure that intelligence drove future operations? The tactical plan was, at least as Mike and I saw it, the easy part (though we were being proven wrong as that pertained to some other commanders). Without a concept for setting up housekeeping afterwards, we could spend days trying to crisis manage our way through these tasks in the midst of emerging events. Failure to plan for these post combat priorities would be an invitation to lose our initiative. If we did not have firm control over our situation, the situation might force us to dance like dolts as it shot at our feet.

We were to have a reprieve, however, at least on the tactical side of the question. ODA 372, one of our sister elements with AOB 370, was led by one Captain Sargent (his real surname). He was a newly arrived captain fresh out of the "Q Course," (short form for the Special Forces Qualification Course) with that dazzled I'm-going-to-combat look in his eye that frightens combat veterans the world over. He was busily politicking with his assigned company commander, Major O'Neill, for part or all of the entry mission that Mike and I desperately wanted out of.

"Some of my guys have been to Panama," he said, "They've been there." Given what I knew about Special Forces missions in Panama, where the biggest danger had been gonorrhea, I had to suppress my urge to put him in his place.

He first approached me when I was roaming through the company area, giving me some song and dance abut why it might be better if they went in first and we followed. It was a convoluted rationale, delivered with the urgency of a child wheedling a favor.

"Sure," I told him. "Sounds good to me."

He seemed so relieved. I know I certainly was.

I told Mike about it. He, too, seemed amused by the whole affair, as well as relieved that we might play a more peripheral role in the "plan."

The time schedule changed with wind directions that day. The guys were instructed to build a pallet for immediate follow on for the mission. They did. Three hours later they were told to break it down and put the stuff in the team room again. A member of 3rd Battalion informed us that building and breaking down pallets time and time again was standard practice for them.

There was another early formation in the morning. We'd briefed plans and changes until the guys were dozing on them. We'd built and broken a pallet. Speculation and rumor was increasing. Bureaucratic stupidity was emerging as a kind of theme. So just before seven that evening, we sent the guys home.

9: The Face Under the Streetlamp

The eleventh of September didn't feel like a Sunday. We would soon lose track of the days of the week. Kyle fired up the 50-cup coffeepot, and we went to that well again and again that day. We packed and unpacked the pallet two more times, exactly in accordance with the procedure the insider had described the day prior.

Mike, Rod, and I stayed out of the packing business, concentrating instead on trying to obtain intelligence. Rod trotted back and forth to S-2, and back and forth to the intelligence representative for ODB 370. He was collecting maps and submitting the Requests for Information (RFIs) that Mike and I were cranking out like machines.

We requested everything imaginable. We wanted a copy of the Haitian Constitution. We wanted the geopolitical divisions of the country. We wanted the names of all the political parties. We wanted the name of the Mayor of Fort Liberte. We wanted the name of the priest in Fort Liberte. We wanted the names of all the members of the FAd'H garrison in Fort Liberte. We wanted aerial imagery of the entire area. We wanted weather forecasts, the depths of rivers, the tides, the names of any unions or cooperatives, the conditions of the roads, the status of weapons and vehicles at the garrison, we wanted everything.

Late that morning, we received what we would get. . . the TIP (Target Intelligence Packet). In it were some of the most useless and generic catalogues of information (misinformation as it turned out) about Haiti and its culture one might find anywhere outside of, say, a fundamentalist mission on the outskirts of Cap Haitien. But what we did have was some of the highest quality satellite imagery I have ever seen on any operation. The overhead photographs were of such a high quality that we used them in Haiti in lieu of maps for the city of Fort Liberte. The photos matched up nicely with the 1/250,000 pilots' maps we had pieced together, and with the 1/50,000 military maps, which we had also built into a broad mosaic.

With the TIP photos, we developed a tentative plan for taking Fort Liberte. We would fly in under cover of darkness, to an LZ selected South of town, move quickly to three mutually supporting positions, sequentially overwatching each position as that position was occupied, seal off access to and from the garrison, demand capitulation with a loudspeaker, and systematically convert the garrison to a rock pile if that capitulation was not immediate and absolute. We only had eight people, and we could not afford to play footsie with a garrison that contained up to 180 armed personnel.

To do the job, we had our night vision capability, anti-tank weapons to heat up the building, machineguns and, of course, AC130 gunship support overhead, which could be called on within seconds to deliver 105 millimeter artillery shells through the roof.

All in all, an imminently functional plan, and one that seemed to excite the team.

We would soon find that we did not have the autonomy to develop our own ground tactical plan for infiltration or for seizure of the garrison. For the time being, however, the team members embraced the plan enthusiastically, with only Rod expressing some trepidation about the manpower ratio; and as I said, Rod tended toward the conservative.

Mike and I were still struggling with the fact that after the takedown, for which there was an easily identifiable desired end-state, we had not yet received specific guidance on the commander's intent for follow on operations—simply nebulous directives like "conduct stability operations." Both of us were becoming comfortable, even cautiously enthused, with the idea of working "by, through, and with the indigenous population" (a favorite phrase of the newly assigned Group

Commander) to rebuild a society in tatters (note the element of both arrogance and unreality in this construction). We allowed ourselves flights of grandiosity, because these flights proved so fruitful at generating practical ideas for establishing ourselves in the community. Nonetheless, that specific statement of observably completed tasks that would tell us the mission was complete was missing. And it would remain missing, leaving us—ultimately leaving me—to fill in the spaces.

On Monday, the 12th, you guessed it, we built and tore apart a pallet. Finally, the pallet configuration was decided upon. Each detachment member would carry a rucksack and a kit bag, containing every item that might be mission essential within the first 24 hours. Every detachment would build three pallets; one with necessary items for immediate deployment. . . spare batteries, extra ammunition, toilet articles, sleeping material, more food, stuff we'd need to operate for a week. The second pallet would be the follow-on, at the one-week mark. This one would have to sustain us until the 30th day after initiation of operations. The last pallet was the follow-on to the follow-on, on which we were told to pack long term needs for the team's operations.

So we packed. The initial pallet was shared with another team, and strictly limited to a bag or footlocker per man and three bags or boxes per team. The second one contained, again, items in accordance with the guidance we were given. The last one we loaded with everything we could stuff on there, to include weights, a refrigerator, boxes after boxes of extra medical supplies that had accumulated, a grill, spare ponchos we'd picked up at DRMO (a kind of army junkyard), coffee pots, radios, everything. This pallet towered to about 75 inches high. I enchant the reader with the details of this load plan only because it would come to have such an impact on our living conditions, the mission, and a number of relationships.

When the pallets were built, Mike and I sent the guys home to spend some down-time with families, while we waited on word from 370, which we intended to pass on to the guys. This worked, with the exception of Ali, the only communicator deploying.

The communications plan was also being batted around so frantically and frequently that it quit making sense. Ali had his hands full just trying to keep up with, and briefing Mike and I, on the constant changes.

The communicator on 370 was a dumb asshole, to put it diplomatically. He gave absolutely no consideration to anyone's input on his plan, which was complex, time consuming, and secure all out of proportion to the non-existent threat. There was not one scintilla of evidence that any Haitian "hostiles" had either the inclination or the ability to monitor or triangulate our transmissions. Ali tried in vain to get him to use high frequency radios with simple secure devices that were far simpler than the Byzantine plan 370 mandated. And a new, revised, more complicated and cumbersome plan had to be briefed that evening, for which I had to regretfully call Ali back in.

Formation the next day would be at 0500.

Each day we were not told until we arrived for work whether we would leave that day or not. Sherry dropped me off each morning, thinking that we might not see each other for six months (the time frame for which we were told to mentally prepare). It was an uncomfortable and tearful experience, that we repeated on the 9th, then the10th, then the 11th, then the 12th. At one point, Sherry became distressed. . . the 11th, I think. . . and said she wished they would just go ahead and go. The mission was giving us a ride on the emotional Tilt-a-Whirl anyway, and this yoyo goodbye routine only worsened matters.

When I was in Delta, I remember, my daughter would glare at me wordlessly if I were caught packing a suitcase. I was leaving her again. I would not know until much later that I was leaving her exposed not only to the absence of her father, but to a parade of activities and characters surrounding her mother when I went away. I left her when she was 13, to go to the Q-Course, moving her mother and her into a nice apartment in San Antonio. A couple of days after I left, a boyfriend moved in. My daughter was left helpless in the presence of this betrayal, a situation in which she was forced to lie about to me every time I called.
"How is everything, honey?"
"Fine."
"Is something bothering you?"
"No. Everything's fine."

I rose at 0330, on the 13th, so I could get a good bellyful of coffee before the embarkation follies began. Sherry got up with me. We didn't say much, and what we did say was very practical and current. "I need to pick up some milk today." "Wanna see the news?" "Guess I need to put on a clean uniform."

The word was finally put out the day prior. Today was departure day. Sherry seemed barely contained, but I had been coerced into a promise not to get emotional. So I watched her move about the house. She was picking up around the house at four in the morning. At four fifteen, she said she was going to wake the kids to tell me goodbye.

We took each other in our arms and held on tightly and silently for a few moments. Then she woke the kids.

Jessie was 11. Jayme was 9. Jeremy was 8. Sherry told them I was going away for a while. Jayme and Jeremy didn't have a good handle on the figure six months. Jessie did, and he cried while he squeezed me around my ribs with his face in my chest.

At the company, Sherry and I took turns lingering more than we'd just resolved not to do. I finally backed away from the car. Her face was bluish in the reflected fluorescence of the street lamp. It was 0445, damp and dark. The car was already moving out of the parking lot, when her face turned away from me. The car crept between the rows of other cars, hesitated at the street, took a right up the last curve in the street, stopped for an instant at the stop sign, then pulled out to the left and behind the curtain of pines.

10: OBSERVATIONS ON THE PLANE

Sleepless, physically tired already, emotionally caught between the sadness of goodbye and the anticipation of an adventure, we filed onto an L1011 passenger airplane before dawn. We dropped rucks and bags planeside, then mounted an American TransAir Airlines charter. The incongruity of our wrinkled uniforms and our weapons with the upholstered, commercial neatness of the interior of the plane and the neatly pressed flight attendants was striking.

We were all hungry by then, and began clamoring at the attendants for food. A couple of the attendants were young attractive women, and the silly posturing began.

It never ceases to amaze me how many men in the army, even men in their thirties or more, who one would think had mellowed, will become painfully self conscious in the presence of some women, and how they will behave even more obnoxiously macho than usual for what they believe to be an appreciative audience.

(I am convinced that the reasons so many marriages fail in Special Forces has much more to do with mate selection than job stress. Insecure men select by a superficial physical standard, mating with thoroughly colonized women, who themselves are selecting by availability and a regular job. Both participants share the belief that these macho boys are really as stable as they pretend. Failure is inevitable.)

Ali was sitting next to me, and we were attended by a friendly, attractive young woman of about 26-27 years. Ali visibly swelled (being a very thick weight lifter to begin with), giving her all the physical presence he could muster, and engaged her in a conversation with a persona I had never seen before. The rugged, no nonsense, former Marine role I had grown accustomed to suddenly metamorphosed before my eyes into a grinning, oily voiced, cow eyed, sexual vulture. Within moments he had learned that she was studying French, which he spoke fluently, and he was playing linguistic badminton with her. Only slightly less surprising was her obvious response to his overtures. . . overtures so greasy and obvious that several of us sitting nearby were squirming in our seats with embarrassment bordering on nausea.

With Ali, I was to see this alter ego again and again in the following weeks, and with my former associate the system was the same. There was a sudden widening of the eyes combined with a softening of the gaze. The lips draw back to expose the teeth in a facsimile of a boyish smile, as the face juts forward, presumably to fill the view of the victim and hypnotize her much like the animated serpent does in *The Jungle Book*. From a distance the perpetrator appears from the side to have a misalignment of the cervical spine, an illusion caused by the improbable forward thrust of the predator's head. This pre-pounce posture is accompanied by verbiage...patronizing, condescending, simple minded. "How 'bout a pretty smile, little lady," or "You're just the prettiest thing I've seen all day."

As an outside observer, I can roughly estimate that this approach, if used like a shotgun blast, that is, over and over on every candidate that holds still long enough for it, until it works, is functional at gaining sexual favors about two percent of the time in the United States (where the vast majority of women see through it within 1.5 seconds), and about twenty percent in Third World nations, where lack of sophistication, naive impressionability, and abject poverty (making all gringos a possible reprieve from desperation) tend to work in favor of the Oilcan Harry who employs it. So if one utilizes the approach fifty times a night in the States, he might get laid regularly. In the Third World, where the competition for affluent gringos is fierce, one only need compromise one's integrity, self respect and dignity five times to achieve the desired result, that is, public conquest of a female to satisfy momentary physical and long term psychological voids.

In the case of Ali, everyone familiar with him has been subjected to long, graphically detailed, play by play recounting of his intrepid forays into the bodies of credulous or desperate women, over and over again, with the storytellers' dick being the protagonist, and the woman (or teenage girl in many cases) being the generically surmounted and conquered "bitch."

Out the window, Cuba appeared.

11 : The Tent

At somewhere around 0830 Local, we arrived in Guantanamo Bay, Cuba. I was sleepless and cranky. Most of the rest of the guys were just cranky.

I have never slept well at the beginning of anything significant, like job interviews or invasions. In fact, I went through my tour in Vietnam on about three hours sleep a night. In Ranger School, sleep deprivation was not my problem. It was going without food that almost killed me. Fast burner metabolism.

We reversed the load drill, packing out on trucks loaded precariously high, driven by civilians who were religious zealots or schizophrenics (I say this because the causal relationship between wildly reckless driving and death obviously wasn't in their frame of reference), who wheeled around corners, nearly up on two wheels, with us perched atop our mile high gear, clutching at whatever straps and buttons availed themselves to our terrified grasp.

When we arrived at our Isolation Site, we did not encounter the expected RFAB constructions, the neatly stacked cases of bottled water, the supplies of Meals, Ready to Eat (MREs) and the identification cards that designated who went in what tent.

This would be the set up I had grown to expect in the Army, but this was 3rd Special Forces Group, as sorry an outfit as I ever had the displeasure of working with in the army.

What we did, in fact, find was an open ten acre field west of the bay, warming with sticky speed in the freshly risen tropical sun, and dozens of tents still packed in the large wooden crates that were randomly scattered about the field.

The view of the sparkling Caribbean was excellent, but we were in no mood to appreciate it. A couple of support units who had arrived by truck shuttle from the airfield prior to us were unpacking more tentage. Dozens of support people were at the high west end of the field, seemingly giving instructions. We downloaded our team equipment where we were told, and I went to the apparent center of activity, asking where we procured our tent, and where it was to be set up. A staff sergeant told me to get one out of that (pointing at it) box, take it over there (pointing again), align it with them (indicating a group spreading their tent on the ground), and make it the fifth tent down this (the index finger again) row. The open field had become an intellectual challenge worthy of Mensa membership.

We followed his instructions to the letter. I whipped up a sense of urgency to get the job done quickly before the midday heat arrived, emphasizing that the sooner we got done, the sooner we could catch up on some sleep.

The tent was a "General Purpose, Large," very spacious, for which we were grateful, since we didn't want to sleep among the clutter of equipment. We worked up a generous sweat, pacing off the distances, carefully measuring the dimensions, pounding the stakes into a granite-like accumulation of coral, spreading the heavy thick canvas this way and that to determine which end was out, which up.

A different staff sergeant then walked up and informed us that we were not in the right place. We were to move one space down. Somehow, even in the absence of any marking, the spaces were as neatly delineated as cemetery plots.

"What?" I asked, as the perspiration slid down my nose, down my back, down my arms and legs. The entire team was standing around, hands on hips now, looking at the suddenly uncomfortable staff sergeant. No one was smiling.

"One space down," he answered timidly. "The sergeant major. . . says you guys are in the wrong place."

"Well, why didn't the fuckin' sergeant major tell us that before we stretched this ten thousand pounds of shit out on the ground, and before we drove all these wooden stakes into this lovely fuckin' coral rock, since no one has had the fuckin' foresight to provide mallets?"

I was tired. I had no idea that it was going to come out that way until it was already out, and the poor messenger was wounded with the figurative shot.

"Sorry. I didn't do it. I just. . ."

My conscience emerged. I apologized, sent him away, and we started the movement to the "next space down," kicking out the stakes that we had laboriously pierced the rocky ground with, tugging and toting the ton of canvas like ants dragging a dead grasshopper.

Within thirty minutes, we were ready to start pushing the poles up under the tent. Another staff sergeant came.

"Yes?"

"The sergeant major says that you guys aren't supposed to use a GP Large. Teams get GP Mediums."

My real self was already warning me that this was just another messenger, not the author of this confusion, and that he deserved no abuse. I had severely strained my left trapezius and right brachioradialus in an exercise two weeks earlier. My Motrin had worn off, and I was in pain. A demon possessed me, one that really liked bad words. I was cannibalizing staff sergeants.

"Look, goddamit! You fuckin' people have been here for two fuckin' days. No one's done shit to prepare this fuckin' site. One of you tells me one motherfuckin' thing, then another one another motherfuckin' thing, then another motherfucker changes it again. My fuckin' people lack sleep. They're in a bad mood. I'm in a bad mood. Just who in the fuck engineered this goat fuck, anyhow? Maybe the fuckin' sergeant major would like to set the motherfuckin' tents up his motherfuckin' self. Maybe we'll just sleep under the motherfuckin' stars. It don't look like fuckin' rain, now, does it? What the fuck has been going on here for the last two days? Sunbathin'? Shell collectin'? Sippin' cocktails on the fuckin' veranda and watching the fuckin' sky change?"

"Look, man. . ."

"No, Staff Sergeant! I ain't a man. I'm a fuckin' Master Sergeant in the United States fuckin' Army, who has eight people here who are gettin' a jackhammer up the ass from the disorganization and incompetence of their support people, and it's very close to pissin' me off."

"Roger, Master Sergeant. But. . ."

"What if we just decide not to put up any fuckin' tent at all?"

Mike intervened. He reminded me that I was shooting another

messenger. I took a minute or two to calm down. I called the staff sergeant back, as he walked away with his head down, making me feel like a heel. For the second time in an hour, I apologized.

By one thirty in the afternoon we were set up. We all laid down to cat nap or gaze blankly at the ceiling of the tent. When I'd summoned the energy, I hunted down a broken piece of plyboard, on which I mounted the team planning maps and overlays.

Rod was a shower freak. He took as many as he could fit in each day. He brought starched fatigues to Guantanamo, for God's sake, for a deployment to Haiti. It was part of his character, like praying before every meal and jump, like always being cautious. Leave it to Rod to find a shower.

We had settled in after the arduous first day. The Rangers were moving in down the plain from us. A huge shower tent was under construction, to be completed on the following day. Just uphill from our tent city was the Naval Guest House, kind of a hotel for traveling active duty folks.

At about six that evening, Rod showed up at the tent, smelling like Irish Spring, wet headed, and smiling like a shit eating cat. He told us he had found a shower. Where, we asked.

The Naval Guest House had left the door unlocked on one of their rooms. . . a room with running, hot water. He suggested we each slip in one at a time to clean up. Within ten minutes, there were seven Special Forces troops lounging around the suite, paging through the magazines, channel surfing through the cable TV with the remote, and rotating through the shower.

Just as the last man, Dave Grau, came out of the shower, we heard a key scratching in the door.

Everyone leapt to their feet, signaling silence with fingers across the lips, and looking for a way to go. We piled up by the back door (there was a front and back door), and waited for the other door to open, whereupon we barreled through ours. We were confronted by three SEAL-Delta-JSOC-types, that is, guys with nice civilian clothes, longer than average hair and mustaches, and prima donna stamped across their foreheads.

"You guys renting this room," asked one prima donna.

"Why, are you?" responded one of our guys.

"Well, what is your room number?" asked the prima donna

spokesman.

"Well, we don't have one," I said. "The room was open. We were taking showers."

"Well, take a hike, guys," said the prima donna spokesman. "This room has been paid for."

That sure put us in our place.

"Well, we were on our way out anyway," said one of our guys, as we hustled out the door at the end of the hallway.

We had a good laugh over that one back at the tent.

For the rest of the evening, we futzed with our equipment, speculated wildly and inaccurately about what the mission would be like, and eventually went to bed, where squadrons of mosquitoes feasted on our flesh for the remainder of the evening.

12: SKINNYDIPPING

We had to get on track with a schedule. So we rose at 0600 on the 14th of September for Physical Training. By 0640, we were slogging at a dispassionate pace down the Northbound road that paralleled the bay. It was a reconnaissance run with salt water access as the objective.

Everyone was residually listless. All of us were strained by the anticipation of a profusion of bullshit. Every mission, good or bad, training or real-world, is preceded by it. It's an officer thing, the profusion of bullshit. So we were searching for a private team space to loosen up in from time to time.

An unerring collective sense of direction turned us down a dirt road toward the blue-gray horizon. We blew past the concertina wire that indicated limited access. We turned right at a fork in the road on a mental coin toss by me. We ran directly past the RESTRICTED sign laying on the ground, and saw the "beach."

It was at the end of a steep drop in the road, between rock outcroppings populated with ten or so marine iguanas. Hoping to frighten us off, the iguanas bobbed their heads at us. The "beach" itself was made of dozed up sand and a great deal of crushed coral. Through the clear water, the sand and grass bottom was clearly visible. A seawall had been dozed up against the surf, great boulders of coral, just under the level of the water, adequate to break up the high waves.

I turned around, and propped the RESTRICTED sign up against an old saw horse that was on the side of the road, placing the warning squarely in the center of the wheel tracks. With that I had claimed the place for ODA 354.

There was a concrete dock built over the South end of this little lagoon. A lifeguard seat was centered on the craggy pseudo-beach like a deserted fire tower. The latrines were at the North end, back from the water. The outer walls were piled with scrap wood and other signs of refuse. Centered and back from the beach sat a tin roofed bohio. In the middle of the concrete dock was an aluminum picnic table.

In the rocks adjacent to the "beach" were a half dozen homemade sea crafts, rafts made of 55 gallon drums, sails made of tattered blankets, one with a rusty remnant of a five horsepower motor. They'd been abandoned at sea when the US Coast Guard had intercepted them, with Haitians refugees aboard, and the current had grounded the crafts here on the rocks. I was astonished by the resourcefulness of the constructions, awed by the courage or foolhardiness of venturing onto the open sea with these puny vessels, like tiny corks on the heaving belly of a capricious god.

We shucked our PT clothes on top of the picnic table and leaped into the warm water, buck nekkid every one.

It was positively amniotic. I love warm salt water. I could float around in it for hours. Getting out is a feat of willpower.

Rod refrained from entering the water. Rod grew up in Puerto Rico, but he did not like swimming, especially naked, especially in the sun. I had learned from the other guys and from association, Rod was a very modest guy. He was also very homophobic, and this all-male skinny dip had a very limited appeal for him. Finally, Rod (as reported by his associates from trips to the Dominican Republic) avoided sunlight as much as possible. He is very light skinned for a Latino, and in the Caribbean, light skin is prized, even by dark skinned people, the ancient imprint of European colonizers on the collective psyche.

The visual irony of our pale, naked bodies bobbing and splashing in this lagoon during isolation for combat proved irresistible for potential amateur photographers among us, and we all agreed to return for another swim, with cameras this time, that very afternoon.

We left the water reluctantly, just in time to jog over to the chow area, where breakfast was a delicious T-Ration, canned food with enough preservatives to give it that cat piss smell and that polyurethane flavor. It is a fact that after only 24 hours eating the stuff, one's own urine begins to smell like the rations.

We began a working isolation in our tent. Mission analysis of our little part in the Gonaives infiltration was difficult in light of the fact that, under pressure from Captain Sargent, the mission was changing with each rustle of the palm fronds. Sargent was still pressing for the "cool" entry mission at the Gonaives caserne. I had walked past Sargent's tent on two or three occasions, and remember him being very excited about the prospect of having to shoot people. I had a laugh about it with Mike. Mike, true to his East Philly origins, called Sargent "a fuckin' geek."

Late that morning, a message went out instructing all Special Forces personnel to stay out of the guest house rooms. . . they were off limits. . . reserved only for VIPs.

"354 is still at the cutting edge," I told Mike.

13: REHEARSING DEATH

At 1200, still on the 14th, we walked about a mile and a half down the open black asphalt in the midday heat with full combat gear for a rehearsal of the Gonaives infiltration/assault. The site selected for the rehearsal was the edge of a large mud flat adjacent to a mangrove swamp.

Mostly we just practiced getting into gaggles that reflected our tentative aircraft load plan, then walked to our assigned locations around the simulated caserne, which was illustrated with white cloth tape stretched out like an immense floor plan.

Sargent's team now had the mission to go through the breach, while we followed on to clear what was assumed to be barracks in the back of the compound. 352, Captain Sargeant's team, now had responsibility for clearing the two buildings of the main compound, a fact welcomed by Mike Gallante and I every bit as much as it was welcomed by Captain Sergeant and his "been there" boys.

The most peculiar thing we did, in fact one of the most peculiar things I have ever participated in with regard to operations, was to occupy a notional security position while the Headquarters section, under the command of Major Mark O'Neill, practiced approaching the front door of the compound and knocking on it to demand capitulation. Over and over, we practiced the contingency of him being killed while doing this. In the past, I had always learned that if you are planning a course of action that has a high probability of unacceptable casualties, you change the course of action to preclude that contingency. Yet here we were, practicing the commander's demise again and again.

Mike and I were utterly incredulous. Our first inclination was to speak to Major O'Neill about the wisdom of clinging to death as a deliberate course of action. After some discussion, however, we agreed that the less central a role we played in this Major's plan, the better off we would be.

Major O'Neill was newly assigned to this company command, and understandably overwhelmed by the magnitude of the events overtaking us. He was a nice guy, personable, initially interested in the welfare of his people, and in all fairness, he was handed a heaping plate (of shit as it would turn out) to eat with this mission. We had been told that all Haitian garrison commanders would be contacted in advance to arrange their capitulation. We were being directed not to initiate hostilities. In theory, it was a good idea, one that might prevent casualties on both sides, but the interpretation of this concept now had us doing weird shit like rehearsing our own suicides.

Mike and I were sticking to the idea that just because we were demanding surrender was no reason to go in acting too friendly, and we clung to that throughout the mission.

What we did not understand at the time was that the fix was in. Plans were already on the board to put these paragons of police virtue, the FAdH, back on the street.

We reversed the death walk, laden with 100-pound rucksacks, back to our happy camp, back to another pigeon sized T-Ration meal washed down with pale watery Kool Aid.

Ali and Mike had to participate in a communications rehearsal that evening that lasted into the wee hours. These COMEXes, as they were called, would become a regular pain in the ass event. Ali returned each time in an agitated state. No input was being accepted from the detachments. The communications security plan was cumbersome and overdone. We were treating the communications security threat as if we were faced off against the former Soviet Union, when the threat from Haitians was non-existent, and the chance of Cuban intervention based on intercepted traffic was about as probable as being struck by a comet.

Despite all the doctrine that exists to guide commanders toward realism in their assessments and priorities, we were still managing to overestimate the mouse turds and underestimate the mountains.

14: Schism

We swam again for PT, but not until the morning of the 15th. Cameras came with us. The skinny dip lasted for about 30 minutes when the Navy police interrupted. There were two of them, one male, one female. The young man sent his partner back around to the other side of the iguana rocks, then descended the hill to confront us. We could not swim there, he told us. Couldn't we read the sign (the one we had propped up ourselves the day prior) that said the area was restricted?

Rather than explain how we had placed the sign there to stake a claim, we left. On the way out, we pitched the sign back into the weeds alongside the road.

For breakfast, we ate T-Ration "bread pudding." I am a fan of good bread pudding. When it's done right, it can be a delectable finale to a meal. This stuff in the cans was a grey-brown gelatinous brick with millions of tiny bits of "bacon" in it. Bacon. No one finished it even in the face of our unsatisfied GI appetites.

The team spent the rest of the day reacting to nickel-dime demands to move this here, carry that there, give us this list, revise that list. Mike and I dropped by periodically at the AOB tent to see if any information was forthcoming on our intelligence information requests.

Not only were they not forthcoming, they never would be.

We coined a name for the AOB leaders that day, based on their superlative organizational dexterity, their firm resolve, their professional tactical plan, and their mature composure. O'Neill, CPT Connors (the Executive Officer), and Sergeant Major Tinney were now the Three Stooges. In all fairness, using the acuity of hindsight, they were only partly responsible for their own bumbling.

I walked out with Mike to find the Group Headquarters so he could call in a favor from the warrant officer (a neighbor of his in Fayetteville) who ran the Rigger Section (guys who pack parachutes). Mike wanted to get his damaged rucksack sewn on their heavy duty sailmaker sewing machines. When we found the riggers, they had arranged themselves around a swimming pool on top of a hill with a spectacular view. The worker bees were in tents, but the bosses and their support cadre were in air conditioned buildings. Who says the military doesn't reflect the larger society?

That day our follow-on to the follow-on pallet arrived for no apparent reason. It wasn't due to follow us for a month, but there it was. Our team refrigerator was conspicuously sticking out of the frayed plastic cover.

This would become a huge source of controversy. The Three Stooges all came by and told us to break down the pallet and get rid of the refrigerator. We explained that it wasn't for immediate deployment, and that a mistake had been made. Finally, they told us to get cardboard and cover the refrigerator up, since it "looked bad." In the military, perceptions are always more important than facts. This mission would prove that beyond any doubt.

On the 16th we swam, did sit-ups, ate bird sized, ill-tasting meals, and reacted. My neck and forearm were hurting to the point I was ready to look up a doctor for a shot of cortico-steroids. My temper was short.

Major O'Neill had developed his plan to the point that each detachment now understood the sequence in which it was to occupy its respective target. Fort Liberte was second to last, being far, far from both Port-au-Prince and Cap Haitien. The major had decided that he would fly over with each infiltration accompanied by a reaction force. I believe now that this decision was driven by his innate caution, but at the time I was convinced that he was shooting for glory and merit badges, as officers have a tendency to do. I was getting testy.

I had been talking to Somalia acquaintances in the Ranger tents the day prior, and had discovered that Lieutenant Colonels were taking grenadier positions and weapons away from junior enlisted men just to make sure they were on the initial assaults. Many officers will deny that this goes on, but it's not just a lie, its a goddamn lie, and everyone in the army knows it is. There were more bronze stars awarded in Grenada than there were captured Cubans (no correlation implied, just a point to be made), and the same shit happened in Panama. This is interesting, given the fact that the former was an invasion of an island with the population of Leesburg, Virginia waged to save the world's strategic nutmeg supply from socialist domination, and the latter was a "surgical" strike (resulting in mere thousands of civilian casualties) into the heart of a country that we already militarily occupied.

At any rate, this was what I thought Major O'Neill was doing, especially since someone had glanced across the shoulder of one Captain who was hunched over his laptop in one of the tents, pre-writing the narratives of his own awards for the Haiti operation, which had yet to begin.

We were being force fed a ground tactical plan that we did not feel was consistent with our objectives. Our complaints were vocal and frequent, and a shrift was beginning to develop between us and AOB 370, our immediate higher unit. It was directed that we would land with an entire platoon of Rangers, who would accompany us as security to our target garrison in Fort Liberte. I was adamant in my opposition to this option, and I became obnoxious about that opposition, to the point where I felt guilty for what seemed like bullying of Mike, whose opposition was not as obdurate as my own, into accepting my argument.

It was, nonetheless, a sound argument. The Rangers had no language capability. They were still smarting from Somalia. They are a heavily white unit, with more than a little of the aforementioned disposition for racial animosity. They would attract civilian crowds, whom they would fear, misunderstand and fail to control to their own satisfaction, whereupon we would have an ugly incident involving the probable loss of innocent life. This would damage every post infiltration mission we (ODA 354) anticipated, all of which were predicated heavily on the establishment of rapport with the local population.

My tentative solution was to leave the entire platoon on the Landing Zone at the edge of town, under Gonzales' control, guarding our pile of equipment, while the remainder of the detachment seized control of the garrison. Mike concurred, and that part of the plan became fixed (for now).

We were simultaneously fighting for possession of one or two of the Squad Automatic Weapons that were being allocated to the teams, but it appeared that the teams organic to 370 were about to receive them, even though our request for these weapons had been the very first submitted.

I was in the process of ranting, saying something like "I don't trust O'Neill or any of those other motherfuckers," to Mike, when O'Neill walked into the tent, at which point I felt like an asshole, knowing full well that I could be heard through the thin canvas walls.

Mike and I switched to a more diplomatic demeanor, and told Major O'Neill about our concerns.

"Do you think I'm fucking you over?" O'Neill asked, seeming genuinely hurt. O'Neill was really another messenger we were shooting because he was the most visible messenger. I would spend a good deal of time on this mission regretting little things—like hurting O'Neill's feelings and feeling like a heel—in an effort to avoid being involved in something I would regret every day for the rest of my life—like loss of lives, American or Haitian, because someone was detached from reality.

"We just need a SAW (squad automatic weapon). We don't need Rangers. And we don't need a loudspeaker team." The loudspeaker team was also being pushed on us. They are teams of privates from so-called psychological operations units (propaganda units), who broadcast silly taped messages at local populations in the "target" language.

"How are you going to escape if you need to, if no one's there to secure an extraction site?" asked the Major.

"We are not leaving. It's not in the mission statement. . . leaving. When we get off the helicopter, we are staying in Fort Liberte."

"What if you meet resistance?"

"We'll eliminate it."

"What if you can't eliminate it?"

"We'll back off and let Spectre drop 105 rounds into the garrison."

"I think you are underestimating the risk."

"I think you are underestimating the risk to our long term objectives if you let those trigger happy skinheads loose in our town."

Again, Mike signaled for me to let up.

So Mike and the Major hashed away at components of the plan, our plan. A big problem the Major seemed to have was with Mike's mission statement. Mike said that our mission was to "neutralize" the FAd'H. . . to us, the right word. It encompassed all options from capitulation to total destruction. The end-state was to neutralize them, with the minimal force necessary. O'Neill said "neutralize" seemed too much like annihilate. On the contrary, we argued, "neutralize" was the most accurate way to express the variety of contingencies. Use the word "control" he told Mike. This is the kind of semantic crap that staffs can argue about for hours, but in our case it was a symptom of the mutual hostility and distrust growing between us and the AOB.

Oddly enough, other teams were asking for more support. One guy on an adjacent team was heard to moan about "suicide mission" on more than one occasion. We were talking about going up against elements with absolutely no significant training, little operable equipment, and no battlefield experience. It had Mike and me scratching our heads. Our confidence had everyone else scratching theirs. The buzz was picked up, we were "cowboys." Total crap, actually. We were just paying attention to the facts we had about Haiti.

September 17, 1994

"PS-Let's move to a place in the Caribbean. The water here has moods. The sky could sustain life with its colors. The breeze is like a cool pillow. We would like it. I.L.Y. -S"

I folded the letter up, three days in the making, and dropped it into the mailbox at the front of the guest house. It was the first thing I mailed to Sherry.

At 1300, we officially "briefed back" the Major at our tent. Briefing back is reviewing your plan with your next higher commander to ensure that your plan is consistent with his overall intent. . . with good commanders. With poor commanders, it is their opportunity to nitpick, pointlessly alter, or rewrite your plan. The business of "control" versus "neutralize" came up again.

We were receiving handouts from Civil Affairs, Psychological Operations, and the Public Affairs Office. They were telling us about Haitians, very pejorative stuff. Just short of calling them sub-humans.

Advice, ostensibly gleaned from the camps, was being disseminated not to put Haitian detainees in the front of vehicles (they'll think they're being killed), not to handcuff them behind their backs (they'll think they're being killed), not to wear sunglasses (they'll think you are a Macoute and that they are about to be killed). Public Affairs was giving us guidelines on speaking to the press. In it, we were instructed to state our mission as "neutralize the FAd'H." Mike doubled up laughing when he read it.

That afternoon, we were scheduled to have our aerial imagery reviewed by a specialist in photo interpretation from the intelligence section. He arrived at around three. Rod, Mike and I carried our photos from the Target Intelligence Packet (TIP) to him.

He was a skinny, bespectacled, blonde-headed captain, with a nasal voice.

"What is this?" we asked, pointing at items on the photos.

His responses were instantaneous, like he was on Jeopardy.

"That's a truck." "That's vehicle storage area." "That's a tree."

He started studying two of the photos of Fort Liberte, on which one had a tree in front of a building, and the other did not. Suddenly, he became agitated.

"I want to know what happened to that tree. What are the dates on this photo?" On and on he went about the tree, speculating that it had been cut to clear fields of fire in preparation for our arrival.

We told him that we had been told that some of the imagery had been doctored to make it clearer. He insisted that the tree was a problem.

"Haitians are lazy motherfuckers," he stated. "They don't go to the trouble of cutting down a tree for nothing."

"What do they build with and cook on?" I asked.

He ignored that.

We listened to this pretentious, bigoted little prick for about another half an hour, wherein we were given the height of every wall, and the identification of every structure adjacent to the garrison as vehicle storage.

For the record, when we arrived in Fort Liberte, not a single shred of what this so-called, highly trained, professional military intelligence photo interpreter had told us was even approaching accurate. The questionable tree is standing to this day, though the Haitians have overcome their innate laziness enough, apparently, to cut other trees in the area and turn them into charcoal and lumber. The truck he identified was apparently parked in the middle of a three-foot sidewalk with space to spare on each side. The six foot walls were 15 foot prison walls. Not only was there no vehicle storage in what turned out to be a quiet residential neighborhood, one would be hard pressed to find more than ten vehicles in the entire city of Fort Liberte on any given day. In a nutshell, like every bit of intelligence we would receive on this mission, it was horse shit.

Two notable things happened on the 18th. Our target intelligence packet (TIP) got burned and we rehearsed again.

The Three Stooges demanded that we turn in all written material for security on the evening of the 17th. We complied.

On the morning of the 18th, Mike and I wanted to review some of the aerial imagery again to assess some ideas we had for fine tuning the plan. We sent Rod over to fetch the TIP. Rod returned and told us that all the material we had sent to the AOB had been burned. This, apparently, was how they were going to secure it. In the packet of "written material" was our meticulously and tediously produced Evasion and Resistance Plan. We were livid.

Fortunately, Rod had hung on to some of the best photo-imagery to look at the night before. At least that had not been burned to secure it. Just as fortunately, we had all committed the key locations and signals for our Evasion and Resistance Plan to memory. Unfortunately, we were obligated to send our specific plans to the staff intelligence representative, and Rod had to reconstruct and rewrite that. This incident did not enhance our already flagging confidence in the people who had been appointed to supervise our activities.

Adding insult to injury, we were obliged to attend another mud flat rehearsal. Mike implored the commander not to practice being killed at the front door of the caserne any more. Humanitarian impulses had finally overwhelmed Mike's desire to distance himself from the AOB tactical plan.

We determined that it wasn't necessary to carry the 120-pound rucksacks in the midday heat again, just to practice moving from position to position. This we considered an exercise of common sense.

So we initiated the first rehearsal. Each element departed its notional helicopter and moved to its designated staging location. From there we each moved on signal to our respective sub-unit missions.

During this whole thing, Mike and I were cutting up a bit. Ali theatrically pretended to be forcing a notionally captured Haitian guide named Harvey through the notional caserne. We had ceased the pretense of disguising our disdain for the patchwork operation we were planning here. One question that Mike and I pondered on more than one occasion was, What if there are really big crowds? What would we do if they interfered with our movement? Shoot them? It was like no one had a shred of imagination on this thing. This was a town we were being briefed had 150,000 people living in a small area. Most of them had seen a neither a helicopter nor an American soldier before. Wouldn't they sort of flock to the scene of all these landings?

We kept to ourselves, because we were thoroughly convinced that none of this plan was going to go as it was planned anyway. For instance, this entire operation was predicated on aircraft loads of 48 personnel with entry equipment. The airframe was CH-47, and we were prepared to bet paychecks that no one could stuff that many heavily equipped people on these airframes when they were equipped with long range fuel bladders. If the Aircraft load changed, then so did the whole plan. One of the landing sites selected was a cemetery, which in the photo was covered with above ground tombs. Another no brainer. Problem was, we had interjected on this plan so many times that our voices were no longer welcome. So we decided to shut up. We would execute our plan at Fort Liberte, as much as they would let us.

On the second iteration of the rehearsal, we planned to practice actions on enemy contact, a standard rehearsal priority. When we were moving like separate columns of laden ants to our assigned targets, the commander called out that sniper fire had been received from a building a block away (he was rehearsing a contingency, you see), whereupon he proceeded to maneuver large components of the main force away from the caserne, to (one must imagine) crush the sniper with certain and irresistible force. This was a slow, cumbersome, confusing move that would have caused fratricide in real life, and for which we stopped all movement toward taking the principle objective, the caserne.

Mike and I looked at each other. I had taught Principles of War at West Point, and Mike had studied them there. This was a violation of the principle of Objective, which states that every military operation must be directed toward a clearly defined, decisive and attainable objective. This little maneuver just redirected the primary force away from that objective. It was a violation of the principle of Economy of Force, which states that the prudent use of combat power must be used to accomplish a mission with minimum expenditure of resources. Here he was directing the bulk of his force toward a one shot sideshow. Finally, it was a violation of the principle of Offensive, which states, among other things, that the commanders must maintain the initiative, setting the pace and determining the course of battle. . . making the foe react to your actions, not allowing the foe to divert you into reacting to enemy actions.

Mike and I had a lively discussion about this one, the he and the she of which, we decided, must be communicated, however unwelcome, to the commander. Piddley shit like a sniper could happen, we figured, and we did not want to be part of an operation that fell into pandemonium through overreaction to a contingency. This was no longer an issue of inefficiency, but one, we thought, of our personal physical security. So Mike reluctantly got up and walked over to Major O'Neill to explain our position.

He did very well. He was deferential and diplomatic. He recommended a concrete alternative. He pointed out the folly without making it seem we considered it stupid (which we did). To our pleasant surprise, the Major quickly comprehended the implications of this action, and announced to the whole force, that in order not to lose the initiative in taking the objective, any exterior threats would be dealt with by dispatching a squad of Rangers to take care of it.

The whole affair only momentarily disabused Major O'Neill of the "cowboy" portrait he was painting of Mike and me in the gallery of his harried mind.

15: The Soft Option

The evening of the 19th was to be D-Day.

We were quickly learning that our efforts to plan at the detachment level, a decentralization heavily emphasized in both training and doctrine, were given short shrift on actual operations. Individual teams did not get individual requests for intelligence, equipment, ammunition or anything else. Each team was generically parceled an identical everything. This was especially galling with regard to ammunition. Our plans were very specific, and we were very pro-active in requesting what we wanted, yet when we received our issue, it was a generic "detachment" bundle.

Part of the problem with this whole operation was that it was conceived as a very decentralized product, but for security, the individual elements were locked out of the planning process. Consequently, Battalion staffs and above were trying to anticipate questions that rightly were the province of teams.

This is common practice in the military. We preach decentralization, initiative and leaving ground tactical decisions to the highest ranking person who will be in the line of fire on an operation. What we preach is in fact sound doctrine that would yield generally good results. When the operation is a real one, however, especially an operation that we are ultimately sure we will accomplish (like overcoming the Haitian "military"), the command emphasis quickly changes to preserving appearances, seeking glory for favored officers, and establishing extreme top-down control to prevent embarrassing incidents. Good results are exchanged for mediocre ones in the quest to manipulate perceptions, write up awards, and protect careers.

The military preaches latitude in which to make mistakes for the purpose of learning. Every leader has heard of this concept in leadership courses. Unfortunately, the reality for officers is that even the perception of error can have disastrous results for his/her career, depending on who is writing that officer's evaluation. Consequently, even the most talented of officers, who might be inclined to be self-starting, creative, and audacious, finds him/herself in a position where scrupulous caution must be constantly exercised, even if it hampers the mission, and careful attention must be paid to every psychological tic of one's immediate commander, who has near absolute power over the disposition of one's career. This system is called OPMS (the Officer Personnel Management System), and it produces better bureaucrats than it does warriors. Good officers do manage to percolate up through the ranks. But far more back stabbers, cheese eaters, and ass kissers move into positions of authority than good officers.

Fortunately for our current system, these assholes are just what are needed to sit in the board rooms of corporations with hugely bloated, pointless defense contracts, as soon as they retire.

Two things besides the illicit hot showers had been discovered at the guest house. In the morning, they had a pot full of fresh hot coffee. Being an unabashed caffeine addict, I found myself every morning, immediately after a quick void, ferreting into the side door while the check-in clerk was looking the other way, to snatch two styrofoam cups full and slink back outside, where I could enjoy them at the round, concrete picnic table with a view of the breezy Caribbean. The other thing the guest house had was a large screen TV, which by now had been dedicated to CNN in the afternoons and evenings. All pretense that we were on an Emergency Deployment Readiness Exercise had been dropped.

It was on the morning of the 19th that we started hearing something about a delegation to work out a deal with the Cedras people. I had heard so many rumors that I blew it off and told the guys to do the same. We would continue to do what we were doing, which was prepare for the mission we had received.

This advice was, as always, not taken. Soldiers are world class rumor-mongers. SF soldiers are among the worst. The only thing they like to do more than share rumors is speculate about the consequences if the rumor is true. It's a very stressful pastime, but they seem to like it anyway. The speculation for that day was, What if. . . the Carter delegation gets a deal and we go in "soft?" Does that mean we don't get CIBs (Combat Infantryman Badges) or CMBs (Combat Medical Badges)? These particular badges are the Army's most coveted merit badges. They are visible "proof" that the wearer has been "in combat." Officers were rotated in and out of theater in Grenada, Panama and the Gulf War, during those "conflicts" to ensure receipt of a CIB. The Army will deny it, but the denial is a lie. In fact many wearers of the coveted CIB have never seen a shot fired in anger. But the badge itself seems very important to a lot of people, and it seemed very important to my guys that day. Suddenly, I saw a deflation of motivation. Interest in the mission fell away. Skye, Ali, Rod and Kyle all said they'd just as soon go on home.

The irony was, only the first few moments of our infiltration had any significant probability of combat anyway. The six months we anticipated being in Haiti were anticipated to be civil-military operations, involving a lot of glad-handing, social mixing, and tedious, hard work. Nonetheless, without this instant that would qualify them for their badges, members of the detachment had decided that they did not want to do it at all. This was a distressing discovery for me, and that devastation was a monument to my own timeless naiveté.

I had touted the abilities of my team to everyone who would listen. I had lauded their professionalism and expressed my absolute confidence in them. They had a reputation as the best team in the Group. They had not batted an eye when I told them we would take down a 180-man garrison with eight people. They had joined me in derision of individuals who were whining about "suicide" missions. I believed I had, even with the quirky personalities (a part of any organization), a fully functional SF A-Team that would go anywhere to do any mission. Now they were balking because they might not get a fucking badge.

I expressed my dismay at this sudden change of heart, and I was not delicate or kind in my expression. I believe I told them that if the badge was all that fucking important, they needed to look for a job on another fucking team. Skye, the recently assigned weapons sergeant, still desperately seeking approval, persisted that I didn't care because I already had a CIB. It was that childish. I walked out of our tent and paced for over quarter of an hour.

That evening, we watched "Showdown in Haiti," now a well know CNN drama, and went white knuckled as the 82nd Airborne lifted off to invade Haiti, even as Jimmy Carter, Colin Powell and Sam Nunn were still in the National Palace giving Cedras his last chance.

It is history what happened.

An agreement was announced, even though Cedras refused to sign, and Jonaissant (the illegally appointed President) signed instead. No details. No nothing. The planes were turned back to Pope Air Force Base, and the delegation left. People in the TV room at the guest house in Guantanamo Bay left with surprisingly little noise. Disappointment was tangible.

I too was disappointed. I truly believed that the FAd'H had to be destroyed if Haiti was to have a chance. What I did not realize until much later was that besides the destruction of the FAd'H, we needed to destroy the FRAPH, if Haitian democracy was the goal. With high resolution hindsight, I can say that Haitian democracy was never part of the plan.

I didn't even go into the tent at first. The CIB discussion was raging again, and I didn't want to lose my composure. Mike and I talked outside. We had a lively discussion about whether the accord changed our actual tactical plan at all. He wasn't sure. I was adamant that it should change not one iota of our plan. Not in terms of approaches, positions, contingencies. Only the Rules of Engagement (ROE) had changed.

Members of the AOB were already discussing "softer" infils. Mike and I agreed that investing our complete trust in this hokey agreement, with the lives of our own people at stake, would be a big mistake. I felt a distant and familiar discomfiture at the direction the "soft option" planning had begun to take within minutes of the news of the Carter sellout. I smelled Vietnam. I smelled El Salvador. I smelled collaboration.

16: RULES OF ENGAGEMENT

Did you tell a member of your team that Vietnam was a race war?

Yes.

You don't think that's seditious?

Where did this word "sedition" come from? I am still entitled to my own beliefs, am I not?

Of course, of course you are. But "race war?"

Were you in Vietnam?

No, I'm afraid that was before my time.

It wasn't before my time. I was there. In my opinion, regardless of what the national objectives might have been, on the ground it played out as a race war.

It seems you are awfully sensitive about the subject of race.

On the 20th, we rehearsed loading 48 people on each helicopter. We did not bring our rucksacks for that rehearsal, even though loading the equipment on and off the helicopters was an integral part of that action. Without rucksacks, we barely jammed in 48 people per lift. The birds, as many of us had speculated, carried the swollen, space stuffing, long-range fuel bladders.

Mike and I exchanged one of our increasingly frequent conspiratorial looks.

"It won't work," we said.

That afternoon, before our last delicious T-Ration supper, Mike and I were going over the Rules Of Engagement (ROE); the rules we were obligated to adhere to in the event we had to use force. The set of rules we suddenly found ourselves under were called Permissive (non-combat) ROE, as opposed to Non-Permissive (wartime) ROE. Originally, the rules stated that anyone wearing any type of Haitian uniform who carried a weapon may be "engaged." Engaged is a military euphemism for shot. Like "servicing targets," which means shooting or bombing them. Like "target rich environment," which means a lot of "enemy" personnel and installations. Now, with the "soft" option in effect, we were permitted only to "engage" (shoot) if the "target" (person who might be hostile) was threatening our life or someone else's.

This restriction in invariably a subject for great debate (1) because as it is stated it has a lot of room for interpretation, (2) soldiers will always look for the loophole that allows them to shoot someone, thereby fulfilling a condition of manhood, and (3) experienced soldiers know that rules, however ambiguous, can and will be held against them whenever, (A) it is convenient to exact revenge for the perception of a bad attitude, (B) the soldier does whatever he does for the pure hell of it, because he thinks he can, and (C) the unforseen consequences of an action reflect badly on the command, and a scapegoat is needed. Mike and the guys were involved in a heated debate.

For the first time since I had re-entered active duty military service the last time, I was able to profitably draw on my experience in the "private" sector, where I trained SWAT teams to protect the Martin-Marietta run Department of Energy nuclear weapons production facility in Oak Ridge, Tennessee, from terrorists, anti-nuclear activists, and environmentalists who might find out about all the stuff that the plant dumped into the local water table. At any rate, I had received and given a good deal of training on the subject of the application of deadly force, as it applies to police. This was good training, clearly explained and reinforced, with a simple formula for the rapid decision that a cop might have to make when confronted with a potential deadly force scenario. As I reviewed the new ROE, it occurred to me that the cop criteria was made to order.

I told Mike that I wanted the guys to strap on their pistols, clear them of ammunition in front of each other, and meet me behind the guest house, where I wanted to run a few Situational Training Exercises (STXs) relating to the ROE. He seemed skeptical, but he humored me.

What was explained was that deadly force could only be applied when the subject in question had "the means, the opportunity, and the threat to cause serious bodily harm to oneself or someone else, as perceived by a reasonable person." Means was explained as a knife, gun, club, overwhelming size advantage, et cetera. Opportunity was defined as the capability to utilize the means, for example, I may be so much larger than you that I can break your neck, but if there is a twelve foot chainlink fence between you and me, a reasonable assumption is that I do not have the opportunity. Threat is determined by the situation and action. To carry the situation a bit further, if I have overwhelming size advantage over a ten year old kid, and I am close enough to that kid to do serious bodily harm, but I am talking calmly, no reasonable person will perceive a threat. However, if the same situation exists, only I have seized the ten year old by the neck, as I shout and turn purple, one might reasonably assume that I intend to commit serious bodily harm. The question now becomes how to stop the situation. In the throttling incident, one might be able to stop the action without the application of deadly force. But if the assailant has a knife, a gun, a club or serious size advantage over that person intervening, and an order to desist does not produce compliance, then deadly force is authorized. . . not for the purpose of killing, but to alter the perceived course of action. This last is an important distinction, inasmuch as an alteration in the course of action may occur without the potentially deadly force actually having lethal results, whereupon the use of further deadly force is no longer authorized.

I explained this in detail, emphasizing the split second nature of the decision, by demonstrating that if I held a pistol at my side, and another person had a cocked pistol pointing right at me, but that person had to wait until I moved to pull the trigger, I would tie them or beat them every time. This "reaction disadvantage" is the reason for training people to assess a situation with the three simple criteria; means, opportunity, threat.

We then went through scenario after scenario (those considered likely in Haiti, fights, robberies, beatings, and so on), and critiqued each one, until it was obvious that each member of the team understood where the lines were drawn. The entire team expressed a higher level of comfort with the peacetime ROE at the conclusion of training. Mike expressed satisfaction as well.

This would prove to be as valuable as any two hours we had ever spent in training. ODA 354 was to be the first team under AOB 370 to enter a deadly force situation.

17 : GATOR

At the end of the day, on the 20th of September, efforts Mike and I had initiated behind the scenes to increase our strength paid off. Two members of other detachments, Jay Stubbs and Clayt Hulin, who had been assigned to duties with Headquarters elements had approached us, looking to be attached for the mission. Jay was a communicator and Clayt was a medic. Both had just finished a stateside Spanish train-up with their organic teams. Both were physically fit, smart, disciplined and eager. Unfortunately for Jay, communicators were a highly prized asset with all staffs, and he was denied. Clayt was approved that evening however, and he stopped by to tell us the happy news. We offered congratulations and welcomed him to the team. His reputation as a worker and team player was good. He was also sniper trained. Mike and I believed he was a very positive addition to the detachment. We instructed him to just get his stuff in the morning and link up at our tent, where we would integrate him into the plan as simply and painlessly as possible.

Clayt was from Louisiana, true Cajun, but about a generation removed from the culture. He spoke no French, though he recognized many words in French when they were spoken, and would explain the customs of Clarence Cochon, the Easter Pig, and Gaston the Gator, the

Christmas Alligator, with enthusiasm and humor.

Clayt was personable and pleasant, conversing easily with the rest of the guys, and he seemed very pleased with the attachment order assigning him to us. He was easily accepted, with his reputation for competence, and his apparent high level of physical fitness, a big factor in the minds of the team members.

His nickname was Gator.

Gator would not be an easy person to lose one's temper with. He was just too easygoing and too professionally responsible. I was to lose my temper with him, with cause, but with a loss of my comportment as well, though we couldn't have known it then, and he was to be the only person who would forgive me for it. That loss of comportment would provide the first powerful catalyst for a team coup.

18: Logjam

The loading rehearsal *without equipment* of the previous day was paying off in total disorder. Every plan based on that rehearsal had to be scrapped and redesigned from scratch for the simple reason that we could not fit into the helicopters with our mission loads. I remembered reading in Che Guevara's *Guerilla Warfare* that the first thing he learned in beginning of the revolution in Cuba, where we now stood melting, was that the hardest and most critical part of every operation is to leave, and the second hardest part is to arrive.

It became apparent when they tried to fill the first helicopter that the projected aircraft load of 48 was a hallucination. Twenty-two was to become the new norm, and at that personnel would be packed like smoked oysters in a flat can. With every load plan now defunct, the priority was to re-plan the airflow, while we passengers sweltered and sweat and asked what the hell was going on for over four hours. 354 was mentally prepared, because Mike and I had told them the day before that there was no possible way we were going to fit everyone inside those helicopters with all the equipment.

I had to piss so badly by the time Haiti came into view my eyes were glazed over. For four hours we had been superhydrating to prevent becoming heat casualties. Now I was in danger of having a ruptured bladder in the back of the helicopter. Several people had already started pissing into empty water bottles. I was sitting next to Ali near the tail of the aircraft, watching the prop wash leave a trail of ripples in the sea's surface, as our helicopter armada flew low and fast toward Port-au-Prince. To accommodate my shy urinary tract and to prevent piss from blowing into Ali's face, I grabbed an empty water bottle and waded over humans and equipment into a tight space between the starboard fuselage and the fuel bladder, where I filled the tiny one quart bottle. I could have filled three of them, but it was enough to prevent me becoming a medical emergency before we arrived on the shores of Haiti. I recapped the bottle and put it in a convenient space under the edge of the fuel bladder. . . a little surprise for the crew later on.

The Isle de Gonave which sits in the Bay of Port-au-Prince is supposed to look like a goddess riding on the back of a whale. From the air, positioned in the long arc of the Western coast, it looked like a little fish being drawn into the maw of a huge fish's mouth, a fish whose mouth stretched out over the horizon.

The air flow around PAP (as we would come to refer to the capital) Airport was overwhelming, an air traffic controller's version of "Tales from the Crypt." Every conceivable kind of military aircraft was landing, taking off, or orbiting. It was a beehive, and we were one of the bees for what seemed an interminable time. . . probably about ten minutes.

Not only was the charging heliborne assault that officers so enjoy fantasizing about not necessary, having landed in the middle of the most well secured airport since the Amal militia took Beirut International, it was not possible. We were dressed in body armor, Kevlar helmets, 40 pound web gear, slung rifles and pistols. We were dragging off boxes and bags and gun cases and the precariously bulging rucksacks. Once everything was out, we buddy dragged the rucks into a superfluous perimeter (not knowing what else to do), and laid down behind the rucks, not to take cover, but to catch our breaths. From this position, we took in the ground activity, Hummers (the nickname for the big, durable Army replacement for Jeeps), ambulances, MP vehicles, flatbeds, reporters' vans. . . crawling in fifty directions like drunken beetles.

No one came out to meet us. None of us knew where to go. No plan had been briefed for what we were supposed to do when we arrived. The staffs had been too busy planning the detachments' missions for them to attend to these coordination details which were supposed to be their primary responsibility.

I told my team to remove their helmets. Within moments, everyone was doing it. Many men, having shed their gear, stood to piss in the grass with ecstatic sighs of relief.

We were sitting there. The adjacent aircraft load was sitting there on our right. The other on our left was doing the same. Up and down the line, were clusters of twenty-two or so people, sitting in little circles, doing nothing. No one from the flurry of human activity over 600 yards away was making any move to approach us. I had a vision of us sitting there as the sun went down, with no one knowing what to do. Worse, there was a sinister looking bank of storm clouds stacking up to the North.

I told Mike I was going to find a vehicle before we got washed down a gully in the storm that was coming. He agreed.

I walked for what seemed a long way before I encountered two security police from the Air Force. I asked them where the Special Forces were staying. They said they didn't know, but warned me that I could not cross the taxiway hardstand to my front on foot.

I was in the process of explaining the flawed logic of a large group of men sitting half mile away with an airstrip between them and the hangars (where I assumed we would be staying), with an obligation to move to those hangars, and a concomitant prohibition against crossing the hardstand. . . unless of course they wanted us to (1) stay out in the rain (2) circumnavigate the earth to get to the hangars, when a Special Forces Major showed up in a pickup truck. The major pointed out a large maintenance bay across from a cluster of dead, antique airplanes. The Major said he would send us a vehicle as soon as he could free one up.

The cloud bank grew. The cloud bank darkened. Jets of cool air began to sprint across the airfield. I returned to my team in the grass.

"Pick up everything you can. We're walking."

Like gypsies with our wagons on our backs, we began the heavy trudge across the grass, across drainage ditches, down the long edge of the forbidden hardstand. When we looked back, other groups were saddling up as well and moving out. It was a migration, and we had started it. The Officer Personnel Management System, which rewards staying out of trouble, by implication, rewards refusing to take initiatives. I sometimes wonder if we would still have been sitting there, had an enlisted man not made a decision.

Our gear was pressed against the locked down sliding vertical doors of the maintenance hangar, under the protection of the eaves. We jammed in between it. Other teams encamped with poncho hooches under the junked aircraft across the concrete strip. Helmets were removed. Body armor was removed. LCE was dropped on the ground to air out our salt caked, dripping uniforms. The rain started to fall. Within moments, it fell hard.

It is now appropriate to digress about uniforms and uniformity. Uniforms are important to the military. Not only are they required by the Geneva Convention and the Law of Land Warfare, in order to de-legitimize unconventional and partisan forces who can't afford them, and to identify ourselves as combatants (so we can be legally butchered). Uniforms are handy tools to discriminate our soldiers from their soldiers, assuming, of course, that they are not someone we've supplied in the past with our uniforms. Anyone with significant combat experience can tell you that a large share of the casualties in any engagement is caused by something we call, paradoxically, "friendly fire." "Friendly fire" causes so many casualties because (1) everyone is excited and scared and behaving recklessly (2) the friendlies are closer to you, so their rounds have a better chance of hitting you (3) in the excitement, people tend to run in front of each other (4) sometimes its dark, so we just shoot at everything. Uniforms are good, because without them, we would shoot even more of our own people, and the enemy would shoot even more of their people, and war in general would be even more costly, barbarous, and stupid than it already is. Uniforms are also a way to save soldiers from the stress of rising every morning, confronted with that awful dilemma, What will I wear?

Uniforms standardize the way we recognize military members who outrank us, so we can avoid ass chewings for failure to refer to someone as sergeant or sir or your majesty, or for failure to salute them. Uniforms allow us to wear coveted merit badges like paratrooper wings and CIBs and Ranger Tabs. Some uniforms are made to look like vegetation, like the American Army's woodland camouflage pattern, which fooled a lot of Haitians into thinking we weren't an occupying force at all, but a reforestation project. When all is said and done, I have to say that uniforms are important, and I support the wear of uniforms by military people unconditionally.

Uniformity is a different matter. Uniformity is the refuge of the dull-witted in the military, a kind of dogma that's lost its moorings with reality. A first sergeant in an infantry company doesn't need to know how to execute correct infantry doctrine. He doesn't need to understand the difference between an emerald and a dog turd. He doesn't need to know how to spell emerald. He does, however, need to be able to look at a group of soldiers and instantly pick up on anything that looks "different." This is his criteria for correct . . .the same. You, Private, are wrong, because your shit does not look the same as all the other people's shit. To be fair to NCOs (since I was one), dull-witted officers or officers who work for dull-witted officers will frequently measure all sorts of intangibles by uniformity. Discipline is measured by uniformity. Morale is measured by uniformity. Esprit is measured by uniformity. Any private being subjected to it can tell you that this is dumb, but officers persist in it anyway, even when lack of uniformity may be due to differences in body type, differences in heat or cold tolerance and differences in mission tasks. Leaders persist in it especially if there are sundry gaggles of journalists bolting around with cameras and camcorders that could transmit pictures of lack of uniformity back to anal-compulsive fellow officers in the Fatherland. (Is anal compulsive spelled with a hyphen?)

There was no "enemy threat" inside PAP Airport. We were invisible to the public, hunkered down behind buildings full of equipment, and the 10th Mountain Division had circled the Airport with concertina wire, bunkers and machine guns, thinking that since Somalis are black and Haitians are black, Haitians must be just like Somalis. We could have run around naked where we were with no risk of being wounded by anything bigger than an *Aedes aegypti* mosquito. But LTC Jones, my battalion commander, and a man possessed of a good degree more common sense than most of his peers, came past in a surly mood and told us to put everything on—LCE, body armor, helmets, long guns, all of it—and leave it on until further notice. His no-nonsense demeanor, in contrast to his generally relaxed and friendly manner, left us no doubt that this was a directive from 10th Mountain Division, who had been foolishly put in charge of the entire Haiti operation.

The discontent of the team was instant and noisy.

"Just do it, goddamit," I said. "We'll be out of here tomorrow."

I would soon learn to avoid such reckless prophecies.

Darkness fell rapidly in the rain. We were wet, hungry, odiferous, uncomfortable, and literally as well as figuratively in the dark. Things had to get better, because they couldn't get much worse. Or so, in my eternal innocence, I thought.

We had been lifting, toting, walking, waiting in the heat, sweating and emoting in response to a steady stream of changes and miscalculations all day. We sat among our stacks of equipment under the eaves, shelled in Kevlar like armored lizards and napped.

The appearance of precision and order are so important to military commanders because they are generally idiots who couldn't plan a decent cocktail party, especially the bureaucrats who float to the top of the Officer Personnel Management System. They require the appearance of precision and order because their operations, this one being emblematic, are goat fucks.

No one should ever overestimate the intelligence of the military, the Army, or especially the Special Operations community. My apologies to Tom Clancy and other well-heeled war-worshippers.

19: The End of Innocence. . . Again

Sometime between 1830 and 1900 (6:30 pm and 7:00 pm), Mike and I received word that LTC Jones wanted to meet with all team leaders and team sergeants by his Battalion Headquarters, set up in a cargo shed with a long row of wide loading docks. Mike and I looked forward to any information to fill the void.

We were about to be shocked.

LTC Jones stood atop a stack of ration cases in the dark. He was silhouetted against the cloudy night sky. Our helmeted heads pressed close to him like a hungry herd of turtles. He told us to make friends with the FAd'H (*Force Armee d'Haiti*, the Haitian armed forces).

I caught my breath. Mike didn't breathe at all.

"I know this is a hard transition to make," said Jones. "But you're all soldiers, and I know you'll follow orders. Get to know them. Watch them work. Take some notes on what kind of equipment they need. Let 'em know your here to help them become a more professional force."

Help them? Help them! It hit me in my solar plexus. These were

107

the people we had watched in our last moments with the wide screen TV in the Guantanamo guest house lobby, wailing the shit out of unarmed civilians for celebrating, cracking their heads and breaking their arms with batons. This was my formerly fire-breathing battalion commander talking. I simply didn't understand. I didn't want to understand. I wasn't here to participate in another El Salvador! I wouldn't do it! What kind of underhanded, bullshit betrayal was this, anyway? I was flabbergasted. My old nemesis, that hot cascading uncontrollable rage, was back. I was being swallowed up in it, even as I recognized its approach.

"Bullshit!" I said, too loud. Helmets turned in the dark. Jones kept talking.

"I know this isn't easy. . ." he said again.

"Bullshit!" I repeated. "I won't fucking do it."

Mike grabbed my arm. "Cool it." It was an order.

I could feel Mike's discomfort. He recognized the hot, red space I was in, and he knew that I might put him in the middle. . . caught between the directive from his commander and me, his chief enforcer, who stood here swearing mutiny. My rage has always found a victim. Sometimes they are innocent.

Then again, I never claimed to be the perfect soldier. That fraud had been perpetrated by people I worked with. If being a perfect soldier meant continuing to follow any fucking order I was given, then I would have to settle for being a mediocre soldier.

The implications were converging on me too fast to sort them out. This was to be the one mission I could be proud of when I had a clear look back at it. We were not going to side with moneyed interests. We would be genuinely restoring a democracy, no matter how it may stumble in its infancy. The people would like us for what we were doing. I was going to be shriven for Vietnam and all the places after. All this seemed to be going out the window.

I wanted to vomit. I wanted to go home. Here was the badge I sought, disappearing before my eyes. I had wanted so badly to do this one thing. One decent thing to salvage me and my country. One decent thing to make amends for remaining silent about the old woman in the potato patch, for rationalizing the Indians scavenging in the hopeless trash dumps of Guatemala, for ignoring the torture victims in El Salvador, for my ignorance of the Third World that existed 30 miles from Ft. Bragg in the poverty-racked Black communities of Eastern North Carolina. Just one decent fucking thing as absolution!

"Do you see what they're doing?" I growled at Mike as we headed back to break the news. "Do you see?"

"I can't believe this," he said. Even Mike, ever the middle-of-the-roader, ever the devil's advocate, could find nothing for which to advocate. We were in shock.

I would find months later while rummaging through the microfilm at the public library, that unknown to us the mission purposes were changing by the hour. First we were not to interfere in "Haitian on Haitian violence," the euphemism for cops and thugs beating the living shit out of unarmed civilians. Then we were to prevent Haitian on Haitian violence (always qualified by saying that also meant civilian violence against police—widespread as that was). Then we were not to be police. Then we were to assume police functions until Haitian police were trained. So it would go.

At this stage in the game, US soldiers were sitting behind bunkers, aiming machine guns at curious but harmless crowds, and as we had witnessed prior to deployment from Cuba, Americans were standing by as Haitian cops and Attaches (auxiliary thugs) executed business as usual tactics against the general population. Ever since our first view of those images on TV, we had itched to intercede against the Haitian police and military. But 10th Mountain Division was still running the whole show, and they would continue to avoid real contact with Haitian citizens for the duration of the mission. In fact, Ali and I had talked to a kid on bunker guard, and they had been indoctrinated to watch out for "voodoo powders" and other such horse shit, as well as told not to smile, speak to civilians, or drink locally sold Coca Cola.

I felt trapped between my sincere conviction against collaborating with the monstrous Haitian state apparatus and my responsibilities to family; a family who had a lot to gain if I started drawing my full military pension in one and a half years. It was as if my retirement had become one last appalling extortion scheme.

I reacted as I've been trained to. I completely lost my mind. "I won't fucking do it, Mike! They can send my bony ass back to the fuckin' States! I won't be a party to this one! Get Jones. I'll tell him right now!" This tirade had Mike squirming. I was wrong to do it, and I had absolutely no control over myself. For two hours, I kept Mike on a tightrope, wondering if he were going to have to continue the mission without his trusted team sergeant.

When I was spent, I laid down, rolled up in my poncho liner on the concrete, and stared up at the stupid fucking stars that were just starting to peek through the stupid fucking clouds. The aircraft that took off and landed were stupid too. Every dark figure that walked up and back past us was stupid. The dead airplanes across the street were stupid. The whole night was stupid. . . and sleepless. I wanted to cry. It grew untropically cold. It was one of the worst nights I spent in Haiti. . . and the first.

Off to a good start.

20: Dialectic

I was too tired to stay agitated, as the "early born rosy fingered dawn" began beating back the eastern night. I knew one thing. If we remained stuck out in the open, we were available to be fucked with. I got they guys up and put them to work breaking in to the American Airlines maintenance bay. I remember procuring a hammer and beating on one of the locks. Other people began prying and sawing and twisting with whatever they could scrounge up. Within twenty minutes, we had gained access. A couple of other teams from our company were helping by then. We looked to the left and we looked to the right. When the coast was clear, we slid the door up a few feet, and we scrambled, men and equipment, to the inside, whereupon we slammed the door back down.

Inside was semi-darkness, trucks, forklifts, mysteriously unidentifiable aircraft maintenance stuff, wire mesh storage cages, toolboxes . . . Light!. . . someone found the switches, the electricity worked, and the huge overhead florescent bulbs came to life. There were two offices along the left wall. 354 grabbed the first, smallest one, because we spotted the wall unit air conditioner inside.

It had been very chilly the preceding night, but we knew the heat would return that day with a vengeance.

We stacked our gear around our new office, as other teams started staking claims. We moved the furniture out of the office, with the exception of the desk. A card game broke out around open bags of MREs. The latrine was located. Rod took a shower. I cranked up my Whisperlite to heat coffee. The air conditioner was hooked up, and found to be functional.

I pulled Mike off to the side, and apologized for my total loss of bearing the night before. I also told him there was a way to ensure very few changes in our mission concept.

He again appeared skeptical, but, God bless 'im, he let me have my head. I had figured a way to meet whatever FAd'H collaboration bullshit directives we might receive with minimal compliance, and to maintain the core of our original plan, by emphasizing "force protection." Force Protection is a blessed bovine that no officer will argue with. That's because the slightest incident involving US casualties does not need to be accompanied by whistleblowers at a later date saying, "I told you so. We didn't have force protection. I told him so." Mike caught the gist, agreed wholeheartedly. I felt better, for the moment.

Time began to drag after the tenth card game. I opened a steel, sliding shutter on the great, locked, metal garage doors leading to the street in front of the airport, and suddenly had contact with real Haitians. We were able to talk to them through a wire mesh screen that was welded over the aperture at head height.

Ali began speaking French with several of them. We soon had a huge crowd of Haitians at the little aperture. This was our first contact with the overall friendliness of the Haitians, and with the smell of unsanitized crowds, wafting now through the wire grate. It is a smell that many people remark on with distaste, but that never bothered me, and that in fact I came to kind of enjoy it.

Nothing worked throughout most of Haiti. Electricity, vehicles, machines, running water. And with the embargo having reduced a nation in poverty to a nation hanging onto survival by its fingernails, everything had become an unaffordable luxury. Not that the embargo was keeping anything from the rich. For them, the embargo leaked like a chicken wire canoe. But for the rest of Haiti, scented soap, deodorant, perfumes and the like are wicked luxuries. Haitians, I would discover, are almost compulsive about bathing. They wash every chance they get, and as thoroughly as they can. But they can not afford the American preoccupation with the eradication of natural human scents.

The water scarcity in Port-au-Prince was so severe, that people could be seen washing the dust from their face with urine in the most horrific of slums. So crowds smelled human, in a way we were not familiar with in our super-sanitized culture.

This would be the subject of much commentary. That commentary would be a source of great irritation to me, as time went by, for it flowed out of a racialized consensus, and continued even as we ourselves blended in to the general aroma. My clothes had already taken on a damp sour aspect that would grow stronger and take many washings to get off both the clothes and my skin.

A Captain White showed up at the portal as well, a Special Forces officer who was working with Civil Affairs and who spoke fluent French. He was a friendly, sensible seeming guy, whom I would learn to personally like, as time went on, for his ability to get along with Haitians, and for his irreverent attitudes toward the military. He explained that he would be attached to our element, until we broke out of Ouanaminthe, to enter Fort Liberte.

We began pumping Haitians for any information we could get, and they were generous with it. What we discovered very quickly was that the embargo had only hurt the poor, the Cedras regime was almost universally despised (contrary to the "balanced" bullshit view portrayed by the media), that Aristide had been elevated by the brutality of the Cedras regime from popular political figure to potential savior, that (again contrary to media crap) the vast majority of Haitians were absolutely ecstatic that we had intervened. As far as they were concerned the quicker we got out of that airport and into the streets and outlying areas the better. The military and police were continuing their terror with a renewed urgency. The three most asked questions, none of which we could answer with any certitude, were: (1) When would the embargo end? (2) When would we begin to filter out into the actual neighborhoods and towns? (3) When was Aristide coming?

Mike and I began discussing the lack of information, the lack of coordination, the lack of organization, and the lack of preparation, on the part of planners for this so-called infil. We agreed that if we had executed a plan as fucked up as this one, we would have been summarily relieved. It seemed like instead of focusing on unsnarling the unmitigated mess we had, with everyone and their brother clogged up at Port-au-Prince Airport, they were putting out one message after another to the various chains of command, emphasizing the policy on uniformity (helmet, body armor, LCE, long gun). It was understandable, I suppose, given all the media coverage, we had to give the impression of organization through uniformity, even if no one in charge of anything there could find his ass with a radar.

21: Escape from Alcatraz

Boredom got the best of me by noon. I got it in my head that I wanted some fruit. . . fresh fruit. . . and that it had to be out there in PAP. So I decided to find it.

I reconned the wire until I found the vehicle, just beyond the last maintenance hangar. I then looked up an acquaintance with the battalion headquarters element, and asked him what we needed to do to check out a vehicle. He was embroiled in a cauldron of confused activity, and told me just give him the bumper number, and I could use any Hummer that was available. People were driving vehicles up and down the length of the airport. Harassed as he seemed, I didn't have the heart to agitate him with more details, like destinations off the airfield. Confusion can be a magnificent thing.

I located our Battalion's line of Hummers, and found one with the top off. The steering wheel wasn't even chained and locked, so I cranked it up and pulled up in front of our team area. I asked who would like to go with me to get some fruit. Kyle, Skye and Ali, instantly taking in what I was up to, all volunteered. We were going into Port-au-Prince, away from our little prison, and away from all those 10th Mountain people. Mike asked suspiciously if I'd cleared the trip. The vehicle was cleared through Battalion headquarters, I equivocated. I

115

assured him that I'd to bring him back some fruit.

We suited up like Robocops, and headed out the gate as if we knew exactly what we were doing. The kid with the machine gun at the bunker there didn't even bat an eye. He was too busy watching the Haitian crowds that had gathered in front of his bunker. They were cheering and talking and begging. He had listened carefully to the intelligence briefing, and his eyes were peeled for voodoo powders and hand grenades.

"Don't get an ulcer, Bud," I told him as we drove out.

As soon as we faded from the view of the last 10th Mountain position, we shed the helmets and the body armor like new lovers coming out of their clothes. The breeze blew through our sweat-sopping uniforms. The open streets were full of curious people—civilians—not a helmet or machine gun in sight. At last, we were in Haiti. Everything was new. Freedom sang.

We weren't prepared for the welcome. We were being cheered in our lone vehicle as we meandered, clueless about the location of the market, blindly penetrating the streets of PAP with the mountains on one side and the ocean on the other to stay oriented. Patton's Jeep lost in Sicily. It was not polite applause, but feral, shrieking, singing, dancing, frenzied celebration. Everyone we passed believed we were the first of many come to stamp out the detested FAd'H, the attaches, the macoutes. Assuming the other three men felt as I did, I was completely overtaken by it, exhilarated beyond words. I made up my mind then and there to do everything I could not to betray the hope that flooded around us.

We asked around for directions to the market, not too hastily, since the ride itself was a great deal of fun. Eventually we arrived. When we parked, Skye stayed with the vehicle, swamped immediately by a growing crowd of awestruck, weeping, cheering Haitians. Kyle, Ali and I entered the huge open market, in which there was only a smattering of goods (because of the embargo). As we meandered through the market, we dragged an ever-increasing trail of cheering, dancing civilians. Before us, we saw the wrinkled toothless grins of market women break into song. For the first time but not the last, we would see an old woman stand, raise her arms high and to her sides, and swing her breasts rhythmically from side to side as she looked straight at us and laughed. This seemingly sexual display, we would find, was no more or less than a universal, Haitian female display of joy. We were to see this again and again in the days that followed. That and the dances, and the chants, and the wonder of Haitian smiles.

We found a little rice, pasta, some meager vegetables in the market. The crowd we were drawing at every turn was making it impossible to shop around. So we waved, shook a few hands, and retreated amidst the cheering to the Hummer, where Skye was alone atop the Hummer in the middle of another appreciative crowd, overwhelmed and no longer happy, shouting, "Stand back! Stay back!"

As we drove around some more, we noticed a few solitary merchants with oranges and bananas on the corners. To claim we had accomplished our stated purpose, we grabbed a few oranges here, a few bananas there, and when we decided we had been gone long enough to start making people uncomfortable with our absence, we reluctantly headed back to the airport.

Nearing the 10th Mountain Zone, we donned our helmets and body armor.

Fruit was distributed. Other teams in the building realized that we had "blown post" so to speak, and they started a buzz. 354 are crazy bastards. Mike called me aside.

First on the agenda, be careful, because professional jealousy may cause someone to drop a dime. Noted. Second, we were not leaving today, and there was no word on leaving tomorrow. Third, the uniform thing had taken on proportions beyond belief, since we left. Any infraction of the uniform policy, no matter how minor, would result in relief of the individual, his team sergeant, his team leader and his company commander. This bit of cosmic prioritizing from General Meade, commander of the 10th Mountain Division, and new king of Haiti. Meade, it was reported, hated SF guys. His Command Sergeant Major, Jesse Laye, was someone I knew, who hated SF, an insecure, hyper-macho posturing, regulation-quoting pinhead, whose politicking and back stabbing I had encountered in the Ranger Regiment.

So I put the word out to the guys that uniform infractions would be an easy way to get rid of Mike and me, if anyone wanted to. At this point, that was no one's desire, with the possible exception of Dave Grau, who had begun to rankle at being an "officer" (he was a warrant officer, a kind of technician) without a leadership role.

22: THE BASEBALL FACTORY

That evening, we were asked if anyone wanted to escort a vehicle over to the "industrial complex." It was off the airport, so Ali and I volunteered.

The industrial complex was a gargantuan manufacturing facility, less than a mile from the airport, devoted in the past to being the world's largest supplier of baseballs. Security fences, fuel storage, warehouses and enough buildings to convert into air conditioned offices, mess halls, a Post Exchange, and so on, in conjunction with proximity to the airfield, made it a handy place to establish the Task Force Headquarters. The tents on the airfield simply wouldn't do for all that brass.

What those of us who were interested would find out was that the facility was leased from the second richest family in Haiti, the Mevs, who also had fortunes based on monopolies in sugar, children's school shoes, and plastics. The military paid a very tidy sum indeed to lease the facility, throwing in a lot of free improvements. It must have been a very convenient arrangement, what with the Mevs having access to the new military rulers, and the US military officers having the opportunity to deal with the people they most enjoy sucking up to. . . the rich and the powerful. Surely, the Mevs were converted to the wisdom of US intervention against their patron, Cedras, with this windfall and assurances that this democracy talk didn't include any space for the foundling forces of anti-neo-liberalism to maneuver against Wall Street or the World Bank. There's a very good account of all this in an anthology of essays, *The Haiti Files, Decoding the Crisis,* edited by James Ridgeway.

As an aside, the Mevs have never admitted to supporting Cedras, though he could not have survived without their support. Only one Haitian family, the Brandts, has more money than the Mevs.

The trip turned out to be boring, miserable even. When we passed through the gate and parked, waiting for whatever business was being conducted inside, we were told to put our K-Pots (helmets) back on by three people within ten seconds. We didn't know who they were, because it was getting dark. We also noticed that no one was speaking to anyone, and that people were moving around like robots.

Meade and Laye, in their inimitable way, had so terrified every officer on the island that all human spontaneity had gone out of the 10th Mountain troops. It was like we were in a world of Stepford soldiers. So to kill time and break the tension, we started saying "Hi, there," to every dark figure that passed. No one would answer us. It got to be funny. So we did it some more. Still no response. Whereupon we started making loud satirical commentary about the complex, its leadership and the 10th Mountain Division. Loud jokes about being lost in a world of androids.

We heard at least three accidental discharges of weapons on the complex in the hour we were there. They were wound so tight their guns were going off.

It was a strange and instructive interlude.

It was through this imposition of near absolute control that the 10th Mountain Division managed to ensure that their soldiers could stay in Haiti for months and never, never be contaminated by the society they had lighted in.

23: Shenanigans

23 September, 1994.

Ali and I had become the cultural adventurers. We were habitually exiting through the gate, shooting the breeze with locals, walking in and out of local streets and alleys, peering into huts and stalls to investigate voices, street wares and very seductive cooking smells.

We rose early that morning and went across the street. We dickered over the exchange rate, then bought coffee, rice and vegetables. All of it was cooked over a primitive, three-legged charcoal stove. The rice and vegetables were cooked in a savory, brown pork gravy. Ali bought bread, which was incredibly expensive thanks to both the embargo and our own rube status there.

Midmorning, Major O'Neill called Mike and me over to his poncho shelter. It was strung under the wing of an old DC-Something passenger plane (the one in that old Hitchcock film, I think). He was haggard looking, unshaven, red-eyed.

He told us that General Meade had visited Camp D'Applicacion, the Haitian Military Academy in Port-au-Prince, where SF was setting up a local Headquarters. Upon entering Camp D (as it would come to be known), four or five Special Forces soldiers had raised up off the bench in sequence, raising both arms, then sat back down in the same sequence, a maneuver known by soldiers and students alike as "the wave" for the catchy rippling impression it makes. This cheeky bit of choreography failed to amuse our intrepid General. In fact, said Major O'Neill, Meade was intensely pissed off. In retaliation, Meade had put an indefinite hold on the deployment of any SF Teams. We were being collectively punished for the impetuous maneuver at Camp D. We were undisciplined, he said, and disrespectful.

Mike and I could barely contain our laughter at the "wave" thing. The consequences, however, were draconian. Mike and I were anxious to respond to the need, urgently expressed by people in the street, to fan out to the countryside where hideous abuses were escalating in the wake of our arrival. But those abuses, it seems, were not nearly as important as the bruised ego of Major General David Fucking Meade.

Major O'Neill did not find the humor in it. His professional ass, along with every SF commander there, was now on the line. Meade had put out that anyone violating uniform policy was going to be charged with "disloyalty." Anyone displaying a less than totally respectful demeanor would be charged with "disloyalty." None of us had ever known anyone charged with disloyalty, whether it was a real charge, or if it was, what the penalty might be. Anyone who was caught in town without authority would be charged with disloyalty. That one caught my attention. Anyone who did anything to demean the conventional forces would be charged with disloyalty. Again, caught my attention. We were also told to remove the magazines from our weapons. I had the funny paranoid feeling that some of 354's actions were in large part responsible for the specificity of these directives and threats. I also had the hunch that stool pigeons resided among us, choked on the seeds of professional envy.

So we had to wear body armor and helmets everywhere we went, presumably because there was danger. But we couldn't have bullets in our guns. On the surface, this seems pretty stupid. But in all honesty, the issue wasn't danger, it was publicity, uniform crap because of the cameras, and avoidance of accidental discharges by people who hadn't been properly trained on their weapons (most of the army), because it invited embarrassing questions.

According to Major O'Neill, if we stayed completely out of trouble for a whole day, General Meade would let us go do our missions the following day. What a mensch!.

With the whole day to kill, we found buckets and attempted to wash some of the funk out of our clothes. We took showers. We changed uniforms.

Guys were now leaving the sliding door open on our maintenance bay. Several people warned that if we continued to do so, someone from 10th Mountain would see that we had something livable and take it away. So we looted some stencils from the American Airlines office, and painted a sign that said RESTRICTED AREA--AUTHORIZED PERSONNEL ONLY. The sign was hung on the back of a chair outside the door, which was lowered to half mast in order to limit visibility.

That night, boredom drove Ali and me back to the street. From outside, we could see the perpetual crowd around the mesh windows looking into our bay. We were completely obscured by the Haitian night and the failure of the Port-au-Prince electrical grid. Inside, every American was lit through the apertures like little television screens.

Ali and I lurked in the back of the Haitian street crowd, signaling silence with fingers to our lips. Ali spoke out in his Haitian accent. Speaking five languages, he had a real talent for accents.

"Why are you here?" he asked from the darkness.

"To save your country," answered a blonde staff sergeant, who stood with his shirt off, trying to inconspicuously flex his muscles for what he perceived to be the awestruck, undernourished natives.

"What ess your name?" inquired Ali.

"Arnold Schwarznegger," Blondie replied.

"You are not Arnold," retorted Ali loudly. "Arnold is a big man. You are a little man. You are a pencil neck. How come you Americans are all so skinny?"

SSG Blondie was deflated and utterly confused. He couldn't decide whether he was disappointed or angry. The insult had been so articulate and unexpected.

Before he could recoup, Ali stuck his face in the window so the light would hit it, and started laughing. Everyone inside joined in. The Haitians found it funny, as well, though most understood nothing that had transpired. . . only that it was a joke. Practical jokes are very popular in Haiti.

This was just too much fun, so we proceeded further down the street to a door that led from the outside directly into another team's quarters. They had not opened that door since we'd been there. One paranoid individual on that team had sarcastically asked us if our forays into the street were for the purpose of checking how big our balls were. Probably worried about "voodoo powders." He feared black people in crowds. We feared field grade American Army officers. Our fears in many ways define us.

Outside the door, I knocked. Rap rap rap.

"What the fuck!" we heard inside. There was a commotion. More questions. . . "Who the hell. . . What do they. . . "

Rap rap rap.

"Go away!"

"Allez! Allez!"

Rap rap rap.

"Who's there?"

"Pizza," I said.

"What?"

"I dunno. Someone says its pizza."

"You can't order pizza here. . . can you?"

Rap rap rap.

"Who is it?"

"Flowers," I said.

Agitated whispers. Metallic noises.

Rap rap rap.

"Who is it?" the voice came back, angry and authoritative now.

"Land Shark," I said.

Ali and I were by now in convulsions. We cackled like idiots, brayed like jackasses.

A crack appeared in the blinds of the window, and we stuck our faces into the escaping light. The door unlatched and opened. As we entered, the men inside joined us in a general hilarity. My own laughter died down a little when I saw how many people were clearing the rounds out of the chambers of their rifles.

24: Through the Looking Glass

At eight o'clock in the morning on the 24th, we were told to pack it up. Today was the day we would infiltrate into Gonaives. So we plucked our clothes off the expedient lines, counted weapons and sensitive items, repacked, reviewed our plan for this mission, and reviewed the aircraft load plan that Major O'Neill had just briefed.

We waited on the grass infield where we had landed three days ago. It was 1000 hours by then. By now the mysterious delays and inevitable changes were *de rigueur*.

At around noon, the first lifts took off. It was nothing like the plan starring Captain Sargent's team, commando assaults executed with clocklike precision to overwhelm the garrison, but a shuttle. The impression was of stupefied, overburdened mules. A couple of aircraft flew to Gonaives, then returned and picked up more people, and so on, until we all arrived.

It was there on the infield of Port-au-Prince Airport, as the guys played cards, told lies and watched seagulls, that Danny MacDonald, team sergeant for 356 and perpetual bearer of news and rumors, strode over on his long, bandy legs, with catbird smile, and told us that the first aircraft had dropped their personnel. He confirmed the misgiving Mike and I had articulated in Cuba. There were "about 10,000 motherfuckers" on the landing zone (LZ).

Danny looked forward to this scenario. He and Lee Guitierrez, one of his men, had only days prior been discussing the merits of various blunt instruments as "NBCs," shorthand for Nigger Brain Crushers. A scene of pandemonium would be just the thing to afford Danny an opportunity to act out his Aryan fantasies.

We loaded at about 1300 (1:00 PM), on a CH-47 Chinook helicopter, complete with the excessive baggage with which we had started and various useful items "liberated" from the American Airlines maintenance shed.

The flight to Gonaives was uneventful. We flew over land the whole way, which I found disturbing, since we easily could have followed the coastline, keeping in touch with the forgiving water in case the chopper suddenly experienced mechanical difficulties.

I have been skeptical of helicopters for some time, with sound reason based on bad experience. I always expect them to crash or get shot down.

I have heard that a crash over water is no less forgiving than a crash over land. That phenomena will have to be carefully explained to me. First of all, I can dive into water from a three meter board and invariably survive, whereas if I were to test a three meter dive over land, common sense tells me to expect catastrophic consequences. Furthermore, when that helicopter splashes into the trees and rocks, then catches on fire, which they invariably do, my broken body will be consumed by flames even as I try to claw it free of the wreckage. If the chopper crashes into the sea, at least the water will inhibit the flames. It may be an irrational preference, but I prefer to fly over water.

No rumor from Danny MacDonald could have prepared us for what we saw below as we began the interminable series of spirals over the LZ behind the Gonaives garrison. There were rivers of human beings flowing into a sea of leaping, agitated humanity, thousands of people, with an island of baked earth in the middle, its shore betokened with soldiers facing out into the tide. Stacks of equipment grew in the center of the island with each helicopter that discharged its personnel and cargo.

All of us had to be thinking the same thing. Every plan 370 had concocted had just been annulled by a reality one had to witness to comprehend. We had not the first idea what the right thing was to do. There was no doctrine for this scenario: Several thousand, cheering, happy people. Hostile crowds we were prepared for.

We landed.

354 was nearest the back of the bird, the first off our lift. The roar of the crowd could be heard even above the screaming engines of the Chinook. Not knowing exactly where to start, I opted for the old NCO standby, accountability. I indicated that I wanted our gear put "here," pointing at a place next to the growing pile in the center of the island. I motioned for the guys to stay together, whereupon we moved to the rearmost quadrant of the circle, and fanned across the front of the crowd, tightening the line that was arrayed against a crowd who could have easily overrun us.

The CH-47 lifted off again, blowing a high powered storm of gray dust across our backs and the crowd's front. We had deployed into the face of the most daunting and perplexing scene I had encountered in my career. Little did we know, this would become routine. There were thousands of packed, screaming, cheering, laughing, dancing, singing people, bouncing and swaying to the Afro-Caribbean rhythms of the pro-Aristide/anti-FAdH/anti-Cedras songs we would learn well in the days to come. Many people were smearing halved lemons on their faces. The dust from the incoming and outgoing helicopters was clinging to the lemon juice, painting their faces a pale gray, reminiscent of the river scene in *Apocalypse Now*, when the boat approaches Kurtz's camp.

The crowd was staying back voluntarily, members of it helping push back the inevitable salients that surged forward, as the members of our units moved back and forth, shouting to move back, shouting to stop, unheard for more than a meter in the din. Some of the guys were trying to appear fierce, but the crowd was so obviously and overwhelmingly pleased with our presence that I signaled my own people to assume the low ready position with the rifles, barrels down, not be trained on the crowd. Within moments, all the rifles were lowered or held at a modified port for pushing instead of shooting.

I had to sling my weapon over a shoulder to keep up with the hands that reached for me. Hundreds of slender, dusty fingers sought my hands and arms, touching, grasping and greeting. The slightest gesture or smile was met by an unbelievable outpouring of relief and joy. I saw faces laughing, faces singing, and faces crying with celebration. The hands of old women reached out of the crowd to brush the dust off my face. The hands of children encircled my fingers. Young men fought for a brief clasp of greeting and gratitude. Kisses were thrown. Fists were held aloft in a salute of solidarity. Hundreds of women and girls executed the breast-swinging maneuver. Old men with tears streaking the dust on their faces shouted *"Mesi!"*

Reporters with camcorders for heads or an armory of cameras slung around their necks swarmed like yellow jackets across the front of the crowd. They were on a feeding frenzy. They shouted questions at us that we could not understand. Every touch between American and Haitian was accompanied by clicking shutters. Every attempt to push back an encroachment of the line was recorded. Scenes were playing everywhere.

We had been working the crowd for around five minutes, when I saw the FAd'H soldier appear in the middle of the clearing. The crowd was screaming and pointing angrily at him as he sauntered through the open area, obviously comfortable with his new American associates. He glared out at the crowd, and swaggered a little with his ironwood baton. They had received the word that the American soldiers would be their new friends and associates.

I had seen the newsreels at Guantanamo Bay—FAd'H soldiers using these batons to bludgeon demonstrators and celebrants. I remembered the 10th Mountain standing by and watching under orders not to interfere, powerless to intervene. The stress of the mission ambiguity, that memory, the arrogant gait of the soldier, and the pleading, screaming agitation of the crowd as he walked past, conspired to make me lose my composure. I wanted very, very badly to shoot him. It was an overwhelming impulse, visceral, lust-like.

I unslung my weapon and carried it by the pistol grip in my right hand, like an enormous six-gun, locking my eyes on the FAd'H soldier as I stalked directly at him. He slowed a little in his swagger, averting his gaze from me. The crowd near us had suddenly grown unnaturally still and attentive.

"Fuck, no!" I shouted, glaring straight at him. He stopped. "Fuck, no! It's over, motherfucker!" I marched up to him. Alarm was visible in his face. The sound of the crowd beside us was suddenly rising. I yanked the baton out of his hand. He flinched at the abruptness of the action. A roar erupted. I slung the baton into the open ground in the center of the clearing. The multitude exploded with a roar of endorsement.

The wild chorus of approval from the crowd was deafening, and they flooded toward the now terrified, retreating FAd'H soldier.

I had caused an uncontrollable breach in the line.

The bloodlust of the crowd toward this soldier was palpable. In a split second, I had to convert myself from the soldier's antagonist to his defender, his life suddenly in grave and immediate jeopardy.

My God, I thought, *what have I done?*

A couple of SF guys who had witnessed the breach rushed over and assisted me in the difficult task of calming and backing up the hundreds of people who had poured toward the FAd'H soldier. In a few minutes, we had restored the line. I am not sure where the Haitian soldier went, but I did not see him again until we entered the compound three hours later.

There was no way to know it at that moment, but this was the first act in a series that would define a relationship with the FAd'H that would supplant the mandated alliance we had been tethered into with them. This dissolution would be one of the principle antecedents of my detachment's success. I am thankful to this day that I did it. I am doubly thankful to this day that we didn't lose control.

We continued working the crowd. The crowd continued to grow. Everyone was trying everything they could think of to settle them. Ali was a dynamo, albeit a very hostile one. He reverted to the techniques he had learned in the camps at Guantanamo, where he'd worked the previous year. In French, he screamed and waved them back. *"Eau ni va! Allez! Fe Bak!"* It was not friendly, but it was effective to move the crowd. To my surprise, the crowd seemed not to resent it.

At my request Ali questioned members of our welcome demonstration about the rubbing of lemon on their skin. It took the sting out of the gas, they told us. Just before our arrival, the FAd'H had gassed and clubbed the population.

Shitah means sit down. I'm not sure when I learned that, but it was within moments. My personal tactic evolved into calling the children forward (Ali, how do you say children? *Enfants*.), and telling them to sit down, while I squatted to their front. The buffer of children was one the adults were not willing to step across. Seating the wall of children and sitting down with them was working for me, the only problem being that it did not work in a linear fashion. The children would bounce and jockey for position until I had not a line of kids, but a circle of them around me. We counted our fingers, exchanged names, interrogated one another about our ages. The kids all asked me how many children I had and what was their gender and how old were they. The little French Ali had tutored me on at PAP was all that facilitated this simple intercourse.

The sight of us sitting there, for several other SF soldiers were now doing the same thing, at the edge of the pandemonium became irresistible for some of the reporters. They flocked to us, creating a new problem. The reporters suddenly became the center of interest. Children and adults alike converged on them. In response, the reporters were backing up. The crowd followed. The lines were dissolving around us like a great phagocyte, and we were being swallowed.

I grabbed one woman with a camcorder on her shoulder, and bellowed that if she would just dive right into the crowd and head away from the center, it would help us immeasurably. Fortunately, she understood, communicating the instruction to several cohorts. As the reporters melted into the mass, we were again able to push the line back out to a comfortable location.

Similar problems were emerging in every sector of the perimeter. Flexibility and resourcefulness were the order of the day.

As the situation progressed, however, the circle we protected became smaller and smaller. Only the incoming helicopters, with the gravel and sand in the blade wash stinging everyone back, could open the distance back up. It was not deliberate encroachment. It was merely the natural character of a crowd. Like a tide. And that crowd continued to increase. The minutes added up, and the numbers swelled.

354 had been on the LZ for over two and a half hours, while the Hummer we had slingloaded under the helicopter, a small Toyota pickup truck and a Toyota flatbed wedged through the mob to shuttle the pile of equipment to the inside of the garrison, less than a block away. The last truck load went out, and the swarm of people closed on us like water from a broken dam.

The trucks pushed through the masses like ants caught in honey to pick up the US personnel and get them through the crowd into the garrison. The teams were by now completely disorganized, so no one knew exactly where anyone was. I elected to walk.

Moving through the demonstration at first made me fear for the loss of my equipment. With all the jostling, anyone could have taken my canteens, my ammunition, my grenades. But no one tried. While I was in Haiti, I never had a single personal item stolen except by other GIs.

The crowd was so thick, it took twenty minutes for those of us on foot to get inside the compound, a distance of about 100 yards. Our treatment by the crowd was what one might expect for returning astronauts. Had the Haitians been huskier folk, I've no doubt they would have hoisted us aloft on their shoulders and carried us into the caserne. Instead, they flowed around us, urging us forward in a Dionysian wave of song and dance. Not a face among the Haitians failed to reward smile with smile.

As I turned the last corner, next to the vehicle entrance for the caserne, there were three FAd'H members with two GIs, holding the masses at bay. The GIs' presence was all that prevented mayhem between the civilians and the military. Inside was a walled driveway leading to the internal quadrangle of the compound. Several FAd'H members stood within the refuge of that driveway, looking flustered and frightened, and trying vainly to aim menacing looks at the unruly horde. Every street, now, within view of the compound, was brimming with humanity, and the converging rivers of people extended as far as the eye could see in every direction. I entered the caserne and went down the passage, glaring at the FAd'H soldiers, and spat demonstrably as I passed the officer who seemed to be in charge.

That officer was clean cut, uniform pressed to a razor edge, shoes gleaming, mustache trimmed so perfectly it seemed painted on, nails manicured, smelling of cologne, with a high quality Bianchi hip holster containing a well cared for Glock 17 autoloader. In military parlance, he was strak. Very respectable looking, with a quiet air of authority. I would later find his name was Castra, and that he was a murderer many times over.

Haiti is a place where looking clean cut and respectable has a high price, and the poor frequently pay it.

My first priority inside was to count heads. I found Mike and we exchanged the names of those we had counted, then rummaged through the billets to the rear of the inner quad, the Headquarters at the front, and among those in front of the building who had been hey-youed for crowd control. Within a few minutes, we had accounted for each member of 354. We directed them to leave the disarray of equipment in the quadrangle for now and assist in the frontal crowd control until some kind of plan was generated.

Mike and I were caught in a formation held across from a hasty FAd'H formation, where Major O'Neill exchanged professional amenities with the FAd'H commander, Captain Castra. Hands were shaken. The Haitian commander pledged cooperation, and Major O'Neill said something about moving forward together to establish democracy. The FAd'H soldiers looked dazed, staring anxiously at the manifold collection of weapons and gadgets we stacked, stowed and carried.

The formation ended.

I went outside to check on the guys. Rod, Dave and Gonzo passed me in the Headquarters. They said that they weren't needed, that some kind of rotation was being set up for anterior crowd control.

Ali, Kyle and Skye were standing around goofing on the crowds. Some of the Haitians had discovered they could communicate with Ali in French, and they were frantically pointing down the street and imploring him to take some kind of action.

What was up? I wanted to know.

Ali told me they were saying someone was about to be killed.

Where?

Just down the street.

Who was killing who?

Soldiers. *Attaches.*

Already in trouble, I figured, because of the baton incident, I thought what the hell. Let's go check it out since it was just down the street. We waded into the crowd. Enveloped, we began moving away from our own units at the garrison. Just the four of us. The cowboys.

As we progressed down the street, urged forward by our agitated guides, my discomfort grew. Each stride took us further and further from the caserne. We walked half a block, in a file, Ali in front translating, me behind him, Skye and Kyle behind me. Still we saw nothing but the endless crush of noisy civilians. Turn right, they told us. How far, we wanted to now. Over a block away now. A little further, they told us. We went another block, now seemingly miles away from the legal and physical security of the garrison. Another block, and the crowds grew louder and more agitated. Left, they said, left. We turned. I was beginning to be confused about the route back. How much further, we wanted to know. Very near, they said. Another block passed.

It occurred to me suddenly that I had committed an enormous tactical error. We had left the caserne without a radio. This was a dumb rookie mistake, and it put all of us at risk. Every instinct I had said turn back, but the crowd we had pledged to was present. No commander knew where we were. No communication. No idea of what the threat might turn out to be. With the same fatal finality I used to exit aircraft at 12,000 feet into the black night, I pulled the butt of my weapon tightly into the pocket of my shoulder and told the guys to step it out.

We emerged abruptly at the edge of an open circular clearing in the street. Hundreds of people at the edge of the empty circle were screaming and shouting angrily. In the middle of the cleared area, an area half the size of a football field, were two civilians, crouched in hip shooters' stances, pointing M-1 Garands at the crowd. Four FAd'H soldiers with Garands were working the edge of the crowd, wading in and out with rifle in one hand, baton in the other, waylaying random members of the crowd with the batons. Six rifles to our four. They were spread out, and we were together. They could shoot randomly, and we would have to shoot precisely. By any objective military standard, we had no advantages and all the disadvantages. And every one of us knew that we were going to prevail. We knew. We had the initiative.

"Kyle and Skye!" I shouted. "Go to the right!"

We deployed into the circle on line with one another, our rifle butts now locked tightly into the pockets of our shoulders, barrels up and trained in the directions of the six assailants. Ali and I were closing on the two with their weapons ready to fire, while Skye and Kyle edged toward the four soldiers, whose weapons were held in non-dominant hands, the better to swing batons. Skye, Ali and I remembered the key phrase we had studied at Guantanamo.

"Mete zam ou ate! Mete zam ou ate!" Lay your weapons on the ground. We screamed it at them, each of us watching the barrels of the Garands, prepared to shoot if a barrel so much as drifted in our direction. Means, opportunity and threat. Means, opportunity and threat. I prayed that all of them were reviewing the shooting criteria we had practiced in Guantanamo, that all of them were watching hands.

The initial reaction of the attaches and FAd'H was shock. They froze and simply stared back at us. In those seconds, we could feel them measuring the situation. The din of the crowd was unbelievable. But we shouted it again. I can't speak for the others, but the assailants stayed my right index finger by reacting to the second command. I had made my decision to fire, from the nearest threat to the furthest, in sequence, two rounds per man, with a center-of-mass sight picture. The safety of the crowd was the only thing that had restrained me thusfar. We were outnumbered and outgunned, and the longer we waited, the more chance they had to conceive a reaction.

The police and one *attache* placed their weapons on the ground. The other *attache* was roughly between Ali and me. Ali had started consolidating the weapons in the center of the opening. The attache was slowly turning now toward Ali. I leapt toward him and shouted to Ali. Halfway through his turn, Ali had the end of his M16 barrel in the *attache's* neck, and my barrel was pressed to the back of his head. He dropped his weapon. Then Kyle shouted something. A member of the crowd had waded in while Ali and I disarmed the *attache*, retrieved a dropped baton, and clubbed the other *attache* to the ground. Ali had snatched the weapon in front of him, and was moving it to the fresh pile of M-1s in front of us. I had turned to see what Kyle was hollering about, when another commotion broke out to my immediate rear. I looked back, and the *attache* who had just given up his weapon was on his knees, blood running into his eye, with a skinny teenage kid brandishing a baton over him, preparing to deliver another coup. I lunged threateningly at the kid, shouting something unintelligible, and the youngster dropped the baton and retreated a few steps. He was met by companions with hearty congratulations.

"Get them in the middle," I shouted.

We started herding our new prisoners to the center to protect them from the now increasingly impassioned and bloodthirsty multitude. Skye and I were screaming orders to *fe bak* at the crowd. Skye looked frighteningly close to firing, with his weapon leveled and his finger firmly on the trigger. Fuck me, I was thinking. I glanced behind me, at Ali and Kyle. They had taken their eyes off the detainees, who were still too stunned to react. Both stooped together over the pile of weapons, clearing the rounds out of the chambers. The detainees began huddling near us for protection as the crowd started closing the ring on us.

"Fuck it!" I bellowed. "Fuck the weapons. Give them to them by the barrel."

Ali looked up, confused. I had no time to explain. We couldn't move these prisoners out, guard ourselves from them, guard them from the mob, control the crowd, and carry the captured rifles all at the same time. We certainly couldn't leave the rifles for the crowd.

"Make them hold the weapons by the fuckin' barrels, out to the front, butts hanging down, and let's get the fuck out of here." Ali and Kyle looked up, and their faces registered alarm at the new proximity of the crowd. They tried to jam the weapons into the hands of the prisoners, who now regarded their rifles like poisonous snakes. We had to forcefully show them that we meant. . . to grasp the weapon by the end of the barrel. When one of them attempted to touch the stock and carry the weapon normally, I yanked the weapon away, and repositioned it, fixing his grasp at the end of the barrel. The crowd was now within arms' reach, and we had absolutely no way to encircle our captives to protect them.

I raised my M16 barrel skyward and let a round go. The boom of the warning shot was magic. For 100 feet in every direction, the crowd went to ground. Gunfire, I discovered in that moment, even directed skyward, had a most dramatic and remarkable effect.

"Get 'em up and get 'em movin'," I shouted. I was cursing myself savagely for failing to bring a radio. Big, big blunder! Dumb! Dumb! Dumb!

"Fey bak!" we screamed at the crowd, which was getting back on its feet and starting to surge forward again, cheering and singing now, not seeming to mind our angry shouts and commands.

Boom!

I let another warning shot go. The crowd dropped and retreated a bit more, and we accelerated our movement toward the garrison, now 100,000 psychological light years away.

We formed a tight quadrant on the prisoners, moving in periodically to shove one if he straggled, then back out to our points on the walking box formation we were using. I noticed my skin was stinging and my nose was running and my eyes were smarting. Ali sneezed. Kyle was spitting repeatedly. Skye coughed. One of our detainees had activated a CS gas grenade in his initial panic.

The formation took over twenty of the longest minutes anyone could imagine to reach the garrison; twenty screaming, cajoling, pushing, threatening, looking-every-which-way minutes. Kyle would later compare the adrenaline dump to a twenty-minute free fall.

When we reached the garrison to the startled, curious gazes of everyone controlling the crowd in front, Major O'Neill rushed forward.

"What happened?" he demanded. "Someone said there were shots fired."

"Let me get 'em inside, sir," I said, panting like an exhausted dog. "We just stopped them from shooting into a crowd. When we disarmed them, the crowd attacked them. I need a few minutes to rest and calm down."

What a picture we were! Surrounded by crazy people, snot-faced and teary eyed with the riot gas, pushing six terrified men with rifles held by the tip of the barrel, two of them anointed in blood from their lacerations, all of us soaked in sweat and still streaked with dust, we surely made the good major's heart flip over.

O'Neill was going to freak out. That was my expectation. To my utter surprise, he put his hand on my shoulder as we entered the FAd'H Headquarters with the prisoners, Haitian soldiers looking on chagrined.

"Everyone's okay?" he asked.

"Yes sir," I said. "The two attaches over there got their heads busted, but they'll live."

"You go ahead and take some time to cool off," Major O'Neill told me. "We'll get the whole story later." At that moment, I liked Major O'Neill a lot.

Mike, Gonzo, Rod and Dave were inside waiting, relief showing in their faces.

"We heard something about shots fired," said Mike. "Is everyone okay?" Reporters had converged on the kneeling prisoners that Kyle and Skye were now guarding in the middle of the quadrangle.

"We're okay."

"Why didn't you guys have a radio?" Mike asked.

"Good question," I replied. "I fucked up. It all happened sort of fast." I explained how we started thinking it was just out into the crowd, but that we were slowly carried away in the tide of events. I was still smarting with humiliation at the flagrancy of my error. It must have showed. Mike, God bless him, didn't say anything else.

Gonzo and Gator were looking at the two attaches with the cracked heads. One had a nice deep laceration over his crown. The other had a deep three incher above his left eye. I told them to go ahead and clean them up and sew them up. This was against the rules laid down in the Operation Order Medical Annex, so I told them "if you want to." I had my reasons, tactical and political, but I had no time to explain them then.

The reporters ate up the suturing operation, the running blood, the pointed weapons. Dan Glick from *Newsweek* was the only person who seemed interested in what actually happened. The rest of them just wanted photos and footage of the gore. The most significant thing about this incident would be how it ended up altering and setting the tone for US-FAd'H relations and US-Haitian civilian relations in our sector for this operation. That would become apparent as time went on. But the majority of the journalists seemed interested only in the splatter. Context and significance didn't matter a whit.

As the reporters shot their splash flicks and the medics tiptoed through the suturing with double gloves, I explained to Major O'Neill and Captain Gallante what had taken place. O'Neill looked very badgered by the whole business, so I emphasized that under the rules of engagement, the guys could have shot every one of them. We had handled it in a judicious and prudent way. By emphasizing this, I hoped to avoid discussion of why we had taken off without telling anyone.

In fact, I considered the restraint exercised remarkable. At one point when the crowd was converging, I was sure Skye was about to fire. I know Ali and I had taken the slack out of our triggers when the *attache* hesitated to drop his Garand.

Ali, Kyle and Skye all agreed that the deadly force training at Guantanamo had contributed significantly to the non-fatal resolution of a potentially disastrous situation. Hearing the story, Mike concurred. My satisfaction was overshadowed by my keen sense of failure at having taken off without a radio, a basic consideration that I was resolving never to overlook again. Radios and Aid Bags would go everywhere, I decided.

Fortunately, this grave oversight was not taken into account by a relieved Major O'Neill, who did not have to explain anything embarrassing now. In fact, this was turning into excellent publicity. An element that hits the ground and takes charge, exercising restraint under stress. The occasion had turned into a press conference.

The FAd'H officers were pained by all this. They were conversing excitedly with the four soldiers who had been clubbing the crowd back for the *attaches*. Ali overheard their conversation, and interrupted to state the facts of the incident. The Haitian soldiers were startled by his fluency in French. Their conversation was abruptly suspended.

The Washington Post printed the following account on the 26th of September, 1994:

2 HELD IN GONAIVES PORT-AU-PRINCE, Sept 25--In the coastal city of Gonaives, a United States Special Forces team took two men into custody late Saturday when they were seen carrying M-1 rifles, the American military spokesman in Port-au-Prince said today. The two men are "attaches," the armed civilians who supported the military government, the spokesman said.

> *The men were captured during a pro-Aristide demonstration on*
> *Saturday night. One of the men, according to Haitian sources, was*
> *Jean Tatoune [the scalp laceration], a one time opponent of the gov-*
> *ernment who was widely disliked for going over to the military rulers*
> *and was presumed to have informed on his former colleagues.*

I place this article here as an example of (1) failure to get at the real story by the journalists who were there and had the opportunity to get facts, (2) the "accuracy" of information gained from military "spokesmen," and (3) the degree of reality distortion caused on even the shortest report, and thereby, the credibility of any interpretation of facts arrived at through media information.

The dimensions of the courtyard were roughly 25 x 65 feet. In this tiny space, we had placed stack after stack of equipment, unfolded cots, established team areas. The billets filled rapidly with equipment, a large segment of us opting to set our cots outside in the courtyard. Ventilation in the billet was non-existent. The heat was suffocating. The breeze was blocked 360 degrees by walls.

The clutter was overwhelming. We stacked and organized the best we could to minimize our inconvenience and discomfort.

We were informed that our team would be rotated to the front for crowd control within an hour, so we all tried to relax and drink some water. The din of the crowd outside was a constant background noise.

One fortyish, red-headed photojournalist with a bushy mustache and rugged looking Banana Republic attire came up to me as I gazed blankly ahead and drained two one-quart canteens.

"Is there something you guys can loan me to sleep off the ground?" he implored.

"Not sure," I said. "We can check. Why?"

"Someone said they saw a rat," he told me, fixing me with a piercing, pleading look. "I have a real problem with rats."

This diverted me for no good reason, but I refrained from laughing. It was just the raillery I needed at the moment, so I rose and scrounged him a cot. He ended up joining the whole enclave of six or seven journalists who camped in their own little area adjacent to the prison yard entrance, near a pile of empty 55-gallon oil drums.

I stretched back out against a pile of bags on the first story walkway. I was letting my eyes wander up and down the cracked yellow walls of the Headquarters along the weathered, cracked, glassless window sills, into the dirty guard billet beside the offices, along the ivy growing up the back wall, when I saw the tuba.

The old tuba was perched against the wall, dented and tarnished and secured in the grip of the ivy tendrils. I couldn't believe I hadn't noticed it earlier. Just as the cannons lay near the prison archway, pitted and stony, more rock now than iron, the tuba sat, locked with ivy against the wall, its owner in who-knows-what parallel universe. Amid crowds and cannons and blood, here we sat, under the galvanizing tropical sun, between an ocean and a sea. . . the tuba and me. I was dizzily tired.

Dan Glick from *Newsweek* sat down on my cot.

"So what do you think, so far?" he asked.

It took me a moment to figure out what he was talking about.

"I think I don't know what the fuck we are doing here. I think we're sleeping with the enemy. I hate to say it, but this fucking Carter agreement has put us in a real ambiguous situation. One minute we're protecting crowds, the next minute we're protecting their abusers. Absolutely nothing we prepared for has been used, and there's no doctrine for this situation."

I looked at the tarnished tuba. Two FAd'H soldiers stood beside it, looking cornered as they smoked.

"I think we've stepped through the looking glass here."

Dan pulled out a little notebook and flipped it open. "Can I quote you on that?" he asked.

"Well," I said, "we were told to avoid using colorful or profane language. I didn't know we were interviewing."

He laughed. "No. Just that 'We are entering an ambiguous phase,'" he said. "And that 'we are through the looking glass.'"

"Sure," I said. "Write whatever you want. Just say that one soldier said it. It's one soldier's opinion, nothing official. My bullshit and my editorializing is not to be confused with the Army's bullshit and the Army's editorializing."

It didn't matter. None of it was ever printed anyway.

25: First Cracks

Before we caught our breath, it was our turn to conduct crowd control in front of the garrison. The crowds had not subsided. The FAd'H was hiding indoors, with the exception of two nervous lads left posted at the vehicle entrance to the caserne. The crowd was respectful of the Americans, bordering on worshipful in their newfound liberty. The problem, again, was the inexorable advance. The children zipped from one part of the line to another, cutting across the cleared "safe" area, eroding the line with their play. The pressure from the outside of the circle to the center, every person straining to see what drama was in the middle, was ceaseless. The mix of celebration and relief set everyone singing and dancing, and the rhythms of song created a physical encroachment. Many people deliberately broke into and out of the line to stick Aristide posters on the building or wave them between the window bars to the soldiers' billet or hoot at and moon the FAd'H. Every few minutes, we mounted an organized push to reestablish the "line." Each man had his own technique. I used the polite tack. . . Fe bak, *sil vous plait*. Kyle pushed physically. Ali shouted angrily. . . *Eau ni va! Allez!* Gonzo was silent and taciturn, signaling firmly. Rod put on his "stern" face and stood like a statue. In the eyes of the crowd, we were developing personalities.

The remarkable thing was that the most forceful and unfriendly of us was accepted happily by the *manifestantes*, because we aimed no weapons at them and hit no one with batons. The FAd'H watched this approach incredulously from inside the garrison. Certainly the magnitude of the masses was intimidating. Refusing to disperse them was the most startling course we could take in the FAd'H's eyes. It was also the decision, along with our actions thusfar, which won the hearts and minds of the general Haitian population.

People smiled. It radiated across a gaunt face as easily as the breeze blew. There were smiles with great white teeth like horses, with diastemas, with spaces marking the ravages of time, with no teeth at all. There were smiles in the faces of tiny girls with dusty, reddened pigtails. They emanated from young men with clenched fists held aloft. They illumined ancient, skinny grandfathers, bent over canes, with straw hats worn as a jaunty counterpoint to thick, bare feet. Smiles broke across the full, round faces of women balancing huge loads atop their heads, with their sublime self-containment and their perfect posture. In every guise it was the same. Easy. Welcome. Accepting. Hopeful.

We rotated back to the courtyard, snacked and napped. Mike and I talked about lessons learned. We exchanged remarks about how unexpected every reality had been.

Captain McCormack, from 356, came by and told me he'd seen the baton incident at the LZ and that he thought it was cool. Mike backed him. He believed it was risky, but the baton snatch and the detention of the FAd'H and attaches had set the tone for the operation. These had effectively prevented us from entering into too cozy a relationship with the Haitian military. Mike and Mac agreed that snuggling with the FAd'H would kill our credibility with citizens, and that we had successfully negotiated that obstacle.

Captain Sargent came by a few minutes later. He told me that he thought the "stunt" with the baton was reckless. I asked if he believed I should have let the FAd'H soldier start cracking heads. He just thought it was a bad idea, that's all.

You can't please everyone. And his boys had been there.

We greeted the 24th of September on a roving patrol in the hummer at midnight. It was a one and a half hour patrol followed by one and a half hours guarding the front of the FAd'H building from the warm, damp blackness of an unelectrified and totally deserted

Caribbean night.

Based on the heat, the cover of darkness and the job we were expected to do, maintain peace throughout the city, I modified the uniform. The uniform was fatigue trousers, boots, T-shirts, LCE, pistols, rifles, night vision devices, and leather work gloves in case we were forced to enter buildings or scuffle with looters. The only things "unauthorized" about the ensemble was the lack of a fatigue blouse and the fact that some of the guys, including me, were wearing olive drab triangular bandages around our heads like do-rags to provide an undergarment for the night observation devices (NOD) head harnesses.

The patrol was uneventful. The electricity was out in Gonaives. The population had fatigued and gone home. The only exceptions were a few late night revelers in their cups with Clairin, a Haitian everyman's booze. We did drive past the roving patrol from another detachment. The most remarkable thing we noticed during the patrol was the brilliance of the stars over this densely populated city. The only other thing of interest was the distant beating of drums near the poor area called Raboteau. It was in the outskirts of town. We left the drumming alone. It was religious.

The guard shift in front of the caserne was a test of our will to stay awake. Absolutely an absence of activity. It was hard to believe that this was the street so wild with the jubilant masses a few hours earlier.

At three in the morning, we went to bed, utterly exhausted.

At six, dawn broke. People started bumping around the cluttered courtyard. I am a light sleeper and refused to fight a lost battle, rising and boiling coffee on the Whisperlight. The reporters had begun to stir. The Tactical Operations Center in the upper floor of the billets was alive. Some chickens were foraging around the front of the soldiers' kitchen, a hole in the wall along the vehicle entrance.

The first thing we were confronted with was the sergeant major. He wanted to speak with me. The subject was uniforms. He didn't want us running around in some kind of "Apache costumes" at night. That meant T-shirts and "drive on rags," as we referred to cravats wrapped around the head. It wasn't the uniform correction that pissed me off and put me in a fine humor first thing in the morning. It was the apparent fact that someone had dropped a stoolie's dime on us. We had worn a non-standard uniform in the middle of the night, driving without headlights, in a city with no electricity, where virtually the whole place was abed, and someone still spotted us and decided to tattle.

The FAd'H were still rolled in thin blankets on their old army bunks with the unleavened mattresses. Some of the officers had homes, but the FAd'H soldiers lived in this pigsty of a building, sleeping on beds we would have thrown out, eating rice and beans. They had clean clothes, shined shoes, guns that were questionably serviceable, cheap alcohol, cigarettes, and enough water to bathe twice a day. They were poor by any standard. Still, these meager *accoutrements* separated them from the *caille paille* mud huts and the bare feet and the dusty, cracked lips outside the garrison, separated them like a deep, swift river. As with the tuba in the ivy, I couldn't decide whether I was seeing a genuine paradox or a towering distraction.

At around eight or nine that morning, I was told to roust my men. A helicopter was inbound, and we had to provide landing zone security and support. Already, the crowd was re-germinating in front of the building.

Everyone rose groggily. Some of the guys were dragging pretty badly, especially Kyle, and we got the word to be out on the LZ within ten minutes. I raised my voice.

"I didn't say to get saddled up and out there when you fucking feel like it. I want you out there now." I said it to everyone, a shotgun blast. I was sandy-eyed and ill myself, and intolerant of passive resistance.

When the bird came, it was a Chinook with a load slung below it, a hummer loaded down with strapped on cargo. The chopper seemed to draw thousands of writhing dark bodies out of the very earth.

Red-eyed and heavy limbed, we faced another wild crowd. We broke a swift sopping sweat, and were powdered by the blade wash from the helicopter with coarse dirt and gravel that lodged in the folds of our skins, our boot tops, our waistbands, under our LCE suspenders, in the corners of our eyes.

The helicopter had delivered our automatic resupply. Within an hour, having gained experience at crowd handling and transportation the previous day, we moved four more vehicle loads of equipment into the cluttered courtyard of the garrison. The courtyard now started to resemble a miniature cityscape designed by a mad architect.

Ali and I were hungry for something. *Not* MREs! We left the garrison area, strolled a half block up the street, and scored some avocados and lemons. A dollar, total, for eight of each. Returning with our booty, we collected the routine gazes reserved for our team. Some looked on us with satisfaction and approval for "just doing it." Others looked at us with censure and jealousy. Getting avocados did not seem like a big thing, to us. But, as if clones had emerged from pods planted by the 10th Mountain Division staff, many former Special Forces people were beginning to wait for permission to draw the next breath. Either they were being good little boys, or they wanted no part of Haiti, or both.

We were scheduled for patrol again that afternoon, so some folks racked. Mike and I reviewed our Fort Liberte plan.

An integral part of our own plan was going to be what I called the Brady Bill Plus. The rule was to be that no one, absolutely no one, outside authorized security forces would have firearms, and the FAd'H's firearms were to be strictly controlled, inventoried and issued by us. All firearms were subject to summary confiscation. In Gonaives, the FAd'H's weapons had not been confiscated, and it made us nervous as hell. We were sleeping in the same complex as them. On the first night, no one had even designated an internal guard setup to watch the FAd'H. As we realized this, I excused myself to talk to the Sergeant Major about this void in our security.

Somehow, the subject of the Rules of Engagement came up in my discussion with the Tactical Operations Center, and the rules were suddenly being interpreted to mean we had no authority to confiscate weapons from anyone. This made me nuts.

I went back to Mike, very agitated.

"Just what the fuck *can* we do?" I asked. "Can we *shoot* them if they *shoot* us?"

I was not aware of it at the time, but the guidance was changing out of Washington, where who knows what elements were fighting to do everything from install completely new people to restoring the Status Quo. Right at that time, the Status Quo was holding sway. This fact was unknown to us, so Mike and I became heated in our conversation.

I came to realize later, of course, that the Status Quo had always been the only option. We were being jerked around in response to emerging situations, but the goal was clear. Re-install the rich. Protect the big U.S. investors. Maintain control over this society.

He argued that we had to follow the ROE given. Period. End of Discussion. I argued that we had to interpret our ROE independent of the interpretation given by FOB 370, because we were a smaller, more vulnerable element with a much wider area to control. What started out as one of my tirades, and one of his devil's advocacies, turned into a very testy argument. I had legitimate security concerns. He had legitimate professional concerns. We both wanted the same things, but we were tired and dazed by changes. We broke contact for a few minutes, then reunited and acted sheepish while we shook hands.

Ali and I went around back to the prison. There was a huge courtyard there, enclosed by the three interior walls of the cell rows and the back wall of the billets. The cell doors were high, wide, weathered, wooden doors, attached with giant, rusty hinges, and secured with iron hasps and padlocks. The barred apertures were about one foot by two, head high if you stood on the fractured concrete foundation that held the cracked, stuccoed walls. There was a tin roofed shelter for the courtyard guard at the rear.

We peeked into the first cell, and asked the prisoners a few questions. Here we discovered that Haitian prisoners received one free meal a week from the priest. If the family was available and capable, they were permitted to bring food for prisoners. If no family members were available, you died of starvation. They simply accounted for that fact in the mornings, and removed the body from the cell. The cell we spoke with had thirty-nine people in it, and they assumed the same was true for the rest of the cells. Most of the folks were in there for petty larceny, or failing to pay off the FAd'H for protection of bars and/or houses of prostitution.

I stopped and spoke with a couple of the reporters, telling them they might want to talk to the prisoners just to see the conditions in the jail. They exhibited interest, but again never followed through. No pazazz, I guess. I'm sure there would have been a story if there were a couple of corpses to photograph.

We had a turn controlling mobs at the front of the building early in the afternoon. It was only an hour and a half, but the crowds were getting bolder and more raucous. They were having a great time now taunting the FAd'H, calling them names, calling the commander a pervert, waving Aristide pictures in front of their faces. The FAd'H was very self controlled, but it was obvious they'd have liked nothing better than to brandish rifles, tear gas, and batons into the midst of the *manifestasyon*. Dealing with the crowds was becoming more stressful than entertaining. Rod, in particular I noticed, had turned into a silent, stony presence in the face of them.

We were hot. We stank. There was moist grit in our clothes. We were underslept.

Our relief rotation arrived, a short respite, before we were due to conduct a mounted patrol. As I was passing Rod in the courtyard, he was getting very loud with a kind of generalized group of people nearby, including reporters.

"We're just a bunch of trigger happy hypocrites," he was announcing. "Just fucking trigger happy hypocrites!"

I pulled him aside, and asked rather sternly what the goddamn problem was.

"We are about to get in a lot of fucking trouble," he said, louder now than ever. "This fucking team acting like a bunch of damn cowboys!"

I lost it.

"You got a problem with the way this fucking team runs, Rod?" I shouted back.

"Yeah! I got a problem with some of this reckless bullshit! Why we taking sides with those fucking crowds? Why we running up and down the streets looking for trouble? Like that shit yesterday. You got no fucking business running off like that!"

"You weren't there, goddamit!"

Dave Grau tried to intervene. I blew him off like a gnat.

"You weren't fuckin' there, Rod! I was! We did the right thing! You need to start thinking about intelligence, and quit worrying about how I run operations. If you can't hang with the fuckin' operations, then you take your fuckin' ass back to the States! And you better never ever start a goddamn shoutin' match with me again, especially out here in front of the whole goddamn world!"

Silence. Only the crowd outside to provide background noise. Rod stared back at me. His chin quivered. His eyes welled with tears.

"I'm sorry, Stan," he said, then looked down. "I was wrong."

Confused and taken somewhat aback by this abrupt change, I stood up from where I'd been squatting in from of him where he sat. Mike was there, looking a little helpless.

"Let's just calm down," Mike told me.

Mike and I went inside the billet. We talked it out for a while. We agreed that we needed to defuse the whole thing. We called the team together, and told them to meet in the prison courtyard.

I apologized to Rod. Rod apologized to me and to the team.

Everyone agreed that the stress was getting pretty bad, and that we had to pull together, not let it wedge us apart, and that we were still the best thing smokin' at Gonaives. It was a real kiss and make-up council. Rod and I embraced.

I did not know it at the time, but Rod had given me a new nickname which he shared with the boys. Batman. The "caped crusader" trying to save Haiti. In Vietnam it was "fucking missionary." I had caved in to my peers in Vietnam. I made up my mind then and there that I would *be* Batman.

26: Combined Patrols, the Voudon Temple, and the Village of Junk

We went on patrol. FAd'H went with us. We had been directed to take FAd'H on every patrol to let the populace know they were combined patrols; that the FAd'H still retained some authority—and our support.

This was, of course, impossible. The politicians and the senior commanders were under the preposterous illusion that these guys could be effectively re-employed on the street. Why they wanted to do that was baffling. That they believed it was possible was a testament to their absolutely total ignorance of Haitian reality.

Once the FAd'H lost the power to abuse, they lost the power to be. They had never enforced law. They were the worst criminals on the street. Their rejection by the population was virtually unanimous, and, now powerless, their fear of that population was paralyzing.

While on patrol, we passed a group of civilians who were gesticulating and talking excitedly, apparently trying to guide us to some emergency. We followed their rather confusing leads, until it led to a house with a high concrete wall around it. We requested permission to search through and behind the house. Mike and the driver had linked up with us, so we left the FAd'H to guard the truck, telling them under no circumstances to dismount. The proprietor, a thirtyish woman, let us in.

Inside, there were simple line drawings depicting amorphous animals on the walls. There was a dead chicken, for several days it appeared, laying on a stand inside the security wall. On the ground was a pile of smoldering embers, surrounded by wilting flowers, at the foot of a metal cross. I remembered some of the Zora Neal Hurston I had read. This was a little altar to Dambala, chief of the voudon pantheon. We had entered a "voodoo house."

The search yielded nothing, inside or out, and I thanked the proprietress, offering an apology for the intrusion. She was smiling and gracious. We left.

A discussion followed, wherein Skye wondered aloud, How can they be Christians and still worship the devil? This was not the first or the last time I was to hear voudon called devil worship. I think too many people have seen stuff like *The Serpent and the Rainbow*.

The culprit we had been sent to catch, whatever his misdeed, had gotten clean away.

Guard rotations and patrol rotations had continued through the night, and we rose early Monday.

Monday. Days of the week had no meaning, but Major O'Neill had tried the trick of attending mass the day prior to win over a religious population. It went over like a turd in the punchbowl.

O'Neill thought the priest was pissed off because the presence of Americans had been disruptive. That was entirely possible. What was also possible was that, unknown to us since the intelligence failed to cover it, many members of the church hierarchy had been firmly entrenched in the Cedras-Duvalierist camp, and they were not happy we had come to undo it.

The first thing that interrupted our attempts to take the edge off our progressively increasing fatigue with MRE coffee was another aircraft. We spat profanities as we saddled up with gear, and prepared to face the crowds and the dust and gravel and the heaving and hauling of whatever it was they were bringing. It was the rest of everything we had palletized for the duration of the mission.

The support people at Guantanamo had seen an opportunity to

use an "available" helicopter, and they sent forward every stick of pal-letized equipment needed for the first month of operations, all seven teams. So by midmorning we were living on top of our equipment. We walked over the equipment, worked in and out of the boxes and bags we opened and closed and stacked and restacked, played cards on it, ate on it, napped on it, wrote letters and revised operations orders on it. It was absolutely the most cluttered environment I have ever lived in. And it was hot. And it was crowded. And it was noisy.

We stank. The clothes we attempted to wash in the limited show-er water that came trickling down from the roof were hung over handrails and expedient clotheslines made of parachute cord. The sour smell on that laundry wouldn't quite come out. I lost a pair of trousers the first day to some unknown Special Forces soldier. I lost three t-shirts over the next few days, as well as three pair of socks, and one complete BDU uniform. Benefit of the doubt went with all disappear-ances, because of the clutter and confusion, except the fatigues. The BDU fatigues had my name-tape on them.

Ali and I went on a coffee patrol. It was less than a block away. The coffee was boiled in a pot beside the road in front of a small store on a charcoal stove made of battered tin, a type of brazier universal in Haiti. The coffee was hot and thick and sweet as Turkish, and Ali and I savored this pure nectar, before the rapt gaze of dozens of beaming, commenting, curious Haitian onlookers. We had already become accustomed to everything we did being done before an audience.

The crowd in front of the FAd'H Headquarters was only slightly diminished from the day prior, albeit bolder in their derision of the FAd'H soldiers who stayed discretely behind the Americans. The Americans had established a firm line, which was now being pretty well respected, well away from the entrance of the building. As the sun climbed in the sky, the trees at the corners of the building drew people into their shade, as did the shadow of the building in the later after-noon hours. This following of the shade sometimes created a mild breach of our lines. Loudspeakers brought in by the Psychological Operations people were well employed by Creole translators to aug-ment the control efforts. The masses remained largely friendly to the US soldiers, even as the fatigue and tedium of the control effort wore away the thin good will of many of the GIs.

In retrospect, naturally, the seemingly ill-informed directives with regard to the FAd'H make perfect sense. We were being directed to pre-vent Aristide's people from filling a void. All available leverage was being maintained. Haiti, like the rest of the world, was going to be economically "reformed."

27 : Chez Laura

Ali and I had spotted a little restaurant a quarter block down the street from the coffee stand, and decided after coffee to check it out. It was a hole in the wall affair, pretty typical for poor countries in my experience, with an old blanket as the door, backed up by some hanging beads. It was furnished with four tightly packed, rough hewn tables, covered by superficially clean table cloths and old German place mats with cartoon pigs on them. The chairs were too small and covered in goatskin. The smell emanating from the outdoor kitchen back of the dining area was pungent, spicy and warm. The handmade sign out front announced *Chez Laura*.

Laura's name was, in fact, Dicembre. She and her family lived upstairs from the restaurant, behind large, arching double doors, with peeling blue paint that concealed the stairwell from the customers. The customers at that moment were Ali and me.

Dicembre was around thirty, her pleasantly fleshy girth enveloped in a worn cotton print dress and a tattered apron. She had full features, sleepy eyes, and was adorned with a preposterous looking horsehair wig, not unlike those worn by 25 percent or more of Haitian women for reasons I never fathomed. Something to do with the misapprehension of a standard of beauty borrowed no doubt from our own shaved, perfumed, stylized, insecure and anorexic culture.

Ali slipped into his *homme fatale* personae (was he hitting on this woman?), all gleaming teeth and doe eyes, to determine what was for dinner.

Rice, beans and corn with goat.

Was it ready?

It would be ready within ten minutes.

Thirty minutes and a Sprite and Coca-Cola later, Dicembre emerged from the steaming, sizzling, smoking bustle in the back with two plates of rice, beans and cracked corn, heaped onto the plates, by the look of it, with a boat paddle. Onions, garlic and cloves were unmistakable in the aroma. Then came two dishes of goat meat, cooked so utterly it was falling off the bones. It smelled like heaven. Finally, there was a dish with a hot, brown sauce, slightly thickened, and a peppery oil floating over the surface.

Ali and I simultaneously dumped the sauce on the rice, beans and corn, then topped it all with the goat. The result was two mountains of aromatic food. It was unspeakably good. Ali, being capable of consuming a calf, ate all of his. I, having of late taken little food, and incapable of eating large portions, was bloated and pushed the remaining half of mine to a grateful Ali.

The cost of the meals and six sodas was 102 gourds. Each soda cost seven, and each meal 20. The exchange rate was around 15 gourd to the dollar. Soda was imported and therefore expensive.

Goats and pigs are both populous in the streets, roaming randomly, ownership established and maintained by some probative mystery.

Thus did we discover our restaurant of choice in Gonaives—*Chez Laura*.

28: We Have It Under Control

We departed *Chez Laura* in time to prepare for a duty rotation at noon. From noon to 1330, we stood in the blazing midday heat in the front street and kept the crowd at bay. Sweating profusely and consuming gallons of water had become normal operations. I was becoming accustomed to my smell, and could ill differentiate it now from the smell of the crowd. Fact was they didn't seem to care, and neither did I.

At 1330, we saddled up for mounted patrol. Aid bag. Check. Communications gear. Check. CS grenades. Check. Away we went. We were using half a team for every responsibility to better conserve our people. Mike, Gonzo, Ali and I were on the vehicle which was almost immediately dispatched to a "Help Us!" call from 372, Captain Sargent's "veterans."

372 was holed up in a church, located within the hospital compound, according to the account received over the radio. There was a confusing message about uncontrollable mobs and barricades and rice. We rolled up on a church that was besieged. Four or five hundred shouting, shoving Haitians were fighting for position at the front door. Women and children were being seriously jostled, as the stronger adult

155

men pushed them to the rear. No Americans were visible.

We elbowed our way forward with some authority, but efforts to stop the fighting and shoving and shouting were in vain. Even Ali's aggressive French verbiage, delivered in his booming voice, accompanied by his hugeness failed to stop it. So I fired a shot into the air, and the crazed crowd went into the modified quiet prone position. Within seconds, many were smiling and nodding their approval of the control. Then the jostling started again. A second shot, followed by a stream of curses and demands in English from me. I wanted to use my native tongue so the emotion would not be lost. It was not. The crowd was told to move back, which they were slow to do, so they received some help from Ali, Gonzo and Mike, who pushed and flung until there was no doubt about their resolve to make a space between the crowd and the church entrance. The crowd became less clamorous and more responsive to guidance. Ali's fluency in French, as it had been and would continue to be, was a tremendous asset in getting things done. He shouted orders, and now people were listening. We had just quelled the beginning of a food riot.

Captain Sargent suddenly burst out from behind the closed church entrance door, weapon held at high port like some "combat leader" statue, his pleasant, boyish face fixed with determination, and announced, "Everybody stand back. We have it under control." Mike laughed at him, as we would have liked to, had we not been controlling a ravenous mob.

Assistance was offered and taken. Ali used his linguistic skill, booming voice and physical hugeness to browbeat the crowd into shape, forming a line to receive the rice rations that had caused this near riot, and placing primarily women and children toward the front of the line.

29:Jailbreak I

Once the situation was placed under the control of Sargent's team again, The 354 guys mounted up and began patrolling the streets. They were called back to the garrison, where Master Sergeant Louys, the intelligence sergeant for the Advanced Operations Base (AOB), leapt onto their vehicle and started giving confused instructions about an emergency, babbling into our radio. He stated that the emergency was at the intersection of (who can remember?) A and B Streets. I cannot remember why, but I detached from the patrol at this point. Team sergeant meeting, no doubt.

Mike asked Louys if he was going along. No. Well what was he doing on the patrol vehicle. Communicating. Well, said Mike, get the fuck off, then. Whereupon the guys screamed off down one of the designated streets, looking for the intersection. It turned out that the two streets given were parallel, and could have shot around the world without ever intersecting, but that discovery came later. The Hummer passed an excited, beckoning gaggle of people who were pointing to a building, beseeching the assistance of the team.

Mike, Ali and Gonzo dismounted, and ran to the front of the building. It was determined that a confused looking man standing outside the building had a key to the door, so he was ordered to open it. Mike,

Gonzo and Ali stepped in to meet a dozen or so cheering people, who for their own safety were ordered to leave the building. The people did that gratefully. Suddenly, several people were telling the guys that they had released the people who were inside. In the confusion of everyone in Gonaives trying to explain what had happened at the same time, no one ever learned what the people were detained there for, who had detained them, or why the crowd had flagged the vehicle down in the first place. In the absence of even a hope of explanation, Mike, Gonzo and Ali mounted up and left the scene, then reported that they had failed to find the reported incident. They were then told there was no longer an emergency.

"I think we just released some people from some kind of jail," Mike confided in me later.

"Good," I said. "Who were they?"

"We don't know," he said, then told me the whole story.

Welcome to Haiti.

30: The Ouanaminthe Plan

This was to be a very typical episode in Haiti. What people tell you in Haiti means something different to them than it does to you. Cultural distance. One seldom encounters the same story from two different people. For this reason, supported stories in Haiti have high credibility, contrary to what my ethnocentric comrades and others in official-dumb would say again and again to the contrary.

After our duty rotation, Mike and I were called to a meeting with team sergeants and team leaders, held in the AOB headquarters, located in the upstairs billet. Major O'Neill was bleary eyed and sagging at the shoulders, with the wear and tear of seven teams operating outside of doctrine in this powder keg of a city. It was in moments like these that I understood the weight of the responsibility he had been given—and that we were about to receive. I found myself feeling guilty for my criticism of him in times of stress, and a bit more reflective about our dissatisfaction with the failure of higher to provide us with a desired end-state to the mission.

The subject for the meeting that pertained to us was the probable linkage of our team with 352 and 356, designated to go into Ouanaminthe and Belladere, respectively. Kwawn-uh-minth-ee was how the Major pronounced it, based on an accidental "Q" that replaced the correct "O" on our map. He insisted, as well, on pronouncing Gonaives (Go-nah-eaves) as Jen-oh-vays. The option of sending the three teams into Fort Liberte together was being studied, he said. In that way, Fort Liberte could serve as another hub. We could assist each other at the initial infil, then upon establishing a manageable situation on the ground, the other teams could push out to their areas.

When the meeting adjourned, Mike and I started discussing that option. It had some merit, we agreed. What we agreed upon, however, was that though Fort Liberte was a more important political center, the Battalion Command and Staff for Fort Liberte and Ouanaminthe was located at Ouanaminthe with a 400 man garrison, whereas Fort Liberte had a maximum of 185 or so people assigned. We decided to discuss the option of Ouaniminthe as the secondary hub instead of Fort Liberte, first with the other two team leaders, then with Major O'Neill. We were even considering leaving 352 and 354 co-located at Ouaniminthe to reduce staff and security constraints, and free up personnel for operations and rest. Both of us agreed that it was a worthwhile option for study, and that the main sticking point would be potential rivalry and discord among the leaders on operational questions.

We were scheduled for patrol/guard duty from midnight to three in the morning, so we suggested that the guys get what rest they could. Ali and I also told the guys about the restaurant, which pricked up their ears, and their appetites. ODA 354 were eaters.

31: The Pied Pipers of Gonaives

Everyone except Rod headed over to *Chez Laura*. Haitian money was loaned and redistributed to ensure each man had adequate funds (we had no opportunity as yet to exchange money except on the street) to buy his plate of food. It was good food again, everyone getting more than his fill. It was a pleasant respite for the team, albeit hot in the poorly ventilated, tightly packed room. LCEs and weapons were stacked against the walls. Shirts came off, leaving us in T-shirts, with no one complaining about the collective aroma. By the time we finished and reluctantly headed back to the garrison, every man's sleep deficit was compounded by the sack of goat meat and carbohydrates he carried in his belly.

Within minutes of our return to garrison, we were producing a chorus of snores.

We were awakened with a task at around four thirty in the afternoon. The demonstrators outside were beginning what would be a protracted demand for the head of Captain Castra. Universally and rabidly despised, he was being called out by the crowd, who chanted

161

"Castra Masisit," Castra the Pederast. The demonstrators grew surlier and more populous, alarming Major O'Neill. So Major O'Neill spun out a plan.

We were to mount the loudspeaker on the Hummer, and play taped music from it, thereby inducing the crowd to follow the vehicle. Then we were to lead the crowd far away, and come back too fast for them to follow. 354 was selected along with two of the Psychological Operations guys to play Pied Piper. One of the Psyopers, as we called them, had the tape. Garth Brooks.

I expressed doubt that Haitians, whom we had been observing making quite good street music in the course of demonstration after demonstration for the last three days, would show any affinity for Garth Brooks. I was to be proven wrong in what turned out to be one of the more bizarre experiences of my military career.

When we pulled through the crowd of demonstrators, and hit the open street, Garth opened up at 200 decibels with his country white boy lamentations, and the Haitians roared their approval

We eased down the street at around four miles an hour, and a huge chunk of the crowd peeled away from the FAd'H headquarters with us. What's more, the music started drawing people out of their houses and off every street corner. By the time we had made three right turns and were headed toward the edge of town, we were looking back on a growing, flooding, wildly cheering mass, who were gleefully ripping the lower branches off every tree in sight. The branches were help aloft by the dancing masses, a symbol of support for Father Aristide. Beyond the range of Garth, music was erupting spontaneously from the crowd, and we found ourselves at the moving head of thousands. At one point, I could see behind us for almost two full miles, and the entire street for as far as the eye could see was filled to overflowing with demonstrators. We believed we were presiding over the biggest pro-Aristide demonstration and celebration in the country. That may have been true at that moment.

We drove along for seven miles, calling in our location to the Tactical Operations Center periodically, as some members of the crowd trotted alongside the vehicle for the entire distance. We didn't turn around until we were well out of town, and it was nearly dark outside. The problem was, as people fell out of the procession, new people took their places. It seemed there was an inexhaustible supply of people with and inexhaustible capacity for celebration.

When we returned two hours later, Mike had been getting his ass severely chewed by Major O'Neill. The major had gone by his operations center and asked for the status of 354, since we had been gone for quite some time. Someone had cavalierly told the major that no radio contacts had been made by 354 since we had departed, a patent falsehood. The stress-fried major had then burst in on an unwitting Mike Gallante with an unaccountable furor, wherein Major O'Neill gave Mike a glimpse of O'Neill's unspoken thoughts. During the loud lecture about accountability, again, totally undeserved, he referred to 354 no less than five times as "cowboys," and to me as a "renegade."

At last, his true feelings about our team had come to the fore. We had scared him. The seizure of the baton, the arrest of the attaches and the FAd'H, and the confidential rumblings of some of his own timid officers had taken their cumulative toll on him, and he had snapped. Mike caught it square in the face.

Oddly enough, Major O'Neill was appeasing to me when I returned, never raising his voice, and seeming a bit perplexed when I calmly explained that we had made several, fully acknowledged, radio contacts. For all his charm, he was just another career-obsessed officer, who avoided both action and conflict.

32: Sleeping with the Enemy

Everyone is aware how poor Haitians are, without really imagining what poor, largely unemployed people, especially kids, do with their fallow time to avoid feeling sorry for themselves. One thing they do is throw rocks. Haitians, boys and girls, women and men alike, are world class stone hurlers. They practice from a very young age on moving targets. Chickens and dogs. Every chicken and dog in the country is fair game for target practice. If there is nothing else to do, children (and even adults) will pick up a stone and fling it, with near nail driving accuracy, at the unfortunate canine or fowl who has strayed into the impact area. The dogs are especially favored targets, because the marksman is rewarded for his or her accuracy with a satisfying yelp, invariably producing laughter from the marksman and all appreciative spectators.

I believe if there is really a cosmic justice that transcends death, the Somozas and Kissingers and Hitlers and Suhartos and Sharons and Ollie Norths will be reincarnated an appropriate number of times as a Haitian dog.

The main point of this digression is not digressive at all.

Just at sundown, our slumbers were disturbed by a cacophony of agitated voices and a flurry of arm waving activity from a group of

angry Haitian soldiers twenty feet away within the walls of the courtyard. Entering the center of that activity was a tall, rather robust
Haitian sergeant with blood running down the side of his head. An
anonymous member of an outside crowd had hurled a rock across a
four way intersection, over the heads of hundreds of demonstrators,
between two American soldiers, and had found its mark upon the hat-
rack of this now extremely hostile, noisy NCO.

All of us sat up at the unaccustomed excitement. People started to
come out on the balcony walkway from the upstairs billet to see what
was going on. The Haitian NCO's display of "I'm not taking this shit
anymore!" hostility had grown contagious, and the FAd'H members
who inspected the lacerated head and listened to his grievance were in
increasing numbers beginning to point in the direction of the crowd
and at us. The offended man was gripping his sidearm in its holster, as
were a couple of others now. Ali looked at me, and we both picked up
our rifles, and assumed kneeling positions at the low ready behind
stacks of equipment. On cue, other members of our team, then of
other teams, did the same thing. Many people who had been clearing
their weapons upon entering the courtyard noisily charged them now,
and the sound of all the bolts slamming forward caught the attention
of Captain Castra, the FAd'H commander. Castra and two others
rushed over to the agitated group and pointed out that they were about
to be massacred. When the FAd'H soldiers looked up and saw dozens
of kneeling soldiers with weapons in hand, facing squarely into their
midst, all except the wounded one became quiet, spread out, and
adopted extremely non-hostile postures. The one with the cracked
head continued to behave wildly, his arms going here and there, while
Castra physically seized the sergeant's face in his hands. Castra forced
the man to look directly into his eyes, whereupon he told him something in Creole that finally calmed the injured man.

In the interest of full disclosure, dangerously fatigued and fueled
on adrenaline and caffeine, I nourished the secret hope that one of the
soldiers would unholster his weapon. My abhorrence of this garrison
was that strong. My fatigue at the tension between the FAd'H and the
clamoring masses was that great. My violence was that near the surface. It always was. The legacy of this career, the addiction to conflict,
is often something I felt nearly impotent against. I was the moth, and
conflict was the flame. I like to think that's past, but I can never be
sure.

I made a mental note to have Ali translate instructions to the demonstrators to refrain from throwing rocks because it complicated our situation, and put us in a bad situation *vis a vis* the demonstrators themselves.

The tension ever so slowly diminished until people went back to sleep. The interior guard was doubled that night and remained doubled until we left.

On that same evening, the first looters were captured in Gonaives by a team from O'Neill's company. They were brought in to the FAd'H headquarters, where it was discovered they were members of our FAd'H garrison, Haitian military, who had been in civilian clothes. Fate was trying to tell us something, it seemed.

33: MACOUTE

We rose early on Tuesday. We were designated for the eight to ten morning shift on demonstration watch in front of the garrison, after which we had a two-hour mounted patrol. I was disturbed out of a light sleep before six by the activity of everyone who was already up. The bone deep, dried out, foul smelling fatigue that made my insides seem to quiver with the effort of just breathing had me. My will as I rose was the receding flame at the end of a wet match. I had a neurological deficit in slow motion when I tried to make coffee on the Whisperlite. I spilled one cup of hot water, then the stove started getting finicky about the kerosene I was burning in it. So I got outfitted with some effort, and stumbled across the quiet early morning street, where I found the street coffee stand not quite ready yet. At this point, I was utterly demoralized.

I went back to the caserne and found Ali stirring.. I told him the order was in for coffee across the street. Ali poked and pottered in his usual maddening fashion, but eventually we got to the coffee, hot, thick and sweet. I drank four large cups of it, which besides having enough caffeine to wire a rhinoceros, loaded me up with about a cup of sugar. I began to feel human.

Demonstration watch was easy. The novelty had worn off, and by the time a crowd of any volume had started to gather, it was 10 AM., and our turn to leave the garrison on patrol.

Something I started to hear that morning which bothered me, but which I decided not to make an issue of—yet—was commentary by Gonzo and Ali about using the gentle pushing necessary to maintain a line of demarcation to feel the breasts of young women in the crowd. They were laughing lasciviously and exchanging stories about "this one" and "that one," referring to the teenage girls they found mutually attractive. I could have made an issue of it, but there was no way under the present circumstances to enforce any prohibition on this groping. I have found in the past that it is a bad policy to state that you forbid something, when you can't stop it. It is quickly discovered that you are powerless to enforce the mandate, and the perception of powerlessness quickly becomes generalized. It is precisely the reason Mike and I had decided absolutely by then not to establish any curfew at Fort Liberte. Nonetheless, this business bothered me. It was typical SF shit. Fortunately, breasts are no more associated with sex in Haiti than eyebrows or knuckles, being casually displayed and widely utilized in accordance with their biological directive as a food source for youngsters, so the intent of the gropers was not likely comprehended. At least these were my rationalizations, and for them I accept responsibility.

The first order of business on patrol was to lend assistance to a team who was apparently trapped at a food distribution center. We responded, backed up the crowd with the other team, and the rice sacks were brought out into the street. A quick collective decision was made. We slashed the bags open in several locations in the street, so it had to be carried away in hands, cups and shirttails, thereby gaining wider distribution and preventing the strongest males from shouldering the 100 pound sack and making off with it to sell at the local market. Within 15 minutes the situation was under control, although there were a few isolated fights breaking out over the rice, so we departed.

On the way out of the intersection, a man approached us with nothing but a straw hat, cutoff shorts and a bucket. In the bucket he had a dozen or so spiny lobsters of varying size. They had been freshly poked through the head with some impaling object, and were still mechanically shifting their slow limbs in the last throes of death. We dickered and fussed over the price for a while, finally agreeing to purchase the whole bucket full for 200 gourd, at our current street exchange about $15. We would take them to Dicembre, and have them for a sitdown meal after patrol was over.

We also took reporters on the patrol. We used the big, white

FAd'H Toyota flatbed truck. About fifteen minutes after the lobster buy, we passed a small crowd, where we spotted a fellow wielding a machete against several people while the crowd shouted and pointed. We jumped off the truck, leaving Mike and the driver, and proceeded to chase the machete man through the rabbit warren alleys and byways of a densely packed poor neighborhood, with reporters constantly running to our front, directly in our potential line of fire. We shouted for them to get out of the way, and they ignored us. Within two minutes, we had lost our runner. Thank god all was not lost. CNN and others had their precious and exciting footage of soldiers running through the streets.

Mike was justifiably put out at the way we all just leapt out of the truck and took off with no coordinating instructions. On reflection, I found him absolutely correct, and we conducted a quick after action review of our chase, wherein we came up with a more controlled, organized system of response, based on a split team, mounted and dismounted, and supported by a standard system of communications.

We mounted up. Within minutes, another incident occurred. We drove into a fight, where three guys were beating the living shit out of one man. The victim was prostrate on the pavement, and the assailants scattered. We only managed to catch one, whom Ali ordered into the prone position. I knelt on his back to conduct a quick cursory search, then flex-cuffed him. The reporters went nuts again, snapping photos of something that probably didn't amount to a hill of beans, and a shot of me kneeling on a prone Haitian with a gun pointed at him showed up in a Dominican newspaper a week later.

We loaded the dude on the truck, and were headed back to the garrison, when an excited group of young men and women started hollering and pointing to a short, dark fellow who was walking furtively down the street, with a look of anger and disappointment. The crowd was telling us that he had just thrown a pistol to someone or into something, and that he was *Ton Ton Macoute*, the secret police and palace guard organized in the heyday of Papa Doc.

Get on, Ali told him. He did, without hesitation. What about it? Ali asked. Yes, he told us, he was *Ton Ton Macoute*. But he was ready to quit. Whatever that meant.

We looked at each other. What the hell was going on?

Ali talked with him a moment more. Bottom line was the guy wanted no part of a fight with Americans, and he had heard about the incident the first day with the soldiers and attaches we had disarmed. So when we showed up, he got rid of the weapon, by "throwing it on a roof," (god knows where, or if it was still there) and now he was beseeching us for protection from what was, true enough, an increasingly hostile and emboldened crowd that gathered below the truck, demanding that we do various things, like gouge out his eyes or cut off his penis. I'll even tell you the names of other macoutes and where they have their weapons, he told us. So much for loyalty. As a matter of fact, he let us know, that guy right over there is one, too.

Sure enough, there was another man, glaring up at us, as he started skulking away. Off went Gonzo and Skye. Search complete. Handcuffs on. Load. Back to the garrison we went, giving a quick information dump on the whole scenario to MSG Louys, the intelligence sergeant for the AOB.

While we gave the intel to the B Team, the lobsters were toted over to *Chez Laura*, where a deal was struck for their incorporation into a sumptuous lunch for the whole team.

Sumptuous it was. The whole team showed up after patrol. We shed warbelts and fatigue blouses, stacked weapons against the narrow walls, squeezed into the goatskin covered chairs, and killed the hour it took to prepare the food, guzzling cold sodas and congratulating ourselves on what a kickass team we were. When the food was done, it was lobster in a spicy, garlicky white sauce, poured over the clove scented rice and beans. For a while at that table, I was confident in our competence and cohesion. We were tired. We were ill utilized. But we were good.

I was living in delirium.

A couple of guys from another team happened to see the team through the door. They stuck their heads in. Our casual team sitdown over lobster and Coke and coffee among all the chaos made an impression that quickly became part of our evolving reputation as the team that did stuff. The Real Team. The Cowboys. It also let the word out on *Chez Laura*. We would never again be able to find Laura's empty. It was to become the most popular and profitable restaurant in the city of Gonaives. And the prices went up.

34: Iron Jesus

The guys bagged out hard. Their bellies were full. They had been baked all day by the grueling Gonaives heat. We had chased and been eluded, chased and captured, assisted the food riots. So they slept powerfully. Except me. I have never been a deep or sound sleeper.

By four in the afternoon, I was bored and antsy. I knew what it was, but that didn't ameliorate the way it felt. I was going through adrenaline withdrawal again.

By five o'clock that afternoon, Ali and Kyle had stirred. Two fellow junkies. Wanna take a walk around town? I asked. Sure, they said. The guys had followed me to this point, and we had had more than our share of excitement. I was a good bet. That was to change, but not for a while.

We slung on our webgear, grabbed our guns, and strolled on out into the street.

"There goes 54," one of the guys out front said, "Looking for trouble."

"Just takin' a stroll," I lied.

We walked left, past the sight of the first day's confrontation, toward the ocean. Less than a mile from the garrison, in the center of town, we encountered on foot what we had seen several times on patrol, the fallen iron Jesus. We stopped and examined it.

Iron Jesus was not an emaciated, tortured figure, all sagging abdomen and skinny limbs, like the ones I had seen in Latin America. This Jesus was chalk white with jet black hair and beard, and a body out of Gold's Gym. This was a thick, muscular Jesus with perfect drilled holes in his hands and feet, who had fallen from the great white cross. The locals had propped him up against the bottom of the cross, a place generally reserved for the skull of Adam waiting to be reprieved from the dust and original sin. The giant bolts that had formerly suspended the savior had bent toward the ground, fracturing the reinforced concrete of the cross around the anchor points. This messiah was fifteen feet tall and made of solid iron. He must have weighed a ton. We wondered how the people had propped him up again, frail and slender as most of them were. Kyle said he would come by later and assess the feasibility of re-hanging Christ on his cross.

We walked further toward the sea. We encountered water at a small harbor, with three rusting ships and a great deal of trash floating on the gently heaving water. We shifted along the waterfront, chatting through Ali with people as we went. We would talk awhile, until a crowd began to smother us, then move along. Eventually we veered away from the water, and into another warren neighborhood of *caille pailles* (tiny houses made of sticks and mud, the most common architecture in Haiti). The neighborhood, we would find, was called Raboteau.

There are, in places like Raboteau, more pigs in the street than other Haitian neighborhoods. The dogs are even mangier, skinnier and more skiddish. The hair of the dusty, naked children with the roundworm bellies, is redder (a symptom of nutritional deficiency). More teeth are missing from the mouths of adults. The bones of limbs are more prominent. The eyes are wider with hunger, dying hope and fear. The hair is more unkempt and nappy. The flies seem more in charge.

We traversed the neighborhood, and the fear was tangible. Until we started saying, *"Bon soir,"* and waving with a smile. It was as if one moment we were in a scene from *Night of the Living Dead,* and the next moment something had breathed life into them. People would break into wide, teary-eyed smiles, waving frantically, laughing, adults and elderly as childlike in their manner and voice as the children. "Way! Way!" they would say. Look at me! As we proceeded, we created a procession, children at first, then everyone, until we had again formed a singing, chanting, laughing demonstration.

Ali told them to stay back, that we were performing security patrols. The older, stronger and more responsible would then police the younger and more impulsive, holding them back, anxious to assist in their own security, the first they had ever known.

At the outer edge of Raboteau, and as it was, the edge of town, there was an extensive plain, a mud flat really, that stretched for miles to a point where it blended with a distant cove in the ocean, between two smoke blue mountains. South along the flats were farms, green and wet in the distance, a counterpoint to the dry, hot dustiness of Gonaives.

The sun was setting, brilliant as usual, meaningless as ever, over Raboteau, the mud plain, the wandering pigs, the naked children, the hungry homes, the fallen Jesus. Haiti seemed in that moment of exhaustion and perplexity the most insoluble problem in the world. I did not say how I felt to my companions. I felt small, like one does when the distance between stars occasionally asserts itself into your understanding, like when your own death's inevitability leaps in front of you in the middle of the night when you get up to pee.

We returned through the darkened streets. My silence was washed away as we approached the garrison by the lingering demonstrations in front.

In the end, we determined that we could not put Iron Jesus back on his cross. He was just too damn heavy and we didn't have the right equipment.

35: The Priest and the Lieutenant Colonel

My dearest Sherry,

It is 28 Sep and I finally have a chance to write a note. Slept five hours last night. Most I've gotten since our arrival, and I feel better for it. We don't go on patrol until the 2 to 6 shift this pm. 1130 now.

The changing of the rules for treatment of the Haitian military has complicated our task beyond belief. We have to carry them along on patrol, and it incites the population, who bear a burning hatred for them. They catalogue the crimes of each one of them to us as we drive by with the accused in the truck. They call them pigs and dogs, while the FAd'H sits stiffly and absorbs it. They are angry and scared (the military). 54 is partly responsible for that. . .

When moments of rest occur, I sneak out to the prison courtyard to be alone with my wallet photos. I have not done well enough letting you and the kids know how much I need you. I love you.

Stan

177

That morning, the follow on/follow on pallets arrived with every last piece of equipment with which we had deployed, and at last one could not see across the garrison quadrangle without climbing something. All the stuff we did not need yet had arrived. What did not arrive was a re-supply of potable water and food, for which we were critically short.

The latest rumor was gaining strength. FOB 33, the Third Battalion Headquarters, run by Lieutenant Colonel Schroer, was about to move into and occupy a headquarters in Gonaives. This was not taken as good news. LTC Schroer was the former deputy commander of the Group, a man who made his reputation cutting money paid to deployed troops, and forcing them to live on MRE's for weeks at a time, in "field conditions" that were not, in fact field conditions at all, while he bankrolled trips conducted by commanders and staff with full per diem payments, allowing them to stay in swank hotels, eat in pricey restaurants, and rent cars. LTC Schroer had become famous for not only turning down army funds to the troops, but refusing to allow them to receive recompense from the Border Patrol, when the teams were doing work for that outside agency. Besides being so stingy he wouldn't pay a dime to see a piss-ant eat a bail of hay (if that dime was paid to troops), Schroer was a thick-headed, insecure, unapproachable, narrow minded, elitist ass. An officer who worked with him, who shall remain anonymous for obvious reasons, told me once, "Schroer hates everyone who is competent."

His reputation as a world class micro-manager whose sole concern was to protect his job and secure a general's rank in the future had the AOB in a tizzy. In response to the news, let it be said however, the AOB was setting up their Operations Center to look like it should have in the first place, with intel displays, ops matrices, schedules and a timeline for milestones in the accomplishment of missions. (Some did these things as part of operations. Some did it as eyewash.)

We were watching the AOB get agitated, which was entertaining, while we smugly scribbled letters and discussed the imagined and highly coveted advantages of Fort Liberte, isolated far, far from everyone. The other rumor was that we would deploy forward to that mythical sounding location tomorrow.

Mike and I sneaked up on Captain Connors to put the bug in his ear about our "Ouaniminthe Option," putting 52, 54, and 56 into Ouanaminthe together, thus creating a secondary "hub." CPT Connors was impatient with us, given the disorganization and the stress level of the AOB, but assured us that the option was under consideration.

An ancient priest showed up at around 11:00 AM. with the weekly food and religion ration for the prisoners. He was a fragile, pasty-skinned Frenchman, with rheumy blue eyes that swam about in the thick lenses of his glasses, a very agreeable type who smiled readily, and went about the routine he had established in the prison with a slow, deliberate competence. Ali spoke with him in his native tongue, and reported that he had been a prisoner of the Germans during World War II, and that he had logged in over two decades working in Haiti.

The team was in a very casual mood, slowly spinning up for the patrol we were scheduled for from two to six that afternoon. We were trying to figure out a solution to the dilemma of no gasoline. There was no diesel left in our cans, and the vehicles were rapidly exhausting their last drops of fuel. We had notified the logistics guy with the AOB, emphasizing that the choppers were having no problem flying in tons of shit we did not yet need, but that food, water and fuel did not seem to occur to the Einsteins in Port-au-Prince.

354 went out on its own again. Ali and I had familiarized ourselves with most of the local streets. We knew the location of the gasoline black market, less than four blocks from the garrison. So we saddled up with our war gear and a radio and strolled down to check prices. With the street exchange of 12/1 gourd/dollar, we calculated that the price of one gallon of diesel fuel would be eight dollars. We came back and made the recommendation that until we could procure the fuel through the normal channels we should utilize the operational funds to buy the minimal gas required to sustain our security patrolling activity. This idea was met with some skepticism, not because it was hard to do, but (in my opinion) because our group had been conditioned by people like Schroer to pinch pennies, even when it made absolutely no sense.

36: ROBIN HOOD

At 2:00 PM, we were standing by, ready to patrol, alongside a Hummer with the fuel needle bisecting the "E." We were being told to wait . . . wait. . . wait. . . because a chopper was inbound with additional fuel. At 2:30, it arrived.

It was 3:30, when we were topped off with diesel, that we finally initiated our patrol, composed of Rod, Ali, Skye and me, with two FAd'H.

Our first area to patrol was Raboteau. In Raboteau, we encountered an incongruous sight, two well appointed gentlemen with suits, ties and bowlers, walking toward the garrison to report that there had been a horse theft.

Ali patiently deposed each of the men, who explained that two horses had been stolen, and that a food theft was in progress as we spoke. We used the standard list of interrogatives to determine the specifics of the infractions, but found, as always in Haiti, that the point of all these questions is lost on most of the population. The two men continually digressed into an obscure historical account of an ancient property feud between two influential families, each explaining that the family in opposition to theirs (they turned out to be brothers) was an inveterate pack of *macoutes*. They became very impatient with us for not wholly accepting or understanding what they believed to be per-fectly credible, perfectly intelligible explanations of perfectly simple facts. And by the way, those *macoutes* are stealing food right this very minute, not a mile from here.

We loaded the two men into the back of the Hummer, and as we drove out of the cluster of *caille pailles*, we saw a long procession of people, on foot, on horseback, on donkeys, leading donkeys, with bags and baskets of laundry, goods and food, coming from the South.

There they were, said the men.

All of them!? There were over a hundred people.

There they were, they insisted.

At that moment, one man with a jackass laden with two 100-pound bags of rice veered right from the procession, and headed into the warren of *caille pailles*. Our guides became highly agitated, pointing and yammering, not in French now, but in Creole.

Skye, who had been diligently studying his Creole phrase sheet, shouted, "Kampe la!" Halt!

The man leading the jackass let the animal go and started to run. He was too far away to successfully chase, so I popped a warning shot out over the mud flats just on the off chance it would stop him. It did not. He hit his afterburners and shot into the ville. The jackass bolted into the ville on an altogether different route, and the whole procession of people to the South hit the ground. Both bags of rice came off the jackass's back, and I sent the vehicle over to police them up.

Being completely confused, I told the guys to direct the procession into a cluster adjacent to our position, so we could figure out exactly what in the hell was going on.

We waved the reluctant procession into a gaggle of frightened looking, barefoot peasants, which made me feel like a bully. So I stopped the roundup, and asked Ali to ask around and find out exact-ly what was up.

The vast majority of the people were simply returning home after working all day, and not having much contact with us, were simply frightened. We were after all in uniform. We did after all carry guns. And we were mounted on a vehicle with the FAd'H. The man who bolted may or may not have been a thief. No one knew him. He may have simply been afraid, since the two men we were with (the suits) were big property owners, who had close associations with the FAd'H, the *attaches* and the *macoutes*. (We would see the tactic again and again of macoutes calling peasants *macoutes*, a kind of Orwellian bullshit story meant to confuse stupid Americans.)

Send them on their way, I told Ali. We turned to our guides. What the hell are you guys trying to pull, we asked.

No, really, they told us, there really was a theft. Out there. They pointed to scattered groups of people over a kilometer away, who were busy in the fields.

Those are not workers? we inquired.

No, they are organized thieves.

Are they dangerous?

Yes, they all carry weapons.

I decided to approach the situation with some caution, given the claim of weapons. We quickly organized into to two-man elements, who would approach the groups one at a time, with one element providing cover for the other's approach. Skye and I were in one group, and Rod and Ali comprised the second. We directed the two suits to stay with the vehicle, and told the local civilians in the procession to stay away from the vehicle. Assenting nods all around.

We moved on foot, across the wide, plowed fields. When we neared the first group, we encountered an old man with tattered shirt and trousers, two young women in equally plain attire, and three kids, one boy of about eight, and two toddlers. The whole group was foraging among the sparse vegetation for some puny okra. They had accumulated less than two shallow baskets full of it, and there were no weapons in sight.

I signaled Ali and Rod, and hollered for them to go get the other group, two or three hundred meters distant, and to bring them to us. As it turned out, they too were foraging for okra.

With Ali translating, we asked them if they owned the property.

No, they didn't.

Did they work on the property?

No.

Was the food theirs to take?

No, they responded, looking somewhat fearful now.

Then they were stealing?

Yes, they were stealing.

Why were you stealing? we asked, knowing the answer.

We were hungry.

I looked around. The field had already been brought in. The okra they had been "stealing" was what had been overlooked by the pickers. Much of it was being found in renegade plants that had sprouted among briar hedges.

Ali and Rod came in with the other "thieves." Three more women, with five kids.

"This is bullshit," said Skye. "We're not taking them in, are we?"

"God, no," I said. "Round them up, and tell them to come over to the vehicle. Tell them to hang onto their okra."

When we all got back to the vehicle, I told Ali to give them the following lecture, in the presence of the two well-fed plaintiffs we had aboard the vehicle:

"Stealing is wrong. It is very bad. Be careful, because the authorities might punish you, if you steal. Do you understand?"

Ali translated, while I winked at them. The whole group started smiling.

Yes, they all nodded. We understand.

I directed the two property owners to sit at the front of the hummer. Rod cranked the vehicle up. I motioned for Ali and Skye to help me move the bags of rice toward the tailgate.

As we pulled away, I opened my pocketknife and slit the bags. Ali and Skye then kicked them over the back. As we drove away, the group of "thieves" stood watching, until we were over a hundred meters away, then we saw them dive into the piles of rice, scooping it up in their shirts and baskets. The procession of people along the trail broke ranks too, and within moments swarmed on the rice.

37 : Dave Goes Home

When we returned, Mike had been involved in a long conversation with Major O'Neill, with regard to the lack of a stated "desired end-state." Mike had been stressing the points he and I had discussed at length. It was impossible to simply redeploy the FAd'H and force the public to accept them. Many of them would simply have to be stood down, even prosecuted for their crimes (regardless of what horse shit may have been discussed about amnesty with Cedras. Cedras was not the legitimate government). They needed to be thoroughly vetted, and culled with a broad ax. Those remaining needed to be re-indoctrinated, trained, outfitted in new uniforms, and put in only their own home towns to police where they were more accountable to their neighbors and families. Major O'Neill generally agreed, and expressed his frustration to Mike over the whole confused scenario brought on by the Carter-Nunn-Powell bastardization.[1] These suggestions Mike and I had batted around, that were now on the table between Mike and O'Neill, were a crappy compromise with the unpalatable realities we

[1] Former President Jimmy Carter, Senator Sam Nunn, and General Colin Powell were part of the US delegation that "convinced" the Cedras government to take a deal, just as the 82nd Airborne Paratroopers lifted off from Pope Air Force Base to begin the invasion, and avoid the "hard option" invasion. I have always found this last minute "miracle" just a bit too miraculous.

were being fed. Our preferred option was still to go in strong, disarm the FAd'H, establish a provisional civilian constabulary, establish a provisional justice system independent of the old one, and prosecute the old regime for their crimes.

When we were in PAP, we had heard stories of soldiers openly committing armed robbery in the streets as a rather common method for augmenting their incomes. Stories of women being gang raped in front of their families, while the family was held at gun point. Any group of people bigger than three was considered an illegal assembly, and the batons were let loose on them. People disappeared. Soldiers would get drunk and harass the public for entertainment. Loans were routinely extorted by soldiers, with no intention of paying them back. Public executions. Murders in the night. None of this was going to be either forgiven or forgotten. And already, Uncle Sam was pushing the theme of reconciliation. One had to ask, to what purpose?

A phone patch was established that evening; an HF link with a HAM operator in the states, who could facilitate conversations with loved ones over the phone. It was an imperfect patch, but Mike got to talk to his wife, Joanne, for a few moments, before he was cut off. Dave Grau also got through. Shortly after he did, he received a Red Cross message that his newborn boy was ill, in the hospital and losing weight.

Mike and I commiserated with Dave, and coordinated him a seat on the helicopter coming in the following day, so he could return to PAP and catch a flight back to be with his family.

It was just as well. Dave was little more at that point than just another body. His input as the executive officer was reminiscent of a tired private, whining about things we had to do and had no control over. He had taken on a role I denied the team members, that of an agitator, loudly denouncing the mission for placing us in a role he had decided was the role of the military police. Worse still, he had made comments aloud stating that he understood now why the police beat civilians with batons. His Dominican hauteur over Haitians was showing. Dave was a racist of the first order, and Dominican racists have a special hatred for Haitians.

I had seen this attitude coming, but let it be known that articulating it would not be tolerated. Dave, however, outranked me, technically. I tried vainly to avoid the nationality issue, Dave being Dominican. But the prevailing racial attitudes of many white

Dominicans toward darker skin, and the long-standing animosity between the two nationalities, were both well known to me and the whole team, because the Dominican Republic was our primary peace-time area of operations. Dave had never given any hint that he was anywhere outside the mainstream on anything. In fact, he was conservative and arrogant. One of the comments about him when he came onto the team was, "We need to take the starch out of that dude's shorts." Mike had doubts, I sensed, about this tech, but he had been professionally circumspect about voicing them. I had been looking for positives with him, as well. In fact, when we were in garrison, Dave had done quite well at conducting language training, and at using the computer to document our training concepts. He was not, however, enamored of hardship in training (a big minus on this very physical team), and his tactical knowledge and fieldcraft could be recorded on the head of a pin. We patted him on the back, adjusted our plans for the loss of one body, and didn't look back.

38: PRESSURES

September 29, we woke exhausted again from an uneventful night patrol. Nonetheless, we were excited that we were about to leave Gonaives. The friction between us and the B Team, the constraints on our operating modalities, and the eminent arrival of LTC Schroer, were all incentives to get the hell out of Gonaives. The previous night, Mike and I were told we were subject to be relieved if 354 was observed committing one more uniform violation. This time, it was a forearm cuff on the sleeves (Ali and me), an empty M203 vest for LCE (Kyle and Ali), a shirt unbuttoned (me). As the stupidity meter began to peg, Ouanaminthe and Fort Liberte started to seem like impossibly distant Valhallas.

Throughout this mission, our accomplishments would be nearly irrelevant, while our appearance would remain an obsession for every commander in the theater, especially the pudgy little oyster-faced lieutenant colonel who "hated competent people."

I crossed the street and told Dicembre that we would be over for breakfast in an hour, then called a pow-wow for the team. The subject was expectations. A lot of the guys were expecting us to let up as we distanced ourselves from "the flagpole." That was not about to happen, I told them. We were about to go through virgin crowd scenes, FAd'H stress, a more intensive patrolling tempo, closer contact with more Haitians, and a far more challenging peacekeeping scenario. Get it in you heads, we aren't even close to resting yet. I was not receiving the customary nods of cohesion. However the guys did build up the flatbed with all our equipment to carry out to the LZ, a new one designated at the edge of town. The truck, stacked precariously and asymmetrically high, looked like the SF version of the Beverly Hillbillies, and was dubbed the Clampet-mobile.

Batman commands Clampet-mobile.

Then we retired to *Chez Laura*, where we dined on goat, boiled plantains, eggs and rice, with a couple gallons of thick, sweet coffee.

When we returned from breakfast, we were told that we would not leave today. No one even batted an eye. One of the boys said we had been so thoroughly fucked, we didn't make a noise when we farted. We were used to it.

LTC Shithead was coming to Gonaives, and he didn't want anyone to move until he had "assessed" the situation.

After we unloaded the tons of gear we had just loaded from the truck, I asked Mike to talk. We have to come up with an alternative to the FAd'H garrison, I said. He was inclined to agree, but wanted to clarify our guidance. This, to be honest, was his obligation, but I was pursuing the agenda of avoiding being identified with the FAd'H as anything but controllers in the public eye. I still had some security concerns about staying in their garrison, especially since we were now down to eight people in a garrison that had the potential to contain 180 armed Haitian thugs. We had an op-fund, I said. Let's rent a safe house, any residence large enough to accommodate us. We can work out of the garrison, if necessary, but secure our equipment and rest our personnel at a different location. Mike argued that the guys might become "centered" on the house to the detriment of operations, which was a very legitimate concern. I assured him that in whatever case concerning housing arrangements, I would be vigilant in maintaining operational focus. With that concern in the open, he seemed to relax a bit and gave tentative approval to the notion, provided I didn't make too much of it with the boys. Keep expectations low.

Mike spoke with O'Neill, who was entering an altered psychological state; a mixture of drunkenness on the absolute power he now recognized he had over this city, fear that it could all come apart as soon as someone tried that power and found its limitations, stress at the prospect of Schroer's arrival, and cumulative fatigue. O'Neill was in possession of the perpetually oxymoronic (if not just plain moronic) intelligence reports that had driven the apparent decision to hold the teams in the hub indefinitely. Lavalas, who had been characterized by our intel people as demonic from the very beginning, was planning a huge demonstration nationwide. Prognostications were that they would attempt to storm the garrisons with thousands of unarmed civilians, seize the FAd'H and kill them, burn the garrisons, torch anti-Aristide businesses, kill the proprietors, sack the premises, then go home. O'Neill was taking this very seriously.

Mike and I discussed it. We agreed that it sounded overblown, but that we should step up local security to appease O'Neill, who was growing weary of our consistent pro-Haitian, anti-military intelligence proclamations. Our team had spent more time in close contact with Haitian civilians than any team there, and we had the most fluent French speaker, so we had a better gut understanding of the local population. We did not seriously believe this population would risk driving us into the camp of the FAd'H with reckless bullshit. Everywhere we had gone, we pitched our situation to the locals, honestly and clearly. We supported the people. We declared our enthusiastic support for the return of Aristide. But we were obligated by the agreement, and by our commanders, to prevent retribution and chaos. We always emphasized to locals how important it was that the demonstrators not "cross the line" and force us into a state of opposition. We always asked everyone to carry that message back into the streets. We reinforced it with a replay of the detention of the four soldiers and the two attaches on the first day in Gonaives, which illustrated our position clearly, and which was well known by now to everyone in Gonaives, the vast majority of whom venerated us for that action.

I strolled out front when I was on an "off" shift, as I did sometimes, so I could witness the demonstrations when I wasn't being compelled by duty to police them. I found them exhilarating in a way I still find difficult to describe. From the first demonstration to the last I witnessed in Haiti, I felt a perverse compulsion to drop my war gear, peel off my shirt, expose my wet skin, and simply slip into the crush, where I could have sang the now familiar songs, and let my feet shuffle down the street to the rhythm of the drums, swaying with the West African ghosts that inhabited the music.

Lieutenant Colonel Schroer rolled up with his entourage, vehicle after vehicle, everyone helmeted and Kevlar jacketed, armed to the teeth, automatic weapons atop the vehicles, as they inched through the manifestantes. Schroer was seated in front of the second vehicle, appearing aggrieved. We would find this a fixed expression, comically Napoleanesque.

When the emperor entered the garrison with his staff flunkies, I went by the vehicles poised fore and aft of the command vehicle and asked them to elevate the barrels of their machine guns so they would-n't point at the crowd. They are not a threat, I told them. Then I went to *Chez Laura* for a Coke, where I could monitor the situation remotely. I stayed there, until the motorcade emerged from the crowd and headed off down the street.

When I went back to ask Mike what was up with Bonaparte, he said the colonel was convinced that we had no control over the situation. There were crowds. He had observed uniform violations inside the compound. All this indicated to him that everyone there needed his control. The FOB went to a large house down the street, rented no doubt from a local Duvalierist, where they proceeded to stretch concertina wire, fill sandbags, build machine gun positions, and generally display the bunker mentality so effectively personified by the 10th Mountain Division.

I suddenly felt very sorry for Major Mark O'Neill. He struck me as inexperienced, at times, but I always believed deep down that he meant well, and I now realized that he was going to be stuck in Gonaives (no garden spot to begin with), with The Man Who Hated Competent People as his constant chaperone. I resolved to avoid showing my ass with him any more, or fighting with his staff over less than momentous decisions, which I have to admit to having done out of pure petulance on several occasions.

39: JAILBREAK II

A couple of the reporters were loitering with forlorn expressions, stuck apparently at Gonaives for an extra day, far from visions of hotel rooms, cocktails, clean towels, concupiscence. The novelty of demonstrations was past. Roll upon roll of stills had been shot with action, irony, human interest. The posturing of interviewed officers had become predictable. Game over. They wanted to go back to civilization, to air conditioning, to the next story.

Feeling bad for them, I sauntered over to two Germans and asked them if they'd seen the prison yet. It was less than fifty feet away.

"Where is it?" one of them asked.

I thought back to El Salvador, to the Camino Real Hotel, where every reporter for the mainstream media was quartered, the pool making leaping patterns of light over them beneath their umbrellas, ice cold Pilsners sweating on the tables through the neatly wrapped napkins, transistor radios held to their ears, waiting for the story. Not being a journalist, it seemed their employers were wasting a good deal of money on them, sending them all over the world to stay in hotels and listen to the radio. They accepted tours by the embassy MILGROUP, where they got their bang-bang footage without human rights violations, and reprinted everything the embassy said. They could have saved a lot of money by just having the official version of everything re-printed, which is what they did anyway. It would eliminate the expense and effort of pretending to "uncover" things.

A brace of international reporters were sitting fifty feet away from a prison where 35-40 people were packed into filthy four by four meter cells, eating once a week when the priest brought food, most sick, some starving to death, held without trial, many for refusing to pay bribes or for political activity against the Cedras regime. They hadn't even walked over to peer into the courtyard, hadn't even wondered what was behind all those big, decaying, wooden doors with the rusty bars over the apertures.

Now their interest was kindled. They picked up cameras and recorder and followed me through the courtyard gate.

We were met with an unexpected scene. One guard was leaning back on two legs of a chair, shaded under the tin roof at the back of the courtyard, disinterested, exploring his molars with a finger. Every prison door was gaping open, hanging on the ancient hinges at various odd angles. No visitors were with the prisoners. No prisoners were walking around for their exercise and latrine calls.

We investigated one cell, then another, then another. Every one was empty. When we peered into the cell adjacent to the guard cubicle, we saw where two bars had been removed from the cell window, by scraping out the loose cement to which they had been anchored. A torn knot of rags was still affixed to one of the remaining bars.

We interrogated the guard. Where were the prisoners?

Gone.

What happened?

They all escaped.

How? When?

Yesterday, he thought. The guard had fallen asleep during the exercise period, and every single prisoner had shimmied down a rag rope to freedom.

Just like an old movie, I thought. The guard didn't care. We're not in charge any more, he told us.

Haiti was imploding. Anything under construction appeared to have been suspended. Anything built appeared to be succumbing to decay. Even the occasional sound structures were boxy, homely, sitting as stupid counterpoints to the riotous patchwork of survival that surrounded them. Concrete purchased for the construction of public structures had been generally resold on the black market and replaced by a mixture of sand and saltwater, with obvious consequences.

Major O'Neill was completely unaware that we no longer had a prisoner problem to solve.

40: CASTRA

Ali consented to leave the compound with me at lunch time. We grabbed a PRC-126 radio to keep in touch and told Mike we were just going to do some stroll patrols since we weren't scheduled for duty until that evening.

Ali and I had begun standardizing the discussion we would carry out on patrol. Each patrol then became a focused effort to gain understanding or tactical intelligence. Today's subject was Captain Castra, commander of the garrison. We could not have picked a subject to elicit a more powerful response.

We interviewed dozens of people that day, and every one of them had a story about Castra.

Castra had been, by any standard we knew, the altogether mad ruler of Gonaives for several years. By Haitian standards, he was the perfect martinet. Gonaives was one of the birthplaces of the revolution, and had a proud history of rebellion, so it warranted the assignment of something more than mere ruthlessness; a man who would enjoy his work, who could maintain "order" with relish. Castra's trademark was selecting a few people at random on the street, and ordering them to crawl on their bellies to the nearest stream of open sewage, where they drank up the green drainage as the price for their lives. This practice was to reinforce to policy of averting one's eyes in silence when any member of the FAd'H passed. He also enjoyed shooting his pistol in random directions when he had imbibed a few drinks. Castra was famous for rages he would fly into, whereupon he would take a baton and break the limbs those who were ordered to present them. Ali and I were shown an abundance of scars and deformities. But Castra's crowning glory was the massacre of 27 men, women and children, in Raboteau, just three months before our arrival. This he did in response to rumors of a plot. We would find that the Raboteau incident was known throughout the nation.

At supper that evening, Ali and I spoke with Dicembre, and she confirmed everything we had been hearing about Castra that day. Ali was incensed. He was in a state of extreme sympathy for the Haitians, which he would periodically swing into, seemingly as the equal and opposite reaction to his frequent exhibitions of wrath toward them.

That evening, we reported our findings to MSG Louys, the AOB intel rep. He showed us a list I had never seen with the names of all official Haitian personnel on a list to be detained at all costs—a list that was effective until the Carter-Nunn-Powell "accord."

I walked away pissed off. I was angry because we had never been given a copy of that list. I was angry that we now had to protect this savage, demented piece of pig shit from a population who rightly wanted his head displayed over the central plaza on a stake. And I was furious that no one in our group had been made aware of Castra's history.

I proceeded to remedy the latter.

We were fucked over on the guard rotation by the AOB. It was our first experience of September 30th. Staff Sergeant Bailey, in operations, had mismatched an ops matrix, and our team got stuck pulling an extra shift of guard. On the morning of the 30th, I lost control of myself, and lit into Bailey like a bull with an ass full of picador's darts.

It had been a mistake, but not a malicious one, and after cooling down, I apologized to Bailey.

I found myself apologizing a lot those days. It was a control thing. I have always had it, the compulsion to control, but as time had shown me, the majority of what we would like to control is uncontrollable, and much of what we would like to control is better off without meddling.

Nonetheless, my emotional investment in the idea of making this mission a genuine success (that is, a genuine liberation), had me stretched tighter than a rat between two terriers. References to Batman were becoming more frequent.

ODA 386 arrived in two more hummers that morning while we were doing crowd control thing, again dressed for combat like the cast of *Aliens*, machine guns at the ready in case of overwhelming adulation from the Haitian mob or attack by squadrons of Haitian fighter-bombers.

Still in my controller role, I told them to point their weapons in a safe direction. I used my momentum to malign in advance the generalized overreaction they would be subjected to by their new boss, Il Duce Schroer, whom they had been sent there to protect and serve. They were receptive to both the advice and the characterization of the little colonel, a man who was quickly becoming legendary as a nuisance commander.

I pulled the same stunt with General Potter's security detail, when his helicopter flew in that morning. He had eight Air Force commandos (Combat Control Teams, they are called. . . the Air Force's Delta Force wannabes), who leapt off the helicopter in combat crouches, leveling their MP-5 submachine guns and their CAR-15 assault rifles at the crowd that inevitably encircled the bird. Our team pulled the LZ security, while O'Neill and half a dozen of his flunkies escorted General Potter (at that time the Theater Special Operations commander) to the garrison, where they could piss on his leg about the mission and try to convince him it was raining. I slung my weapon conspicuously, turning my back on the crowd, and sauntered over to one of the CCT ninjas.

Over the whack and whine of the chopper blades as the bird shut down, I told him to let his guys know that the threat was minimal, and that we would prefer it if they didn't train their weapons on the throng of civilians. Surprisingly, he did just that, then motioned for his comrades to do the same.

Moments after Potter's bird pulled pitch and whisked him away to the next stop on his Haitian tour, we heard a commotion that sounded like a demonstration, only thicker, deeper, and stronger. In the distance, the drums were keeping time to *When Aristide Comes, Disarm the Army, Cedras Eats Shit*, and other top forty demonstration tunes. The chorus of voices this time, however, was being carried through the ground like the vibrations of a locomotive. The garrison scrambled.

Every available American was thrust to the front to control the coming deluge. The loudspeakers were set up, and the Creole translators were standing by. Pepper spray canisters were double checked. The FAd'H moved entirely inside the building.

It was the feared Anti-Castra demonstration, and it sounded big.

When it came in view, the horde looked limitless. Thousands of shades of color in the hodge-podge of clothing, on the acres and acres of dark skin, under thousands of tree branches torn off and held aloft like battle flags over the chanting, purposeful faces, came at us like lava.

Three years ago on that date, the Cedras-Francois putsch had ousted the skinny, bespectacled, peasant's priest from office, sweeping aside the modest dreams of a desperate people. Now, they were back. And Castra was the embodiment of their thirst for justice.

As they approached the caserne, we saw the first young men, strong by Haitian standards, wearing the red and white headbands. The signs correlated. *Lavalas*. These young men raced back and forth, shouting orders to the revelers, containing them, guiding them, enforcing a distance between the deluge of people and any buildings, vehicles, and property along the street. When the stream flowed in front of the garrison, the *Lavalas* "police" kept the demonstrators halfway across the street from any part of the building or grounds. Within moments, it became apparent that they were going to do our job, and we all relaxed. The discipline was justifying everything I had stuck my neck out on with reference to *Lavalas*, and I was so pleased, that I went forward to shake the hands of the young men in the headbands.

Then we sat back and enjoyed it. Ali began flirting with every pretty girl that went past, and they readily responded. I held aloft a clenched fist periodically, just to elicit the sure roar from the passing crowd. One marcher carried a twenty foot pole aloft, with a dead cat tied to the top, while surrounding marchers pointed and laughed and called out the name, "Castra!" Gonzo began dancing along the sidelines, to screams of approval and laughter. Clayt smiled his disbelief at the magnitude of it. The loudspeaker was turned over to a seven year old homeless kid with a withered leg and a homemade crutch who had become one of our camp followers, and he announced in his reedy voice, *"Fey Bak!"*, to a storm of applause and laughter. It was Mardi Gras.

When the parade was over several hours later, the standard crowd remained, but they were pumped up by the excitement, and emboldened by the word that we had been on the street the day before, asking about Castra. Within minutes, we had a static anti-Castra demonstration going on.

The name of the game in demonstrations had become push it to the very outer limit. The marchers dearly loved to wag Aristide posters in the faces of the soldiers, to call them names, to moon them, to point at them and tell them how powerless they were with the Americans there. It was a game that amused some of us, and caused others to develop sympathy for the FAd'H (I wouldn't put up with that, and neither would you, they would say). That day the taunts became focused on one man.

Every dog that passed was called Castra. The children chanted "Castra Masisit!" Cassava was held in the air as an offering. (What does that mean? I inquired. It's prison food, they laughed.) The intensity of the demonstration increased, until we were forced to push the crowd back away, and let Castra escape, hunkered down in the back of a FAd'H Toyota. When he was gone, we told the crowd so, and they calmed. We would learn later, that when Aristide limited the concessions for amnesty, Castra fled to the Dominican Republic.

41: The Ouanaminthe-Marine Corps Plan

On the evening of September 30th, we were told by Major O'Neill that we would under no uncertain terms be deployed the following day to "Kwanaminthee" (Ouanaminthe).

Sure thing, sir. We'll be standing by.

No, no. You're going in. With Marines.

Mike sat there with his mouth open.

"WHAT⸮!" was my response.

The shit was on, as they say. I went into my Tasmanian-devil-this-is-fucking-bullshit routine. Mike was trying to plead for sense in a less argumentative manner.

I don't remember verbatim what I said, but to sum: Marines! For what! Is this more of that paranoid, "suicide mission" crap⸮ They're worse than Rangers. Look at the bullshit they did in Cap Haitian. The Marines had killed ten FAd'H under very questionable circumstances, whereupon every FAd'H member in the city fled. . . and the Marines summarily refused to fill any security void except to protect the property of the rich. We do not need the Marine Corps. Are we going to be under their operational control⸮

I was concerned about violations of the rules of engagement. I was concerned about civilian casualties. I was concerned about our operational autonomy. I was dead wrong. But I would find that out later.

Anyway, we fussed and cussed over this bit of stuff for a good portion of the evening. When I had spent my venom on that subject, I went upstairs to operations and got the boys off the guard roster for the 4:00 AM to 8:00 AM shift of guard.

I suspect to this day that the goofy individuals who had cried suicide mission in GITMO (diminutive for Guantanamo) influenced the decision to take Marines into Ouanaminthe.

42: BONAPARTE'S AIR OPERATION

We rose early on the 1st of October, trying not to believe we were really leaving. We were hustling to be packed and in "PZ posture" (ready to fly) by 10:00 AM, at a big open field behind a macoute-owned Hotel.

Prior to moving out, I directed every team member to put his hands on every high dollar, serial numbered item he was responsible for, and give me notification that all items were accounted for and packed. Every man gave me a thumbs up for his equipment.

The aircraft type changed about ten times. The load plan changed about ten times. People were loading and unloading and reloading trucks, with every new change. It was getting impossibly hot. There was no shade. Every bird that flew in and took off, often with no reason, powdered our sweaty bodies with dry, gritty dust.

Mike and I were beckoned to Schroer's Hummer. Yes, Schroer was personally supervising the whole operation, one that could have been planned, supervised and executed by an NCO with some basic air operations experience.

Napoleon Schroer gave us the once over, allowing his eyes to narrow on my rather lush mustache, then rendered a complicated explanation of what we were going to do to load and fly to Cap Haitien, Hinche and (I seem to recall) Limbay. The plan had teams crossloaded, and a perplexing system for picking people up at different locations on the landing zone.

"Why don't we just put each element flying in a spot, drop their gear there to mark it, and ground guide the birds into one after another, until we are all airborne?" I inquired.

Bonaparte attempted a withering look. It was like a withering look from Poindexter. "Just stick to the plan, Sergeant Goff," he directed. "Don't make it any more complicated than it already is."

"I was trying to make it simpler." I blurted it out, and I don't know why.

Bonaparte called Mike aside, where he appeared to be speaking sternly to him. Mike returned, and motioned for us to go.

As we walked, he said, "The colonel wants you to get rid of the cravat you're using as a sling on your weapon, and he wants you to get rid of the double magazines. He says we're not cowboys here, and that we're not in Vietnam."

"How would he know?" I laughed. "He's never been to Vietnam."

"He's a fucking dick," Mike laughed, too. "But lose the magazine and the sling."

While I replaced my double magazine with a single, and removed the cravat from my sling swivels, it dawned on Mike that the cowboy remark closely mirrored the angry comments he'd been subjected to from O'Neill several nights ago. Mike began to get pissed.

"Fuckin' O'Neill! That cowboy shit is straight from fuckin' O'Neill. Otherwise he wouldn'a used the word 'cowboy.' Fuckin' 370 is talkin' shit about us."

"Yeah," I agreed. "They're poisoning the water for us with Schroer."

"God! I'll be glad to get outa here."

"We're gettin' out today."

"They're doin' it because they're jealous of us."

"Yeah."

And so we went on. . .

Another glitch. We were told we could not land in Ouanaminthe, now, because it was within the five-mile air exclusion zone of the Dominican border. We took this news with the greatest aplomb and resigned humor. Typical military shit. Somehow, it was resolved.

43: SEMPER FI

We swallowed gallons of Gonzo's hyperchlorinated water. It was an antidote to the blistering heat on that open dusty plain. We were finally given the go ahead to load one of the Marine Corps CH-46s. The 46 is a miniature Chinook, but in the absence of the ever present Special Ops fuel bladder, there was ample room to put everything we owned, then clamber to the top and find seats.

The flight over the mountains to Cap Haitien, aside from causing me my usual helicopter apprehension, engaged us with mile after mile of lush, tropical, agrarian, mountain vista. It was absolutely enchanting, a Haiti we had not yet seen on the ground. The flourishing vegetation, the patchwork of crops, the relaxed, unceremonious pace of animal activity, began purging the tension of the frenetic activity and grotesque density we had left behind in Gonaives.

Cap Haitien rose at us like a miniaturized PAP, with the clusters of drab military hardware, the cargo aircraft around the airfield ceaselessly in takeoff and landing orbits, with the seaport already bunkered and razor-wired..

We landed on a grassy flat at the Southern end of the airfield. We dismounted and picked out shady resting places in the grass. Some locals who were maintaining a wary distance from US military activity crept cautiously toward us and sold us a few sticks of sugarcane. For over an hour, we masticated like cattle, spitting the cane pulp on the ground, and waited for the word.

The word came. We would go in with a reinforced platoon of Marines, under the direction of a Lieutenant Colonel Jones. It seemed like in Haiti, every leader dropped down at least two levels to be in on the action wherever it might be. We were unhappy with the arrangement, but it was too late to do anything about it, so Mike and I resolved to just go along, until we could execute our own plan in Fort Liberte. What had been resolved was that once on the ground in Ouanaminthe, the three detachments, 352, 354, and 356, would be under the control of Captain Mel Metts (with Mike and Captain McCormack weighing in on decisions), me as the operations sergeant, and Master Sergeant Springer as the intelligence sergeant.

I had reviewed the landmarks on the satellite imagery and the maps so many times that following them as we flew North was easy. I mentally checked off the points on the ground to gauge our progress. We flew past Fort Liberte. From altitude and offset, I could see merely the bay with the peninsula thrust into it, the checkerboard of streets growing off the main artery into town, and a distinct lack of activity. The crazy image of us entering an empty town flashed in my head. The one thing I picked out right away was the garrison building. The target.

When we arrived to circle dozens of times over Ouanaminthe, while the Marines landed, we all peered out the porthole windows of the 46 to gaze down at the hugely imposing triangular FAd'H caserne. This building dwarfed the modest little garrison at Gonaives. The was a castle-fortress perched atop the highest ground in the city. Around it was a clear area of about four acres, sealed with an eight-foot cinder block wall. The only out building was a kitchen next to the pump.

The Marines were staging at the insertion LZ, waiting to move on the castle until we were ready to accompany them. Crowds were already gathering to cheer the arriving liberators, and to watch the ten-helicopter air show.

After a seeming eternity, we landed. The Marines were already pushing up the hill from the landing zone about 400 meters outside the caserne. We had opted to leave equipment aboard while we secured the building, so we simply moved in and around the marine combat formations.

The jarheads were all business, dressed in full combat regalia, advancing in fire-team singular "wedge" formations, weapons held at the ready, while we sauntered along with them, standing upright, waving at civilians, weapons at a casual low ready. We encountered two walls along the way, which we overcame putting one of us on all fours while the others used him like a step, then reaching down with the last two atop the wall to hoist the "stepman" over.

As we crossed the last street before entering the caserne, one that ran between the garrison and the cemetery, there was a confused looking FAd'H member standing there like a doorman with a baton.

It was perfect for infiltration theater, a dramatic setup to win the population over with a symbolic act. Deliberately, this time, I relieved the soldier of his baton and sent him inside the walls, standing in the street, directing the last of my team across. As I followed them in, I placed the baton at an angle against the security wall, and before an already cheering crowd, I delivered a downward sidekick to it with the heel of my boot, cracking the ironwood and folding the baton. There was a predictable approving roar from the crowd. This time, however, the former owner was already inside. All the drama and symbolism without the risk of a lynching.

I was later criticized for these types of actions. Many actions I took in Haiti were thickheaded. Many were mistaken. But I truly believe that actions such as this were productive communicators of our desire to develop rapport with communities, thanks to the incredibly effective Haitian grapvine. When fewer than ten people are ultimately going to be given 1000 square kilometers and a quarter million or more people to "police," the support of the masses of those people, through establishment of a positive emotional bond, is an absolute prerequisite.

We entered the garrison outside the main vehicle entrance and conducted a headcount. The Marines were doing most of the searching inside the building, where they were stacking up hundreds of weapons. The FAd'H, meanwhile, merely stood around among us, watching perplexedly at the developing situation. Many clutched batons, which I walked around and relieved them of, tossing them down the hill, as the crowds perched atop the security walls applauded and cheered from a distance.

Mike and I were standing around figuring out our next move, when a CH-47 Chinook helicopter with a full interior load and a large sling load beneath it, hovered over the huge courtyard, and prepared to land with its gear. We hunkered down, and squeezed our eyes shut against the sandblasting. A moment later, the noise of the crowd changed strangely, and there was an eruption of shouting by FAd'H and American alike.

We looked up, and the entire Southern wall had collapsed before the hurricane-like rotor wash of the chopper. People in the crowd along the wall were frantically calling for help, as people were already being extricated from the rubble. In one glance, I saw four to five figures moving under the fallen blocks, and two bicycles twisted under gray dust and concrete.

The call went out for medics. It was echoed through the compound. I ran to the front vehicle gate where I saw a young man of about 25 years lying in the shattered debris, with a second joint above his knee, and the ashen look of shock on his face. I shouted for the first American soldier I saw, and ordered them to get Gonzo, to tell him to bring his aid bag with the Kendrick traction splint. I seized the foot of the casualty and applied traction along the natural axis of the leg until the deformed femur was straight, and a look of relief washed over the young man's face.

"*Qui parle espanol?*" I shouted at the crowd. Several people assented that they spoke Spanish. In Spanish I told them to tell the man to lay back and relax, until I could apply a splint.

"*El habla! El habla bien!*" someone shouted back. The patient spoke Spanish. He was already laying back.

I explained to him that his thigh was broken, that it was dangerous to move, that he could cause an artery to be cut inside his leg. I reassured him that with a splint this danger would pass. He held stock still.

I had given Gonzo my old, custom-made trauma bag for this mission. The traction splint was inside. Kendrick makes one that is a mere foot long in the bag, which extends into a very sturdy, effective long bone splint. When Gonzo arrived, he seemed a bit panicked by the fractured femur.

"I've never used this splint," he said.

"I have," I told him. "Get my traction."

Gonzo drew traction on the foot, while I applied the splint. Once the traction was taken up by the splint itself, I told Gonzo to go ahead and start an intravenous line on him, while I got the splinted leg lashed to the adjacent good leg, what's called an anatomical splint, to further stabilize it. We hollered for someone to bring some kind of litter.

This kind of scene was going on up and down the collapsed wall. There were eight serious casualties, and innumerable minor ones. All would survive that day, though one would die of septic complications almost a month later.

Someone delivered an opened cot for us to use as a litter, to which we tied in our patient with a number of cravats. Cravats go fast with casualties. That was the reason I used one for a sling, one for a belt, and one for a sweat rag, tied around my neck. All these worn bandages were outlawed by the dress code, even in this environment, for the sake of maintaining uniformity.

The next patient I treated, while Gonzo assisted with the transportation of our femur fracture to the helicopter, was a little girl with multiple lacerations on her head. All were too dirty to suture, and the environment was filthy, so I irrigated her cuts with sterile water, then peroxide, painted them liberally with Povidone, and dressed them. I turned her over to members of the crowd, who said they knew where she lived, telling them to get her to a local facility as soon as they could.

Captain White, the Civil Affairs French speaker, was on the scene, moving up and down the collapsed wall, shouting instructions to control the crowd.

"This is fucked up," he said to me, taking a break. "But you know what? This could be really good in the long run."

I stared at this comment, slowly drifting back out of a state of "trauma management tunnel vision."

"Think about it," he explained. "How powerful do we appear with the helicopters? How competent do we appear treating these injured civilians? And what a symbol! The wall came down."

I took a second to understand him. Cool. But what I saw was a huge crowd now, with no physical barrier between them and the business we had to conduct—getting moved in and coordinating with the FAd'H.

We spent the next two hours holding back the crowds, and shuttling equipment inside the FAd'H compound. Fortunately everyone had learned to back away from the wall when the helicopters came, because a subsequent landing knocked down the West wall. No one was hurt this time.

We were to learn later that the old sand and saltwater trick was used to build the walls, so the bags of concrete could be used to line the pockets of the FAd'H officers, who had it sold at market for embargo prices.

The Marines did a superlative job of carrying out tons upon tons of light, medium and heavy weapons. We reserved enough to issue for garrison duties, and sent the rest back to be destroyed (or more likely to be shipped back as war trophies). When we talked to Colonel Jones of the Marine contingent, we discussed the "let them keep their weapons" option we had been pressured to use.

"That's fuckin' stupid," was his comment. Semper Fi! I suddenly liked this Marine.

I was very glad we did not have to deal with the hardware, and that the Marines were there to help out with local security while we got established. I had to eat my words about how stupid it was to send them. They turned out to be very cooperative, and didn't seem to care a shit about whether our uniform was like theirs or not. Jones even called back and arranged to have a large quantity of concertina wire and barbed wire sent forward to replace the destroyed wall.

I tried to argue for reducing the size of the compound and turning the large Southwestern open area into a public park, but was overruled on the grounds that it seemed too provocative toward the FAd'H. They knew me like a book. So the wire was laid on the ruins of the fallen walls.

The civilians stood astounded, while they watched people who had walked in and disrupted the FAd'H's power, destroyed the walls, behaved like doctors, held back the crowd in three languages, and were now raining sweat as they put to the labor of stretching wire.

44: Moon Over Parador

When we finally moved inside, posting the minimum necessary guards outside, we discovered the total decay of what appeared from the outside as a proud and imposing structure. The smell of stale urine was overpowering. Soldiers pissed wherever the urge hit them. The rooms were piled high in trash, heaps of rotting uniforms, rusting equipment, rat shit and spiders. The absolute absence of any type of discipline was apparent. As search parties conducted a more detailed search, more small weapons were found. Piles of equipment, debris, and clothing began to grow in the vast paved courtyard, under an enormous mango tree.

We started looking for an upstairs wing of the caserne to isolate for our own billets and activities, one that would serve for operations and security. The Western wing was as close as we could find to ideal. With some shuffling and changing, we eventually established one large room as the operations/communications/intelligence center, with two additional rooms as the billet. We brought the engineers from all three teams together, and directed them to get cleaning gear, kerosene lanterns, fuel, cook stoves, and anything else we would need immediately to set up shop.

They were back in less than two hours. Ouanaminthe is separated from the Dominican Republic by a shallow river. The black market flourished, and was the primary economic activity there.
Everything we needed, we got. At the bridge where customs officials
and soldiers hung out on either side, some of our guys contacted a
Dominican officer they knew, who volunteered to get them anything
they needed from Dom Rep. We were not allowed to cross the border
(though it became a regular activity for the team who stayed behind).

Besides the gear, I found a case of Presidente beer, a full bod-
ied German brew, made in the Dominican Republic, and well known
to all three teams, laying in the middle of the billet, with boxes and
boxes of fresh fruit.

I called the other two team sergeants in; Springer and
MacDonald.

"I dunno who got the beer," I said. "But you all know that
O'Neill will be here. The general will be here. God knows who the
fuck else will be here. Leaving a case of Presidentes in full view of the
world is stupid. Talk to your guys and tell them how fuckin' stupid it
is. If they can't be more discrete than that, we might as well just follow the letter of the law on that fuckin' General Order One we got in
Gitmo. Tell 'em to use their fuckin' heads."

I set up a guard rotation, a patrol rotation, an intel/ops patrol
reporting system, and then I called my guys out on the balcony.

As they gathered next to the balcony rail, I gazed down at the
confounded Haitian soldiers, the goat eating grass from between the
paving stones, the chickens foraging in and out of the doorless rooms
in the ground floor, and the piles of stuff.

"It's fuckin' Moon Over Parador," I remember muttering.

I decided to give the team a preemptive ass chewing.

"Listen, guys. Danny's team is over there claimin' they crossed
the border. They're leavin' beer in the middle of the floor. They are
already coppin' the attitude that the work is over.

"Get this shit straight. Ain't nothin' over. Now that we don't
have any micromanagement restrictions, operations are gonna acceler-
ate, not slow down. We got more to do with less people, and we aren't
gonna stay here for more than a week. We gotta get this place on its
feet and runnin' before we can take over our beach resort. Don't let

down your guard. Stay aggressive. Stick to the plan.

"I'll get you the slack you need to slow down when we can. I'll make sure you start gettin' rest, and you get a chance to clean up. But don't cop that vacation mentality on me. That's 56's M.O., not ours.

"On the subject of this alcohol shit, I know I said we hafta refrain. Once shit slows down, however, we're gonna be here a long time. When it's appropriate, I'm not gonna look over your shoulder, but I want everyone to understand big boy rules. We don't need some-one gettin' drunk and shootin' someone, or showin' their ass with the Haitians. So just hang on. We'll get back to a human existence."

Everyone on the team seemed satisfied with this. Some had already said how they looked forward to their first cold one.

45: SPEECHMAKER

The guys were released to their responsibilities, and Mike and I stayed behind. We discussed the infil into Fort Liberte. We were more convinced than ever that vehicular entry was the right answer. The choppers would turn the whole operation into a three-ring circus. . . again.

Mike went to arrange our initial coordination meeting with the FAd'H officers.

That meeting took place just after dark, in the former commandant's office. The floor was rotten and full of leg-breaker holes. There was potential for falling straight through to the bottom floor. We had a desk set up, and I sat there with my notes. On it burned a kerosene lantern that cast an eerie yellow light over everyone. Mike Gallante, Mel Metts and Dennis McCormack stood menacingly half-lighted against one wall.

Mel Metts, detachment commander for 352, and an ally so far in the effort to actually turn this mission into a humane achievement, translated through Captain White. He introduced the captains, himself and me.

Paraphrased very roughly, he said, "We will need your cooperation to restore democracy to Haiti. This is not going to be easy. We are here to insure peace, and that means preventing violence against civilians committed by soldiers, and violence against soldiers committed by civilians. [This was becoming the official "balanced" line of the Task Force—like there was a lot of abuse of soldiers by civilians!] I look forward to developing a good working relationship with Colonel Simone (the FAd'H battalion/garrison commander), with his officers, sergeants and with his soldiers. I ask that you be patient, because this will be a long and difficult process. I look forward to working with you, and I am confident that we will succeed.

"Our operations chief, Sergeant Major Goff (I loved the instant promotion) has a few points he would like to make."

Mel was the good guy. I was the bad guy. I picked up my stack of notes, tapped them against the desk, and very slowly and deliberately slid my horn-rimmed reading glasses onto my nose. I was playing cold-blooded-functionary to the hilt.

"My first concern is for the security of my men." (Pause. Look up. Look around, over the top of the glasses.) "So I want it clearly and unmistakably understood that any threat to that security. . . even the perception of a threat to that security. . . will be met with swift, overwhelming, lethal force." (The faces of the FAd'H froze at the translation.) "Inform your people that if they are under arms, when they are in the presence of my people, they will sling or order their weapons. If they train the barrel of a weapon in the direction of one of my people, if they load a magazine without express authority, if they place their fingers on the triggers, this will be interpreted as a threat. It is absolutely paramount that each and every soldier understand this rule thoroughly. The consequences of a misunderstanding will be grave.

"The people of Ouanaminthe are going to celebrate the departure of the *de facto* government, and the return of Father Aristide. Those celebrations will involve massive demonstrations. Those demonstrations will be permitted. Members of this garrison will be subjected to verbal abuse at times. They will not respond, either with verbal replies or force. Your people will be gradually integrated into the security of the caserne and the community, based on the evolution of the situation, and the directives we receive from our commanders and the Haitian central government. Inform us of volatile situations, and allow us to take the lead in resolving them.

"Community leaders from the civil sector will be contacted. Your leaders will sit down with them and listen to their grievances. We are here to ensure that the armed forces are effectively subordinated to the civil authority. Until that civil authority can be established, the American officers in this room will function as the local government.

"Your staff counterparts will be introduced to you in order to facilitate the possible reorganization or termination of this garrison, and to assure smooth operations on a day to day basis.

"On the subject of batons. Today, I took the batons away from the soldiers. I understand perfectly that the batons are, at least for legitimate police functions, an intermediate step in forceful response, between talking and shooting. Be that as it may, those batons have been used so brutally and so often in the service of abuse that they have become a symbol of repression. Batons will no longer be carried by members of the FAd'H.

"I am very pleased to be in Haiti, and I believe deeply in the justice of this mission. I hope everyone here completely understands me."

You could have heard the proverbial pin drop. As an afterthought, I said, "No one is to enter or pass the wing of the upstairs that we are now occupying. If any of you needs to see one of us, tell one of the Americans, and he will relay the message."

The effect of my open hostility, totally premeditated for the purpose of ensuring our own security in the days to come, was heightened by the translation pauses. I stopped after each sentence, allowing Captain White to transform my menacing into perfect French.

I packed up my papers, and summarily left the flickering yellow glow of the room to the officers to hammer out any details they needed to with the Colonel.

It was my first real speech. I was to make many, many more.

46: BARTERTOWN

Everyone was up by 6:00 AM.

First order of business was to send a patrol to the bridge on the Riviere Massacre (named in memory of a Dominican massacre of thousands of Haitians), to coordinate more supplies from the Dominican Republic. Next, a patrol was sent to find a place where we could establish a safe house with some kind of bathing facility. Finally, Gonzo volunteered to work on the broken pump outside the fortress walls, next to the kitchen building.

Mike and I grabbed one of the vehicles, loaded all the empty diesel cans aboard, and struck out to find the gasoline black market. We intended to use the time apart from the others to start discussing a timetable for the entry into Fort Liberte. With a few requests for directions, in Spanish (spoken by every other Ouanaminthan), we navigated the hummer through the narrow, muddy alleys, sometimes clearing the slipshod Haitian houses on either side by fractions of an inch, until we emerged into a scene that can only be compared to the Mad Max movies. In fact, the gas market would end up being called "Thunderdome." It was absolute squalor and apparent chaos. Hundreds of men, women and children were engaged in loud, frenetic trading. The ground near the caille paille neighborhood was deeply contaminated with a petrochemical soup. Trash was everywhere. Bottles of every shape and size were being guarded, carted, and exchanged. They contained gasoline, oil, and diesel, all of which found its way across the river and past the embargo. Pigs, chickens and dogs roamed aimlessly. Some of the tiny naked children would simply piss or shit where they stood. Every trade was being struck in loud Creole. Every customer was assailed by a flock of sellers, shouting and shoving for the attention of the potential sale. There was an unlikely, disorganized fleet of old cars, new cars, motorcycles.

Mike and I pulled in, with a new, tan Nissan 4x4 behind us. A sandy headed journalist got out, wearing the standard international journalist multi pocketed vest over a t-shirt and blue jeans. We shot the shit with him for a while, then moved in to start trading. Other *blancs* were coming in and out, from god knows where. Illegal fuel had become an international gathering point.

47 : Trusted Agents

When we returned with the booty, we snaked up the gravel driveway of the caserne past the pump, where Gonzo was on all fours with a fleshy, grizzled, light skinned Haitian. Tools were scattered around them, and they were reassembling something. Later on, I asked Gonzo who the guy was, and Gonzo told me he was a guy named Vincent. Knew his shit with pumps. Had the right tools. Said he could've fixed that pump years ago, but wouldn't do it for the FAd'H.

Springer had sent a posse out to find a hotel, and had succeeded in finding a place about 3/4 of a mile away, that had a bed, a nightstand and a shower in each room. It was musty and illuminated with kerosene lamps, but the water in the showers ran. The price of the rooms was something like six dollars a day, so they rented two of them and told the management to leave the place open all the time. I took my first shower in one of the rooms that afternoon. The shower stall was dark. The stream of water was like a thick cord. Something was in front of my feet that was dark and hairy looking in the gloom, so I stood back from it. It never moved, so I decided it was not alive. The shower refreshed me, but not a single set of my uniforms (I had brought three) would relinquish the peculiar sour odor they had developed, no matter how hard I washed them.

Operations took on a predictable, orderly nature, which was somewhat comforting, after long days of seemingly inexhaustible chaos. Patrol reports to intel desk. Intel desk gives patrol a list of desired information to collect based on gaps in local analysis. Patrol departs, collects information, maintains security, familiarizes with area, intervenes and interviews where necessary. Patrol returns. Reports to intel desk. New patrol waiting to hear debrief. Intel rep conducts debrief and updates maps, sketches and logs. Intel rep gives next patrol "collection guidance". And so on. This was a system that was missing in Gonaives, and, we felt, that gave us the greatest gain for our effort. It was focused and flexible. Focus and flexibility had been watchwords for Mike and I from the beginning of our professional relationship. Every leader has some little thing she or he hangs the hat on.

That afternoon I went to visit L'Escale, the restaurant/club we had passed several times, and where we had dropped in for refreshments during patrols. It had a high wall surrounding it, some thatched cabanas inside the wall, and the soda was cold. We enjoyed the privacy it provided inside the walls, having grown weary of the ubiquitous crowds and their relentless and unfailing curiosity.

I went on foot, to avoid obligating a guard for the vehicle. The restaurant was only three blocks outside the garrison. I had left word with Mike where I would be. My purpose was twofold. One, I wanted to a break from my constant contact with our own teams. We had all begun to get on one another's nerves pretty badly. Two, I wanted to start collecting information on Fort Liberte.

The owner of the club was behind the bar when I arrived. He spoke near perfect English. He introduced himself as Freddy, and pulled the top off a Coca-Cola for me. Freddy was around thirty and handsome in a boyish way. He was not light, nor dark, for a Haitian, but about the mean. He dressed casually, jeans and short sleeved shirt with a collar (though jeans are a sign of some affluence in Haiti), and wore a mangled, striped ball cap on his head at a nutty angle.

I asked him to fill me in on the situation in Ouanaminthe, what it was like there before we came, how we were perceived, and so on.

You can see how you are received, he told me. Just look at the way they cheer you. Ouanaminthe has been anxious.

Freddy emerged in the conversation as an intelligent, articulate young businessman, whose interest in politics was solely to stabilize things so he could make a living. He cursed Cedras for the climate of fear, the embargo for being such a blunt instrument, and Dominicans for preying on and exploiting Haitians. My impression was of a young man who was comfortable with his worldliness and his touch of comparative power. He seemed a bit cynical, but vaguely hopeful about what might become of the situation, if only certain things happened; elections were restored, the embargo lifted, and decentralization of the government occurred. He was frank about Haitian misgivings, at least among the intelligentsia, about the Americans. The history of American involvement in Haiti consisted of a Marine occupation that was racist and harsh, followed by the installation of a series of deadly-oppressive regimes, the capstone of which was the reign of President-for-Life Francois Duvalier. He seemed pleasantly surprised that I was at least conversant with the historical facts, and aware of some of the implications. As the conversation progressed, he opened up more and more. We rambled about politics, about history, and finally about philosophy and literature, both of which he demonstrated familiarity with, which was the pleasant surprise for this old English major who has spent a long, long time in exile from literature, my first love.

Vincent, the pump mechanic, lumbered in and sat down with us, introducing himself with a thick-pawed handshake. "Vincent Namours." Vincent, who turned out to be an old CDS (National Department of Health) engineer, proved just as well read, and just as animated on the subject of politics and history.

Vincent's racket was working inside and outside. He was a power broker. He was a salesman. He was a politician. He supported and had numerous contacts inside Lavalas, though he personally didn't "give a damn about Aristide. The son of a bitch means nothing to me, personally. But he was elected, so he is our son of a bitch." Vincent was insulated against reprisal by his past association with the Agency for International Development, for whom he wrote proposals (thereby earning fat commissions), and he seemed to have his hand in everything.

Vincent explained that Ouanaminthe had a slightly better situation that most Haitian communities, because illegal goods were available, due to the proximity to the border, and because there was a certain collusion between the civilian community and the FAd'H, who cooperated in reaping the benefits of the lively black market.

Vincent and Freddy would take turns talking, and they had the most amazing ability to continue each other's script. One would be speaking, and the other would simply integrate into whatever diatribe, with not one whit of disagreement between them. Their perceptions seemed to be identical. It was apparent that they had carried on many, many conversations in the past, and that they had discussed our arrival. The other thing that became apparent, as an incredible variety of people came and went from L'Escale, soldiers, civilians, groups of furtive young men, marketeers, barefooted old men, that L'Escale was kind of a neutral zone, and as such, the public center of gravity for Ouanaminthe.

Vincent and Freddy had Presidente beers brought to the table, and ordered me a Coke. We sat and talked for a good two hours. I was convinced that I had found the "trusted agents" I would need to guide us in the short term through the mysteries of Haitian reality. So I asked them.

Would they help me? Could they provide me with guidance and information to facilitate the earliest possible return of normalcy to the situation. I was very candid about the difference between me and my convictions, and me the soldier obligated to follow orders. I was going to follow orders, even though those orders may not be given in the spirit of establishing genuine democracy, but I was also going to do everything within the stated limitations to facilitate a situation that was good for Haitians, all of them. I told them forthrightly that I had personally leftish political tendencies, and warned them that my personal social convictions were well outside the mainstream of my profession. I was there as a pragmatist, and a soldier, who was going to do the best I could to meet the stated intent of my commanders, which at the time was to maintain stability. My spin was, and remained throughout the operation, that the maintenance of stability would be most readily accomplished with the willing cooperation of a friendly populace. For that reason, I told them, I wanted to establish a good working relationship with popular religious and political leaders. . . in particular, Lavalas.

I noted an exchange of glances. I was coming on fast and furious now, and I suddenly feared that I may have laid my cards down too quickly.

The discomfort of the moment was dissipated when two reporters entered L'Escale. There was a young man, around 35, who worked with Associated Press, and a young woman, around 30, who worked freelance. I had seen them both at a distance, during the infil, and hanging around the garrison where we had ignored them. The introduced themselves as Jim and Claudia. We all sat around and exchanged pleasantries for a few minutes, then Vincent excused himself. Shortly afterwards, a number of customers rolled in and Freddy went behind the bar to help out.

I sat there with the two reporters, they in their clean, comfortable shorts and shirts, encumbered only by cameras and notebooks, and me in my dust impregnated, sour, wet fatigues, with a pile next to me of my webgear and M-16A2. We went through the usual familiarization, where they interrogated me about SF organization, capabilities, and so forth. They congratulated me on our actions the day prior, when the wall came down. The medical response had much impressed them, as well as our crowd handling. I assured them that our experience in Gonaives had prepared us for crowds, but that the medical emergencies were unfortunate and unanticipated.

Everything was just as friendly as it could be.

48: Public Relations

The reporters then zeroed in on what we planned to do. . . now that we were here. I had grown relaxed in the presence of reporters, and had mentioned to Mike that I wanted to make allies of them, wherever possible, in case we could enlist their aid in Fort Liberte to attract non-governmental organizations. (This was naive in the extreme. Once the exciting footage was exhausted, every reporter on the island retreated to the comforts of Port-au-Prince to parrot whatever they were told by the Public Affairs Office. I was also to discover slowly that the NGOs were not the benevolent and constructive agencies I was imagining.) I let them buy me a Coke, and I talked as freely as I had with Vincent and Freddy. I explained our intentions, and our operating philosophy. Our intentions were, at least in our operational area, to maintain a climate where Haitians would be able to come up with Haitian solutions to Haitian problems. Our operating philosophy was that we had to break the psychological hold of the *de facto* regime, to eliminate the climate of fear, that we had to establish a network of relationships with community, political and religious leaders, to avoid misunderstandings and to communicate our actions and their rationales to as many people as possible, that we had to avoid establishing relationships of dependency and unrealistic expectations between

American military and Haitian civilians, and that we wanted to ensure the reversal of the traditional military-civil relationship, that is, to subordinate the military authority to the civil authority. It was a good conversation, one that rambled easily away from the official stuff into where are you all from, how many kids do you have, what did you think of that movie, then back again to the official thread.

I remembered some guidance that had been earlier published and distributed in GITMO with regard to press interviews, but have only recently re-discovered the little wallet card they gave us to carry around.

"POINTS TO REMEMBER WHEN DOING A MEDIA INTERVIEW
- Be relaxed, confident, and professional.
- Be concise; think about what you say before you speak.
- Avoid using colorful or profane language.
- Confine your discussions to areas of which you have first hand knowledge or where you have substantial personal experience.
- Deal in known facts.
- Avoid speculation. Avoid discussing hypothetical situations in any form.
- Label your opinions as opinions. Don't get into political discussions.
- Stay on the record. If you say it, they'll print it!
- You don't have to answer a question, but don't say 'No comment.'
- Don't argue with the reporter. Be firm, polite, but don't get emotional.
- Protect the record. Correct the 'facts' if you know they're wrong.
- Speak plainly. Don't use military jargon or slang.
- Don't discuss classified information."

I did on occasion, in every contact with reporters, use some profanity. It was unconscious. I had a soldier's vocabulary. Other than that, I followed this guidance very carefully. The only thing that is preposterous is the prohibition against discussing politics. How can one discuss anything about an operation like that one without discussing politics. It was a purely political operation. If we mentioned democracy, was that political? If we discussed the mission, was that political? Within five minutes of this operation beginning, every commander that came within the noise radius of a reporter had said something that could be construed as political. Alas, the little card was a guide, not an order—something they made to keep the Psyops printers busy. Some officer, somewhere, received a favorable "bullet" statement in his Evaluation for that card.

Jim later told me at the garrison, prior to moving out to Fort Liberte, that Claudia was very favorably impressed and even a bit "infatuated" with my apparent grasp of the situation and my "understanding treatment" of Haitians. Flattering as it was, I would soon cancel that bit of admiration.

49: The Les Cayes Directive

I believe it was that night we received word that a Special Forces soldier had been shot in Les Cayes while taking a shit. FRAPH had taken the credit, and two of the gunmen were killed in the encounter. Two others were captured. Colonel Boyatt, the Group commander, was enraged. I believe the order we received to detain all FRAPH, *attaches* and *macoutes*, without hesitation, to be held for questioning, was an order he issued on his own, but I can not verify that. What I can verify is that I was energized. This was exactly what we needed—a free hand to slam the opposition once and for all.

50: BRIDGES

3 October, 1994

I slept in until 6:30 on the 3rd. By the time I got dressed, prepared a canteen cup of MRE coffee, gulped it down, and headed to the shower hotel, it was past seven. In the street, I encountered Ali and Kyle returning from the shower.

Neither of them had fatigue shirt on. Neither of them had their webgear. Neither of them had a hat. Ali was wearing shower shoes, and Kyle was wearing his aqua socks. They had picked up the mood of relaxation and run with it—typical of these two, especially together.

I stopped them and told them both not to leave the garrison again without all the gear required in case a VIP showed up. Mike and I could be summarily relieved if these two had been caught like they were. I got some smart response about them just hiding until people left, whereupon I interrogated them about what actions they would take if they were suddenly fired upon. Would they run through the streets in their lounge about footgear? Would they holler gas, and hope someone believed they really had the CS grenades? Ali and Kyle together enjoyed playing the big mavericks. Their immaturity was synergistic. I

237

told them not to pull a stunt like that again, and that was the end of the discussion. They stalked off, Ali acting chastened as a whipped puppy, and Kyle barely concealing his bile. Another click in the ratcheting up of my tyranny over the team. Not the last.

Across from the hotel, after my shower, I stopped and ordered a triple helping of hot, sweet coffee and three dipping-size baguettes. I dipped the bread in the sticky coffee, just as the Haitians were doing. It was a fine breakfast.

Around nine that morning, there was a stir about the border. Apparently, Mondays were border-crossing day for the Haitians, and huge crowds showed up to cross and procure black market items. The problem was, the FAd'H was afraid to control the Haitian side, partly my fault because of my prior menacing of the Haitian soldiers, and the Dominicans were threatening to shoot members of the surging mass, if they crossed without adhering to procedures. So 356 was dispatched to seize the bridge and establish control. Some sort of melee was in progress, and the team had to fight their way forward, where they resorted to pepper spray and a great deal of heaving and shoving, *a la* the Gonaives food riots, to get control of the crowd. I drove out with Rod to deliver a couple of five gallon water cans (the heat was already murderous) to our guys, and out of the crowd emerged Danny MacDonald, the team sergeant, carrying one of the riot batons we had taken from the FAd'H two days earlier. He was strutting and smiling and swinging the baton like a beat cop, laughingly telling us as he approached about how many of them had just peeled off the structure of the bridge when the pepper spray hit them in the face. It was all great sport.

I asked him what he was doing with the baton. He told me he was waiting for the chance to knock some heads. I told him to put the baton in the Hummer, and lectured him on how politically stupid it was to carry a baton like the FAd'H did, how it sent the wrong message. He balked, so I ordered him to relinquish the stick. He threw it in back of the Hummer, snorting, "If I can't hit the motherfuckers, I guess I can just shoot 'em," as he stalked away. Click. Click.

Rod sat silently through the whole episode. Rod disliked crowds immensely, and had expressed his empathy for the FAd'H using their batons when we were in Gonaives. But he knew better now than to provoke me, especially on the subject of treatment of Haitian civilians.

So far, that day, I was making friends with everyone I came in contact with. To get away from the interpersonal pressure, I decided to head over to L'Escale for lunch.

51 : Damocles

Vincent walked in while I was eating my chicken, rice, and beans. He was wearing black work trousers, old sneakers, a white cotton short sleeved shirt, the goofy hat, and the look of a man who had made up his mind about something. He shook my hand as he scooted a chair out and plopped down onto it. Leaning over to me, with his elbows on the table and his ample belly on top of his thighs, he asked me if I wanted the biggest macoute in town.

Sure, I said. This was the test. For him and for me. Put up or shut up. Who can trust whom? I left the plate on the table and downed my soda as I headed to the bar to pay the bill.

I went to the garrison and found Mike there. Did he want to grab the biggest thug in town? I asked.

Who?

Guy named Damocles.

No, who is going to grab him?

You and me, right now.

Mike had been left out of a lot. He had his webgear on in seconds.

We loaded in the hummer, me driving, Mike in back, standing and holding on to the roof brace, like Patton in Sicily, Vincent in the passenger seat. Vincent directed us to a house that was almost across the

241

street from L'Escale.

"Vincent, I don't mean to be arbitrary, but this better be real."

He acted like he was hurt and offended. "It's real. You'll see."

I set the brake, and leaped out, heading to the front door. Mike scrambled to keep up. I freed a set of flex cuffs from my LCE and staged it over a canteen cap for easy access. My pistol was already out, rifle slung across my back as was now becoming our SOP for urban operations. Mike moved up behind me as I assumed a door position. I checked the seam of the wooden double door. It opened to the inside, and only a light deadbolt was visible through the centerline crack. I stepped in front of the doors, and delivered a sharp front kick to the deadbolt area. The doors snapped open and we leapt into the room. I cleared right, where I could see in a millisecond there was nothing, then proceeded straight to the couple sitting at their table eating, weapon trained on Damocles, but watching the hands of them both. Mike was already alongside me.

I had shouted *"Kampe la!"* as I burst in. Now I was shouting *"Les mans au l'air!"* Their hands went tentatively up, as they pleaded *"Ayitien! Ayitien!"*

I don't know why they were telling us they were Haitian. We knew that.

We hustled him outside, put him against the side of the hummer, and I cuffed him. Then we assisted him onto the back of the hummer, where he glared at Vincent. A small crowd had already started to gather. Members of it were standing with their mouths open. The whole procedure took about a minute, and we were off.

On the way back we missed the turn to the garrison, and had to turn around at the city arch at the edge of town, retracing our path until we arrived at the right turn. As we drove through town, people began to applaud when they saw Damocles on the back with his hands bound behind him.

Vincent even mounted the steps to the garrison, as we led Damocles up and past the FAd'H duty personnel at the front desk. We told them to put him in jail until further notice.

Vincent told us there was one more, if we wanted him. So off we went. That one was not home, but we certainly made an impression on the neighbors when we burst into the empty house.

As we said thanks to Vincent, and went upstairs to recount our little adventure, I began to be seized by the first germ of doubt about Vincent. Had he directed us on this venture as a power play for himself? Had we just been duped into settling a personal score? Haitians were constantly trying to use us to do just that in Gonaives. This was a more sophisticated Haitian, one that had been married to a Swede, went to an English university, discussed Hesse, and could charm a snake. But I was suspicious nonetheless. That actually made me more suspicious. To no avail. I had cast the die with this man, and I had decided to see things through with him. If worse came to worse, and we discovered we had been manipulated, Vincent would share the cell with Damocles. At this point our power was that absolute.

Less than two hours later, the man whose house we had raided when he was absent showed up at the garrison, asking what it was we had wanted at his house. The neighbors must have told him the Americans visited. We put him in jail.

52: L'ESCALE

Ali was rummaging through his gear like a Tasmanian devil. This was not an unusual occurrence, and everyone knew that when he became so obsessed to give him a little space. Just let him fling and curse. That's what he did for over an hour.

Mike and I were sitting on opposite cots, discussing what we had done, and what we planned on doing in Fort Liberte, when Ali came by. He was straining to appear casual. What he told us was not in any way casual.

The AOB in Gonaives was demanding an item by item account of all serial numbered equipment that evening, and Ali could not find one of the satellite communications radios, a small thing that cost tens of thousands of dollars. Could we please have everyone check their baggage to see if they had accidentally packed it?

We did that, but as it became apparent that no one had the SAT-COM, as it was called, Ali confessed that he may have left it in a box on a pallet in the courtyard at the garrison in Gonaives.

Mike looked panicked. This would be another accountability gig against him if it got out. The last one had been caused in the Dominican Republic, when Ali had lost some ten thousand dollar solar battery chargers, then tried some unsuccessful flimflam shit to cover it up. Ali had ended up footing the bill, for which he blamed the "fucked up army", instead of himself, and Mike had received an ass chewing and a questionable rating on his OER.

I took Ali off to the side and got in his face. He had lied when he gave us a "thumbs up" on all equipment before we had boarded helicopters in Gonaives. He had taken the lazy private way out, hoped for the best, and blown off the inventory. This was the second time in less than a year he had lost track of expensive equipment, and now his commander may be relieved because of his irresponsible bullshit. I was on a roll. Ali, as usual when he had lost the moral high ground, gave his whipped puppy in the gargantuan body act.

I told him to get on the horn with Gonaives, contact an enlisted person with their commo cell, have him check the container in question to confirm that the SATCOM was still secure, gain an agreement to load the radio covertly on the helicopter that was scheduled to visit from Gonaives the next day, and be there to meet the bird when it came.

I then dismissed him, fighting the suicidal urge to strangle him, went in and bummed a cigarette of one of the commo guys in the Ops Shop, and started smoking again for the first time in two years. I smoked and leaned on the balcony rail, as the daylight faded, staring down into the *Moon Over Parador* courtyard, with the goats and chickens and the mango tree, and I wondered if I would die in Haiti of a bleeding ulcer.

That night, when our last patrol was in from 354, I slipped off on foot to L'Escale, where Vincent and Freddy introduced me to a guy who looked like a bum, who was bent over a beer on the table, his feet bare, his pants ragged, his shirt threadbare, his head covered by another cheap, beat up ball cap. This was Ronnie. Ronnie mumbled, so you had to lean really close to him to understand him.

As I got to know him, he explained that he was there to check on his pig farm outside Ouanaminthe. It was his hobby. He owned a pharmaceutical company in PAP, had a PhD in chemistry, and could discuss French history and Nietzsche and American politics in the same breath.

So there we were, Vincent and Freddy and Ronnie and Stan, having a great time discussing politics, literature and philosophy.

Skye came by for a while, and engaged Freddy in a knowledgeable conversation on the relative merits of various reggae artists.

I had a genuinely good time. It was like being in school again. At one point I made a comment about people making asses of themselves because they denied their mortality. Ronnie leaned into me and gave me a faint smile. Haitians make asses of themselves, he told me, but mortality is our daily companion. I felt chastened and told him so. No matter, he said, you just went home for a bit.

When I left that night, past midnight, while young Haitians were still dressed in their almost elegant clothes, dancing and talking politics with great animation, Vincent told me to bring my maps and aerial photos of Fort Liberte to L'Escale the next day.

53: The Pascal Plan

Do you think you are pro-Lavalas¿
What does that mean¿
Do you think you favored Lavalas over other groups¿
What other groups¿
Groups other than Lavalas¿
I don't know of any other popular groups besides Lavalas¿
Do you think you are anti-FAd'H¿
Yes.
Why are you against the FAd'H¿
Have you talked to Haitians about what all they did¿ They're criminals.
But we were told to work with them.
I did. I worked with them every day.
Your team members said you showed unremitting hostility to them.
I was ordered to work with them, not like them.

Major O'Neill and his entourage flew in from Gonaives early on the 4th of October. A buck sergeant who worked with his communications people slipped Ali's wayward SATCOM to us in an aviator's kit bag. Ali became relaxed, almost giddy. He was off the hook.

A noisy crowd, *de rigueur,* had formed outside the front gate, by ten o'clock. Someone was on the Psyopers' loudspeaker, and they were getting a loud response from the crowd. On investigation, I found several well-dressed men standing on the balcony in the front of the caserne. One of them, a gentleman of about my age, 43, was giving a speech. The crowd was waving their hands excitedly and disapprovingly in the air and chanting him down.

Captain White was there, and explained unnecessarily to me that the speaker, who happened to be the mayor of Ouanaminthe, was very unpopular. The crowd, he said, was demanding his removal. Some were demanding things more severe, like the removal of certain body parts. I observed that the crowd was getting pretty rowdy, and Captain White agreed. He asked for the microphone.

White didn't even begin speaking, before the Haitians cheered wildly and started smiling again. Haitians are very demonstrative. When Captain White started speaking, he issued the same lines we had been dispensing from the get-go. Cedras was out. Aristide was coming on the 15th. Democracy could begin in Haiti again. Every single thing he said was greeted by riotous jubilation. He could have been appointed mayor. At that moment, he could have been appointed king.

Later at L'Escale, with my imagery in hand, Freddy, Vincent and a Spanish speaking native of Fort Liberte, Charles, who was also introduced as my contact with Lavalas, met me for lunch. They puzzled over the aerial photos and the maps. The perceptual shift to "seen from above" graphics was very difficult for all of them, and we spent a great deal of time trying to figure out what was where. Once I identified the arch, the French Fort, the FAd'H caserne, and a few other landmarks we had identified, some incorrectly it turned out, from the intelligence, they were able to work with the photos. The map, they explained, was dicked up.

Vincent recommended to me that I pick up a man named Pascal Blaise for detention, and any of his "gang." I asked him why this person with the famous backward name was so vital. Blaise, he told me, with Charles nodding assent as he received the translation from Freddy, was the head of a gang of thugs, *macoutes*, in Fort Liberte, who did most of the dirty work for the local FRAPH. He was widely feared, and without his detention, we would have a difficult time gaining confidence or cooperation from the locals.

Fort Liberte, they further explained, was the political nerve center of a wide area, and was heavily populated by *attaches*, *macoutes*, and FRAPH. With up to 10 percent of the citizens opposed to Aristide, this made Fort Liberte a *macoute* stronghold. Neal Calixte, the owner of the swanky hotel on the bay, was the former ambassador to France under Francois Duvalier, and Calixte was the financier for most *de facto* government activities of an unofficial nature there, particularly FRAPH. At least, Calixte's wife was. She was old French money.

The town itself had the appearance of having died in the last few years. They compared it to the setting in *One Hundred Years of Solitude*.

Get Blaise, they emphasized, and everything else will be easy. This was exactly the kind of information I wanted. I decided then and there, to push for an infil into Fort Liberte on the next day. I did not want the Haitian grapevine, the most remarkable non-technical communication system in the world, to alert our pigeon Blaise. I told them that I would need a guide. Vincent said that when I gave him a time and place, he would link a guide up with us, and that he himself would follow us into Fort Liberte to help facilitate our setup.

Before I left, I asked what the problem was that the public had with the mayor. Vincent and Freddy told the story of how hundreds of bags of rice had been sent to Ouanaminthe for distribution from food centers. With the enforcement of the FAd'H, the mayor had confiscated all of it, and under the FAd'H's protection, he had sold every grain of it at the local market. This was unlikely to ever be forgotten. What will happen with him, I wondered. I think he'll be leaving soon, now that you boys are here, Vincent told me.

That day, Vincent bought wheelbarrows, shovels and brooms, hired a dozen or so locals, and had the streets of Ouanaminthe cleaned. Vincent was riding our coattails, and the locals loved him.

That afternoon, I asked Mike if we could go in the following day. I gave him an intelligence dump and the reason for my rush. He quickly agreed, and we set about making coordinations for the operation.

We had to set up a meeting with the commander from Fort Liberte. We had to coordinate for support from 356 for the infil. We had to prepare the big Toyota flatbed for the trip, and load all our equipment on it. We had to request Close Air Support, not that we needed it, but we wanted AC130 (a specially modified C-130 airplane, a flying weapons platform, with computerized aiming systems) on station as a threatening gesture for the FAd'H. We had to ask for one of the Civil Affairs guys, so we chose Ken, a Sergeant First Class, who had spent time as an operator in tenth group. We had to top off with fuel at Thunderdome. And we had to request permission to make the move from the AOB in Gonaives. It was a busy afternoon and evening.

The activity drew reporters like flies. They smelled something. One of them who showed up was a big, fiftyish bearded fellow, named Tony Marcelli. He was the Reuters representative for this part of Haiti, and had lived in Cap Haitien for the last 22 years.

Everything went smoother than could be expected. The only glitch was the Close Air Support, but we'd decided that it was gravy anyway, not necessary to make the move. We warned the guys not to let on about the Blaise business. Many of the reporters had already been to Fort Liberte on their own, interviewing people, and hoping to catch us coming in. Our plan was to get in before daylight, before the crowds could gather, without helicopters, coordinate the FAd'H's virtual surrender, account for their weapons and personnel, find quarters, and locate Blaise's house before he got out of bed. We held out only dim hope that our guide would show up. The trick was for a team, Kyle, Gonzo, and Ali, to slip away from us and the reporters, so no one would see them snatching him out of his bed (still a gray area in the rules of engagement).

We were informed by the AOB that we would comply with the FAd'H commander's request from Ouanaminthe, that we take along a FAd'H interpreter to stay with us while we were in Fort Liberte. He would act as a liaison between us and the Fort Liberte garrison, which was subordinate to Ouanaminthe Battalion Headquarters. Colonel Simone was the Battalion Commander. The caserne commander of 18th Company, Military Police, at Fort Liberte, was one Captain Pierre Ulrick. The interpreter/liaison was named Lieutenant Percy.

Ulrick showed up before dusk for a meeting with Mike, Col. Simone, and me. He was a hugely fat man, around fifty, with large owlish glasses that gave him a cornered look, and a wide diastema. He started scraping and bowing and vowing cooperation even before we started to threaten him, which I did. His most panicked reaction was when I told him he would have to sit down with the Mayor, one Adele Mondestin, within a week, to work out how his garrison would be subordinated to the civil authority. He protested that she hated him, to which we responded, why. He called her a political radical. So we told him we wouldn't let her kill him. We also told him there was to be no preparation, no gassing, no batons, no crowd control measures, preceding our arrival.

Percy was linked up with us soon after. He was a tall, slender, bespectacled sort, looking a little like a bookish jock. He was quiet, slow to muddle through English, and extremely polite. I liked Percy, even though he was FAd'H. He didn't have that vicious edge to him. That was the first chink in my armor of generalities about the Haitian Armed Forces.

That evening, I told the reporters what we were going to do, and that they needed to be up by 3:00 AM, because we were rising at 2:30, and would leave by 3:30. We just hung around and shot the shit for a while, before everyone went to bed. The reporters who had been there told me that it was a "shithole", where no one did anything, the streets were hot, dusty and empty, and people peered suspiciously out of their window shutters.

Great, I thought.

My fatigues were getting nastier smelling by the day, even with the cursory washes I gave them. I was smoking again. I was dog-tired. I knew I wouldn't sleep that night, and I didn't.

54: The Longest Day

This was it. At 0300, I went to each team member's bunk and woke him up.

I was tired enough and stretched thin enough to obsess, and that is what I did. My obsession was Pascal Blaise. His capture and arrest would be a defining act, one that would send all the right messages to all the players in one fell swoop.

I was growing comfortable with acid smell of me, mixed with layer upon layer of insect repellent, applied through the night. I smoked until my tongue was bitter and cracking.

Mike was ready within five minutes. In the 3:00 AM darkness, the boys muddled around, brushing teeth, boiling coffee, pissing outside the vehicle arch, folding cots, stuffing their sleeping gear into their rucks, and jamming the rucks into the potential spaces of the top heavy Toyota flatbed, parked in the courtyard. I woke the reporters at 3:30. Tony Marcelli, the Reuters man, asked if I'd like a cup of brewed coffee from his Thermos. Gratefully, I freed my canteen cup from my LCE and accepted.

Captain Joseph, an English speaker from Colonel Simone's staff, was designated to guide us, but he had not shown up, and in my obsessive sleepless state that tardiness became a source of intense pressure.

I finished my coffee and started warming up for my Tasmanian devil role. I could feel it coming. Control, the ultimate burden and the ultimate necessity at this juncture. I started snapping like the Alpha hyena; Why isn't the truck strapped in yet, get everyone over here by quarter til, wherethefuck is that fuckin FAd'H captain, we're getting on the road by four or else, eat that cold goddammit and get moving—you can eat on the road.

356 was up, and I believe I took a moment to hint at browbeating their captain if they weren't ready on time. Are the radios checked? Well, where the hell is mine. Fuck me with a jackhammer, we've only been waitin' a thousand years to do this, this is it, this is our mission, are we gonna be late for it too. Oh, I was in fine form. Click. Click. Click.

At quarter to four, we sat the team down. We reviewed our actions, who goes where, who does what. The key thing was the sub-element designated to get Pascal Blaise. When I saw the reporters focused elsewhere, I would discretely signal the boys to move on Blaise. The problem we anticipated was using the locals. Ali could talk to them in French, but Tony spoke French and Creole. I could use Spanish, but Claudia spoke Spanish better than I did. I would have to be pretty cagey to elicit the location of the house, without the reporters figuring it out.

356's job was just to establish a loose perimeter around the front of the garrison to hold back crowds as they developed, and to guard our gear until we could find a place to unload it.

It was already hot, and my acrid damp fatigues were already being resoaked with sweat.

Captain Joseph did not show. So at ten after four, with me in a near rabid condition, we departed. I felt myself calm down, the minute we passed through the town arch on the road out of Ouanaminthe. We moved at a snail's pace over a dreadfully pitted road through as black a night as one can imagine with a clear sky. The sounds of the engines, the Toyota, the Hummer, the three reporters' 4x4s, cut a wake in the unmechanized silence of the Haitian night. The headlights played over huts, *raket* hedges, slipshod fences, roaming livestock, and an occasional timid and fearful eye peering out of a slumbering domicile.

We encountered a confusing fork in the road about thirty minutes out, and that's when Captain Joseph's jeep slid into the convoy out of nowhere. Joseph got out smiling and told us to follow him.

An hour out of Ouanaminthe, we entered an area almost devoid of structures, nothing but rolling grassy fields beyond the *raket* that lined the roadside. Suddenly we were in a town, and no sooner were we in the town, than we passed under the yellow concrete arch, announcing FORT LIBERTE. Under the name of the town was inscribed, LA DULCE DANS L'EFFORT. The sweetness is in the effort. I don't know why, but *Arbeit machen frei* jumped into my head.

The first hint of dawn was sneaking into the east as we pulled up in front of the garrison, and the soldiers began streaming out onto the porch of the caserne to get an anxious look at their new reality. The streets were otherwise empty.

356 deployed at both ends of the street. I sent everyone else inside. Each man had something to look at, construction of the garrison, weapons, sleeping quarters, latrine facilities. Mike was escorted by Percy and Joseph to talk again with Ulrick. Ali had all the soldiers turn in all their weapons to the arms room, a filthy, spider ridden room, heaped with old mildewed uniforms, forgotten documents, hundreds of weapons in various states of serviceability.

I slipped down the street to the corner, where people were singing at 5:00 AM. It was the big round pavilion we had seen on the satellite imagery that Vincent and Freddy had identified as a big Baptist Church. I motioned a somewhat surprised master of ceremonies to the door. The preacher said something to the two dozen or so worshippers, then came outside and offered his hand. He spoke English. I was in luck.

I asked him if he knew of a Pascal Blaise. He assented and asked what it was we wanted with that man. I said we needed to contact him. Did he know where Blaise lived? Down that way somewhere, he pointed, to the North. He was sure it was nearby. I thanked him, afraid I may have already tipped Blaise off. I was beginning to have supernatural expectations of the Haitian grapevine.

I rejoined our group at the garrison. The reporters were having a field day, shooting pictures of the disoriented Haitian soldiers, popping flashes at the stacks of accumulating weapons. They're attracted to the same stuff as adolescent boys. Guns, gore, cheap drama.

The mosquitoes were like a biblical plague. They started eating us with such ferocity that we were getting to the point where we could barely function. Our rucksacks with our repellent were still loaded aboard the truck. Claudia, the freelance reporter produced a tube of cream repellent, and offered to share. One by one, we polished the tube off like locusts.

Dawn was lancing further and further into the sky with brilliant yellow and salmon rays. A small crowd was beginning to amass on the street. It was not yet a demonstrative crowd, just curious. I approached them and asked who spoke Spanish. A very dark-skinned man stepped forward and began conversing in perfect Dominican Spanish. He told me he was a fisherman from Fort Saint Joseph, the neighborhood at the North of town, across the "causeway." His name was Dumas. He said he did a great deal of business in the Dominican Republic, and that he had lived several years in Santo Domingo with members of his family. I asked him if he would interpret. He agreed gladly.

The members of the crowd eyed us suspiciously. The reporters they glared at with open hostility. I briefly wondered what the problem was. I decided to give a short speech.

"I am the operations chief for the team of Special Forces soldiers you see here. My name is Stan," I began. "We ask that you not interfere with the operations of the American soldiers. There are so few of us. We are obligated to protect everyone in the city. That includes you and the Haitian military." This brought some grumbles. "Do not worry about any more abuse from these people. We will supervise their every activity, until the central government of Jean-Bertrand Aristide decides what to do with them." Aristide's name brought a little cheer. The crowd was beginning to swell as people entered from every corner. "We understand that you not only fear the soldiers, but that there are *macoutes*, FRAPH and *attaches*." Demonstrated understanding of this fact met with much nodding and murmuring. "They will not threaten or harm you any longer." The excitement grew in the gathering. "We are here to restore the rightful government. We are going to ask your help in this task. There will be only eight of us staying in Fort Liberte. We need you to act as our eyes and ears. We need your leaders to exercise restraint, and to prevent violence or revenge.

"You have not been allowed to demonstrate your happiness at the return of Father Aristide. That is now permitted. You may fill the streets with celebration if you like. The only thing we ask is that you do not attempt to enter the garrison or make contact with the soldiers. I am a soldier under orders to protect all people from any form of violence, and I ask your cooperation, so that I may stay firmly on the side of the people.

"Most importantly right now I need for you to keep your distance from the entrance to the caserne, so we can finish our business here and get established. Within the next few days, my captain and I will attempt to meet with all the leaders in Fort Liberte. Especially with the leaders of Lavalas, with whom we have had good relations in Gonaives and Ouanaminthe.

"Lavalas has exercised discipline in preventing retribution and counter-violence against collaborators with the *de facto* government. We desperately need the cooperation of the people of Fort Liberte in taking this first critical step toward democracy."

The speech met with strong, general approval, and the original climate of suspicion seemed to have evaporated. I then called my Spanish speaking fisherman friend over to the side. I explained that I needed his help locating some people, but that we would have to be discrete. He was very keen to help.

Did he know where Pascal Blaise lived? Yes, of course he did. Would he guide us there when I gave the signal? Yes, he would, but what did we want Blaise for? To arrest him, I said. He became so animated I had to tell him to calm down, lest the cat get out of the bag. Was there anyone else I wanted to arrest? I wanted Blaise's inner circle. I wanted the leaders and members of FRAPH. I wanted to question Neal Calixte. All this met with profound approval and an excitement he seemed barely able to contain. I told him to wait on the corner, until the big man who spoke French came to get him.

I pulled Ali, Gonzo and Rod out and pointed out the guide. I told them to mill around until the reporters seemed to be distracted, then grab him and go get Blaise. Then I told Mike that we were about to execute the move against Blaise. Mike asked if they had commo. I assured him that they did. Ali had the 126 on his LCE. Mike called for a commo check. Ali acknowledged.

Suddenly, the guys took off. They weren't waiting for the reporters to be out of the way.

Holy Shit! I told Mike. Look at that.

The three were walking purposefully down the middle of the street, with the guide in tow, and the reporters were dashing off behind them like sharks on a chum trail.

Mike and I were frantically calling on the 126, telling them abort, abort, abort, but no one acknowledged. Mike and I started skipping off behind them, preparing to stop the detention face to face.

We didn't catch them. Blaise's house was so close they arrived even before the reporters caught up. Behind us, the crowd was trailing. We caught up with the reporters, and rounded the corner to the left, to see Ali already pointing a weapon in the space between two houses, shouting orders in French.

Fuck it, I said. I dove into the middle of it. A man was face down on the ground, and Ali told me that Blaise was in the house. I told him and Gonzo to go through the back door, while the reporters were busy snapping pictures of the prone man, so they wouldn't see our guys make the entry.

Ali and Gonzo emerged in less than a minute, with Blaise, half dressed and sleepy-eyed. Is that Blaise, I asked the fisherman. He nodded. Show me the rest, then.

Mike asked what was going on. Ali explained that the man on the ground was Blaise's chauffeur, and pointed to Blaise. I explained that we were going ahead with a general roundup, now that the shit was on. Mike concurred, and gave me the go ahead.

I told the fisherman to show us the people we wanted. Crazily, he pointed out three people who were in the street by now, watching all the commotion around Blaise's house. They were dumbfounded as we pushed them to the side and flex cuffed them. The crowd now joined in. They understood what we were doing. More people were pointed out, some now as they slipped away from the crowd, seeing the danger of detention. Within two minutes we had rounded up ten detainees. The reporters were confused and excited, snapping pictures and rolling tape, and jockeying for position. Some were rapidly changing to faster film to accommodate the not quite light, predawn conditions. Miraculously, no one had witnessed the actual entry into Blaise's house through the back door. Not that it mattered. The reporters were less interested in rules of engagement and shades of gray therein, than in getting the best pics.

We ordered the crowd to stay back, and members of the crowd echoed the commands, eager to help their liberators. We decided we had enough. I told them to move the detainees back to the caserne.

In front of the caserne, a couple of FAd'H stepped out to talk to Blaise and the others, and I snapped at them to move back and shut up. One of the Creole translations of "shut up" is *shut up*, a holdover from the Marine occupation. All but one of the prisoners had assumed his place in single file, and were kneeling as instructed. I stormed over to him and told him to get down. He gave me a look between defiance and fright, so in English I barked "Get down, Goddamn it!," pushing down on his shoulder and foot-sweeping the back of his knee. He dropped down with finality, then lowered his head in surrender.

I looked up and saw Claudia, the freelance reporter who had declared her admiration for my humanity to her companion two days before, and she was crestfallen. The reality of force had replaced her admiration with disillusion. She came over to me, the chill in her attitude visible, keeping her distance from the smell I was exuding, and asked if we were applying any "rules of evidence or due process" to this roundup. Where would I present that evidence? I asked. In the local court? Maybe I should run the "evidence" over to the local Haitian forensics lab! I was ordered to detain anyone associated with FRAPH. The people who gave me that order would decide what to do with them. As far as I was concerned, Fort Liberte was under martial law. She scribbled officially and stalked away, secure in her comfortable, bipolar, petit-bourgeois morality.

356 was heavily occupied maintaining the standard crowd line around the front of the garrison. Fort Liberte was waking up, and they wanted to know what was going on.

The caserne was near condemnation. There was no way we would be able to live there. I sent Kyle and Ali to recon for a house. They came back in twenty or so minutes, telling us they had found a first class hotel, something none of us would have hoped for. It was the hotel owned by Calixte, the former ambassador to France under Papa Doc. Kyle was excited by the prospect. He was keen to move into comfortable quarters, and Calixte had offered to put us up for the nominal fee, provided we keep the unwashed mobs from ransacking him. Ali insisted that we provide security for him, too.

Ali was a sucker for anyone who spoke pretty French, himself despising the plosive cadences and simplified conjugation of Creole. Kyle's problem was different. Kyle epitomized many of the criticisms I had of Special Forces. He was ignorant of doctrine and pretended he was superior to it, a case of buying into the SF mystique. He was more concerned with how he looked than how he performed. He assumed because he understood the engineering part of his job that he was exempt from other "soldier" skills and tasks. He felt he was entitled to higher levels of comfort than conventionals and Rangers—that the austerity they endured was for the simple minded and not for "special" people like Green Berets. From my first days on the job, he had resented my opposition to that sense of entitlement, and my insistence on mastery of basic military doctrine as the foundation for conducting "special" operations. I hated the mystique. So our antagonism, while never loud and open, was early and consistent. He would take the refusal to use the Hotel Bayara as our quarters as some kind of personal affront.

I told them to send two FAd'H to the hotel to guard it, with instructions to merely prevent entrance with minimal force, and to bring Calixte to me.

Were we going to make a deal for the hotel, they asked, seeming very much in favor of the idea. I doubt it, I said. I'm going to arrest him. Both men looked taken aback, but both knew I was sleep deprived, single-minded and cross, so they went back to the hotel to detain Neal Calixte. Could we just take the hotel over, like appropriate it? they queried. Just bring me Calixte, I said.

When they came back with Calixte, he was stiff backed and indignant, demanding to see someone in charge, with an absolutely outraged French wife in tow. Both were in their early sixties, well kept, accustomed to command, her more than him. We told her that she was not under arrest, but she refused to leave his side, and we decided not to wrestle an obstinate sixty year-old woman. She stayed. We sat them both down in the courtyard of the prison with the rest of the detainees, where they immediately wanted to talk with Blaise. All were told not to utter a sound.

Ali and Calixte were engaged in an animated conversation, and I asked Ali to translate the gist of it to me. Calixte was a former ambassador, he said, and claimed to have diplomatic immunity. This claim caused some hesitation on Ali and Rod's part. Mike was there by then, and seemed curious but disinclined to intervene. As far as he was concerned, the operation was going grandly, and there was no reason to fuck with success. He was going to let me have my head. So I overruled the hesitancy of Rod and Ali. Fuck him, I said. Tell him he is the local chief financier for FRAPH, that we know it, and that he is going by helicopter to Port-au-Prince tomorrow. Ali translated.

The question of food came up. How do the prisoners eat? We decided to give each detainee an MRE and to allow them to eat it. We had to remove all the flex cuffs. Mrs Calixte did not have cuffs on, since she had not been detained. She was detaining herself.

Calixte never lost his *hauteur*.

They're still death squads. Were we ordered to work with them, too?

No, you weren't ordered to work with them. But it sounds like you harassed them.

I arrested them when I had permission.

You arrested a man with diplomatic immunity, too.

How can someone have diplomatic immunity in his own country when he's not an ambassador any more?

Didn't your own team warn you that you shouldn't arrest Nyll Calixte?

My team also wanted to move into his hotel. I ran the team.

At around 8:30 AM, Vincent, Ronnie and Freddy showed up. They cruised through the caserne and assessed what was going on. Vincent told us we had done marvelously and had detained exactly the right people. He asked if we needed anything. Yes, I told him. A house. We still needed to unload our truck full of supplies and establish communications with higher headquarters. And we may need a little help with the ever swelling, now dancing-and-singing mass of spectators outside the caserne. I told him we would communicate with the FAd'H strictly through Percy. As we stood there in the lobby of the caserne, we could hear Ali talking on the radio he had set up to talk back to Ouanaminthe, between translating for the rest of us. In English his every other word was fuck, fucker, motherfucker, and the female reporter from the *Los Angeles Times* stood there amusing herself by repeating the cascade of expletives to one of her companions. It created a weird male-female echo: fuckin'-fuckin', motherfucker-motherfucker, this fuckin' shit here-this fuckin' shit here.

In front of the caserne, Vincent gave a short speech to the crowd. They cheered him, then broke up and dissipated into a handful of people. 356, who was growing impatient, relaxed a bit, and collapsed their perimeter onto the caserne porch, in the shade, protected from the sun which was growing more viciously hot by the minute. Time was passing more quickly than we had imagined. Before we knew it, it was 10:00 AM. I began to stress about getting a house, and clearing 356 out of there.

During one respite in the frenetic activity, the reporters got to me, and asked why we had arrested all those people. I explained what I had learned before we left Ouanaminthe, and they all exchanged knowing glances. That was why everyone was so hostile, they concluded, when they had been in town the day before we arrived. The people they had interviewed, thinking they were speaking with the leaders of Fort Liberte, had been Neal Calixte and Pascal Blaise. They had hobnobbed around with these guys in public, slavishly writing down everything they had said, and reported to us how unfriendly Fort Liberte was—how people peeked suspiciously out their doors at them. They had been interviewing the two most feared and hated citizens in town. I decided then and there that I needed to get out of the military and become a journalist. I, at least, did some of my homework.

Then Vincent showed up with a young Frenchman, who could only be described as blonde headed, blue eyed and pretty. He seemed so pretty, in fact, that it was hard to imagine him here in Haiti, in Fort Liberte, the land that time forgot, where beauty was not manifest in prettiness, but in the stark business of survival. He was introduced as the administrator for Doctors Without Borders, and he had a handful of keys that, Vincent explained, were to our new house.

Doctors Without Borders had left Fort Liberte during the "troubles" with the Cedras regime, and this administrator had remained behind, in his own words, as a witness. We were here, now, and his job was done. He would be leaving, but the house had a current lease, and he wanted to let us use it.

We walked two blocks South from the caserne, and he led me up the porch of a block house, painted yellow, with a small carport on the left as you faced it. It was a concrete porch, half wraparound, with houses on both sides within four feet. We went in, and the place was covered in grime and cobwebs. The bathroom had a sink and a toilet, but no running water in either. The shower had a head, but the tile shower floor below it had been built with one small oversight . . . there was no drain. Obviously, the shower had never been used. The Frenchman told me that there was a 1500-gallon cistern atop the house that had to be pumped full from the underground cistern, which he showed me on the East side of the house. There was a comparatively large living room, on the wall of which was perched a huge black spider, and an adjacent hallway, leading to two small bedrooms on the West, two large bedrooms on the East, and one more large room in the North or back of the house. There was no kitchen. There was no electricity. But there was space, space enough to move in and store our gear. I thanked him enthusiastically.

Kyle, Ali and Gonzo started bitching as soon as we began to unload our cargo into the house. They wanted to move into the hotel, and they felt that I was fucking over the team, making then live in the "shithole." It was better than anything they had lived in since we got to Haiti, but Special Forces—as I pointed out—suffers frequently from brattishness.

I told them shortly and sharply that I didn't want to hear their whining, and that there was no way we were going to move into that hotel, giving the appearance that we (1) were going to simply appropriate anything we needed, and (2) that we were in bed with the bad guys. Our comfort was still secondary to the mission. This was a concept that was lost on them and would remain lost on them. It never really occurred to them that we shouldn't simply impose our will on Haitians, and that it was more important to win their loyalty than it was salve our own pride. These attitudes were serious indicators, and I slapped them like mosquitoes. Click.

The spider on the wall had left me with an uneasy feeling.

We posted two men on the garrison, then brought everyone to the house to quickly download all the equipment. The hot bull labor reminded us that we were frazzled, exhausted. When we were established, albeit by a mere figurative toehold, in the house, I let 356 go back to Ouanaminthe. It was noon.

Vincent, Ronnie and Freddy came by to say they would be returning as well. I thanked them all from the bottom of my heart for their help.

Mike, the reporter from the *Los Angeles Times*, and I went over to talk with Doctor Max Mondestin, the regional surgeon, head of the regional hospital in Fort Liberte, and cousin of Adele Mondestin, the mayor whom we had not yet met.

Max asked that we refrain in the future from bringing rifles into the hospital. We apologized and agreed to comply with his wishes. We assured him that we wished to be as non-disruptive as possible, and asked his assistance with explaining our mission in Fort Liberte, since he probably came in contact with more people than anyone in town, and because he had the reputation as a public benefactor who was apolitical. He said he would do what he could, but that he wished to remain outside politics and military operations. We assured him that we understood and promised to stay in touch. Our objective was to educate the local population about our mission and to provide stability as quickly as possible. We were not there to solve Haitian problems. We had neither the understanding nor the resources to do that. He seemed pleasantly surprised by our low-key approach we expressed our intention to follow. We talked casually for a while, and learned that he had done his residency at Boston College and that he had returned to Haiti to do what he could for his people.

A year later, when I would return, Max would be packing up to take a job with the World Bank. So much for first impressions.

The rest of the day proceeded with the cleanup of the FAd'H head-quarters, inventory and confiscation of weapons, and ordering the house. We hung a canvas field shower in the bathroom, but had to root through the liberated American Airlines tools to find a large punch, which we used to knock a hole in the tile for a drain. We started rotating members of the team into the shower, and people started dropping their fatigues into buckets of water to soak.

Percy stayed with Skye and Rod at the caserne, where he translated in his halting way, occasionally taking time to explain that we had to watch out for the people, because they were planning to storm the garrison and kill everyone.

By mid-afternoon, we started vehicular and dismounted patrols, partly to provide a security presence and partly to familiarize ourselves with the layout of the town. The reporters had described the place correctly as a town that died during the day. The streets remained nearly deserted, and I began to fear we had inherited a ghost town, that the morning's crowd was some kind of crazy hallucination brought on by fatigue and dehydration.

I made a decision to eliminate any patrols that night, except for emergency, and to drop down to a one-man radio watch, rotated hourly. I wanted everyone to get a solid good night's sleep. I detected an attitude on the part of the guys that the mission was over, and everything else was a denouement. I attributed this to exhaustion. I would find that this was one of the worst miscalculations I would make during this mission.

Just before dark, we got the call that the helicopter was inbound to pick up our detainees. Rod had recorded their names, date of birth, ostensible employment, and anything else he found out that seemed pertinent. Kyle, Rod and Gonzo went out to the landing zone (LZ) we had identified in a field about a mile out of town (chosen to prevent helicopters from blowing the roofs off of houses, a problem that had cost considerable sums to repair in Ouanaminthe).

When they returned, we were reviewing what had to be done and what needed to be done, and what the goals were for the immediate future in Fort Liberte. Emphasis was on maintaining stability with patrols and ready reaction to monitor demonstrations, making contact with community leaders, and a systematic expansion of our influence to outlying communities. October 15th was our milestone, because Mike and I agreed that once Aristide was back, the excitement level that anticipated his return should drop off.

While we were meeting, the drums started, somewhere off in the South end of town. It was dark, and the beat pierced through the darkness over the broken rooftops, with the syncopated chanting. Manifestacion. And it was coming our way, to the garrison. Everyone automatically started donning his web gear. We knew the drill well. We delegated. You and you, on the vehicle, follow the demonstration, watch for any troublemakers, and watch the buildings around the demonstration to make sure no one attacks the demonstrators. Be obvious about the protective mission. It'll keep the crowd friendly. You and you, to the front of the garrison. When the demonstration halts there, the vehicle guys will dismount and assist in holding the line. You and you, maintain security and radio watch here at the house. Get us a quick commo check all 'round. Make sure the aid bag is in the vehicle.

Within five minutes, we were posting. We followed the demonstration, and as we predicted, they ended up in front of the garrison. The FAd'H soldiers stood on the front porch of the caserne, blustering and terrified. There were only about ten of them left for the evening. We had sent the others home.

What we were treated to was interpretive dance. As the demonstrators settled into their static rhythm, several members of the crowd, children and adults, leapt into a clearing that the crowd made to provide a stage. There, to the beat of the drums and the cyclic crests of the converted African melodies, scenes of choreographed violence were dramatically rendered; police batoning the people, people being dragged away and beaten and shot, women being raped; the performance was amazing, not just for content, but for its production values. I regret that I did not have a video camera.

The production seemed to satisfy the crowd. They began moving off to the South, directly toward our new team house. Which is exactly where they went. We moved with them. We sat on the porch blocking their way in, so a wave of enthusiasm didn't crest them directly into the house. We had gained a lot of experience. We guarded covertly, sitting and smiling, not standing with weapons at the ready, providing a line, which we enforced by gently guiding people back into the crowd, especially youngsters, who were the point persons for crowd advances. We sat on the steps and the wide concrete porch rail, and the crowd sang to us in welcome. The ubiquitous tree branches, symbols of solidarity with Father Aristide, were used by young girls, to fan our sweaty faces, while hands young and old reached out to touch us, to seize our hands, by children to feel our white skin. We left the Hummer headlights on the crowd, to aid surveillance, and so we could see each other in the non-electrical Haitian night. We were surrounded by a sea of smiles, by the sour smell of a throng, by the ever more familiar music of the street, by tears of gratitude.

Behind my confident smile, I wondered, as I had since we arrived, if we weren't about to betray them all. Fraud, a voice kept saying. Judas. Tool.

Mike made his last journal entry for that day, when the host of people had gone to bed, and we were left with snoring and the steady hiss of the SATCOM radio and the gentle Caribbean breeze whistling over the roof. "GREAT DAY!"

55: Sweeping the Street

We rose before daylight. My own sticky, itching skin and vinegary smell had stirred me several times during the night. A one-hour guard and radio watch rotation had broken each team member's sleep once during the night as well.

The quiet of the windless, pre-dawn streets was near total. The background silence underlined the scuff of early feet on distant street corners, and the Baptist minister's sermon at the pavilion two blocks away. Roosters had turns crying out at one another.

We scuffled around by yellow kerosene light. We bolted instant coffee and portions of cold MRE's, then headed over to the garrison, leaving Kyle and Gonzo to start assessing the house for priorities of improvement.

The FAd'H was confused. Most were still waking. They were lost, clueless about how to react to us. Mostly they stood still and stared like deer fixed in the beam of headlights. Nothing in their experience had prepared them for how they found themselves before us, any more than anything in our experience had prepared us for it. No one was fighting. No one had gone into hiding. None of them were yet in prison. None of them were any longer in charge. And none of them were dead.

That counted for something. Our every encounter with the FAd'H now confronted us with mortally frightened men. Their capricious use of near absolute power in the past—and the sudden reversal of fortune—left the newly defanged soldiers with the baldest kind of apprehension about our own potential capriciousness. Our discipline and circumspection in the handling of prisoners, our lack of brutality, was the twig in the sea of their fear that they all clutched. They adopted a non-demeanor, like rabbits in the open holding perfectly still to avoid being noticed by a hawk.

So I behaved harshly and erratically before them, a bit of theater to further ensure no one tried to take advantage. We knew the rules of engagement. It was not to our advantage for them to know them. Through trial and error, the potential resistance to our team [Note: I do not say American forces, because many forces had by then already demonstrated their willingness to crawl into bed with the FAd'H, and to protect only the interests of the elite.] would find our limitations.

I had already begun to form the idea that we needed to be alert for an opportunity to blur the lines wherever possible, to muddle any conceptions about "fair play," about due process. Every faction had to believe, at least initially, that we were a powder keg not to be toyed with.

At the headquarters, we began where we left off, inventorying, cleaning, counting heads and trying to elicit an accurate personnel status (this was to become a daily battle). The street in front of the garrison was paved in the litter of the previous night's demonstration, mostly the trampled leafy branches waved above the demonstrators' heads as a symbol of support for Aristide.

I located a couple of brooms. Rod and I began sweeping the street. Rod seemed to take comfort in sweeping, in the quiet street. He needed the breather from all the tension and uncertainty, which challenged his seemingly congenital watchfulness and insecurity. Sweeping was a natural activity in a unit like Special Forces, where there are no privates, and everyone from commander down participates in the most banal necessities. It was not normal in the eyes of the FAd'H.

The sun was almost visible, and in the yellow light, the FAd'H soldiers were stepping out on the porch of the caserne to stare. My age and my imperious pose had given the soldiers the impression that I was the leader. They were astounded that I was sweeping a street.

In a few moments, two, then three FAd'H soldiers appeared alongside us with brooms. Now five of us were sweeping the street.

Civilians were stopping on their way to the market, stepping out of their houses with sleep in their eyes.

One, then two, then four women emerged with brooms from the nearby habitations, and there was a veritable squad of us sweeping the street. Mike glanced out, saw what was happening, and scrounged a broom.

Small clots of people gathered at each end of the street and watched. When we were finished, we said mesi to the women who had participated, mesi to the soldiers, and we quietly went back into the caserne.

Mike and I were on the same wavelength. We went inside and agreed almost simultaneously that we had stumbled upon a model for future actions. Cooperation and community. We were to explain this model to the other team members again and again, and too late we were to realize that they may have failed to understand or—more likely—failed to agree to the notion of community with Haitians.

At 9:00 AM., Mike, Ali and I went to the *Biblioteque*, where the city offices were located, to seek the mayor, Adele Mondestin. We were guided past a host of functionaries, each offering his or her hand with a name and a welcome. At long last, we were led into the office of a short, heavyset, fiftyish woman of severe appearance, short hair straightened and plastered straight back, tight on her head and wearing large-lensed glasses that made her protruding eyes look very owlish indeed (I would later learn that Adele was plagued nearly to incapacitation at times with an eye disorder, probably glaucoma, which causes proptosis, or bulging eyes).

She was very stiff and formal. My first impression was that she was frightened of us and trying very bravely to conceal it. Nevertheless, she invited us to walk through town on a kind of orientation.

Adele, Ali, and I visited the hospital again, the city square, the cathedral, several water pumps, schools, government offices. As we walked I took every opportunity to impress on her that we were there to support the return of Aristide, and to facilitate a transition into management by the legitimate government as soon as possible. We had received valuable support and assistance from Lavalas thusfar, and we wanted to continue working with them. We also pointed out that Captain Pierre Ulrick, the commander of the garrison, was no longer in charge, and that in fact, until the central government found itself in a position to function, that she as the mayor was the highest authority in Fort Liberte.

She told us that many weapons were still hidden by the old guard, a claim that we would hear from fearful Haitians for the rest of our stay, and that she was a target of the old guard. She had been threatened and arrested by the FAd'H in the past, and since the coup she had lost all authority.

Ali translated a promise that we would publicly announce that all legitimate officials, and she personally, were under our protection, and that any action taken against those under our protection would be met with the most draconian measures, to include summary arrests of all *attaches*, FRAPH members and FAd'H officers, and house searches of anyone remotely associated with the old guard. With this, Adele visibly relaxed.

My thoughts turned to how we would arrest *attaches*, when we obviously didn't know who they were, so I frankly asked Adele if she would assist us in identifying them in case they became the target of a future operation. Maybe, she said. A mental note to have Rod set up a file.

We then discussed setting up a meeting with all elected officials included in Ft. Liberte Commune, religious leaders, community representatives, and officers of the FAd'H. She assured us that such a meeting was possible, and offered the largest room in the *Biblioteque* as a conference room. We set the meeting for ten o'clock in the morning.

When we walked Adele back to her office, a gentleman of about fifty years greeted Adele warmly, and Adele introduced him as Bernard Fanfan, the mayor of a remote community named Perches. M'sieur Fanfan was about my height, 68 inches, well fed but not corpulent, and dressed in inexpensive work slacks with a cotton short sleeved shirt. He was a few days past his last shave, as are most Haitians, grizzled with rheumy looking eyes and one of his front teeth missing.

He was deferential to a fault on introduction, but once we asked his business in town, he became instantly emotional. He launched into a tirade about a sergeant with the FAd'H, the *attaches* in his community, and a stolen automobile, with such suddenness and detail that he completely lost Ali, and as Ali attempted to translate, the confusion became generalized. Only Adele seemed to know what he was talking about.

We asked him to calm down and go slowly, allowing Ali to elicit a bit at a time, and allowing me to clarify the situation with questions as we went along. This routine was becoming normal in Haiti, as well. All pleas we encountered there were emotional and presented as narratives that assumed much. Factor in our near complete ignorance of Haitian norms and values, and every conversation became a (sometimes tedious) lesson in local anthropology.

The story as we finally sorted it out centered around a soldier, sergeant Brunot Innocent, aka A Te Plat (meaning "flat on the ground," a command Brunot was widely known for). Brunot was from Grand Bassin, the town next to Perches, and spent a good deal of time in Perches. He was alleged to be in cahoots with Captain Ulrick—also a native of Grand Bassin—in a variety of extortion and bribery schemes. Brunot was widely feared in the area (Adele nodded a stern confirmation of this), being a violent, often drunk, and unpredictable bully.

Brunot had somehow talked Bernard Fanfan into loaning him the official automobile of the town of Perches. That automobile was for M'sieur Fanfan to conduct official government business. It was community property. Brunot had taken the car to Port-au-Prince and returned car-less. Bernard said Brunot was spending a great deal of money—ill gotten by Bernard Fanfan's account.

We were mildly interested in his story, but wanted to defer action. We had higher priorities for the time being.

We released Ali to go back to the house and help out with the renovation. Mike and I headed back to see what was happening at the garrison. When we arrived, Colonel Boyatt, the 3rd Special Forces Group commander, was there. He had flown in on a chopper we'd heard landing outside of town while at the *Biblioteque*. Rod and Kyle had gone out to the LZ (about a mile out of town) to carry him in.

He asked a few questions. But mostly he congratulated us and himself for a mission that "so completely utilized our capabilities as Special Forces soldiers." I took this as a good sign. At that point, I, too, was convinced—in spite of all misgivings and self-doubt—that this was the ultimate mission, if for no other reason than the learning curve was so steep. He was happy that we were using trusted agents from the adjacent community and encouraged more of the same. He was very pleased at our rough and ready entrance with all the arrests. He was still quite emotional about one of his soldiers being shot by FRAPH people. We briefed him on our proposed meeting, our plans for the FAd'H, our intelligence collection concept, and our ideas on community participation in labor intensive projects as a means of jump starting initiative on Haitian solutions to Haitian problems. We told him the story of the street sweeping. Colonel Boyatt seemed appreciative of our insight, our initiative, and our aggressive enthusiasm. And we basked for a moment in the approval.

Not long after the Group Commander left, a Toyota Land Cruiser drove into town with two United Nations Officers. One was from Ireland, named Jerry O'Donahue, and the other was from Djibouti, named Harun. Both were very friendly. Both looked over our work in progress with a great deal of approval. They asked about the Hotel, and we told them that the owner was under arrest.

That evening we were informed by radio, that M'sieur Calixte was, in fact, no longer under arrest, having been set free in Port-au-Prince, on a Presidential Order from the United States. We were further told to leave Calixte alone. I accepted it with minimal complaint, but my uneasiness about the objectives of our mission suddenly ratcheted up a notch.

Kyle complained that we should have left him alone in the first place so we could have used his hotel to live in. Mike looked up at me, and I at him. We had already discussed Kyle's frequent regressions into petulant, spoiled adolescence. Kyle was seriously starting to get on my nerves, and I made a mental note to take some time out real soon to yank a knot in his tail and put a stop to his shit. Mike could read my mind. If he gets away with it, it will become contagious.

We had made a great deal of progress on the house that day. Water was still a problem. The pump that filled the roof cistern from the ground cistern was tiny. It had a ten inch handle that worked the operator half to death to push minimal water up through the half inch pipe. Gonzo had some ideas for building a more efficient pumping system, but in the meantime, we planned to make water runs every day to a very clean, functional pump we'd located out of town by an old windmill.

At dusk that evening, a wild crowd approached the house. Most of us went out to meet it, and when we got there, a circle of determined young men had a man with his hands tied in the center of the melee, and the young men were pushing angry crowd members away from the restrained man. The crowd's mood was ugly, rabidly so, leaving us very little doubt that the ring of protectors was saving the captured man's life.

We tried several times to make sense of what was going on, but the crowd was pressing more and more tightly against the circle of protectors, wherein Ali, Mike and I were now contained. The pushing and gouging and screaming had closed in on us to the point we could not function, and the situation was becoming alarming.

I unholstered my pistol and let two rounds go into the air. The crowd scattered back and dispersed. Many of them dropped to their hands and knees. I followed the shots with a loud, insane sounding string of English obscenity to reinforce my dangerousness, then asked Ali to figure out what in the holy hell was going on.

Mike had had his back turned to me when I fired the warning shots, and it startled him.

"Fuckin' lemme know when you're gonna do that!" he barked.

"Sorry."

Ali determined that the crowd was calling this man, named Rene Mozart, the president of FRAPH. The men protecting him identified themselves as Lavalas, and said they had seized him from the crowd to protect him because we had asked their cooperation in the prevention of violence. They added, without necessity, that they were not sure they could protect him indefinitely, and asked us to lock him up. This seemed like a very reasonable course of action, and we relieved them of their burden, told the crowds to go home, and took the silent M'sieur Mozart to the garrison with the intention of getting to the bottom of things without a lynching. As we escorted Mozart away, the formerly angry mob gave out whoops of approval for his arrest.

On the way, Ali spoke with the man. Rene Mozart stated candidly and proudly that he was, in fact, the president of the Northeastern Department FRAPH.

At the garrison, we told the ever more confused soldiers that if he escaped, all of them would be summarily arrested in his lieu. Ali and I arranged a small, now dark room, with an old chair, a small, plain table, and a kerosene lantern, to look as much as possible like the interrogation room from an old Peter Lorre film.

Mozart was led in, where Ali, thick and huge, waited in the yellow lamplight. I stood in a dim corner of the tiny room, with my patrol cap forward, a silent eyeless menace in the dim corner. Ali then put on one of his most entertaining performances as the evil French policeman, switching back and forth between a sneering, oily sarcasm and a raging, impatient beast. I occasionally repositioned myself in the room, never speaking or uncrossing my arms. One time I glanced out the black square of the glassless window to the courtyard, and saw the top half of Mike's head. He was standing in the dark outside, suppressing his laughter.

Though obviously uneasy and off balance, Mozart was impressive. Of all the members of the old guard we ever dealt with, he was the coolest and the least intimidated. He would fall silent at Ali's shouted command, then resume quietly, controlling the tiniest tremors in his hands, his explanation that FRAPH was merely a political organization, pro-American at that, committed to progress for his beloved nation. Yes, he had a weapon in his home. That was not illegal. No, he had never participated in, nor ordered violence against anyone. Yes, he supported the coup. Aristide was a communist, a man who would incite the masses to anarchy, a burner of the American flag. Later, of course, we were to discover that indeed the FRAPH was a creature of the Central Intelligence Agency.

After we put Rene Mozart to bed in his cell with an MRE to breakfast on, I told Mike that I believed Mozart was a dangerous man, not physically dangerous, but dangerous for his composure and his guile. In Mozart, I felt we had just encountered our most calculating and potentially menacing foe.

We requested a helicopter to come get Mozart. Our headquarters said the chopper would arrive tomorrow.

Mozart would be released three weeks later, and I regret to this day not having given him secretly over to the masses. We were hamstrung, but they were not. They had earned his ass many times over. That would've been my due process.

56:The Meeting

Percy had been relegated to the front room, and instructed not to come back to the Operations/Communications Center we had established in the back room. His body in the house made us nine.

We had one toilet, and the mornings—as we were discovering—were an exercise in patience, visceral discipline, acceptance of the idiosyncracies and the smells of every other soul in the house. The toilet was only flushed after it was completely full of shit—never just to rid ourselves of urine—because water was hauled from afar and that labor dramatically increased its value. We flushed with a bucket at first. The bucket proved not to have adequate capacity, so we later learned to open the large mouth on a five gallon water can and pour vigorously to achieve the necessary hydro-momentum for a good flush. We learned that Ali liked to take long bucket baths, and Gonzo liked to shave for a long time to get the perfect result, and Rod fussed with his hair.

We rushed through on the 7th of October, prioritizing the bathroom for people who would have to transport Rene Mozart to the inbound helicopter for temporary incarceration in what was reported to be a now brimming facility in PAP.

Mike and I were very excited about the meeting we had arranged.

It was to go at ten that morning. We had gotten the word out for civic, religious, labor, police and student leaders to attend. I was constructing a list of points we would have to make. I recently found that old list laying around. It read:

MTG c COMMUNITY LEADERS 7 OCT 94 FT LIBERTE

\# POLICE--LEGAL PROCESS: NEED LAWYER

\# NO HARASSMENT OF IND POLICE--WE DON'T ALLOW THEM TO DO IT. CIVILIANS DON'T DO IT

\# SO FAR, SO GOOD. . . . . . LAVALAS DEMONSTRATIONS HAVE BEEN DISCIPLINED, CREATIVE, ENTERTAINING

\# INFORM OF 7,000 TO 3,000 DOWNSIZING (of security forces), DON'T KNOW ABOUT TRANSITION--PATIENCE/ FLEXIBILITY

\# Tx (medical shorthand for treatment) OF ALL PAX (military shorthand for people) WILL BE EQUITABLE

\# NO MOB ARRESTS

\# HAVE PUBLIC PRESENT CONCERNS/APPEALS THRU CIVIL REPRESENTATIVES, THEN REPS TALK TO US. CHECKS AND BALANCES.

\# PROVISIONAL REHABILITATION OF CIVIL AUTHORITY

\# CIVIL-MILITARY "LITTLE PROJECTS" THINK SMALL-ACHIEV ABLE. COHESION. RECOMMENDATIONS?

\# WEEKLY MEETING TO GAUGE PROGRESS/EXCHANGE INFORMATION

\# OUTLYING COMMUNITIES--SPREAD THE WORD

\# SEEK CREATIVE SOLUTIONS

\# EDUCATION

\# INTEL COLLLECTION

\# SOME PEOPLE DON'T WANT US HERE. WE ARE SOLDIERS. WE ARE HERE. THIS DET WANTS TO PARTICIPATE IN PROGRESS. PLEASE COMMUNICATE FRANKLY AND OPENLY.

\# ALL GUNS ARE HEREBY ILLEGAL. TURN THEM IN OR FACE ARREST. MILITARY AND POLICE INCLUDED. NO PRIVATE FIREARMS.

When Mike, Percy and I walked in to the *Biblioteque*, at ten of ten, we were subjected to a whirlwind of introductions. I had the opportunity to practice my French salutations around thirty times in a row. I lost track of the others. I would listen for the surname, repeat that surname with the appropriate title, claim to be enchanted by each of them, and move on to the next. We were being received like foreign kings and it was a little embarrassing.

Captain Ulrick stood outside the door, subjected to a hostile silence by the majority, with a few well-dressed exceptions.

We took the lead in manual labor, arranging the chairs for a meeting, and everyone quickly threw in. In moments we were arranged more or less in a circular pattern at Mike's and my insistence. Adele and the others wanted to stage us in front of a crowd, like preachers before a flock. We had very good reasons for dispensing with the idea of leadership.

The principle reason for the meeting, in the minds of Mike and me, was to explain up front what our limitations were. Our credibility was linked to the realism of Haitian expectations. We had decided to assertively deny leadership in any realm but security.

The meeting began with Adele introducing us. We in turn asked each participant to introduce him or herself. The introductions took a good fifteen minutes, and already the packed room began to swelter. Sweat made rivulets down the face of almost everyone, and the tart aroma of canned humans gave us all a determined intimacy.

Attending were teachers, FAd'H officers, students, farmers, mechanics, school superintendents, priests, community workers, cobblers, city inspectors, artisans, bookkeepers, housewives, accountants, voudon priest(ess)s, and two "athletes" from Pascal Blaise's soccer team. Also attending were the mayors, acting mayors, or consensus representatives from every community in the Fort Liberte Commune.

Many questions came up for discussion, and many of them were the questions that would recur throughout the mission.

The first was why hadn't we arrested all the *attaches*, all the *macoutes*, all the FRAPHists, and specified members of the FAd'H? We had just received message traffic the night prior that directed us to start applying the most stringent "rules of evidence" to detain anyone. Claudia the freelance journalist, it seemed, was now directing our policy. We were further told that we must acquire the evidence on those in custody in order to retain them there. As it turned out, Emmanuel Constant, chief of the FRAPH, realized that his membership was being caught in a shit storm, since the shooting of the SF soldier, and our subsequent orders to round all of them up. A presidential order to release Calixte certainly factored into the thinking of American commanders. I explained, frankly, that I'd like nothing better than to round them all up and pack the jails with them, but that I had rules under which I operated, that the courts were in no way prepared to adjudicate matters of the past, and that it would be imprudent to allow "mobs" to level accusations as a way of conducting our daily business. I requested their help in collecting and documenting evidence, and explained that the reinstitution of a viable court should be a very high priority. I also explained that we were merely eight people.

They still have guns, they pleaded. After the stiff, rather formal introductions, we would find, a typical community meeting would quickly degenerate into persuasion by decibels. We found ourselves repeatedly depending on the more authoritative members of delegations and groups to quiet the raucous and reestablish order.

We knew that guns were hidden. We had found dozens of firearms ferreted away by FAd'H members. On the other hand, we had searched several alleged weapons caches, to absolutely no avail. I, again, told them this in the most straightforward way I could. I further stated that any firearm violation would result in the most severe measures imaginable, to include house to house searches of every known *de facto* government sympathizer. I told them that anyone except American forces, or FAd'H directly under their supervision, who was seen with a firearm was subject to be shot. This seemed a very satisfactory response, and even garnered a flurry of applause. I asked their help, but warned them that we could not respond to endless false alarms, and that if we suspected we were being used to settle old scores, we would be very upset. There was nodding all around.

The feedback at every session, under every circumstance, from Haitians, became critically important for gaining and maintaining rapport. Haitians are, by and large, very emotional and ingenuously expressive. The feedback of their faces and their body language, I found rather quickly, was the key to effective communication.

Adele Mondestin had sternly followed the general line of thought, and waited for a millisecond of quiet to interject. As she began talking, the repressed rage she felt about whatever it was she was saying (I had not received the translation yet) smoldered. A breeze slipping into the steamy room might cause her eyes to burst into flame. Her deep voice took the drum-like cadences of Creole and cracked them like a whip. As she spoke, the steel control she exercised over her speech was belied by the tremors in her nervously fluttering hands. At pauses in her narrative, she would press her lips tightly together, and tap a series of tiny nods with her head. The great bulging eyes fell on the crowd, on me, and on Pierre Ulrick, in turn. Each time her eyes met with Ulrick, they would narrow, and Ulrick would shift in his seat.

The translation started to come through. Percy was visibly uncomfortable with what she was saying. He was equally uncomfortable with English, and consequently the translation was slow, forcing us to beg frequent pauses.

She gave a rather patchwork account of the past three years, telling us how she was arrested at Ulricks's direction, threatened with a necklacing (being killed by a burning tire placed around one's neck) by Pascal Blaise, how Luis Cassinir, the only humane garrison commander they'd ever had, was run out of town by his own mutinous troops, how people were beaten by batons without provocation, and how trash was thrown into the street at night to discredit her politically.

With every reference to Ulrick, the bulk of the assembly would nod and grunt their assent. With the mention of batons, the room exploded into a hundred baton stories at once, with people pointing to where they had been struck and jabbing their fingers in the direction of Ulrick and the garrison.

I interrupted at this point. I told Percy to translate accurately and slowly.

"Yesterday, we cleaned the garrison."

Percy translated.

"It was a pigsty."

Translated.

"We hauled out ten truckloads of trash."

Translated.

"Every baton in the garrison. . ."

Translated.

". . . was carried away in that truck."

Wild cheering followed by applause.

The baton thing worked again. I was learning to be a politician. The cheering spread to the outside. Hundreds of onlookers were peering through the holes in the masonry from outside, and thereby cutting off any semblance of ventilation, and we soon had a "Viv Aristide!" chant going up. Ulrick was the only person in the room who appeared to be sweating more than me.

Things settled after a fashion, and others spoke. We heard the plaintive requests for economic assistance, for electricity, for irrigation, for education, and we responded the same way each time. We sympathized with them, but we were only eight soldiers, here to ensure security, and we had neither the mandate nor the resources to work in those other areas. Moreover, I repeatedly told them, American solutions would not solve Haitian problems. The solutions had to come from Haitians. I said it there, and a hundred times more before I was sent away. Organize, Organize, Organize. I was figuring some things out about our own Task Force and where it was headed, and my subtext was: "Get ready, we are going to hang you out to dry."

The other high point of the meeting, for me, was the revelation from Adele and confirmed by others that there was a list of all the *attaches*. We did not have that list, we responded, or we could at least ensure that those people received special attention in the event of trouble. He has it, Adele declared, pointing at Ulrick. Ulrick simply stared straight ahead, while laughter erupted, and heads nodded, uttering *"Oui. Oui."* Ulrick cast his eyes about, apparently looking for help from some quarter.

I leaned over to Percy and told him to pass on to Ulrick: We get the list by tomorrow, in duplicate, or we promote one of the lieutenants to the position of garrison commander. Neither Percy nor Ulrick knew, of course, that we had no such authority.

Mike indicated that it was time to close the meeting. My fatigue shirt was so soaked that sweat was dripping from the hem onto the floor. I announced with relief that we needed to get back to our responsibilities.

We closed with a series of formal thank-you's around the room. We would host a weekly meeting such as this one, every Friday at 10:00 AM, with political and community leaders as a way of maintaining communication and dispelling rumors. As a postscript, we thanked Lavalas again for their restraint, their willingness to pursue peace, their patience with the slow business of seeking justice, and their friendship.

Our departure was met with yet another ovation, and with a five-minute queue of handshakes. We stepped out into the open midday air. The southbound breeze off the sea hit us. It felt so good I got goosebumps up my legs, and I lit a cigarette.

Mike and I walked down the street, elated, congratulating ourselves on making history . . . that is, bringing the opposing sides together and having a discussion without violence. We needed this bit of self-delusion for our morale, beset by a thousand misgivings.

57 : DEATH DRIVES A TOYOTA

We were working around the house, arranging the Operations Center, and refining the field shower, when a Land Cruiser arrived with a portly black gentleman and three white women. On the side of the vehicle was written *"Medicines sans Frontiers,"* Doctors Without Borders. We exchanged introductions with the Ugandan-born Belgian doctor and the American nurses. The doctor spoke French well, but not English, so Ali was drafted to accompany Mike and the doctor to the doctor's appointed residence three blocks away near Max Mondestin's house.

Shortly after their arrival at the doctor's residence, in the course of a conversation Ali was translating between Mike and the doctor, the 38-year-old doctor appeared to start choking. He quickly fell to the floor and began to convulse. Ali was sent running to the hospital two blocks away to fetch Dr. Mondestin, while Mike administered CPR to the man, who had quit breathing and had no pulse. Resuscitation efforts continued until after the ambulance arrived at the hospital, where Max terminated the efforts and declared the Belgian doctor dead.

Meanwhile, hospital officials had sent a vehicle to the Team House to tell us what happened. The whole story was excited and garbled. We couldn't make heads nor tails of it. I understood hospital and dead,

285

so I sent Gonzo with an aid bag to see what the hell was going on.

By and by, I arrived myself, where I found everyone circled around the corpse in one of the hospital rooms, Max, Mike, Ali and Gonzo, along with two Haitian nurses. Outside in one of the multiple porticoes, sat the three American nurses, wet-eyed and stunned. I introduced myself and offered condolences. They barely heard.

We offered to see if an American helicopter might be used to transport the body back to Port-au-Prince, since the long, hot ride aboard a tiny Land Cruiser seemed not only a sanitation hazard, but a terrible ordeal to put the nurses through.

While walking back to the house—Ali, Mike, and me—Ali launched into a tirade about setting up communications between us and the hospital, and about getting more radios to keep ourselves in constant contact. Mike nodded and said he's see what we could do. Ali started shouting at Mike that he would do it, and that was all the fuck there was to it, et cetera. Mike tried to calm him, which only seemed to make Ali more belligerent. The hair began to stand up on the back of my neck.

"That's a captain you're talking to, Ali," I warned him.

Ali persisted in bellowing and cursing.

"Ali!" I shouted. "Be at fucking ease. . . Now! Now! You are dangerously close, young man, to being given a ticket back to North Carolina."

We all walked back in silence.

Shortly after our return, I was sitting on the porch smoking. Ali came out with a whipped puppy expression. It was a weird contrast with his hulking size.

"I'm sorry," he said. "I guess it just got to me. I never saw anyone just die before." With that, he abruptly began crying, almost uncontrollably. I instinctively put my arm around his shoulders, at least as far as it would reach, and said something intelligent, like hey hey hey hey hey, all the while feeling like a heel for not figuring it out. All the killer talk by the troops sometimes obscures the fact that most of the guys are, at bottom, fragile, middle class, insecure men, who just happen to be physically gifted.

58: Rangers, Recons, and the Man at the River

The 7th was a crowded day. It was early afternoon, after the evacuation of the FRAPH leader, after meeting with the FAd'H, after the meeting at the *Biblioteque*, after the doctor dropped dead, when we received word. The Rangers were coming. The bridge at Trou du Nord had to be assessed for an impending 10th Mountain convoy. Kyle and Skye had to drive out to Grand Bassin and Terrier Rouge, and a helicopter had to be coordinated to extract the cadaver that lay in storage at the hospital. Adele promised to prevent any demonstrations for a couple of days to give us the breathing space we needed, and she was good as her word on that one. . . mesi.

The Rangers arrived on a Chinook helicopter. The crew blew us off on our request not to land in town (because of the roof destruction problem). They landed in a big soccer field on the South end of town, thankfully not blowing away any roofs. They did, however, create the inevitable wild crowd scene. Haitians, it seemed at this point, would never tire of the spectacle of helicopters, especially as they represented such extraordinary power in the service of their perceived liberation.

The officer in charge of the Rangers was Lieutenant Colonel Curley, the Regimental Operations Officer for the whole Ranger Regiment, and a former associate. LTC Curley was always friendly and supportive of me when I worked at the Regiment, and a gregarious person by nature. I had treated him twice, medically, once for an ingrown toenail, and once for severe dehydration on a road march. He saw me on the LZ, and ran forward to blow through my salute and give me a bear hug.

Over the roar of the Chinook engines and blade whack, I asked him to have the local security refrain from pointing weapons toward the people, hundreds of whom had created a circle around the ship. The threat was nearly non-existent, I explained, and he shouted instructions into the ear of a man I didn't know. The man trotted back to the perimeter, and within moments, all weapons were trained on the dirt in front of their owners.

LTC Curley and a contingent of four other people were then led through the teeming masses to the hummer. We jammed them aboard. I called for a Spanish speaker from the crowd. When one volunteered, I asked him to pass the word to the crowd to maintain a prudent distance from the chopper for safety.

As we crawled off through the rocky, pitted streets of Ft. Liberte, LTC Curley and his entourage, all outfitted to the eyes in the full battle uniform, body armor, helmets and all, seemed to be enjoying themselves. They appeared to fancy the mixture of strangeness, anarchy, and joy—an exotic scene out of a film in which they were the conquering heroes.

When we arrived at the team house, all were led into the operations center, provided with anything we could find to sit them on, relieved of their helmets and body armor, and provided with a jug each of bottled water. Mike took over and began what would become an expanding, standard briefing, explaining our activities to date, the situation as we saw it at the moment, and our plans for the immediate future. . . accentuating the positive, of course.

LTC Curley positively glowed, calling us great Americans, and congratulating us on what he perceived to be a superlative job.

A major eventually chimed in, getting down to the business of coordinating signals and Landing Zones for the eventuality of our evacuation under duress—the purpose of the visit. The Rangers had been tasked with emergency evacuation planning for each site.

When we prepared to carry our guests back to their helicopter,

LTC Curley took Mike aside to stroke him again on how well we seemed to be doing. After the departure, Mike and I were positively pumped up with flattery, and we passed on to the team that they had consistently left a good impression throughout the course of the mission to date, both on counterparts and Haitians.

Ali had disappeared after we picked up the Rangers. I was pissed. I knew exactly what was going on. Ali had been chatting up a Haitian girl before the choppers came, and he had gone back into her neighborhood to get laid. When I confronted him, he admitted that this was exactly what he had done, and that he would be sure to not disappear again.

Kyle, Ali, and I drove out that night to check out the bridge at Trou du Nord.

The bridge at Trou du Nord is a one lane, steel girder affair, built in 1934, by engineer units in the United States Marine Corps, with forced Haitian labor. There is only one road across Grand Riviere that links Cap Haitien with Ouanaminthe, Fort Liberte and the constellation of smaller communities around them. It is an absolutely essential bit of transportation infrastructure for the Northeast, because without access to Cap Haitien, goods cannot be moved to the Department, and the alternative, as during the embargo, is to use the Dominican Republic. Using Dominicans has a terrible price for Haitians.

We did not know, as we approached Trou du Nord for the first time that night, that the surface panels of the bridge were crumbling, that the girders were nearly rusted through. We had not seen the bridge yet to know of the hundred foot drop to the shallow river bed, the fording site on the South side of it where women washed clothes with their shirts off, enjoying a respite from the heat and men, while naked children played in the water. We did not know of the serpentine, muddy approach to the ford, or the piles of garbage stacked for the pigs on the city side. We new nothing of the market that began on the West side of the bridge, or of the perpetual traffic of donkeys laden with sugarcane, led by gap toothed, shrivelled men on the East side. We did not know that Trou du Nord would become the site of a meeting with leftist Christians, that we would conduct murder investigations there, that our FAd'H soldiers would lose their weapons there, that we would slip in to raid houses at night on motorcycles, that we would meet our most reliable trusted agent there, that the Haitians would form a community watch there, that we would discover a restaurant there, that we would get into trouble with our commanders for silencing American propaganda there. All we knew was what we saw—miles of mud huts discretely back from the road, among palms and gardens, blacked out and sleeping as the whole Department seemed to do in the absence of electricity, with only an occasional candle behind the shutters.

I believe that Haiti has an inscrutability not because of "voodoo" and all the crap that the media has done with the idea of "voodoo," but because the place presents travelers with so many unaccountable events. Things happen there for which there is no readily available explanation, at least to the untrained northern eye. No one knew we were coming to look at the bridge. We stopped at the Eastern edge of the bridge and dismounted. In the black stillness, we slowly walked out onto the wooden runners, then out on the bridge itself. Our footsteps spread like coughs into the gaping valley below. Kyle stopped occasionally to kneel down and finger the struts. At the far end of the bridge, a cable was stretched across the bridge to prevent vehicles crossing, and a short, chubby man stood there as if he were waiting for us in the dark. "Bon soir," he greeted us.

All of us froze for a moment, then Ali and I chorused a bon soir back at the man in the dark (Kyle refused to attempt even a greeting in any language other than English, in Haiti, and by reports, when he was in the Dominican Republic). Ali confirmed that the man spoke French, and began interrogating the man about the condition of the bridge.

The bridge was unsafe for vehicles to pass, he told us. If we wanted to drive past, we would have to use the ford. Could he show us the ford? Of course he could, with the greatest pleasure. And so he did. He also led us through the route that would have to be taken if approaching from the Cap Haitien side to enter the fording site.

We scribbled the details on a notepad under a flashlight, and thanked the man, who then bid us good night and left.

I felt very good about the reconnaissance as we made the bumpy 45-minute return trip to Fort Liberte, knowing we could give very specific instructions for the convoy. The kind of specificity we would provide is the essence of good reconnaissance work, and it was, frankly, another tiny feather in the cap of 354, who was, at this point, gaining a widespread reputation for getting things done.

I will never know who that man was or why he was there. I didn't think to ask. It was just Haiti. Understanding would have to wait. Acceptance was all we had now.

On the 8th of October, we slept in. I told the team to sleep until they couldn't sleep any more, just keep rotating the guard every hour until someone decided to stay awake.

I was never a great sleeper. Nervous energy has been both blessing and curse for me for as long as I can remember. At 6:00 AM, after little more than six hours sleep, I was wakened for my shift. I went ahead and made coffee on my Whisperlite camp stove.

The house buzzed with snoring and with mosquitoes. On the back porch, the acacia leaves were beginning to stir with the dawn breeze. Roosters debated each other across town. Hens ambled in and out of the walled quadrangle of the back porch, through the house, between the buildings, pecking at things I couldn't see. I could hear the distant, screeching Baptist hymnals from the pavilion. (A people so musical could find neither melody nor harmony in the bloodless, inhibited, Victorian wailing, no matter how accurate the translation into Creole.) A jackass brayed to the south, already under the lash. I turned up the squawk box on the radio, and carried my steaming canteen cup to the front porch, where I could squat on the steps and sip, watch the chickens forage, and feel the dawn light slowly infuse everything with colors.

Only when I have been conscious could I relax well. For as long as I remember, I have read at night in order to let sleep ambush me. If I rise to do so much as piss, I have a difficult time falling asleep again. I used to break out in hives when I went to bed. It may be caused by Agent Orange exposure, but I have often believed it is a psychological rebellion against turning out the lights on reality. I have struggled with sleep for most of my life. I now rely on Atarax to regulate my patterns, and even now I find myself shifting into the schedule of a hound, napping and roaming at random, neither nocturnal nor diurnal, dozing off when the sun hit me just right, obsessing at 3:00 am.

Eventually, one at a time, the team members woke, stumbling to the bathroom, heating MREs, making coffee, checking the hand washed uniforms on the parachute cord clotheslines, tidying their areas (Rod and Mike, the neat freaks). The rest had been long overdue, and sleep was only reluctantly loosing its grip on any of them.

59: Conflicts

At around 11:00 AM, two employees showed up. James and Magda. One was the 14 year old kid Gonzo had begun using as a general factotum. The other was the young woman Ali had hired as a cook, laundress, and housekeeper. They begged for the work, and the boys begged to hire them.

James was the size of an average American ten-year-old, bone skinny, dark skinned, with close cropped hair. He had the Haitian belly button, protruding from his abdomen like a big grape. His feet were thick soled, and he had a sleepy eyed moon shaped face. He had no last name. Just James to us, whereas the locals called him Chakono.

He worked alongside Gonzales, handing him things, fetching things, holding things in place. Gonzo worked on the pump with James, sent him across the street to the empty lot to burn trash, had him scrub the masonry on the porch, patch and pump vehicle tires, wash vehicles, carry water. James watched Gonzo's every move. James spoke fluent Spanish, having family in Santo Domingo with which he had lived with for some time.

Magda spoke Creole. Nothing but. Her name, in fact, was Magdalene, but everyone used the diminutive. She was around five feet tall, deep mahogany black, and bony. Her hair was scratched up and back, giving the appearance that something had exploded in front of her face. Her brows crested flatly, giving the impression that she was perpetually angry.

She was shown the shed on the back porch, which we were in the process of converting into a food storage site and field kitchen. She told Ali that she would need charcoal and a squat stove, and that she would need to go to the market. All business.

James approached me slyly, when I was working on the information board in the Operations Center. He gave me a Latin American high sign to indicate he was about to talk about someone, a flicker of raised eyebrows and pursed lips in the direction of the subject. Magda.

"*Una mala*," he whispered. She's bad.

"*Explicame*," I said. Explain.

"*Ladrona*," he replied. She's a thief.

"*Seguro que si?*" I asked. Are your sure?

"*Si*," he said, with a bob of the head for emphasis, brows knitted to show sincerity. "*Todo el mundo sabe.*" Everyone knows it.

I assured James that I would mention it to Ali, then in a fit of god-knows-what, I asked him if he was a Christian. He said he was. Then you know, don't you, I lectured, that we must always believe that people are capable of change. James nodded, deferentially told me to be careful, and left.

I passed James' warning to Ali. He duly noted it, saying we should give her a fair chance. I heartily agreed.

Gonzo and Skye had taken to dashing out on the porch every few minutes, hollering "*Allez! Allez!*" at the shifting clots of curiosity seekers, admirers, and children who appeared in front of the house.

I asked them what the problem was.

Skye complained, "I can't stand the motherfuckers watching every goddamn move we make." Gonzo seconded.

Be patient, I cautioned. Rapport was still our most critical task with the locals. . . all of them. There were eight of us, and hundreds of thousands of them. This was a directive, not an option: Smile, and wave, and say pretty please until it hurts, then do it some more.

They wore the expression of two hogs staring at a wristwatch. "Why?" was straining to pass their lips. I watched them transform into an obedient deportment, but it barely concealed the weariness that they were beginning to feel at my close supervision of such behavioral details. Click.

Later that day, Skye saw a dog he became attached to. The dog was out in the street in front of the house, harboring a healthy suspicion of humans. Skye opened a chicken-and-rice MRE and began tossing spoonfuls of it out to lure the dog closer. I was returning from the FAd'H headquarters where I had been conducting an inspection, when I happened onto this scenario.

Several children stood enviously watching the dog eat.

The dozens of people who had been by the house to beg for food, had had it explained to them that we were prohibited by military order from giving any food away. In fact, Mike and I had issued the proscription, knowing that the introduction of free food would have disrupted all operations and set Haitian against Haitian in the scramble for food. All of us remembered the food riots in Gonaives.

Yet here stood Skye, tossing food to the dog, after earlier bellowing at people to go away.

I passed through the front door, opting not to say anything for a few moments, for fear that anger would garble the message. Instead, I went to Mike's cot and told him about it. It was a tactic I learned in my family of origin, triangulating messages to avoid confronting an issue. Mike agreed that it was "real fucked up." My composure gradually returning, I saw through the tangle of emotions, returned to the front porch, and calmly asked Skye to come around back.

To my credit, I explained the problem calmly and rationally. Skye became resistant, rationalizing, defensive. People bring their situations on themselves, he wheedled. Animals are innocent.

"So the dogs are morally *superior* to the Haitians?" I inquired, feeling the bile rising again. He was absolutely blind to the implications of what he was saying. He was attuned, however, to the thunderstorms of my personality, and saw black clouds gathering on the horizon. He appeared to reflect for a moment, then concluded that it was probably a bad idea to feed the dog on the porch, and assured me that it would not happen again. Click. Click.

Skye had showed up on the team after the notorious external evaluation in Fort Bragg, the one that had me accused of stealing aircraft and running renegade around Sicily Drop Zone. He had not had that opportunity to go to the field with us, and get used to my peculiarities. He was in a Non-Commissioned Officer's development course at the time.

When he did return to the team, we were already steaming forward with component skills training for reconnaissance and free fall parachute infiltration. He was a little taken aback by the accelerated pace of things, and even more taken aback by the physical training regimen we had implemented.

Skye was a fire plug, short, stocky, thick through the legs. Running was not his forte. Neither was rucksacking for speed, though he was capable of shouldering heavy weight for moderate distances at a slow pace. (The team was carrying 85 pounds over body weight for five miles, at fifteen minutes a mile, once a week.) When Vern Brown was phased out of the team, Skye became the slowest man on the team, which was hard on him. He had been something of the team pariah before I arrived.

ODA 354 was cliquey. The had grown cliquey on the Dominican Republic trips, where they had all drank and whored together with great conviction and enthusiasm. Ali, Pedro, Kyle, Frank Harris (the self-proclaimed Nazi), and Rod had gone through the Special Forces Qualification course together, and Ali, Pedro and Kyle had been the original team members, when 354 was first re-activated three years prior. Rod and Frank had come from other teams. The exception on the drinking was Rod, who was a tea-totaler. Vern had come from another Special Forces unit, and had subbed as the team sergeant, after the last one was fired for incompetence. When Skye arrived, for whatever reason, he was excluded, much as a new kid is in a junior high school.

He had made one Dominican trip, where he had reportedly performed well, teaching a subject he was unqualified to teach, in a language he was unqualified to speak. He had pursued the teenage Dominican females with all the ardor of the other team members, guzzled Presidentes with the same gusto, but there remained something about Skye's personality that put them off.

That isolation was formative for Skye. He was very motivated to prove himself, and to be accepted.

The first time we piecemealed to Normandy Drop Zone to conduct free fall training after Skye returned from the NCO Academy, I caught a ride with Skye. He drove a red car (I'm no expert on cars), one of those "muscle" cars, the kind that go from zero to two hundred miles an hour in a nanosecond, burn off the back tires in less than an hour, and get two and a half miles a gallon with a nitroglycerin and gasoline fuel mixture.

The two things he talked about that fastened onto my memory were Kung-Fu and race. Skye wanted to implement Kung-Fu training as part of our physical training program. He had a friend who would teach it. And he told me that he considered a race war inevitable. He told me that he was already in possession of a small arsenal to fight that war.

"I hope you're wrong," I said, feeling diplomatic. "A lot of people in my family might not know which side to fight on."

That truncated the conversation. His face turned to puzzlement.

Minutes after the confrontation with Skye over the dog, Magda returned from the market. She added condiments to the aromatic pot of rice and beans that were cooking, then called me slyly out onto the back porch.

Gason la (James, she meant) was *pa bon* (bad).

"*Por quoi?*" I was asking stupidly for an explanation that she could not render and I could not understand. And she couldn't understand my shitty French. I didn't know yet that Creole for "why" is *poukisa*.

"*Pa bon,*" she said again, wagging a finger to underscore her denunciation. "Pa bon!"

60: NAPOLEON GETS NERVOUS

Ken and Rod went to Derac, one of three dying, deserted company towns on the edge of the largest defunct sisal plantation in the world. The rest of us stayed around the house, and entertained serial visits.

First came the bishop's secretary, a soft, feeble, pale creature, speaking passable English, French by birth, ancient. His handshake was positively frangible. Ali carried on the bulk of the conversation with him in French. He was quick to point out, not for the last time, that our uniforms reminded him of his days in France during the war, where for a time the Germans had detained him. He invited us to come by his residence, one of the three most palatial in Fort Liberte (the others being the bishops house and the residence of Nyll Calixte), any time. He applauded us for employing Magda, whom he said needed the work, having two children at home to feed, and her without a man. He let us know, as diplomatically as possible, that M'sieur Rene Mozart was a long-standing acquaintance of his, really quite incapable of criminal activity or violence. Here was the Church standing before us, split in Latin America between the hierarchy supporting the bourgeoisie and the rebellious clerics of liberation theology, like Aristide. The Bishop, Duvalierist to his roots, ensconced in his palace lived only three blocks from the local priest, an ally of Aristide.

299

Throughout Haiti, we would find, the upper echelons of the church sided with the elite, and the parish priests tended to be Lavalas.

LTC Schroer flew in that day, and failed to hear what we told him about anything we had accomplished. He wanted to reemphasize, ad nauseam, that we were not the police, and that we had to apply the rules of evidence to further detentions. I got the distinct impression that he heartily disapproved of our earlier detentions. That would have been compatible with our experience of LTC Schroer. He was not a man who did well with controversy or initiative, and we felt sure that the Presidential order to release Nyll Calixte had stung him badly. He also seemed obsessed with the subject of uniform violations, the rolling of sleeves (he wanted them down; we wanted them up), the cravat that I had retied to my weapon, and the double magazines that I had reinserted. (Little did he know that I now used the double mags so I could roam around without my LCE [Gasp!], fully believing that I no longer needed teargas, hand grenades and 400 rounds of ammunition.) He threatened Mike with relief if he saw the cravat on my weapon again.

Schroer started the operation as a clueless asshole, and he would end it as a clueless asshole. I guess it was a character trait. It's generally easy to tolerate a clueless asshole if (1) he is not in charge of you, and (2) he is not unreservedly arrogant. LTC Schroer was in charge, and his arrogance was matched only by his stupidity.

The final visit that day was from Major Fox, not the Major Fox of our own organic company, but another Major Fox, who under the incredibly confusing realignment for this mission, ran our immediate Headquarters, ODB 310, in Cap Haitien. The "310" Major Fox was the picture of All-American manliness. Tall, slender, innocently handsome. A real Joe Armstrong. He was quiet man, who seemed a little disturbed by my own innate hyperactivity, but friendly and polite nonetheless. He simply reviewed our setup, listened attentively to Mike's rundown of the situation, and shook hands all around. As he prepared to leave, he quietly reminded us that the priority of "higher" seemed to be uniforms, so be careful.

This uniformity obsession would continue. Uniform changes for specific tasks used to be a decision made by the senior NCO on a site. Now it was an issue for Generals. Someone told all of them that we lost in Vietnam because we had fucked up uniforms, I think, and they believed it. Stupidity is a tough, fecund thing, like crabgrass.

We did not know it at the time, but we were beginning to see the routine that would develop for us in weeks to come. Check on the FAd'H. Talk to the steady stream of visitors on the porch. Enter notes into the intelligence files. Prepare, send and receive messages on the radio. Improve on the team house. React to emerging situations. Sleep. Pull radio watch. And so on.

61 : THE FANFAN STORY

One of the visitors on the porch, late that afternoon, was Bernard Fanfan, the mayor of Perches, a community 40 minutes away by hummer, high in the mountains between Grand Bassin and Acul Samedi. He related for the second time his trouble about the theft of a municipal car by one Sergeant Brunot Innocent, a member of what was now our garrison.

I don't remember who I sent to fetch Brunot Innocent from the garrison. It didn't seem that big a deal at the time. I only remember that Brunot was no longer at the garrison. He was reported to be staying with acquaintances in Fort Liberte. I decided to go to Perches that evening with this mayor to remove the most threatening people, according to him, a group of three *attaches* who had promised violence if Mayor Fanfan returned to Perches. The detention for questioning of Sergeant Innocent would have to wait until the following day. I regretted that decision more times than I can count.

In later investigations we would learn that Brunot Innocent, a birdboned man of small stature, with a Leprechaun face, was the single most feared man in uniform in our entire sector. If anyone was questioned about Brunot, from Fort Liberte to Trou du Nord, from Caracol to Acul Samedi, recognition and fear were combined in response to his reputation for savagery. Some did not recognize his given name, but all knew his nickname; A Te Plat, translated as Flat on the Ground, a command he made universally famous.

What we did not know was that he and Pierre Ulrick had grown up in the same town, Grand Bassin, and had for years been co-conspirators in countless schemes and acts of thuggery. Ulrick, being the garrison commander, realized that we were looking for Brunot. The next day, when we began searching in earnest for Brunot, the good sergeant had vanished.

Ulrick, Innocent, and a first sergeant, Alexis Frandieu, were the three most feared and despised men in our Area of Operational Responsibility (AOR). I squandered, in my ignorance of the situation at this early stage of operations, the last chance we might have had to put Brunot Innocent into custody.

We speculated that Brunot had lifted the municipal car from Perches and sold it in Port-au-Prince.

Skye, Ali and I departed at dark with Mayor Fanfan. We knew by now that Haitians, in the absence of electricity, retire quite early. We believed our chances of seizing the *attaches* were exponentially increased by the cover of darkness.

The drive out was the first trip I made on the twisted, precipitous mountain road connecting Terrier Rouge with Grand Bassin, Perches, and Acul Samedi. As we left the flatlands of Terrier Rouge and began our ascent, the air slowly cooled and dried. Shadows of thick, tangled, tropical trees drifted past, falling down and back into darkness, the diesel growling and clattering up the side of the mountains. Pinholes of candlelight pierced out of an occasional hut. From time to time, a child, a skinny dog, or a man leading a burro would get reeled into the glare of the headlights, all staring yellow-eyed straight at us, with no thought for the blindness we left behind. Potholes, raket hedges, primitive fences, entered the light in front of us and slid back into night before we reached them.

I drove. Skye and Ali stood in the bed of the Hummer, leaning on the anterior roof strut to keep from falling out. Bernard Fanfan sat in the front passenger seat. We seldom spoke. The diesel was too loud. We would ask Fanfan for directions at the few intersections in the road. He was slow to respond, seeming preoccupied, and on one occasion, Skye became very threatening and short with him. I, in turn, became short with Skye.

"That's a mayor you're talking to, not some rowdy kid in the street."

Skye withdrew sullenly into his silence. Click.

The plan was to have Fanfan direct us to each house, where we would cover the front and rear, demand entrance and seize the *attache*. We were prepared to assault the house with a two man clearing team (Ali and me, both of us having been trained for room clearing) if we met armed resistance.

Entry into the town was abrupt. One moment we were climbing and twisting up a steep ascent, and a moment later, we had burst in to a central plaza, with a park and a cathedral surrounded by buildings.

I directed Ali to instruct Fanfan to show us quickly to the first house. Fanfan showed us an adobe structure with one front door flanked by two windows, and a modest porch. The house had been freshly painted sea green. Plastered all over the front of the house were posters of Jean-Bertrand Aristide. We turned to Fanfan and asked him what was up. This was obviously the house of an Aristide supporter. Where was the *attache*'s house? This was the house, he assured us. The Aristide posters were a clever ruse. Are you sure, we wanted to know. Oui, oui, oui, he was sure.

We inspected the structure and found no back entrance. Ali and I positioned ourselves along the wall next to the door. Bang, bang, bang, Ali pounded his fist on the door. He called in French for the name Fanfan had given us to come out with his hands clearly in view. Low urgent voices muttered to one another inside with confusion. Bang, bang, bang, bang. Ali bellowed the order to come out this time. Urgent female voices told us to please wait, wait, they were coming.

The door cracked. Lamplight. We pushed in past the middle-aged woman in the door, and cleared the two-room house. Two children were still asleep. The woman was frightened and red eyed.

Ali asked where the man was who we were looking for. He had gone out earlier with a friend. She didn't know where.

Again, I looked around the kerosene lighted house, noted the wobbly little table, the crooked, handmade chairs, the tick mattresses, the frightened woman, and the exhausted children. Again, I felt like a loathsome tyrant. Guilt was beginning to be something I carried everywhere, like my canteens and my pistol.

The scene was repeated twice more. Only one of the men we were searching for was home. He was flex cuffed and put in the hummer with Skye and Mayor Fanfan.

While we were there, I decided, we needed to go ahead and draw a crowd, introduce ourselves, explain our mission, and do a bit of PR. I pulled into the plaza at town center and parked, leaving the lights on. Within five minutes, we could hear the music heading toward us. *Viv Aristide. Cedras Manje Caca. Dezame Lame. Lavalas-la.* All the top tunes we had come to know and love.

The main body of the demonstration was preceded by a group of a dozen or so people, strangely all old men and young boys. They stood, taciturn, at the edge of the headlight glare. Fanfan said something to Ali.

"Stan, something's wrong!" Ali blurted.

"What? What?"

"Stan, he says these people are all *macoutes.*"

"Huh?"

Once again, I felt caught in a whirlpool of confusion. These were old, barefooted men, and skinny, ill-clad kids. One thing we had noted so far was that *macoutes*, the real article, were comparatively well dressed.

We had Fanfan dismount and stood him in front of the little assembly. Ali directed him to explain. Fanfan pointed at one of the old men, this one standing ramrod straight with a straw hat on. Fanfan said the man was a *macoute*. The old man's black eyes flashed indignantly. He appeared to draw himself up into an even more stately posture, took a step forward on his thick bare feet, and glared at Fanfan from a foot away.

"*Ma-Coute!?*" he spit the word back into Fanfan's face.

The other men and the boys began chattering like parakeets, pointing at Bernard Fanfan, telling us HE was the *macoute*. HE was a thief. HE was the collaborator with the *de facto* government.

I think I said something intelligent, like "Oh, fuck!"

We decided it would be prudent to separate Mayor Fanfan from the incoming demonstration and the now excited group to our front. Skye escorted him into the darkness at the other end of the plaza and stayed with him.

In they came, up, out of the darkness of a street that snaked down toward a valley, drums beating, whistles blowing, flutes and basoons made of bamboo, the chorus of voices mostly young, the snap and bounce of lean half-clad bodies, all now predictable. Predictable and safe. We had grown to the point where we considered a demonstration anywhere away from a FAd'H garrison an absolutely benign occurrence.

I gave Ali his instructions. Stay friendly. We are happy and honored to be here. Explain our limitations, and issue an open invitation to the house in Fort Liberte. Aristide will return on the 15th (the one thing we said repeatedly that qualified as seriously sticking our necks out). The day of the soldier with the baton, the *attaches*, and the *macoutes* was past (okay, so we missed on this one, by and by, too). We know about the poverty and the hunger. We can not solve it. We are only here to provide security for the Haitians to determine the solutions to their own futures (as it turned out, our necks were out here too. . . me knowing nothing of the future actions of the whole coven of international financiers, US diplomats, spies, propagandists, and a cancer of NGO's). Then, I told Ali, get to the bottom of this shit with Fanfan and our detainee.

The speech led, as always, to cheers and gratitude, *Viv Aristide, Viv Meriken.* But the story that emerged from the typically anarchic conversation with the growing crowd was revealing our ignorance and naiveté once again.

Bernard Fanfan was universally despised in his home town. Yes, yes, we elected him, they admitted, but he had become a creature of the FAd'H, and a corrupt, avaricious one at that. The car he had come to have us help him recover was in fact one he used personally, purchased with public money. In fact, Fanfan and Innocent had been seen together in it on more than one occasion. But isn't Bruno Innocent the notorious *A Te Platé?" Oui, oui,* that's him. And Bernard Fanfan had been chumming around with him from Grand Bassin to Perches for quite some time.

"Stan," said Ali, as an aside, "I think we fucked up here."

"Understatement of the Week," I offered. "So who're the guys we were fixin' to arrest?" I was remembering all the Aristide posters plastered on the front of the first house we violated.

Ali asked me for the list of names. I rooted in my pockets until I produced it. Ali held the list sideways to read it in the headlights. Who are these three men?

Everyone murmured and smiled. Why, those are the three most important people in town on the Committee of Lavalas.

I lit a cigarette. "Skye!" I hollered to the darkness that contained Skye, the detainee, and Fanfan.

"Yup!"

"Release the detainee, and tell 'im to come 'ere."

"Huh?"

"Send me the detainee."

The crowd cheered as our recent prisoner emerged into the light. From the crowd came another man, a tiny man, no more than five feet tall and bone skinny. He told us that his was one of the names on the list. We asked where he lived. In the freshly painted house, that way, with the Aristide posters.

Ali and I conferred for a moment. Ali apologized to the entire town for our error, and in particular to the men whose homes we had entered, and again in particular to the members of the families whom we had frightened in the process. Ali explained Fanfan's story and the source of our misunderstandings, and the crowd actually found it all quite amusing. There was a great deal of laughter, especially when Ali announced that M'sieur Fanfan would be passing the night with us in Fort Liberte. The crowd insisted that Fanfan not be allowed to return to Perches at all. To appease them, we announced that we had as of that moment suspended his mayoral authority.

This news was met with applause and singing.

"We need them to chose an interim representative, Ali," I said.

Ali asked them who they would have to represent them at our community meetings, and for the purpose of representing the interest of the town generally. Overwhelmingly, they pointed to the little man whose house we first invaded.

Ali's sense of drama was impeccable. Amid the clamor, he picked the little man up effortlessly (Ali loved to be the strong man), held him aloft, and announced in French that this, then, was the new mayor. A rousing cheer went up. The smiling man was passed from Ali to the crowd, who began to caper about the plaza with the man held aloft.

Amid this all, we bid adieu, mounted up with a silent and sullen Fanfan, and returned to Fort Liberte, where M'sieur Fanfan was given a room in the Hoosegow Hotel for the evening, and an MRE for his breakfast.

We weren't even through our toilet rotation the next morning when Adele showed up in tears. She had been to see Bernard Fanfan, her friend, and he had told her how *macoutes* had sent people out to act like Aristide supporters in order to trick us into taking him into custody. Adele was stricken. She was worried that tricksters would have us putting her in jail next.

I smoked with her on the porch, assured her that no one had the least intention of jailing her, and tried to explain how the night's events had unwound.

She would hear none of it. Bernard Fanfan had been her friend all her life, and he would never engage in corruption. She began to well up with tears again.

Christ! this seemed like an awful pickle. We had Perches in hand, because we arrested Fanfan, but we stood to lose the loyalty of our key civil official in the political center of the area. Moreover, I liked Adele, and seeing her weep made me feel like a heel.

"Ali," I said, "tell her that Bernard will be released this morning, then go to the garrison and let him go." Ali started to tell her.

"Sorry," I interjected. "Tell Fanfan not to return to Perches, if he has somewhere else to stay. Tell him it's not safe there for him. Don't tell her I told you that."

Well, as it turned out, Fanfan had not the least desire to return to Perches, especially in any official capacity. He gave us ample assurance.

But the story of Bernard Fanfan and Adele Mondestin was not over yet.

That very day, the 9th of October, I sent Rod and Gator down to check the garrison, and told Rod to have Piggy Ulrick hand over the list of *attaches* immediately, or look for a job peddling dry fish in Derac. We received a battered list, with a poor carbon, with a list of 180 names. It was quite a piece of intelligence.

I determined then and there to plot the locations of the *attache* homes on our satellite photo imagery for future operations if necessary. Mike mentioned the policy of maintaining these lists in the garrisons (since *attaches* were in fact employees of the garrisons, Auxiliaries was the official term) to our commanders in the daily message traffic. We were the first to obtain such a list, but the commanders seemed strangely unconcerned with the importance of it.

The list was set aside. It was a busy day, as all of them had been. Ali and Rod and I went to Terrier Rouge, in response to a letter from one Paul Pierre, who claimed there was some kind of emergency there. There was, in fact, absolute peace, followed by great curiosity as we met with M'sieur Pierre. But the main thing we did there was draw a crowd and give what was becoming a standard speech. We discussed on the way back to Fort Liberte how we were developing the *Stan and Ali Travelling Show*, and how that concept needed to be used with each initial visit to each new village and town. More on that later.

On the 10th of October, we visited facilities; pumps, wells, generators, windmills. Adele notified us that there would be a small demonstration, which there was, with no problems. It was hectic and hot, but essentially a low adrenaline day.

A chopper flew in that afternoon around four and dropped off Mermite containers full of food. There were steaks, baked potatoes, salad, green beans, bread and koolaid. It was gratefully consumed, then we had to rush out and return the Mermite containers just prior to six, when the chopper flew back through.

We were winding down, bellies full, patrol out, someone at the garrison, Mike on the radio (it was his day on what we called Radio/House duty), and Rod and me pouring over the confounding stacks of accumulating intelligence. We had taken notes on everything. People were now corresponding with us from the villages. Paper was piled all over the field table that sat below our wall mounted imagery, which now had strings pointing to key locations, with information sheets on each location at the other end of the strings.

I was absently smoking and scanning the names on the *attache* list, just to do a cursory mental file on them in case names would recur in the future. Near the end of the second of three pages, I suddenly sat up at a name.

Fanfan, Bernard.

"Mike," I called. Mike was across the room, hunched over a notebook writing messages. "You need to see this."

I got up and dropped the list of *attaches'* names on the table in front of him.

"What's the third to the last name on that page?"

There was a moment of silence as he searched.

"Holy fuckin' shit!" The vocabulary of strong emotions is limited in Special Forces.

Bernard Fanfan was the mayor of Perches, and he was an *attache*.

The list was passed around. Ali became very excited over the discovery. We would later find that the true mayor of Terrier Rouge was an *attache* as well. By then our capacity to be surprised was diminishing.

I tried to think of a way to tell Adele without shaming her for her credulity.

Two days later, when Adele was over, I asked if she would look at our list and make a mark next to any names she knew who were residents of Fort Liberte. She accommodated happily, ticking away at easily one in every three names, as I watched over her shoulder. I saw the pencil pause imperceptibly as it passed Fanfan, Bernard, and Adele seemed to have a longer than usual respiratory pause. Nothing else.

When she was finished, I thanked her and shook her hand. She said I was welcome. I asked if she would stay for a Coke, but she said she needed to get to the *Biblioteque*. . . work waited. . . she was, after all, the mayor. She was very self contained when she walked away. Sadness settled on me, as I watched her go.

She never brought up the subject of Bernard Fanfan again.

10 Oct
Dear Sherry,

We just ate a huge lunch. I am having a cup of strong coffee to get woke up. Magda, the cook we hired, fixes enough to feed a herd of cattle. Rice and beans today. Yesterday we had rice and beans. Tomorrow, something new. Rice and beans. Condiments change daily. We've also hired a factotum. James, 14. James says Magda is a thief. Magda says James is a devil. We arrested Magda's cousin, but she didn't like him anyway. We also arrested James' uncle, but the uncle never claimed the nephew, so no love lost. Everbody in Ft Liberte is everyone else's relative. Adele, the mayor, has something like 36 brothers and sisters spread between here and Santo Domingo. Busy dad. Lots of moms.

We had demonstrations this morning. I wish they'd chose a cooler time of day. I had to give speeches to the cops to calm them down. They think every crowd will explode into a bloodthirsty furor, and that if they defend themselves, WE will attack THEM, the cops. Tough place to be in. Brought it on themselves. No easy solutions here.

Two guys just interrupted me, trying to get us to settle a civil dispute over water. Told them we are not a courthouse. I've not, since Vietnam, stayed so tired all the time.

Last two hour interruption. Interviewed a farmer. Sent two guys to control a crowd. Dispatched the vehicle to meet a resupply helo w water, diesel, a cooler w raw steaks in it. No mail.

Friday, we will discuss state of cooperatives with the mayor and some local econ reps.

Gotta go. Can't stand the fucking interruptions.

Sherry, I love you. Your letters came yesterday. Got one from Celia. One from Mom. Love you, need you, miss you awful. Some day.

Love, Stan

10 Oct
Dear Sherry,

    A note while I am on radio watch. I wish I could begin to describe all the contradictions. I locked up the mayor of Perches the night before last. He lied to me to get me to lock up Lavalas. His town calls him a macoute. Adele almost cried. She says he is a good man. I released Fanfan, the mayor I locked up. He cried. I felt like a heel. Had to, or I'd have lost Adele as an ally. She is instrumental in keeping calm here. Receive a list of over 200 attaches (secret police). Number 138 is Fanfan. Adele is Lavalas. It's all crazy. Pigs roam the streets. There was a cockfight in front of our house this morning. The animals have a better idea of what the fuck they are doing than I do. The skies are gorgeous. No power = no pollution. Perches looks wet and green as Panama. Everything we think of as the basis of an economy is non-existent. Prices out of control because of the embargo. . . what a fucking blunt instrument! Very hot today. We got steaks, but no generator, no fans. I bathe with a bucket and a plastic water bottle cut in half. Recognize a lot of faces around town already. Bishop's secretary is old, doddering, half deaf, sweet natured old Frenchman. . . probably a Duvalierist. Always tells me the same stories about WWII. I shake a hundred hands a day. Busy. That's good, 'cause I don't think of missing you so much. Love you, Sherry. –S

62: The House

The team house was a yellow structure, made of concrete, with louver windows and no screens, a shower without a drain, and a carport too small to fit a car into. By Haitian standards, it was upper middle class...out of reach of 95 percent of the population.

The porch was constructed of concrete arches and columns with a low wall stretching across the south-facing front of the house, wrapping partially around the east wall like a fallen L. The cinder block walls separating the house from the two adjacent houses were within three feet of us, creating narrow alleys on both sides of the house. The alley extended all the way to the back on the west side. On the east, there was a recess constructed behind the great room on the southeast corner of the house, where the cistern was located.

In that recess, we strung parachute cord, as we had on the back porch to hang wet clothes. We also stretched barbed wire along the two adjacent property walls, which doubled as an additional clothesline. All these clotheslines were perpetually full. The combination of 90+ degree heat every day, the coastal humidity, and the ubiquitous dust, kept a steady supply of rank Battle Dress Uniforms moving through the plastic buckets we washed in on the back porch.

We hung a haphazard lattice of barbed wire at the street end of the eastern alley to limit access around the house, with the enthusiastic consent of our neighbors who wanted to keep the local children from mounting the dividing wall. The wire did nothing, however, to impede the chickens and cats that hung around the house. Frequently, in fact, chickens would traverse through the house, where members of the team would shoo and chase them.

There was an acacia tree that grew in the middle of the cracked concrete on the back porch, providing shade for us and our back porch neighbors. A wall separated us from them as well, with an opening to pass from one property to another.

The storage shed was in the rear, at the Northwest corner, and was used as a kitchen. We stored our MRE's there, our T-Rations when they arrived, and the staples we bought at the newly opened market; bread, rice, beans, eggs. The kitchen was outfitted with a Haitian charcoal cooker, a shallow metal dish mounted on three ten inch metal legs, approximately a foot and a half in diameter. Next to the "stove" we kept a large sack of charcoal (35 gourds apiece).

The technique we learned from Haitians for lighting the charcoal was to arrange it evenly across the bowl of the stove, ignite a couple of splinters of lighter knot (also sold in bundles for a half gourd), then fan the flame lightly with a piece of cardboard until the flames grew. When the charcoal was well lit enough to withstand stronger fanning, the cardboard became a bellows that accelerated the burn rate until a nice bed of coals was established.

Eventually, after several unsuccessful tries, we acquired a generator that and thereby developed a new technique; a merger of the Neolithic age and the twentieth century. We filled the stove with charcoal, then soaked the charcoal with kerosene from the supply used for our lamps. We set the stove in front of the back bedroom, where Kyle and Skye and Gator were sleeping, and lowered one of the fans purchased from the Dominicans in Ouanaminthe, aiming it at the coals. We ignited the fuel, turned on the fan, and the flames gained strength. Then we turned up the fan until the stove looked like an operational solid fuel booster. Whole process, ten minutes. Great bed of coals!

From the back porch, there were two doors, the one leading to the rear sleeping quarters, and the one entering the open room on the northwest corner that functioned as our Operations/Communications/Intelligence Center. The Ops Center, as it was called, was visible through the aperture in the wall leading to the rear neighbors' domicile, and therefore visible to the steady traffic created by their comings and goings, our alley being the only easement they had to the street. So we suspended ponchos in a kind of vestibule to prevent civilian intervisibility with our maps and schedules and so forth.

We opened an extra cot along the north wall on the back porch to provide a place for people to sit, read, eat, bullshit. Moving around the back porch usually required a good deal of ducking and dodging to avoid the clothes, dripping, damp and dry, that hung everywhere.

Doors had been built all over the house. There were two doors on the front porch. One led into the living room. The other led into the western hallway. A door connected the living room and the hallway. Another door straight across from the latter connected the hallway to the carport-that-was-too-small-for-a-car. The carport-that-was-too-small-for-a-car door and the hallway-living room door both opened in to the hallway, and banged into one another when opened simultaneously. One step further down the hall, and the door to my bedroom (the hottest, tiniest cubicle in the house) opened into the hallway as well, hitting the bathroom door, also a hallway opener, directly across from it. The door opening into the second largest bedroom (where Mike and Rod slept) hit the door across the hall that led into Ali's bedroom. Mike and Rod's room had an additional door that led to the cistern.

The woodwork on the doors had been done by hand and was nothing less than exquisite. The doors had been hung perfectly, each one swinging effortlessly and noiselessly and fitting perfectly into its frame. It was almost a metaphor for the general dissonance of our mission in Haiti. These perfectly designed, perfectly installed passageways beat each other when they were used, conspired to form barricades, had not been integrated into the overall design of the structure for which they were built, and could unexpectedly smack you in the face.

The plumbing and the house routine evolved symbiotically, reminding us how central water is to the human experience, and how much we take it for granted.

The water in the cistern was under a concrete cap. The cap had been finished before the surrounding concrete, so the completion of the surrounding porch had resulted in a thin seal of cement that essentially closed the cap on the cistern. We could not see, therefore, the level of that cistern, which we had been told received its water from the public pump, and old diesel affair, located at the river.

Gonzo had experience digging wells, maintaining pumps, working on oil fields, driving trucks, the kind of labor experience that made him the *de facto* hydroengineer of the operation. Kyle's *forte* was in construction trades, and though he had some knowledge of these matters, he deferred to Gonzo's experience.

Gonzo discovered that a hand pump, with a ten inch handle, mounted on the Eastern outside wall, was what was available to move the water in the ground cistern through a tiny 3/4 inch pipe up into the 1500 gallon reservoir that was built on the flat, concrete roof. We all soon discovered that before one man could pump that hand pump enough to fill the reservoir he would have developed arms to rival Lee Haney or died of exhaustion. Gonzo determined that what we needed was "an electric 1 1/2 horsepower pump with a four inch hose to do the job right." We did not have that, so we soon used what little water was in the reservoir, then went looking for water from another source.

We discovered early that the shower stall had been connected with the reservoir by a pipe into the shower head. The bathroom was been nicely tiled, with a high louvered window to ensure both a breeze and privacy, but that the builder(s) had overlooked the detail of installing a drain. The workers themselves had probably never used a top flowing indoor shower. We ended up knocking a hole in the floor with a punch and a hammer (courtesy of American Airlines in Port-au-Prince), where the water could at least run into the space under the house.

We hung a field shower up in the stall with a carabinier attached to parachute cord, and built a shower curtain with a camouflaged poncho. The field shower was a five gallon, water repellent, heavy canvas bag, with a plastic shower nozzle located bottom-dead-center. The nozzle was operated by twisting it right to allow flow, left to stop flow. For conservation, we mandated that the bather wet himself, stop flow, soap up, rinse off, get out…this procedure affectionately called a Navy Shower, since it is used to conserve water on ships.

The toilet required water to flush as well. The rule on the toilet was only flush feces. "If it's brown, wash it down; if it's yellow, let it mellow." It took the best part of a five gallon can of water to effectively flush the toilet, and with eight people, regular as sunrise from a diet high in rice and beans, that meant eight of the thirteen five gallon cans we owned were used up every morning in sewage disposal.

Each man had to shave, brush his teeth, and each of us did laundry.

We drank as much as five gallons of water per man per day during the initial, crazy, clockless days in Gonaives and Ouanaminthe, with the loading and unloading of choppers, the incessant moving and stacking, the ceaseless patrols, the standing in the sun to barricade crowds. Even with the order we had begun to establish in Fort Liberte, the consumption was as high as three gallons a day per man. For potable water, we had to pump the acquired water through a Katahdin pump to remove the encysted protozoa, then bleach the water to kill bacteria that might slip through the ceramic filter of the pump. I asked Gonzo to trust the pump and hold the bleach down to three parts per million, but Gonzo was the assigned medic, and used his prerogative to keep the water closer to a hefty six parts. . . a practice that was noted by the other men who complained that their innards were probably as white as a new pair of Jockey shorts. MRE fruit flavored drink mixes were very popular, and almost overcame the bleach on one's breath. Later in the mission, as the supply system became more efficient, we were to receive a steady supply of bottled water.

Gonzo had located a very clean well with a functional pump about two miles out of town, in an open field with a windmill that surprisingly worked and kept a steady dribble of water running into the surrounding earth. We began a practice of sending a vehicle with two to three people out to the pump every day to fill up the water cans, both morning and evening, to keep up with our incessant need.

Another practice that developed in a short time was for the men to take their toiletries with them to the pump and bathe there with a bucket. Water runs, then, became an affair that could take more than an hour. The bathing rituals became a source of great entertainment to the rural Haitians who used the pump as well. They would cluster at a respectful distance and marvel at the thick, muscular, well-fed bodies of the blancs, and the children would giggle at the men's genitalia. The latter practice led to some insecurity among my men.

Water cans were lined up in the hallway, and as each was emptied, it would be moved out onto the porch, where the next water detail could toss them into the back of the hummer and head to the pump.

The living room was soon stacked to the ceiling with MRE's, T-Rations, and eventually the bottled water. Percy had a cot in the living room, as well, to separate him from the Ops Center, for we suspected quite logically that he had been ordered by his superiors to spy on us.

Mike and Rod were both very tidy, and their room was always picked up and presentable. My room seemed always halfway between uses of some kind. Ali's was heaped into a corner. Skye and Kyle kept their room like pigs. That is a serious indictment, coming from me.

For the first few weeks, no one would come to take the ever growing collection of confiscated firearms from us, so along the Eastern wall of the Ops Center was a bristling stack of M-14's, M-1's, G-3's, shotguns, Thompsons, and an assortment of museum pieces that even included one Sharp's .50 caliber.

The guard/radio watch roster was advanced an hour each night, so that if you pulled guard from 11-12 tonight, you would pull it from 12-1 tomorrow night. The roster started at 9 p.m. each evening, and ended with a general wake-up at 6 a.m. each morning. Kerosene lanterns were lined up on the two Ops Center windowsills, and one was kept burning all night at the radio desk. The guard was in possession of a flashlight, which he would periodically flash around the outside of the house just to prove our 24-hour vigilance to whomever might be interested.

A day watch was also established, in which one man would be responsible to stay at the house from 6 a.m. until 9 p.m., and monitor the radio. This became an onerous responsibility in its tedium, so many of us used this day to catch up on letter writing and reading.

A couple of the guys had brought along some soft core smut, which they would pour over for hours on radio watch, which has always struck me as a peculiar form of masochism. Only Ali and Skye were sexually active with Haitian girls, and only Ali with any regularity. Everyone else restricted themselves to imagination and autonomy. As the mission progressed, the hook lock on the bathroom door was closed with more frequency.

The lack of screens gave total access to the mosquitoes. This was a source of concern to us in an area where dengue fever was endemic, though when we saw how little trash accumulated in our region, some of the fear was dispelled. The *Aedes aegypti* mosquito is the vector for dengue, and they generally hatch in old tires and cans, trash dumps. Haitians do not let such resources go to waste in a dump. Nonetheless, the *culex* and *anopheles* variety of mosquito were abundant. When one woke in the morning, the outside of the mosquito net would be covered in them, perched like hundreds of microscopic vultures. If one or two managed to find a breach in the net, one might wake and slap, finding under the assaulting hand a stamp of blood from the intruder feeding again and again during the night.

Fine red dust was everywhere and insidious. Dusting and sweeping were necessary twice a day. It collected in the weave of your clothes, it powdered your cot, your locker, the radios, your weapon, the crevices in your skin. Our eyes were always inflamed, with dark crusts forming in the corners, our fingers eternally excavating our noses, and it seemed the clenching of our teeth would invariably grind with dust. Many things wore us down on this mission, work, heat, prejudice, conflict, loneliness, power, powerlessness, frustration; none of us recognized it at the time, but the dust, in its obscure relentlessness, may have worn us down more than anything.

All of us had a favored area to relax. Mike and Rod both stayed to their room, the airiest and lightest in the house. Ali and Skye and Kyle preferred the back porch, because they disliked dealing with passing Haitians, who out of curiosity, need, or avarice were wont to impose themselves. Gonzo slept in the front room with Percy, then by himself when Percy left. Gonzo could be found mostly at the side of the house, where he seldom relaxed, working compulsively on the water or the electricity. I liked the front porch.

My favorite time was in the morning, when I had last radio watch. I turned up the radio squawk box so I could hear it, fanned up a bed of coals, boiled a pot of coffee, and stood out on the front porch, while the dawn seeped in. The air was cool with the morning breeze stirring. The marketeers, one at a time, or in discrete groups, were ambling sleepily toward the markethouse, leading donkeys, carrying baskets of produce on their heads. The chickens foraged erratically below the porch and in the street. The house slept, and I had my moment of quiet solitude under the hopeful eyes of dawn. The coffee was hot and sweet. A quiet *bon jour* could be exchanged with passing faces.

Later in the mission, we would come by an electric pump, courtesy of Brown and Root, Inc., in Cap Haitien. I would take a hammer and open up the cistern. We would receive a decent generator, and we would restore rationed electricity to Fort Liberte. Bottled water would become the norm. Food would become so plentiful that it was wasted. Security would become so well established that we would find time to build chinning and dip bars to exercise, weight benches with improvised weights, we would swim in the bay, jog unarmed to the well, sunbathe. The house would fill with fans and souvenirs. But things would have happened by then; things that had fragmented us, that made the collective meals on the back porch quiet and pressured and irrevocably divided. As the need for teamwork and resourcefulness diminished, so diminished our cohesion.

The house would come to feel like a prison to me and my men, and my insurrection would come to trip over theirs.

63: PERCY

During the initial meeting with Captain Pierre Ulrick, the meeting at the Ouanaminthe caserne, where we succeeded in convincing the good commander of the 19th Military Police Company in Fort Liberte that we would meet any failure to cooperate or aggressive action on the part of the garrison with an unspecified retribution on a biblical scale, Mike and I were introduced to Lieutenant Percy. I have forgotten his last name and confess to not having recorded it in any of the notes I still have. He was our FAd'H interpreter. The lieutenant was a lean, rangy, dark-skinned fellow, faultlessly pressed, with a square head, upon which sat the shiny twin ellipses of his large horn-rimmed glasses. His impeccably vertical posture and the lenses that concealed the details of his eyes lent him the aspect of a cold, machinelike functionary.

The moment he was introduced, however, he extended his hand warily. His voice was timorous as a shy child, his English precise and atonal, like a recital. His head pitched indefinably, as if bravely awaiting a blow.

I'd seen this bearing before. It was the demeanor of a first year West Point cadet, no longer on the edge of his first day terror, but habituated to the humilities of a prolonged initiation. In spite of my intentional pose of malevolence toward all FAd'H at that point in the operation, I found myself wanting to put him at ease.

I had been a "soft" instructor at West Point when I taught Military Science there in 1986-87, one the new cadets could relax with. I had an aversion to the "fourth class system" there, a euphemism for the officially unacknowledged combination of servitude and hazing, designed to fragment the first-year cadet's personality in order to reassemble him or her institutionally. The young lieutenant's comportment aroused my old rebellion and my empathy. He just seemed vulnerable.

Checking my inclination to ask his first name, we continued that meeting which I described earlier, the first "sweating out" of Capitaine Ulrick.

A young lieutenant was instructed to present himself to us at 2:30 a.m., packed and prepared to travel.

The morning preparations were feverish and preoccupied. When the lieutenant came, I briefly shook his hand and told him he could ride on whichever vehicle he preferred. His manner was very courteous and deferential, and again I found myself wondering what all this must be like for him.

"What is your first name?" I asked.

He seemed perplexed by the question and hesitated.

"Excuse me, Sirzhint Goff, I do not understand"

"What is your Christian name?" I rephrased it.

"My name? My first name?"

"Yes. What does your girlfriend call you?"

With an involuntary smile and a dissembling drop of the head, he responded, "Percy."

"My name is Stan."

It would take some days and much reiteration before I would induce Percy to call me by my first name.

Percy was twenty-three years old. His family was from Port-au-Prince, where he had gained acceptance into the Haitian Military Academy, at Capt D'Applicacion, indicating that his family had some influence. He must have been very hopeful about his future, by Haitian standards, before we invaded, as even starry-eyed American junior officers are. His temperate deportment would lead one to disbelieve Percy capable of the mayhem and thuggery associated with the FAd'H. The intuitive inference I drew about Percy, under my conscious skepticism about all FAd'H, was that he had, as yet, been comparatively uncorrupted. He was a young professional embarking on a heartening journey into the future.

Young professionals, I reminded myself, sympathetic as they may seem with a disarming modesty, are always necessarily invested in conservatism. Conservatism, here, meant the baton. That said, I found Percy very likable, and I wondered how astonishing the changes in his life must have seemed, when the old order had just been erased, and no one was articulating any plan for the future.

When we arrived in Fort Liberte, Percy acted as the interpreter for Skye and Ken and Rod, as they cleaned out the arms room, inventoried the mountain of weapons, attempted to find accurate personnel records, and began separating the piles of trash and worn out gear from what was still serviceable.

As the house was established, and we began assembling the Operations/Communications/Intelligence Center, Percy was given a place in the front room, furthest from OPS, with Gonzo, to set up the cot and mosquito bar we provided for him. He was told, firmly but gently, that he would not enter the OPS area. This directive necessitated him walking around the house to get to the back porch, where we ended up taking most of our meals.

The second day in Fort Liberte, Percy met a man at the garrison, who sold him a dilapidated 100cc Honda motorcycle. Percy spent a good deal of his spare time for the next two days fooling with the cantankerous machine. It is a great credit to his mechanical aptitude that he finally coaxed the thing to life, and managed to have it parked in front of the garrison when the first, big Lavalas supported demonstration demanding the disarmament of the Haitian armed forces took place.

Percy had the doubtful privilege, described earlier, of being the translator at the initial civil/military get together at the *Biblioteque*. I admit to feeling a little divided and guilty on Percy's behalf. Not only was he a fumbling, nearly inept translator, with his rudimentary grasp of English, he was in the particularly unenviable position of being the soldier designated to tell superior officers, on our behalf, that their power had been essentially terminated. Moreover, he was obligated by his duties to translate civilian complaints to us about the members of his own profession. In the end, however, he handled the duty with aplomb.

"Sirzhint Goff," he approached me on Saturday, the 8th of October.

"Stan."

"Sirzhint Stan."

"Stan. Just Stan, Percy."

"Yes. . . Stan. . . I ha-a-a-af a request." He was very nervous about whatever this request was.

"What is it, Percy?"

"I would like. . . to know. . . if it would be permission. . ."

"You want permission?"

"Yes."

"Permission to do what?" It was like pulling teeth.

"I would like. . . to be free. . . tonight."

"Why, sure. What's up, Percy?"

"I have. . . a date."

"Ahhhhhh," I couldn't help smiling. "So you are already making friends here?"

Percy was smiling and looking around the room with a blush.

Mike happened through the room.

"Mike, Percy has a date tonight. We can get through the evening without him, can't we?"

Mike laughed about it, and started to rib Percy a little, asking if she were pretty, and was he going to be in before curfew, and so forth. We told him to enjoy his date, and not to rush home, but to make sure he announced himself to the radio watch when he came in.

Percy was in the field shower within ten minutes. An hour later, he left the house, dressed in civilian clothes, reeking of cologne. The shocks on the little motorcycle were compressed to the limit, when the six foot three inch suitor rode away .

Percy was privy to many conversations in which Mike and I, as well as the others, openly discussed the FAd'H's abuses, the likelihood of future prosecution for those abuses, our own revulsion at some of the activities, our distaste for Pierre Ulrick, and my conviction that the armed forces needed to be completely disbanded, with a new civil police force built from the ground up, starting with community watches. I also vented frequently about the economic stratification of Haiti, and about the necessity to redistribute the land, source of most wealth, if a long-term solution was to be found. The latter view met with consternation among my own team members, and there can be little doubt that Percy was uncomfortable with all of it.

Percy called me aside on the 11th of October, and asked if he might say something. He seemed very somber. "Of course," I assented, and opened myself to his soliloquy.

He told me that he wanted to speak to me not as a soldier but as a young Haitian. He said he loved his country, and hoped only the best for its future. He said that, as Americans, there was much about the culture of Haiti that we could not understand.

I agreed.

Percy told me that he was worried that, even though some of the soldiers looked upon us as a possible way out of hopelessness, everyone, including himself, were worried about Haiti, and about the Americans in Haiti, because our fates had now been tied together for as long as we were there.

I found some of his sensitivity and insight engaging, and I listened attentively to see where this would go.

He told me that progress in Haiti was not possible without an end to violence. He admitted that in the past the armed forces had committed excesses. It was important, however, that I realize that not all soldiers were murderers and thieves, and that some of them were genuine patriots, committed to a better future for their country.

In a few days, he said, when Aristide returned, hundreds, even thousands, of people would take to the street in celebration. Haitian people, he explained, were mostly children, understanding only the advantage or excitement of the moment, and easily led to excess.

Not knowing our experience in Gonaives, Percy told me that I could not conceive of the numbers that could appear in these street demonstrations. There would be, he said, an ocean of people, and they would have sticks and hoes and machetes.

There will be agitators among them, he claimed, and indeed we had experience culling agitators from crowds to prevent mayhem. They would be whipped into a frenzy by those who want to tear Haitian society apart, Percy stated, and they will go over us, all of us, Haitian and American military alike, killing us to the last man, before they loot the town and burn it.

Percy begged me to reinstitute the FAd'H prohibition on public demonstrations. I suddenly understood where the intelligence had been coming from, warning of disaster again and again, since Gonaives.

The 10th Mountain Division, and the senior commanders of every component, sympathetic to the military, almost to a man anti-Aristide, joined at the information hip to the CIA and thus the FRAPH, attracted to the well-heeled, French speaking, business owning elite, suspicious of all those rambunctious, uneducated "negroes" in the street, had been listening to the FAd'H, scribbling notes, and calling that Intelligence.

I thanked Percy for his concern, and explained that I could not see my way clear to implement prohibitions against demonstrations, and that I was unconditionally confident that we would prevent violence on the 15th or any other day.

The last statement was one of the few lies I ever deliberately told Haitians. I wasn't sure of anything in Haiti any more than I am sure of anything in Hot Springs, Arkansas, or Fayetteville, North Carolina.

Percy's utility as a translator had proven limited. He was simply all the FAd'H had to offer us, and he had been offered without solicitation. Even James, the fourteen year-old Spanish speaking kid we had hired as a factotum and translator, had more value as a translator, because he was fluent in Spanish, which most of us spoke. My gut feeling was, Percy really believed what he was telling me, and he told it to me out of fear and affection. My professional skepticism required that I look at the possibility that Percy was a "plant," attached to us for the dual purpose of reporting our plans and propagandizing us. I spoke to Mike about the conversation that afternoon, explaining my beliefs and my reservations. I made the case that we weren't using him much anyway, and that he was being daily humiliated by his status in the house as an outsider. I asked Mike if we shouldn't thank him for his services, wish him godspeed, and send him back to Ouanaminthe to be a FAd'H lieutenant again. Mike agreed, and Percy was driven back to Ouanaminthe the following day after a friendly thanks and goodbye.

I saw Percy again, two or three times, briefly, during motorcycle forays into Ouanaminthe. He had begun working out with the 352 guys on the dip bars and chin-up bars. His arms, shoulders and chest had thickened, and his face was filled out with good eating. He seemed content that he would remain in the army, as an officer, and that his future was no more in question than the future of any of us, even those who take for granted everything. He did not mention the inaccuracy of his prognostications. Neither did I. I was happy to see him, and to see him doing well. I believe the feeling was mutual. I hope he has learned as much as I have since then.

64: ALI

He checked his notes and referred to my reported comments from the incident that Special Forces was a racist organization. Had I meant that?

Here we were. We were on the subject of the "dirty little secret."

I told him I found a lot of racism in Special Forces, that I had seen racism in the Q-Course, that racism was openly tolerated on the teams and overlooked by the commanders. I didn't realize it at the time, but I may have been saving myself.

He wanted to know how I defined racism.

Disparate treatment of people by other people and institutions based on skin color. (It was a half-assed definition, but it sufficed for the moment.)

Do you consider members of your team racist?

Yes.

Do you know of any racist commanders in Special Forces?

Yes.

How come you haven't reported them?

Because being a racist is not against the law in the army. The threshold for proving racism is very high.

Don't you think, he asked, don't you think that sometimes you might be a little oversensitive?

No.

The night of the 10th of October, as promised by Adele, there was a demonstration. It was a small one by our standards, and we simply put two men on the garrison porch, two in the hummer to follow the crowd around (more for their protection than anything else), two men designated for the house, and two with a radio to wait at the garrison with the FAd'H Toyota pickup and respond to emergency calls for assistance if necessary. The follow vehicle had Ali and me, and we enjoyed the music and the dancing, which led us from the river to the market, through Sicar, back to Fort St. Joseph, picking up people as they went, and finally to the garrison, where the manifestation lingered.

Ali and I dismounted, and I sent Rod upstairs in the garrison, because the crowds always seem to upset him, and because I wanted someone to observe the dark streets behind the crowd for possible threats to the demonstrators. Gonzo was already on the porch.

The dancing became even wilder and more overtly sexual, if that is possible, with various couples springing forward of the crowd, and to the tune of *Desame Lame* (Disarm the Army) and other demonstration favorites, simulating and syncopating graphic scenes of wild copulation. Many of the men and boys, frenzied on music and Clarin (which flowed freely that night), kept the beat in a wide legged stance, pelvis forward and thrusting up, heads back, one hand firmly cupped over the genitals. Women and older girls tore off blouses or pulled them behind their necks, in response to the heat, and rocked their breasts to and fro, stamping a rhythm on the ground, with their arms stretched wide. The collective voice of the crowd alternated choruses with cues.

Gonzo later stated that the dancing was "turnin' me on."

The dancing was directed at the FAd'H like a challenge, the people now feeling safe to taunt them, and bursting to do so. Half the crowd was children. One fellow, Ti Jo from Ft. St. Joseph, became louder and louder in his taunting of the FAd'H, and spontaneously mooned them to the applause of his companions.

The three FAd'H on the porch stood stony faced, backs to the wall, while we Americans sat casually forward on the porch, warning individuals back where they tried to breach the imaginary line. This was, by now, almost routine. Our rifles were laid harmlessly across our laps, and we allowed ourselves to smile at some of the antics, while goodnaturedly repelling attempted breaches. Gonzo, on a couple of occasions, lost patience with the incursions at the building, and became stern and menacing.

"*Allez! Allez!*" he would shout. Go away! This command would become so customary for Gonzo throughout the mission, that it would become his nickname among some of the citizens of town. Allez allez (pronounced Allay allay).

Adele was at the back of the assembly when they were walking through town. She was walking hand in hand (as all Haitians do, male and female) with a young woman, dressed top to bottom in denim, with a red kerchief about the head. It would be rumored that this woman was, from time to time, Adele's lover. They swayed and bounced along, like everyone, until arriving at the garrison.

In front of the caserne, I lost sight of Adele. She had been tipping at Clarin through the evening, and breathing fumes when I had greeted her earlier in the street. Her mood had been high and hopeful. Then I saw her near the porch of the FAd'H headquarters, at the edge of the light provided by the Hummer we had parked with the headlights on.

She was not smiling. She no longer moved to the voices and whistles and drums. Standing stock still, her prominent eyes were hooded over and locked on the double front doors as if she were in a trance. In her cups, she smoldered, fired by some buried anger and pain. Adele looked dangerous.

Moments later, Ti Jo began spitting epithets, not musical, but like gunshots and lashes. The music suddenly began to fade, and suddenly we were facing a very surly mob, whipped alive by Ti Jo's insults, feeding off the smokey silence of Adele. Angry choruses began to explode with unsettled accusations and unexpressed misery.

Ali took the initiative and did exactly the right thing. He turned to the FAd'H members on the porch, targets of this dangerous animosity, and spat a loud order to go inside. He added a growling "right now!" to the injunction, both to speed them inside and to play to the delighted crowd's approval of his curtness.

It was a minor masterstroke. The edges of the assembly began to unravel, and within ten minutes the street was empty.

Ali Tehrani spoke five languages; English, French, Italian, German and Spanish. His father was an Iranian, a businessman living in San Diego, and his mother a German. Divorced while Ali was still young, Ali was placed under the tutelage of a stepfather from Luxembourg, where Ali's first language was German, and the stepfather sternly obliged Ali to learn French, English and Italian. Ali said that he hated it while he studied it, but that he was forever grateful that languages had been impressed upon him.

He mentioned all three of those adults, but never elaborated on them to the point where one might gain an impression of their personalities. Instead, he was most impressed with his maternal grandfather, who he said was in fantastic physical condition, a bodybuilder, even in his seventies.

Ali talked most about his friends in Germany, and without saying so, it was apparent that both he and his friends were financially well off, able to indulge in travel and parties. Ali's favorite nightlife pastime was Karaoke, and he fancied himself an Elvis impersonator. I had even seen old pictures of Ali, dressed like Elvis, before he had bulked up on protein and steel; a skinny kid going prematurely bald.

Ali lifted weights like an animal. He did a standard forty sets at any workout, always lifting heavy. He seemed possessed in a gym. His personality seemed to wave at you from far away. He became something that grunted and growled, almost angry. He was big, thick, inhumanly strong, and outrageously vain about it. He was perpetually dissatisfied with himself, and obsessed with the dense belt of fat that wrapped around his waist and defied his most strenuous efforts, his strictest diet of vitamins and tuna fish. Ali had no ass to speak of, either, and the whole effect was more dangerous than aesthetic, like a rogue bulldozer.

He was remarkably insecure about his physical prowess, given his incredible strength. He hated running because he was not fast. He hated Ultimate Frisbee, which the team had taken to playing occasionally for Physical Training (PT), because he could neither throw nor catch the disc. He hated basketball, football, soccer. He did not feel apathetic toward them, as I admit I am, but despised them as one would despise a threat, because Ali wanted to be all things to all people.

Swimming he could do, especially the distance strokes (side and breast), which he had learned and practiced to absurdity while in the Marine Corps, his prior service. He ended up in Force Reconnaissance, the elite of the Corps. After a break in service, he joined the Army, where he worked as an infantryman in the 82nd Airborne Division until he made Sergeant, whereupon he entered Special Forces.

In Special Forces, he had found a place where his language capabilities set him apart from and above the mass. His physical size, his linguistic skill, and his Marine background made him the stuff of minor local myths, and he embellished his uniqueness by being Muslim.

Ali wore a red, stained glass pendant on a chain around his neck, with a crescent moon and Persian script. He liked to let people see it. He liked saying he was a Muslim. He liked playing the minority, and denying his Christianity for the shock value. But no one ever saw him go to a mosque. He drank heavily at times. He was an inveterate womanizer, and had the reputation (which he enjoyed) of being a pervert. He really never displayed the slightest religious inclination in his day-to-day life. Mention of Muslims in America, however, especially the Nation of Islam, sent him into tizzy of petulant indignation about their religious impurity.

Ali was a bigot. I say this without speculation, having heard him repeatedly perform caricatures of a black dialect, refer to black soldiers as "Joe Boof." and do monkey imitations when he was complaining about the support signal detachments (mostly black soldiers). That said, when Ali went "downrange," to the Dominican Republic, he sought out the blackest women he could find. Everyone commented on how much Ali liked black skin on a girl. While Ali and the other team members were quick to point to this as evidence for Ali's contention that he was not a racist, I found it, in fact, to be an indispensable ingredient of his prejudice. It was the perfect marriage of his contempt for women and blacks, and I would see that contempt in action in his later approaches to Haitian women, girls really.

I do not know if Ali was indoctrinated into his beliefs as a child, as most people are, or whether he acquired them from adolescent peers, as many people do. The inclusive and focal motivation for Ali seemed, to me, to be a profound insecurity. That insecurity appeared to stand behind his every action, alongside an urgent craving for approval. Much of his behavior, however motivated, was reprehensible. Much of it, however, was endearing and valuable. His vulnerability, obvious to me, which he hated to show, forced me to like Ali in spite of how much I disapproved of many of his actions. His international formation and facility with language gave his considerable intelligence a breadth that exceeded his fellow team members.

His favorite film was *Kiss of the Spider Woman*, a remarkable choice in the homophobic world of Special Forces, though a good deal of his affinity for the film was attributable to his obsession with Sonia Bragga, the Brazilian actress whose nude photo he kept taped to the lid of his foot locker. He and I were the only two people I knew in Special Forces who approved of women who allowed the hair on their legs and axillae to grow. We were both fans of Albert Camus, which he read in the French, and we were the only two people on the team who even knew what the Holy Roman Empire was. Both of us relished thick, sweet coffee and street food, and Ali was always the first to understand how and why we trained as we did in Fort Bragg for the Reconnaissance mission. Ali was a superb marksman, and we shared an enthusiasm for long range shooting on the Known Distance range.

In some degree, I believe I was, if not a father figure to Ali on the team, at least an uncle. I wrote the first impact award he had ever received. I listened to him when he lectured me on communications, and incorporated his ideas into training. I chastised him when he went too far. I confronted his racism relentlessly, and he always repented willingly.

On one occasion, when we were discussing the possibility of the Haiti operation, back in Bragg, the subject of Haitians surfaced with regard to the camps in Guantanamo, where Ali had been detailed to work for a month. He had grown, in that concentration camp environment, with its built in oppression and frustration, to abhor Haitians in a special way, and concomitantly he had come to believe that he was now an expert on "them." During the conversation about the possible operation, in which I was not participating, he said something, I can't remember exactly what. Something about thousands of Haitian children who would die from AIDS. Ali's blurted response was, "Good."

I swallowed my reaction about that comment and stayed at my work on the laptop, but it ate at me the rest of the day. Every time Ali would approach me, I was a little cold, and the rest of the team noticed that I had withdrawn.

At the end of the day, I could keep it in no more, and I asked Ali to step out behind the building so we could talk. I told him what had disturbed me, and tried to explain why it bothered me. He was relieved that it was being aired and told me that he could tell something was bothering me. He apologized, sincerely I believe, and admitted that the camps had poisoned his perspective on Haitians, assuring me that he would behave professionally and humanely when the time came. He even made some of the standard protestations about how many times he had demonstrated his lack of prejudice. The point is, Ali was sensitive to how I regarded him, and he genuinely sought my counsel and approval.

Approval was what Special Forces gave him. That, and validation. He received it from his friends, for his strength, his intellect, and his often very amusing clowning. Belonging demands many things in Special Forces, and a shared sense of superiority is usually one of them. This came naturally to Ali Tehrani. Belonging also implies a fiercely blind national loyalty, and for an affluent European-Persian Muslim, this was the acid test. Ali would have made an excellent covert operator, because he would not question certain nationalistic axioms. The only weakness he would have had in that regard was sex.

He was preoccupied with his appearance to an extraordinary degree. His greatest preoccupation, besides his musculature, was his hair. Ali was naturally bald. He had a large cross-shaped scar over his occiput, where he had receive scalp reduction surgery. His hair was transplanted in the front. He kept it long, combed it straight back, glued it carefully down with something black in a spray can, and even occasionally painted the bare skin underneath. Once he put on a hat, the hat was not removed until he could enter a bathroom, and rearrange the rows of hair in private.

Ali was married to an immigrant from Costa Rica, a woman who sported large tattoos, rode a Harley-Davidson, and drove a truck for a living. There were rumors, which I never cared to confirm, that they had "an understanding." That money was an issue in the household I was sure, because I was the listener for Ali's constant expressions of anxiety about his finance. His apprehensions were familiar to me, having been in a money-obsessed and dysfunctional relationship with my former wife. I had also been in a relationship where adultery was the weapon of choice in the quest for anesthesia. Ali seldom talked about his wife, but frequently talked about his conquests. He kept pictures of "his" Dominican girls in the team room, all pretty, all black, and all incredibly young.

Ali liked girls between 16 and 18. In Haiti, he was paying close attention to them at 14. Younger girls are more worshipful. Poorer girls are more eager. Racially self-loathing girls are more grateful. I watched Ali romancing the girl who lived next to us in Haiti, an aging 20 year old with two children. She was middle-class by Fort Liberte standards, and she saw a chance to "put cream into the coffee" of her next offspring, a Haitian preoccupation with lightening the family, and the most obvious manifestation of Haitian internalization of post-colonial racism. She and Ali disappeared. The next night, she showed up again on the porch, asking for Ali. I fetched him. When he saw her, he treated her with a cruelty and disdain that was stunning. She was deflated and beaten. He went back into the house, apparently not thinking twice about it. When I asked him what that was about, he said, "There are hundreds of them."

I liked Ali, in spite of Ali, but sometimes it was hard. I especially liked him professionally. He was, without parallel, the greatest asset we had among the team members. He was also the biggest danger to the team, in his terrible, arrogant irresponsibility. His fluency in French, the best in the battalion, gave us an accuracy of assessment and a streamlined ability to organize with Haitians that no other team possessed. I believe that Mike and I had made all the correct connections on Operations, we had successfully determined where our focus should be, and Ali gave us an implementation capability that was matchless. Ali believed that, too. Then he got tired. Then he grew weary of Haitians. Then he was given the choice between the approval of his peers on the team or the command element.

Ali and I went everywhere together, in Haiti. For many Haitians, the Americans were Stan and Ali. There was no comparison to what we could get done, with the author of the operation and the ultimate translator present. Ali had come to the point where he could anticipate my responses and my goals, and frequently translated without having to ask me what to say. Occasionally, this went awry, and I would stop him and redirect. I did not know it at the time, but this was the object of a powerful resentment.

On one occasion, Ali had helped me translate some comments to German journalists. They had asked if the United States had any hand in the coup itself. I disclaimed that I was only giving my own opinion, but that people couldn't be blamed for assuming such, given the record of our past foreign policy in the region, and especially that of the CIA. I felt this was an essential admission for our own credibility, but Ali would later tell me that it greatly disturbed him.

I had grown accustomed to confiding in Ali at odd moments. We were strolling down the street one day in Fort Liberte, and Ali began interrogating me for war stories from Vietnam. I told him that had I been Vietnamese, I would have been VC (Viet Cong). I told him that Vietnam was an economic war for the big shots, and that on the ground it had degenerated into an obscene race war. He gave me a peculiar look, like something had closed inside him, and walked silently the rest of the way to the house.

Ali liked me and admired me, I think, in a peculiar way. With all our disconnects, we had some connections, too, very personal at that. But the combined force of peer pressure, resentment, and chauvinism would—as I have said—make Ali my personal Brutus, even as I had taken on that same role with the Task Force itself.

65: THE BULLY

On the 11th of October, we had received instructions via radio to prepare for a massive, nationwide demonstration. Fort Liberte was considered a high-risk area, because it was a political center, albeit one in
a comparatively small town. Our gut feeling was that the town had
celebrated hard the night before, and no demonstration could be any
tougher to handle.

There was not the least stir on the street to indicate either rest-
lessness or anticipation, but Mike and I considered it the prudent
course to prepare. We got the team together after everyone had eaten
breakfast, loaded up on coffee, and cleaned up.

In our meeting, Mike explained what our guidance was and
remarked to the guys on what an excellent job they had done the night
prior and throughout the mission so far.

When I had the floor, I covered a checklist for the day: Patrol locally, record status for the FAd'H, start asking about *attaches* and where
they lived so we could plot their residences on our overhead imagery,
draw water, stand up an aircraft reception for the FOB 33 people.
Sergeant Major Stone, the Operations officer, and an Intelligence
Officer would be coming out to check on our set-up and our progress.
Then I got down to business on planning for the expected/unexpected

demonstrations.

I told everyone, frankly, that I did not expect any trouble, but that in preparing for the worst, which we had been told by the Intelligence people (again and again) was eminent, we could debug our options for the arrival of Aristide, when we expected wild celebration and possible right-wing skullduggery.

The task organization, the weapons and equipment, the communications plan, and contingencies were discussed with a minimum of confusion or dissent. Everyone was accustomed to me planning, and no one felt inclined to question my experience or authority. Yet.

Mike and I had visited Fort Dauphin, the ruins of the French fortress constructed on the north-jutting peninsula in Fort Liberte Bay, the day prior. We were both impressed with its beauty and historical value, and equally impressed with the ugliness of a boxy, yellow, concrete and cinder block building with a tin roof, that had been constructed atop the fort by the FAd'H. We had agreed that a civic action project early on, one that cost nothing, was labor intensive, and could involve us working with the local population, was to tear down that eyesore. That it was a FAd'H structure made it a doubly desirable objective, because of the symbolic significance.

We returned to the house excited about our project. We decided to bring it up in a meeting that evening, prior to our deployment for the impending mob scenes that intelligence seemed so concerned about. Meanwhile, we wanted to start the serious assessment of the water system.

We had asked Gonzo to start analyzing the water distribution system for the city, several days before, and where he had seemed enthusiastic at first, he had turned unaccountably recalcitrant about civic action in general. We chose Gonzo, because water sources were more or less in the bailiwick of the medic, and because he was knowledgeable about pumps, wells and hydrodynamics. He had been out to the public pump, which had been constructed by an Agency for International Development project several years earlier at the entrance to Sicar on the main road. The repair of the pump had been followed by another breakdown, followed by another repair, and another breakdown. Gonzo had been scrounging parts, each time, and each time, incorrect use or overuse caused another malfunction. What seemed to bother Gonzo was not so much the cyclic breakdown of the pump, but the lack of demonstrative gratitude by the people.

Gonzo, it needs to be said, had been cranky from the first time I met him. He was 38, and seemed to rankle at younger people (me not being one of them) being in charge. He had come into Special Forces as a line medic, with no infantry experience, yet during training, prior to deployment to Haiti, Gonzo was always the most bull headed about arguing extraneous tactical details, and missing the main point of the training.

Eventually, I came to understand that Gonzo was one of a large number of people who believed that infantry doctrine was some simple-minded process of common sense, refined by a futile game of what-if. This is a common belief among non-infantry people in the military, and one that has consequences. Infantry doctrine is not only complicated, but its application to real situations is an art that requires long practice to intuit. Like skiing, the natural "common sense" reaction to lean back as one loses one's balance, is often exactly the opposite of what actually stabilizes. There is nothing natural about close, armed combat, and natural responses can be fatal. That is the reason for an emphasis on combat drills. Drills, performed repeatedly, can imprint reflexive actions contrary to nature. I used drills extensively, and Gonzo always wanted to assume an adversarial attitude about each iteration of those drills.

Gonzo had a romantic problem, as well, of which I had not seen the genesis. Mike had. He explained that Gonzo, since meeting his present girlfriend, had changed—become more mercurial, more morose, less focused. Gonzo had sent his wife and children away to Texas only a couple of months prior to the Haiti deployment, and had moved his girlfriend into the house a few days later. This attachment manifested itself in unusual surliness when our mail was mis-forwarded for the first month in Haiti, leaving us out of contact with our loved ones.

What we had directed him to do was find the source of the water, the master pump, the reservoir, and the lines for the city water, which was pumped into the cisterns built adjacent to houses throughout the city. The system had not functioned since shortly after the coup. The diesel required to fire it was embargoed, as were replacement parts. He was also to locate each well pump, like the one at Sicar, so we could plot them on our maps and track repairs, if and when we received resources to do anything. Gonzo had located one pump at the hospital, which was reserved for Hospital use only, the one at Sicar, and one that was next to the central plaza, across from the church, near Adele's house, at the north of town.

Gonzo headed out that day to the Sicar pump, to fix it yet again, and Mike and I decided to check the water situation ourselves, because both of us had grown suspicious of Gonzo's reliability. We secured the city map, with Gonzo's penciled in notations, and took the Hummer out to see each one. That was the day we discovered two things. One was that Fort Liberte had an unnecessarily complicated and disjointed systems of valves and pipes for the sequential rationing of water to five different areas of the city. Two was that Gonzo had begun to lie.

Two of the pumps he had plotted did not exist. He had just penciled them onto the map in lieu of looking. Mike and I found two other pumps that had not been plotted, one in Fort St. Joseph, and one beyond Sicar, near the mangrove South of town, which functioned but drew water so brackish it was undrinkable. The latter was used only for wash water, and was at the end of a trail beginning behind the coffin maker's house.

I came back from the pump reconnaissance in a foul mood. My people were lying to me. The thing I needed most from them was a mission focus, and it was becoming increasingly difficult to deny that there was no genuine fidelity to the mission or to Mike and me. Nothing could have distressed me more. We were looking at six months on the ground, and the guys were already losing the fix. I deeply resented it when one of the men deliberately committed an infraction that forced me to become the heavy.

When I got back to the house, my wrath had been feeding on itself, and there was no worse time to present me with unwelcome news. Five people I recognized as residents of Fort Saint Joseph, what we called the "Fishing Village," were standing with Rod on the front porch looking frightened and angry. Rod looked trapped, which was the tip off that something real was happening.

The villagers stated that one of our initial arrestees, a tough, aggressive, young attache, named Smith Edouard, had been released from confinement. He had appeared on the streets of Fort Saint Joseph the night before, inebriated and brandishing a pistol, telling everyone he could corner that he was going to commit random murders in their village on the night that the communist, Aristide, returned to Haiti.

"*Gen temwan?*" I asked. Are there witnesses.

"*Tut moun,*" they replied, excitedly. Everyone.

I looked at Mike.

"Take Rod and check it out," he said.

Rod, all the plaintiffs, and I loaded on the hummer and tore down to the village, me driving. A wire was shorting in my head, and the sparks of homicide were bursting behind my eyes. Goddamn Gonzo! Goddamn this team! Goddamn this mission! Goddamn Smith Edouard!

Rod wanted to take statements, gather evidence, do the deal by the book. Fuck that.

Is this what he did?

Yes.

Everyone who saw him doing it, raise your hands.

Dozens of arms shot up.

Who knows where he lives?

Quiet settled over the agitated throng. Fear is so durable.

Give me two people who can point out the house, and I will drop them off before I pick him up.

Suddenly ten people wanted to climb onto the Hummer at once.

"Goddamnit! *Deux! Deux! Pas anko!*" Everyone was pissing me off.

We sorted it out. Off we went. We crossed the causeway, and hung a left, into the rabbit warren of houses between the local boat-maker and Calixte's hotel.

"*Ici mem,*" they said, as we passed it.

"*Le maison blanc?*"

"*Oui.*"

We dropped them off. They immediately began engaging curiosity seekers in animated conversation.

When Rod and I burst into the house, middle-class by Haitian standards, dirt poor by ours, I had that same ambiguous shame I felt when I violated all the homes of "bad guys." Poor people oppressing poor people, and here comes the rich ruffian to sort things out. Edouard's wife was cutting up vegetables, and she didn't even stop when we burst into her home. It was like she was expecting us. She looked up from her work, and answered us quietly.

Does Smith Edouard live here?

Yes.

Are you his wife?

Yes.

Does he have a weapon?

I don't know.

Where is he?

I don't know.

We lifted the thin mattress, opened the tiny cupboards, rummaged through the trunks, while we interrogated.

Her knife had ceased moving. Her chin barely quivered as the tears flowed silently over her cheeks and dripped off her chin.

"Let's go, Rod," I said, fearful that I would lose the edge of my anger here.

"*Regret,*" I told her, as we left. Sorry.

Our guides directed us to a tailor's shop two blocks away, jabbing their fingers and chattering excitedly. Outside the shop were two FAd'H soldiers, relaxing in the shade of the building, talking with an assembly of six or seven civilians, all well dressed and friendly with the soldiers.

I instructed Rod to cover the front door of the tailor shop, while I went around the back. If there were an entry to be made, I wanted to go in alone, so we didn't shoot each other. I circled the building with my pistol in a two handed shooting grip, trained on the ground in front me, and spotted a comparatively husky young man coming out the back door. I snapped up the pistol and told him to raise his hands. He did so immediately, and began talking rapidly.

"*Pa pale!*" Shut up.

Turn around. He did.

Don't move. He didn't.

In the cursory search for concealed weapons, I pulled a slip of paper from his shirt pocket. I backed away to read it. He was unarmed.

It was the release form given him at the detention facility. The name on it was Smith Edouard. I had him.

I hollered for Rod, who came running.

"It's him. He ain't got a gun."

Move, I told him. He hesitated, so I moved up behind him and slapped him in the back of the head.

"*Marche,* motherfucker!" I slapped him again. "*Marche!*"

Rage was beginning to cascade in me.

I pushed him roughly as we advanced to the Hummer. When he was almost there, as the stunned assembly of soldiers and civilians looked on, I thrust him into the back of the hummer, and caught his wrist in a lock as he dropped his hands to break his fall. I holstered and flex cuffed him, then bounced him off the back of the hummer again. There was a loud, guttural voice possessing me, cursing blindly in English, as he fell to the ground, and I kicked him in the thighs and buttocks. Far, far back in my consciousness, a voice was warning me not to kick higher, or my angry blows would kill him.

"Stan! Stan! Stan!" Rod was calling me from a distance. I looked up, and he was standing right next to me. "Take it easy, man! We can't kill him." Rod was frightened.

The onlookers were frightened.

The wife had been frightened.

Smith Edouard was frightened.

I had become a frightening guy.

Some time later, I, too, would be frightened . . . at what I'd become.

Rod and I loaded him roughly into the back of the Hummer, hands cuffed behind him, with his face in the dusty floor, and his feet sticking up over the edge of the bed. He didn't even attempt to shift his position for comfort, he was that terrified. He certainly didn't look like the intimidating apparition described by the villagers earlier.

I wheeled the hummer to Fort Saint Joseph. On the way, Rod told me frankly that he worried when I got that emotional.

"Don't worry, buddy," I reassured him, after a deep drag on the cigarette I just lit. "I'm not going to kill anyone." I could see Rod relax. I was talking normally, again. "Those were just dramatics," I lied.

The group in the street at Fort Saint Joseph peered into the Hummer and confirmed with nods that he was the one. I returned to the team house, with Smith Edouard still in his awkward position and feeling every pothole on his face.

At the team house, I secured Ali and released a thankful Rod. Ali and I headed to the scrub thickets at the end of the road in the salt marsh east of town. I pulled the Hummer into the thicket, out of sight of everything and everyone. I briefed Ali.

I walked off into the thicket.

Ali lifted Smith Edouard bodily out of the bed of the hummer, and began urgently telling him to give up the locations of all the weapons in town, because his crazy operations chief was contemplating murder. He'll tie rocks to you and sink you in the ocean, he told the now tearful Smith Edouard. Edouard denied knowing the locations. He denied having been in the village the night before. He denied being an *attache*. He denied any ill will towards Aristide. I showed up, emerging like a phantom from the scrub.

Smith Edouard began crying audibly, begging us not to kill him. My rage was gone.

"Tell him to mind his own business from now on, and pass the word on that we won't take a bunch of bullshit from his *macoute* buddies," I told Ali. I had had enough. Now I had begun to empathize with Smith Edouard. Guilt was rising like mercury in my throat.

We maintained the stern demeanor, even as we cut off his cuffs and released him. A hundred yards up the road, someone had been waiting for him on a bicycle. They rode off together.

Forty-five minutes later, seven young men appeared on our front porch, dressed like they were heading down to catch the Sunday sermon. They even had ties on.

We are a delegation, and we desire to speak with the American soldiers.

Come in, we told them. There was handshaking all around. Ali interpreted. Mike and I listened and responded. Some of the faces looked strangely familiar.

I asked them if they would write a list of their names down on a paper for me, just for our records—we see so many people. As they were writing, I remembered. They were the "soccer team." They were the guys we arrested, with Smith Edouard, and with Pascal Blaise, on our first day in Fort Liberte.

They told us they were patriots, good Haitians, who were glad the Americans were there, pro-American in fact. They were vitally interested in the future of Haiti, because they were the town's "intellectuals". We heard stories of Aristide burning American flags, making anti-American statements, allowing mobs to pillage the cities. Nonetheless, they explained, they themselves had come to accept that Aristide was the elected leader of Haiti, and they were sincere supporters of the democratic process. Because they did not support Aristide in the last election, they explained patiently, some of the rabble in town had taken to slandering them, threatening them, trying to get them into trouble with the Americans. They had heard of an unfortunate incident earlier that day with a friend. They were anxious to avoid any misunderstandings.

They were frightened. This fear thing had become really contagious.

Mike let me have the floor.

I was a picture of perfect calm, almost gentle.

Political differences are a fact of life, I explained. Misunderstandings are, too. As Americans, we are determined to stay out of Haitian politics as much as we can. But we are soldiers, operating under orders, and we have been given the responsibility to ensure an orderly, peaceful return of the legitimately elected president of Haiti, Father Aristide. My little piece of that responsibility is Fort Liberte Commune. If the peace breaks down in Fort Liberte, I am held accountable by my officers, as is Captain Gallante here. Until today, everything was very calm. People come and go again in Fort Liberte. The market is open and busy again. The streets are being cleaned. The children play without cares. People are no longer afraid at night. Now it seems that you all are afraid. This is not our desire. Before we came, I am told, the people were hungry and they didn't sleep well because of fear. Now they are only hungry. It is small progress, but it is progress, and we will not step backward. We will not take a single step backward. You need not be afraid. We bear you no ill will. So long as people behave in a civil way, we have not the slightest intention of interfering in anyone's lives. But remember. We will not fail to execute our orders. We will not permit anyone, under any circumstances, to disrupt the peace. The result of our failure would be our withdrawal, and as you can all see, the FAd'H has been rendered powerless. I shudder to think what might happen, how many old wounds might be opened, if we left too soon. I certainly hope I can count on the cooperation of this delegation of intellectuals toward that end.

In the delivery, of course, I would state a phrase, there would be a pause, Ali would translate it into perfect French, then the process would begin again. I have said before, though slow, this kind of delivery can be very dramatic. It was, in fact, the most elegant and understated threat I have ever communicated.

We received assurances of that cooperation, exchanged a stiffly formal goodbye, and watched them saunter down the street, seeming beaten.

Mike and Ali became merry and boisterous, congratulating me and themselves on having accomplished something far beyond the events of the day, for everyone was sure that we would experience no more difficulty with the former strongmen of Fort Liberte. In fact, that prognostication turned out to be accurate. We won something. . . against the old guard, for the general population.

I told Mike I was going to take a walk. He asked me what was the matter. I wasn't sharing in the festive moment. Nothing, I told him. Just need a break.

At the place where the Hummer tracks turned around in the scrub thicket at the salt marsh, I sat alone and smoked.

11 Oct

Dear Sherry,

> *Quick one. On radio watch. Tough day. Caught a bad guy today. Scared his wife to tears. Beat his ass. He was threatening to kill people. Deserved it, I guess. Made him think I was going to kill him. He cried too. Cronies came by, bargaining for peace. All in all, it was an effective action. I was right. I feel like there's something dead in me. Nothing's easy, clearcut. I don't want to hurt anyone. I really really really need someone to tell me that I'm not like him, not like Smith Edouard, not a bully.*

I love you. Stan.

On the 11th of October, I frightened a lot of people. I was a real tough guy. I felt really tough. And I really wanted to just go home.

66: ELECTRICITY AND RAGE

Mike was just delighted with everything those days. We were expanding our influence. The intelligence was flowing like water over a precipice. The town was relatively calm. We were beginning to click on day to day operations. When the boys got tired and stubborn, I nipped at their heels. He was in the catbird seat, so to speak, because all he had to do was bless a decision here and there and participate in operations.

What Mike did not see, partly because he wanted to believe it was gone, was my near explosive emotional state. The only thing really that attenuated my affect was the chronic fatigue. The other storm he failed to recognize on the horizon was the deep rift that was developing between the men and me.

Kyle had already written me off for my lefty political pronouncements as non-credible. He was as actively a doctrinaire conservative as I was a developing mid-life Red. In past detachment regimes, he had been able to trade heavily on his construction skills and hide his faulty understanding of infantry doctrine behind the mutual ignorance of his team sergeants. He had begun resenting me early for my insistence on "back to soldiery basics" first, and special skills afterward. His early attempts at Fort Bragg to test me with loud belligerence had met with

347

my total intransigence. He had the disease of specialforcitis bad; arrogance, a belief in one's innate right to special privilege, vanity, conformity to special operations trends (yes, there are fashions), the belief that operations should look good and feel like a party, and the compulsion to avoid his own decisions while he second guessed his supervisors'.

Ali was chafing at my rigor in controlling his translation, and positively distressed by my willingness to tell reporters, Haitians, and NGO representatives that US foreign policy had been, in my own experience, designed to enrich corporations and perpetuate the regimes of brutal US sycophants. I felt that being frank was helpful to our credibility, especially in a country that had been on the shitty end of a lot of US foreign policy decisions. Ali felt that it was not only a security violation (as if Haitians didn't know that US Marines once occupied the country and massacred its residents), but that it constituted disloyalty.

Rod wanted me to quit dismissing the intelligence reports that Lavalas was about to engage in a massive, armed, anti-colonial struggle against us, even given the fact that Lavalas had been, throughout the operation, the lynch pin of our success. He wanted to pursue a more "balanced" approach, outlined earlier. I was on some kind of indecipherable crusade, in his mind (for he was the originator of the Batman appellation), and I was not behaving consistently with the guidance "between the lines" of our directives. To give Rod credit, he was right. He knew, and I knew, that what the Task Force was trying to do was participate in the wholesale betrayal of Haiti (Rod would have used a different word than betrayal). I was simply executing our directives within the letter of the law (in most cases), while attempting to advance the public declarations of our government that we were in Haiti to restore democracy. Slippery word. . . democracy.

Gonzo was in a permanent state of petulant rebellion, but that was how he'd been since I'd met him. Macho man exterior, passive aggressive manipulative interior. He worked his ass off, especially on projects that allowed him to exercise his considerable mechanical skills, projects that allowed him as little contact as possible with more than one Haitian at a time. His growing distaste for Haitians was barely concealed. Even James, who dogged Gonzo's footsteps, who worshipped Gonzo and had taken his last name, and for whom Gonzo seemed to feel a genuine affection, was startled more and more frequently with sudden eruptions of wrath from Gonzo. Gonzo's general rebellion against any control was beginning to focus on the most frequent proprietor of that control. . . me.

Skye was just trying to assimilate. He bunked with Kyle. Kyle was an incessant purveyor of discontent. There's one in every team, every squad, every platoon in the army. It rubbed off on Skye, because that discontent is what he was allowed to participate in. It was how he got himself included.

I made it easy for them. As the mission progressed, and as things got more tedious, I became a bigger and bigger asshole. It was my job.

The single exception to this trend of resentment I was attracting was Gator. Gator was being an ideal soldier. Mike and I had both commented on it. He concentrated his energy on doing the best job possible, stayed to HIS job instead of trying to do everyone else's and the supervisors', followed instructions promptly and without complaint, and never had to be checked up on. He was thoughtful, analytical, and systematic. He always offered to lend a hand with everything. His racism was no worse than the rest of them. . . in fact, it was probably less poisonous and cunning.

What a shame it was him at whom I exploded.

On the 13th of October, three gigantic tanker trucks full of diesel fuel, some thirty thousand gallons worth, were disgorged from landing craft at the western closure of Fort Liberte Bay. While they rumbled over the disrepair that was the road for almost two hours, General Potter dropped in via helicopter. The house was abuzz with all the activity.

Mike was anxious to display our operational prowess to the Special Operations commander. Gonzo was curious to see if the makeshift repairs he had made on the electric generator near the river worked. The town knew something was happening, and Aristide was due in two days.

We picked up Potter at the helipad in Fort Dauphin amid a cheering crowd, which we now took for granted. Potter's entourage and bodyguards looked somewhat silly with their alert crouches and rapidly shifting eyes, while Mike and I waded casually through the bodies, mostly children, with our weapons slung. Kids would attach and detach themselves from our passing fingers as we escorted our guests to the Hummer. The crowd parted without a cue as we put the vehicle into gear, and we hardly thought as we called matter-of-factly to the press of little ones, *"Atansyon, anfan!"*

Mike was well practiced in his presentation and his guided tour around the town. General Potter was properly attentive and impressed. He was about to retire, and it was easy to see that he was just going through the motions. This mission was getting to him too.

Mike took his opportunity to conduct an end run, and told the General that we still had no word on our two tardy arrivals; Pedro and Dave. This was an issue Schroer had met with perfect disinterest.

The General left. The trucks arrived. What ensued was a massive mobilization of every 55 gallon drum in the entire area, because this delivery, part of a PR campaign called Operation Lightswitch, had not been coordinated.

Adele sent the word out over the grapevine that we needed the drums, and within two hours we were draining the trucks into so many 55 gallon drums that they filled the courtyard at the FAd'H headquarters and surrounded our house. We didn't even approach emptying the three trucks.

The truck crews were kept in body armor and helmets to do the entire job, which we objected to strenuously. It was inhumane to force soldiers out of danger to work in this heat with all that crap. We were told that orders were orders, and uniformity was the highest priority of the mission. Every time we had a chance, we brought the crews inside the house, dropped their gear, and offered them water and soda.

At the end of the day we were exhausted.

I was exhausted.

Gonzo headed to the generator with a drum full of diesel and his Haitian helpmate, a suspected FRAPH sympathizer who nonetheless was the only person in town who had displayed any knowledge of diesel generators.

I left the house at dusk and strolled up to the plaza, where I sat quietly for about half an hour in the dark. Influential people from around town had converged on the house to explain how important it was that we give them a drum of diesel. We didn't seem to be able to overcome the problem of forced abundance. They were sending us tons of food, when we couldn't give food away, bottled water when we couldn't give that away, transistor radios (100) so we could give them away then face the resentment of those who received no radio for weeks to come. . . now diesel. This was infrastructure. Now we would have the lights turned on, for a while, until someone changed his mind, or until we left, or until we were told the embargo was gone and they were on their own. . . and it meant we would have to protect this gain, this electricity, or face a massive loss of morale. In the park, I tried to think of ways we could help Adele find revenues to keep the electricity going after the free diesel was cut off. So much for avoiding the culture of dependency.

I was standing at the corner two houses away from ours, listening to quiet voices in the street that I couldn't understand, when there was a blue flicker overhead. Then another. Then the pale azure light silently covered the main street from beginning to end. Little clots of people were caught in the unexpected light, and a collective sigh went up.

"Lumiye!"

The spirit of joy this little bit of electricity engendered was infectious. I even caught it. . . against my own apprehensions. Gonzo came down the street in the twisted Toyota pickup with his sidekick half an hour later, and I was still standing there. I stopped him and shook his hand for a job well done.

In the house, Gonzo and Gator began the tricky business of deciphering the wiring in order to bring the electricity from the street into our team house. By kerosene lamp and flashlight, they futzed and pottered from one place to the next, puzzling and discovering, until Gator said it.

"Something over here has been nigger-rigged." He chuckled. "Guess I should be careful about saying that here, huh?"

I wasn't even sure I had heard it. Mike confirmed it for me. I heard Mike say, "Yeah, you should be careful. You never know who you might offend."

"Like me!" I announced, bursting into the room.

I have no idea where the fury came from. But come it did. Unbidden. Unharnessed. Of course, I was offended. But my reaction was so out of proportion to the offense that I knew some hidden fuse had just finished burning. Smith Edouard got his, why shouldn't they get theirs?

I can't remember what I said. I shouted. I cursed. I kicked things over. I cornered Gator, who was pale and startled and saying, "Whoa, whoa, Stan, Stan, I'm sorry, I'm sorry!" Mike leapt between us. Someone extinguished the flame on a lamp I had broken. Mike corralled me and aimed me into another room, while I continued to rant about how I hated the army, I hated Special Forces, I hated the bigotry and ignorance I encountered at every turn, et cetera. It took ten minutes or more just to calm me down. I was guilty of insubordination at least twenty times in refusing to follow Mikes's directives, and disrepect another twenty for saying things like, "Fuck that, Mike!"

When I did calm down, I knew that something had changed irrevocably in my relationship to the men. I had taken leave of my comportment in a major way, and had abdicated much of my authority in those few moments. I was so shaken by the magnitude of my response that Skye was emboldened to lecture me out of the contagious noise I had started.

The mistake was not confronting the comment. The mistake, irrevocable, was my total loss of self-control. It was a full-blown tantrum.

Later I apologized to Mike, then to all the guys. None of them even looked up to acknowledge me. My stand had been correct, but my response had made me crazy. I am sure that talk began that very evening among the team members about whether I was reliable any longer. Plenty of people snap, team sergeants included, but not with the history I had developed around that mission.

Mike told me to forget about it and drive on. I knew better.

I was now absolutely alone.

We heard something out in the street. Far away. Drums. The rhythm of bare feet. Signing. Whistles. It was a demonstration.

"Saddle up," I told them. There was only a tiny moment of hesitation by every single one of them, but it was enough for me to understand.

67 : The Belladere Incident

We were talking to army spooks right before we heard about the incident. A secret army unit that does "tradecraft", official jargon for spying, had two members stop by the team house. I still can not say their names or their business, or I would court a great deal of official trouble.

The spooks left, and we were checking radio traffic. Mike was going into another uproar, because 370 was giving us a ration of shit for demanding return of our grill. 354 had packed a barbecue grill, which would have been very handy, and someone in 370 had expropriated it. When Mike tried to ascertain its whereabouts, he received a lecture on uniformity again. There was also a cryptic message about an "incident" at Belladere. Danny McComas' team.

Later that day, Captain White dropped by in a Hummer. He gave us the details.

356 had taken their garrison and turned it into a fiefdom. They were ruling over the mountain town of Belladere in a heavy-handed way, and they had essentially imprisoned the FAd'H, for reasons that were unclear. They were putting the troops through a modified form

of basic training. At night they had them locked into a consolidated sleeping quarter.

The 356 Warrant Officer had recently returned from a stint at the Army's Survival Evasion Resistance and Escape School at Camp Mackall, and he apparently wanted to use some of the more sadistic techniques he had been subjected to there on the FAd'H "trainees". Danny was an unrepentant racist. Bailey, his intel sergeant, was still flashing back on Somalia and waiting for death at the hands of an African. All of them had been drinking since they arrived in Ouanaminthe, though I have no way of knowing whether they were drinking that night. Certainly what happened had all the earmarks of alcohol involvement.

Danny had gone into some kind of rage over an undone detail—like sweeping the steps or trimming the grass—and went to wake the FAd'H by screaming unintelligibly at them through the locked doors of their quarters...in English. The Warrant Officer caught the contagion of insanity from Danny and woke them up "SERE –style" by throwing a hand grenade simulator (a very loud and alarming explosive) outside the domicile. Bailey apparently joined in the melee, adding his voice in English to the shouted demands to come out. The Haitians, of course, were terrified and had no intention of coming out. Danny then told Bailey—who had displayed signs of irrational fear and hatred of Haitians from the beginning of the missions—to "shoot off the lock," a weird command, given that the lock was inside the room. Bailey then began discharging his M-16 through the wooden door, thereby firing blindly into a room full of unarmed, undressed people.

Captain White and the rest of the personnel who had been asleep upstairs from the commotion were now rolling off their cots onto the floors, scrabbling for their weapons, terrified themselves, and thoroughly convinced that total war had broken out. Many of the personnel were inexperienced Psyopers. They came dashing out of their quarters, and were crouching at random all over the caserne with no clue what to do.

Pleading for their lives, the Haitian soldiers, took advantage of a pause in the fire from Bailey to tear open the door and run in a wild panic in every direction. Most were in their undershorts.

One unfortunate soul burst out of the caserne walls and went running across an open field, where he was "perceived as a threat" by a young sergeant from Psyops, who opened fire. Others then joined in, and the running man was shot eight times as he ran away unarmed in his underwear. He would survive, but be permanently and multiply disabled.

The investigation was highly contained. The Warrant Officer, who had failed two evaluations in a row at Fort Bragg, and was on his way out anyway, was eventually relieved as the team's sacrifice. Danny and Bailey and Parker the trigger-happy Psyoper were all absolved and never missed a day of duty.

This was the kind of incident that causes reliefs of command way up, and the kind that terrified Schroer. So Schroer contained the whole incident, and even reports weeks later of an attempted rape by one of the 356 team members, to keep the spotlight off himself. At the same time, Schroer continued to bear down on us for "uniform violations," and would eventually sign relief orders for both Mike and me.

It was the day before the anticipated return of Father Jean-Bertrand Aristide.

That afternoon, we had coordinated for a show of force, a weapons demonstration off the point of Fort Dauphin. We wanted to impress everyone, especially any anti-Aristide forces who might be considering our small size and isolation, with why they needed to behave. The grenade attack days earlier in Port-au-Prince, by FRAPHists against a crowd of Aristide supporters, were still in my mind. We announced the weapons demo to 310 from Cap Haitien, and three officers from 310 came out to watch.

Rod fired a Light Antitank Weapon (LAW) at the FAd'H building perched on the fort, which we were planning to tear down anyway. Amazingly, he missed it—write that Tom Clancy!—and the round exploded harmlessly in the bay. Tony Marcelli, the Reuters freelancer and businessman from Cap Haitien had dropped by with his wife. She asked Rod if she could have the expended tube as a souvenir. Rod said fine.

We then fired several belts of 5.56 ammunition through the Squad Automatic Weapons into the bay. It was quite a noisy show, and it attracted plenty of attention. The guys from 310 looked on and traded bullshit with Mike while we fired.

That night we had plenty of rowdy, drunken demonstrations all over. We zipped around town and responded. By 11:00 PM, the whole ville was exhausted and abed. No incidents.

68: TITID RETURNS

The president returned on October 15th. We had passed out 100 transistor radios to give folks the opportunity to hear his return speech. The exhaustion of the previous two-days celebration had taken its toll, and people were moving about as if they were walking on eggs.

When he made his speech, he promised that he would attempt to move his people from misery to poverty.

We sent all members of the FAd'H home. No reason to tempt fate.

It was the day we had designed all our activities around, and it was underwhelming. Pure anticlimax.

Mike and I counted this a success.

69: Big Boy Rules

On the 16th, we received word of some problems at Terrier Rouge, and 310 sent people to retrieve Gator. We were now seven.

On the 17th, my wedding anniversary, I became very homesick. I was also deeply troubled by the aftermath of the incident with Gator the night I lost my composure. The guys were totally exhausted. The Fort Liberte market was beginning to bustle. There was more activity and normalcy in the street. The FAd'H had returned, not to duty, but to hang out in the garrison and play dominoes across the street in the shade of an acacia. It seemed the mission, at least this phase, was accomplished.

That night I got stinking drunk and swam naked below Fort Dauphin. It constituted a public change of team drinking policy that I would take advantage of time and time again. It would also provide the rationale to eject me from Haiti. It was my wedding anniversary, I told everyone, and we were going to begin playing by "big boy rules." Do your job, drink when it's appropriate, and what happens on the team, stays on the team.

"Let's go," I told every man who was not on duty. Rod was on the radio and Mike wanted to stay behind. I rounded up Kyle, Skye, Ali, and Gonzo. We piled into the Hummer with the bad springs like teenage boys out for a cruise in the convertible. At the little store in Fort Saint Joseph, the fishing village across the causeway from Fort Liberte that sat directly between town and the fallen Fort Dauphin, we bought ten one-liter bottles of Presidente, the rich, Germanic lager brewed and bottled in the Dominican Republic.

The beer had been on ice, and we reminded the proprietress of the store to chill some more. I bought a fresh pack of *Comme il Faut Vert* cigarettes.

The boys began to get giddy as they realized we were headed out to Fort Dauphin for a deliberate toot. For that moment I had been reprieved from my despotism, my atypical politics, my Lavalas bias, my monstrous temper, and all the petty resentments I had authored in each individual. In laying aside General Order One's prohibition against alcohol, I had laid aside my authority for the moment, and I was not a bad guy after all. Their relief at this transitory abdication was exceeded only by my own.

Many North Americans, accustomed as they are to the sweet, bland, lawn-mowing beer available in our ubiquitous corporate food outlets, would not immediately appreciate a Presidente. It is stouter than the pallid brews we sell in cans, richer and a shade more bitter. There is a hint of skunk in the aftertaste.

We, however, were seasoned drunks. . . Ali having grown up in and around Germany, Kyle having served there, all of them already familiar with the Dominican brew, and me having sampled untold gallons of manifold meads in five continents. Each man there took his first deep swallow of the ice cold lager in the same sensual trance, each subjective universe squeezed into a tongue and a throat in cool communion with this wet and bitter ambrosia. No one spoke for a moment as the bottles were set back onto the fenders of the Hummer. Each of us was savoring that satisfied fragile flush that starts behind the eyes and slowly explodes through every cell.

Seizing the freedom that contempt for death brings, I lit a cigarette, drew deeply on it, and took another swallow. The late afternoon breeze, the rippling water, even the gravel underfoot, could not have been more immediate and enchanting.

We smiled at one another again, guilelessly.

Alcohol has always seduced me.

After my first bottle of beer, Ali and I drove back and picked up Adele. She gladly accepted our offer to share a bottle, and we picked up four more bottles on the way back.

By the second bottle around, we were planning a windsurfers' vacation hideaway at Fort Liberte, Haiti, and discussing what kind of music should be featured at the hotels in the evenings. I was building schools that positively popped with children and books. Gonzo was converting the entire energy economy to propane. Kyle was constructing a marina. Ali was becoming an entrepreneur in the local sex trade. Skye was arranging tours on horseback into the mountains near Acul Samedi.

By the third bottle, we were talking cat-shit about Schroer and his stupidity, while we soundly clapped ourselves on the back for being the best goddamn detachment in 3rd Special Forces. We were reviewing the adventures in Gonaives, every night tactical free fall jump we had completed together, the day we arrested ten people in ten minutes upon entering Fort Liberte.

By the fourth, I was getting dizzy. Ali had become my translator again, as I told Adele not to trust Americans and to organize now against the *macoutes* who would come back. With this, Ali became sullen. Skye had remained talkative to the point of irritation, forcing Kyle and Gonzo to sit quietly and nurse their warming beer. Night had fallen.

We were shuttling periodically for more beer. I was smoking like a chimney. Adele was growing tired and sat in the Hummer, where she nodded off. Everyone slowed down on his and her intake except me. It was my wedding anniversary, and I really did not want to think about it.

At some point, I walked away with a half-empty bottle of warm Presidente in my hand, my head spinning sickly. I descended the fragmented French stairs that peeked anciently out of the brush and rubble on the bluff. How I avoided falling to my death remains a mystery.

At the bottom, I heard the Hummer start. Someone was taking Adele home.

I was sure I was about to vomit, so I took off all my clothes and waded out on the dead coral among the urchins and starfish. When I was thigh deep, I launched on my belly across the surface of the tepid water.

The water started to melt away my dizziness, and when I rolled onto my back, hundreds of feet from the shore, the full moon stared into my face with a steely radiance. I stayed in the water for a long time, calling back and forth with the guys who checked to see if I was all right. I would scull with my hands occasionally, but mostly I floated. . . just the moon and me. . . drifting away from the nausea.

I don't remember when I got out of the water or how. When I woke the next day, I was dressed. My skin was encrusted with salt and itching. My head was painful and stony. My stomach was quivering like a fresh killed cat. It was after 7:00 AM and I had not been awakened for my guard shift.

Mike told me later that he had trouble stirring me, that I stank like a gin mill, and that he had pulled my shift. I protested that I was willing to pull it, drunk or not. He told me it was nothing, don't worry about it, just make arrangements next time to have a designated driver. He was pissed. The rest of the guys had pulled their shifts.

We were back at work, and I had knocked the last support from under the pedestal of my authority.

70: MISSION SHIFT

People began to swarm over the island like bees. We had international everything showing up, announced and unannounced, day in and day out, beginning on October 15th. The mere presence of Aristide seemed to have them all concerned. We had International Police Monitor visitors in on the 18th, USAID folks on the 19th, a roaming chaplain and eight survey people on the 20th, Schroer started lurking more frequently, CIA agents dropped by, reservist lawyers who wanted to assess the state of the judiciary, embassy people, and so on.

We had to be prepared to give a briefing in a moment's notice. We also were directed to "vet" the FAd'H to weed out the bad guys, and to keep them gainfully employed. We set up five guard posts around town, where we would post two FAd'H, and their jobs were to tell us if anything happened, not to intervene unless it was life or death. It was eyewash for Schroer and his ilk. The whole sector was enjoying more peace if not prosperity than they had seen in years precisely because there were no soldiers and policemen about. "If it ain't fucked up, don't fix it," Mike and I agreed.

Adele had come by alarmed on the 20th about some "extra-constitutional" police force. Mike and I made a note of it, but were more concerned with producing a plan to move the mission along, even in the face of guidance that seemed to deliberately obstruct anything productive, and to keep the boys busy.

We planned to initiate decentralized operations, with each man having his own area of responsibility and his own Haitian liaison to get his responsibilities done. The goals were both intelligence gathering and civic action. We had developed an outline for area surveys, and took turns sending guys out to the various villes to gather the information. It was civil information, mostly, the status of water, roads, finding out where folks' food came from, that kind of thing.

But I had also initiated a search for Brunot Innocent, the wicked little sergeant know as A Te Plat. I instructed every man to ask about him in every ville, and to gather depositions against him. He had become our next strategic target. We needed him to bolster then public's confidence that we were making progress toward justice. Brunot was their obsession, so he would become mine. It was the single biggest issue on Haitians' minds: Justice. And we were beginning to hear another word with increasing frequency from the Task Force commanders, parroted mechanically in response to every mention of justice. That word was reconciliation.

71 : Jericho

That's perhaps a grandiose title for the story about tearing down the little FAd'H building at the Northern point of Fort Dauphin. But the walls did come tumbling down.

We had scheduled the destruction of the building for Saturday, October 22nd. Originally, Mike and I just wanted to do it. We wanted to get the public involved in the destruction as a way of both restoring the Fort, which at one time was a tourist attraction, and of giving the town a project they could work together on to consolidate a new sense of civic involvement. Part of the plan was also to cut out the old underbrush that had grown over the place, and to sweep off the stones and steps.

Rod was our first dissenter. He wanted to know who was giving us permission to destroy the building. Rod had come to question our every action, as we had come to be increasingly creative in our interpretation of the commanders' guidance. They had told us to reactivate the Haitian soldiers, so we posted them but left them with directions not to act. Rod wanted to know why. Skye chimed in on this, rankling at our constant responsibility for solving disputes. That was the Haitians' job they said. Rod wanted to know why we dismissed the intelligence summaries, and was dissatisfied with our answer that they had consistently proven to be worthless. Rod wanted to know how we could continue to take sides, when we were being told that the FRAPH was now the legitimate political opposition. So we got permission to destroy the building, to satisfy Rod.

We asked Adele Mondestin. She said tear it down. She would organize the work crews to help us clean up the Fort. They had a plan to carry the pieces of the destroyed building to Fort Saint Joseph to construct a little house for an old woman who had none.

Kyle wanted to know why we had to participate. Why couldn't we just let them tear it down? Gonzo muttered his agreement with Kyle.

"Because I fucking said so." I had grown impatient.

Everyone looked at me. Mike nodded his approval. He was growing very weary of the childish rebellion on the team. Ali kept his head down. Click. Click. Click.

Ali had led a Karioke session on the porch the night before. We had picked up a rock station from the Dominican Republic, and they were playing Elvis and other oldies. Quite a bit of beer was imbibed, and the guys were feeling rough. So was I. Last night, they had enjoyed the Haitians. This morning, they hated them again.

Adele showed up at 11:00 AM with around fifty people. They had machetes and rakes and brooms. We came with sledge hammers, claw hammers, and crow bars.

Ali, Mike, and I immediately began by popping the nails up on the tin roof. Gonzo was on house watch with Rod, and Skye was assisting Kyle in organizing the machete crew to cut underbrush. Within minutes, the place had become an event. Women started to flock in with baskets and jugs, congregating on the shady side of the Fort. Children began singing, dancing, and capering around inside the fort, the old armory and the slave holding chambers, both of which are twenty degrees cooler than outside.

Then the hammering began. We hammered at the walls, and the chips hit us in the face. We hammered in blitzes until we were out of breath, then we'd step back, rest our shoulders, and begin another hammering frenzy. We would spell each other, and more and more Haitians became involved in the building destruction. Two Haitians found Pierre Ulrick's signature in the concrete of the foundation, and they began chipping his name off with little Haitian hammers. Later, we took wire brushes inside to vainly scrub at the massive amounts of graffitti on the inner walls.

Within half an hour, Kyle and Skye had completely quit. They were standing on the Hummer watching everyone else work. It was a little rebellion, and I took note. Skye had hungered for acceptance, being the outsider on the team when the mission started, and now he had found a way. He was helping form a subversive clique. I was succeeding in my mission to build cohesion on the team, but in a new way now. I had given them a common enemy. Me.

Adele took me aside when it was almost done, and again pleaded for help with an illegal policeman near Malfety. Hora was his name, and the public was terrified out there because he was still at large with a weapon.

Not a single intelligence briefing had so much as mentioned section chiefs. Their badges say *Police Rural*, but they were known as *chef d'seksyon*, and they were a notorious group. Adele was patiently explaining this to us, and we were only partially understanding it all.

72: Roundup

The afternoon after the building was torn down, Ali, Skye, and I set off for Malfety in search of Mesidor Hora, the section chief. We had his name written on a slip of paper.

When we arrived at the outskirts, we asked if anyone had seen him. Sure, he's right down there, they said, indicating a side road that ran along the river. We were taken aback at how easy that had been. Does he have a weapon? Yes, of course he does, we were assured. Is he a bad man, we asked. At this, there were some suspicious glances all around. They were wondering which side we were on. We were wondering the same. One boy behind the gathering crowd was staring intently at us, trying to catch our eyes. Ali spotted him and nudged me to look. Ali asked the crowd again if Hora was a bad man. More mumbling, but the boy gave us a definite, if discreet, nod of assent. Yes, he is a bad man.

Mesi, mesi.

Off we went down the side road. It was a thickly green trail, with *raket* right up to the edges and plenty of deep grass, mangoes, and palms. We had gone less than half a mile, when we turned a corner and found ourselves face to face with a horse-mounted man with a shotgun, not fifty feet away. Skye stopped the vehicle, and Ali aimed his rifle at the man.

"*Le mens au l'air!*" Ali shouted. The hands went slowly up past a face with a questioning look. What's this, his expression seemed to say.

Skye and I closed with him, pistols drawn, and Skye relieved him of his shotgun. As far as we knew, this was the first act in the disarmament of the section chiefs across the country.

Hora spent the night in jail, while we tried to figure out what to do with him. We called back, and no one even seemed to know what the section chiefs were. The fact that they were called rural police gave some people pause, who began to wonder if we weren't supposed to be helping them out, given the changes in commanders' guidance that edged ever closer to collaboration with the security forces. Rod, of course, began fretting that we had exceeded our authority again.

We finally got hold of Boyatt's headquarters, where we frankly asked permission to go through our entire sector and disarm them all. Boyatt still regarded us as favorites, precisely because of our initiative, and gave us a green light to round up the weapons, but not detain the people. We were instructed to release Hora with an advisory that he was summarily retired.

We set out over the next two weeks to identify all *chef d'seksyon yo* in our sector. By the 1st of November, we had completed the disarmament of them all, 21 total, from Fort Liberte to Vallieres to Trud du Nord. Two had already lost their weapons to angry populations. Two had sold theirs to the 10th Mountain Division in Cap Haitien, where they had initiated a "weapons buy-back" program. We had the finest collection of old Browning 16-gauge shotguns available.

Officially relieved of their "duties" were Brunot Iliomer, Charles Louis, Cezaire Louis, Dorsaint Marcelin, Desgravier Declamus, Fleurimond Charite, Mesidor Hora, Jean Josue, Jospeh Cleon, Joseph Deluis, Joseph Charles, Jean-Baptiste Joseph, Gaston Auguste, Montreuil Yves, Pierre Altidor, Pierre Eliophat, Vilfort Salvant, Joseph Flarentin, Lafosse Stobert, Noel Pierre, and Dezana Francisque. Before we left, we were already hearing how Dorsaint Marcelin had regrouped with a band of *macoutes*, in the hinterlands of Gros Roche, to become a local Jesse James. I never got the chance to go after them.

73: VETTING

We began vetting the soldiers in earnest around October 24th. It wasn't hard to do. You could get a group of citizens together, and call off the names. They would respond with bon or pa bon. If a soldier consistently received pa bon assessments from every ville we talked to, we assumed he was pa bon.

At each stop, we would have to explain that we were helping decide which soldiers would be permitted to become part of a new police for Aristide. That was not a story. It was a lie we were being told by our own commanders, most as unwitting that it was a lie as we were.

It was tedious work, the vetting, but it was successful. We were achieving consistent results, and felt we had very firm ground to stand on with our recommendations. The populace was also very encouraged by this process.

Eventually, we recommended the exclusion of 41 names as absolutely unacceptable to any sectors of the population. Nineteen were still with the garrison. Nine had deserted, including Brunot Innocent. The rest were not former FAd'H, but the members of Blaise's "soccer team", which included Smith Edouard.

Weeks later, when the initial training was scheduled for the new

Interim Police Security Force (IPSF), every one of those lads, good, evil, and in between, leapt aboard the Blackhawk to attend. The whole vetting process was blown off. It was eyewash from the beginning.

74: The Mennonites

We were told in no uncertain terms by "higher" that we would begin redeploying the FAd'H immediately. That was on the 24th of October, after much foot-dragging and argumentation on our part. Our success to date in conducting "stability" operations, in our judgment, was based on credibility with the population. That credibility was built on two things; we accepted the account of the general situation given by the vast majority and based our operations on that account, and we neutralized the FAd'H, FRAPH, *attaches*, and miscellaneous *macoutes*. We explained this again and again, thinking we were exercising the most rudimentary logic. It seemed logical to us. We had no idea how much concern it was causing every level of command above us. . . that we were actually doing it.

It was an order, unequivocal, and we were given no option. We would redeploy the FAd'H. The first place we were to redepoly them was a sizable town across Grand Riviere, halfway to Cap Haitien, named Trou du Nord.

Ali and I informed Captain Ulrick of our intent to redeploy in the presence of about 20 members of the company who were loitering in the shade tree across the street and playing dominoes. The result was pandemonium. The whole crew was jabbering at once, obviously protesting, including Ulrick. Ali had to roar at them twice to quiet them enough to hear one at a time, what was the problem. Ulrick went first.

They are crazy there. It is dangerous. They will kill us, he went on, to the vigorous assent of the others. A now-familiar weariness settled on me. I could tell it was on Ali, too.

We were going to have to force a selection on three unwilling soldiers for Trou du Nord, three more for Grand Bassin, and two for Terrier Rouge. A made up my mind then and there to commit a stupid error. Of course, I didn't know it was a stupid error at the time, but I decided to simply go through the roster, and assign people arbitrarily to the various villes in our sector, of which Terrier Rouge, Trou du Nord, and Grand Bassin would be the first three. The order to redeploy was arbitrary, so I became arbitrary in its execution. It's a soldier thing.

Several soldiers declared that they would desert if forced to go to Trou du Nord. A fair number already had, and that didn't concern us in the least. If they'd all desert, we would have one fewer administrative hassle. They still weren't getting paid, and we were still feeding them, and I wouldn't have blamed them for leaving.

Quite all right, I assured them. Go for it. There are plenty of folks out there who will be glad to see you, alone and unarmed.

Many were remaining in the garrison because they were afraid of the general population, and many remained because there was little else to do. Some remained because we fed them. Some were still waiting for their "new" jobs as rehabilitated police.

We departed the next morning with six soldiers, two for each ville.

In Terrier Rouge, we had two volunteers. One in particular, named Gabriel, a tiny man of about fifty, who enjoyed his Clarin, and who seemed universally liked, declined even to bring his rifle. He and his compatriot were greeted enthusiastically by the residents of Terrier Rouge.

At Trou du Nord, we dropped off two very unhappy troops in a garrison building that had been gutted and defaced in the absence of any authority.

Then we headed up the mountain to Grand Bassin, where we dropped off two soldiers who had been residents of Grand Bassin, and exhibited no fear.

When we passed back through Trou du Nord, all hell had broken loose. There was a very excited and agitated crowd around the bridge that extended back to the garrison adjacent to the West bank of the fording site. Ali began questioning people to piece together what had happened. It was not pretty.

Immediately upon our departure, a very rowdy crowd had cornered our two intrepid troops in the garrison. Several agitators had whipped up emotions, and the crowd took on a surly aspect. The soldiers were admonished none too gently to leave, and when they attempted to make their escaped across the river on foot, members of the crowd had pounced on them. They had both received ass-whippings as they struggled free from the crowd and fled back toward Fort Liberte. They had lost their weapons in the melee and the weapons had fallen into the hands of a local hooligan called Ti Ben. Ti Ben was believed to be headed to Cap Haitien to sell the M-1's to the 10th Mountain Division under their weapons buy-back program.

Ali was stunned. Normally, I would have been, too, but I was particularly exhausted that day. For reasons I still can't discover, I found it funny. It was like we had reached some final act in a great geopolitical burlesque. I got tickled, and Ali became irritated with me for my mirth.

"What the fuck are we supposed to do, Stan?"

I told him to establish communications with Mike in Fort Liberte, and to get the serial numbers off the rifles. Skye could check the inventory sheet from the garrison, and see which rifles were signed out. Then we could call into 10th Mountain at Cap Haitien, give them the serial numbers, and alert them to detain Ti Ben when he tried to sell them. Accounts from the locals had indicated that Ti Ben was not some great liberator, but a pretty run of the mill thug, who was suspected in a number of local robberies and rapes.

We couldn't bring anyone up on FM with a whip antenna, so Ali decided to use HF with a doublet antenna. This is a fairly laborious set-up, and we needed plenty of room. The doublet is a T-shaped affair of wire that is around 100 feet wide and that has to be elevated high overhead. We needed plenty of space and some trees to snake the lanyards through to hoist the antenna. It's a bi-directional antenna, so it has to be "aimed" at the receiving station. That meant we would have to aim it at Fort Liberte, then re-aim it at Cap Haitien. The only appropriate place we could find was the plaza near the bridge in front of the biggest church in town, where there was a wide swath of space ringed with several two-story buildings and three mango trees. It gave Ali something to do that he was very good at, and helped cool his anxiety.

When we were nearly finished setting up the first commo shot to

Fort Liberte, I was standing up in the back of the hummer, and two civilian 4-wheel-drive passenger vehicles loaded to the hilt with white people pulled into the plaza. They slowed nearly to a stop to gawk at us, and we gawked back.

Certainly, it was unusual to see US troops in a single pair, when across the country 10th Mountain had a policy of deploying only entire units. It was also unusual to see troops without helmets. And it was extremely unusual to see them interacting directly with Haitian civilians in an unoccupied area. I was passing a bottle of water around with a pack of kids who were perched on the tail of the hummer. Ali was squatted under a mango tree with a handset in one ear, munching a baguette in a gaggle of onlookers, between attempts to raise Mike on the radio.

"Hi," I said, silver-tongued devil as always.

"Hi," came several back. They were American.

"Who are you guys?" I asked.

They introduced themselves as members of something called Christian Peacemaker Teams. They were intensely curious about what we were doing.

I gave them a brief account of our adventure, then asked them what they were doing. They said they had come to have a meeting with the representatives of a collections of local organizations. Two were wearing Lavalas ball caps, and one wore a Lavalas T-shirt. I mentioned that it was unusual, that most of the evangelists I knew of were busy saving Haitian souls and didn't particularly care for Lavalas. I was frank in sharing my opinion that evangelizing wasn't what it seemed was needed here.

"That's not what we do," said a handsome blonde-headed woman, who introduced herself as Carla Blutschi.

"Good," I said, and we all seemed to turn some kind of corner. No one was fulfilling anyone's expectations. We established within minutes that we were both pro-Lavalas. I explained how we were operating through the community groups, and how we had yet to establish any relationships in Trou du Nord, frankly asking if they would mind our attending the meeting.

Carla towed me off to one side, and we sat together on the foundation for the church fence. Obviously, this was a dilemma for her. But she was interested. It became apparent that she was in some leadership role here.

As we conversed, she pointed out that if we were doing what we described, the way we described it, then we were not behaving like any other military she had seen. While I suspected as much, it was a little disconcerting to hear it. It was disconcerting because it reinforced my gnawing suspicion that we were operating far outside the expectations of the task force command structure. And it was disconcerting because I feared what this might mean other military units were doing...like collaborating with the old power structure.

"I admit I am not religious," I told her.

"You sound as if you might be," she said.

"I'm an atheist," I explained. "And I think I might be a socialist."

She smiled, seeming to actually find that reassuring. "Then I don't think we're very far apart."

I cautioned here that I was talking about me, and that this is a form of blasphemy in the military. Ali was safely distant, shouting into the handset to elicit the serial numbers of the stolen weapons from Skye on the radio.

"The meeting will be out that way," she motioned to the South. It's in a cock-fighting ring. Everyone knows where it is. Just ask. We'll start around two. I'll ask Etias if you can come. If they won't let you attend, I'll have to ask you to leave."

I couldn't ask for more than that.

"What church supports the Christian Peacemakers?" I asked.

"We're Mennonites."

Ali accomplished the communications. It was a good plan. The only glitch was that the 10th Mountain never even attempted to look for the serial numbers. It's possible that no one attempted to relay the message. We would find again and again that no one in the task force ever seemed interested in doing anything except making their scheduled contacts, accomplishing resupply, and avoiding as much as possible doing anything with the Haitians. The whole task force was withdrawing inside concertina wire compounds, setting up VCR's, stockpiling cheap novels, and doing the absolute bare minimum required of them. They could care less about stolen guns or Ti Ben.

We were allowed to stay at the meeting.

First we had a long series of formal introductions from an alphabet soup of organizations. Each representative then was given a short time to explain their situation, their analysis, and their needs. There was a fair amount of polemicizing, but it seemed to be a therapeutic necessity.

Carla translated. She had spent 13 years in Haiti and spoke Creole like a native. She also gave me a code to discuss *macoutes*. Call them MacIntoshes, she instructed, because the word will always engender an animated discussion that will sidetrack the meeting. During the meeting, she advised me that CDS, the sanitation department that Vincent Namours worked for, was known as a "MacIntosh" organization.

So my worst suspicions about Vincent were probably true. He was a con man, and intriguer, and probably a *macoute*. Now the team at Ouanaminthe had appointed him the mayor. And I was more than any other single person probably responsible for his rise to power there.

For the hundredth time, I felt like a babe in the woods.

When all grievances were aired at the meeting, and all points of view were on the table, Carla introduced me. The suspicion was palpable. Not only among the Haitians, but one particular Mennonite, a young man of about 30 with a fine great beard, who appeared to be writing every word that was said in a microscopically small script on a composition notebook, sat next to me and glared up at me when he could take a breath from his recording. His hostility seemed amplified each time I would shake loose a *Comme il Faut* and light it.

So I waded in very carefully. Ali was now a mere bystander, his translation not being required, and me being the spokesperson.

The history of US presence, and especially US military presence, in Haiti has not been a happy one, I acknowledged. This was necessary to simply establish the most rudimentary credibility, in my judgment. I saw Ali shift uncomfortably. One older Mennonite, around sixty, also with an excellent full beard (it must be a Mennonite trait), smiled and nodded approvingly.

I then recounted the affronts to Haiti, beginning with US assistance to oppose the revolution, through the Marine occupation, through US complicity in the maintenance of the Duvalierists, and probable CIA links to the FRAPH. Ali had a clearly disapproving look on his face, but most heads around the cock fighting pit had begin to nod assent. I had succeeded in surprising them.

Then I crossed the line, at least with Ali.

I told the assembly that there were strong indications that the head of FRAPH was closely connected to the CIA, and that this justified the suspicion that the CIA may have been involved directly in the Cedras coup against Aristide. Ali was obviously livid.

I was not saying anything that was not already public knowledge, but I had taken a giant leap forward in trust-building.

The point I was making, I told them, was that while we were officially in support of Aristide for the moment, they needed to begin preparing for a future of their own making. Foreign policies change, I warned. We might be completely withdrawn in six months, and the *macoutes* had not been disarmed. They needed to begin now organizing and building support among the population to protect themselves.

I explained the rules I was obligated to operate within; that we had to push an official line of reconciliation, and that we had to react in like ways to any and all forms of violence, regardless at whom it was directed. I reviewed our good experiences with Lavalas thus far, how Lavalas had helped us ensure no reprisals, and by extension avoided the twin possibilities of the heavy-handed introduction of conventional troops, and of orders to us from the task force to crack down directly on Lavalas.

It was not subtle.

There was a flurry of outraged protest at what was perceived to be an implicit threat. The apparent facilitator, a baby-faced gentleman with a slight lisp, named Etias Seville, who had obviously understood that it was not a threat but a friendly warning, calmed them down, giving me a chance to explain.

I did not want to crack down on anyone. I personally supported the President and Lavalas, but I was a soldier in the American Army, and I could be made to do things I did not agree with. It was an open admonition to trust neither the US government nor the US military.

They had questions, lots of questions, clarifying questions. This was good. They got it. They were asking questions to determine exactly where the existing boundaries were. We were in dialogue. We were collaborating.

These were the groups that represented the popular will, so technically I was supporting Haitian democracy. This was Operation Restore Democracy, was it not? But I could not have been more disingenuous. The democracy we were supporting as an official policy had nothing to do with popular will. I knew that. I had seen it elsewhere. We were building a ersatz democracy again. A technical democracy, where everyone had the opportunity to vote in an election where every other process leading to those elections would be controlled by the people with the money. A democracy where we pretend that the power of money has no connection to the political process.

Democracies like Chile, like El Salvador and Guatemala, like in the United States. Democracies where we can rationalize why we continue to give it all to the rich.

The meeting was a rousing success by my estimates. Each Haitian and each Mennonite shook our hands, even the glum fellow with the busy tablet. Etias agreed to act as a standing contact with the team for Trou du Nord. Carla, seeming a bit surprised by the whole development, sent us off with a warm good-bye.

Ali was stonily silent in the hummer on the way back.

"Alright," I said. "What's eatin' you?"

"I don't think you should trash the United States to foreigners," he spat. "I don't think we should be saying shit to anyone about the CIA and all that."

"It was necessary," I said.

Just West of Carrefour Chivry, we picked up one of our mugged FAd'H soldiers that had been run out of Trou du Nord. He was stumbling down the road with a stick in his hand, a torn T-shirt, some scratches and bruises, and a very sad face. We took him to the garrison at Fort Liberte and dropped him with his colleagues, who gave us I-told-you-so glares as they commiserated with him.

75: BRUNOT

In the statements my men wrote against Mike and me for the 15-6 investigation that was coming in December, four people described my obsession with FAd'H Sergeant (some were now referring to him as corporal, a point I never cleared up) Brunot Innocent.

Brunot had been at the garrison when we arrived. I barely remembered what he looked like. The only vague impressions that remained with me were a pinched face and very small stature. He was from Grand Bassin, as was Ulrick, and I came to understand that Brunot was Ulrick's principle enforcer.

Brunot had a reputation that extended all the way to Cap Haitien, but not everyone knew him as Brunot Innocent. He was far more widely known by his nickname, *A Te Plat*. The nickname came from his most frequent command to anyone who ignited his aggression, and it meant "flat on the ground". Ulrick most likely used him as an enforcer not because they were homeys, but because Brunot was thoroughly mad and the entire population was thoroughly terrified of him. Ulrick, a consummate coward, was probably afraid of him, too. Like Castra in Gonaives, Brunot was fond of making people lap up the green effluvia in sewage streams. He beat people unmercifully at gunpoint for the slightest perception of an affront to his authority, and was even known to have shot a rock that he tripped over in Terrier Rouge. It was a Lavalas rock, he had shouted. Bang. Bang.

The first time I had gone to look for Brunot was when the mess happened with Bernard Fanfan. Brunot was a kind of accomplice and-or material witness in that convoluted drama. Like several soldiers who saw the handwriting on the wall, Brunot had fled. We had told the population when we first settled in that we were going to begin deposing people for future trials over police and army misdeeds. Brunot's were abundant.

Every time we questioned anyone about the past, officially or unofficially, Brunot's history was resurrected, and the picture began to emerge of a very sinister little man whose return the general population still feared. In discussions between Mike and me, it was decided that the capture and prosecution of Brunot would be a strategically pivotal act. It would go a long way toward annihilating the psychological vestiges of police terror, toward a public sense of justice, and toward razing the barriers to the vaunted "reconciliation" we were being pressured to promote. It would also go a long way toward further increasing our stature, of course, and as the mission progressed the task force's direction was eroding that a bit each day with their bald collaboration.

The boys were right. It definitely did turn into an obsession.

The reason it preoccupied me more and more, however, was that the task force was, I believe, giving the man refuge. In October, I had heard that Brunot was visiting his home in Grand Bassin on a number of occasions. Every time we went past or through Grand Bassin, we would pay a visit to his house to see if he was there. We always did so with our pistols drawn, making quite a show of it, knowing that we were not going to catch him, but hoping our public displays of intent to arrest would discourage his presence anywhere in the region. That much, at least, worked. But we eventually became privy to rumors about him having been taken in by the garrison in Croix du Bouquet.

When we first tried to confirm the rumors, our own immediate headquarters in Cap Haitien took an extremely lackadaisical attitude toward the whole issue. People almost smirked at me when I explained that I wanted him sent back to face a trial. I am sure they never passed on my requests to inspect the garrison at Croix du Bouquet. So I began to include the whole story, the charges that had been made, the symbolic importance of his capture, his notorious brutality, in the official written radio reports. That way the reports became part of the official record, which is generally the best way to begin breaking up bureaucratic logjams. Those reports disappeared into a black hole, burned most likely, to secure them.

Finally, after weeks of frustration with the regular chain, I had Ali string up a powerful HF doublet antenna and look up the frequency and callsign of the actual team in Croix du Bouquet. When I had a direct conversation with the team sergeant there, he told me they had never heard of Brunot, nor had they received any radio traffic about him. He had lots of new soldiers, he told me, and it might take a while to figure out who they were. This was about the time that the task force began to shuffle soldiers from one garrison to the other without letting the local teams know what they were doing. They were accommodating the wishes of FAd'H commanders who were hiding their people from prosecutions before the judges were re-seated. The team sergeant was collegial on the radio, but he came across as a little befuddled as to why I would even care about one Haitian corporal. The issue of Brunot's crimes seemed to be irrelevant to him.

I was still isolated, and still for no good reason assumed that other teams were doing what I was doing, and that only the task force commanders were being obtuse.

Fritz, the Haitian-American Navy interpreter, accompanied me for several days to various villes, where we accumulated dozens upon dozens of depositions against Brunot Innocent. One day, we spent several hours at Derac.

Derac is a dessicated collection of decaying cinder block row houses just above a salt marsh near the east end of Fort Liberte Bay. Its inhabitants live on the bare margin of starvation with a few puny salted fish, and what they can scrounge of what passes back and forth across the nearby Dominican border. It was built by a giant sissal company as a company town for the workers of Plantation Dauphin. When nylon replaced sissal as the principle material for rope, the Texas company pulled up stakes, and left the former subsistence farmers—turned wage laborers—sitting on this parched and valueless plot with nowhere to go. The whole town is the color of dirty salt, including the people who are powdered like pastries by the incessant dust. At midday, it hurts the eyes to gaze ahead, so everyone simply seeks the little shade there is and looks mostly at the ground. In the middle of the place, like the monolith in the eerie scene from *2001 Space Odyssey,* there is a smooth, precise structure, part box, part dome, with a pipe extending over a well crafted cistern and pouring a steady stream of bright, clean water. On top of the structure are the glaring slate gray slabs of two solar cells. It is a solar powered pump, built years ago by World Vision, one of the cancer of Non-Governmental Organizations that provide "services" to Haitians. The Deracans will tell you that the machine provides good water, but it doesn't work right at night.

Fritz and I gathered together a crowd in Derac, and he explained that we were collecting evidence against Brunot Innocent. A chorus of *"a te plats"* rippled through the gathering. We had a great deal of difficulty explaining what we meant by evidence. It was pretty clear to them that he was guilty. The notion of proof for those who knew Brunot was a kind of superfluous absurdity. He was *A Te Plat*. He was bad. He did these things. Are you going to put him in prison, like you did Rene Mozart? Will they let him go, like they did Rene Mozart?

Patiently, dripping in the white-hot sunlight, I explained through Fritz, who himself occasionally needed further explanation, that the rules were such that we could not guarantee if we caught Brunot, we could keep him. To do that, we needed evidence. When asked what kind of evidence, we told them witnesses, temwan.

Fear ran through the whole group like a current.

What could we do to ensure their security? they wanted to know.

I 'fessed up again. If he came back after we left, I told them, I couldn't make any guarantees.

What would I do if I was still there, and the court let Brunot go?

I did make a promise then. I told them that if Brunot was released to Fort Liberte, he would show up in the Plaza at Derac one dawn, bound hand and foot, and the community could administer his justice. When Fritz relayed this, a jubilant atmosphere spread through the Deracans.

We ended up writing down statements for the next three hours, detailing the crimes of Brunot Innocent.

When we were finished. I didn't feel like returning right away. I took a wad of rags out of the hummer and tied them into a ball. Then I set two sets of rocks out on each end of the street. The children knew what I was doing right away, and exclaimed happily, *"Futbol!"*

I decided to do some social engineering.

"Jeune fils, solemente," I announced. It was to be a girls only game. It was an effort for Fritz and I to keep the boys off the "field" and to encourage the girls to get out there and play. But when they did, they

went at it with enough wild, fall-all-over-one-another enthusiasm to more than compensate for their lack of skill. It was great fun, and the entire ville became the spectators.

Brunot, with the assistance and complicity of the United States military, is a free man roaming around Haiti to this day.

76: Frags in the Colonial Well

It was just a day, one where I ran out of excuses for putting it off, when I threw the two hand grenades into the well. I don't remember the exact date, only that it was after I flew off the handle at Gator, and during the time we kept receiving indications that the "authorities," whoever the hell they were, wanted to release Pascal Blaise.

Vincent was the one who first told us that Blaise's henchmen had hidden their dead bodies in a well, "The Colonial Well." Vincent didn't know exactly where that might be, and when we asked the locals, they only knew where "the well" was. That well was the one located beside the USAID pump, the one we used for water, in the field with the windmill, beside the road to Ouanaminthe, near the turn-off to Ferrier, just past Carrefour Chivry.

I had inspected it briefly, finding it not in use, and stuffed to the top with tough, dry sisal plants. I knew the first time I saw the sisal, that clearing the well was going to be a rigorous task in the heat, so I had procrastinated.

I don't know what day it was. It was after my tantrum at Gator, but it was in response to the newly urgent necessity to keep Blaise locked up. It was at the time when the Team and I were going through our emotional divorce, when they began to be petulant with my every directive, and I, in response to that petulance, became ornery and resentful. It was when all of us had to engage tremendous will just to leave the house, because the sum of official circumscriptions on the mission had canceled our power and monopolized our time, and the team members had begun to weary of my Australian Shepherd method of leadership (adopted in response to a collective recalcitrance). Every action seemed only to occupy time, and none of us wanted to see any civilians, the men because it obligated them to deal with Haitians, and Mike and me, because we had to explain that, with the rules we were now operating under and our inherent limitations, there was really very little we could do. We had become diffused. Each of us, hiding from the heat and the dull reality, was maintaining the maximum possible distance from all of the others, sipping coffee, reading, writing, hardly talking, spread equally like molecules of solute in solvent.

And so we went.

I know me, so I know how I must have steeled myself for the effort, because it was an effort, and I knew it would be an effort, and all efforts were more arduous these days, because we couldn't do what we needed or wanted, so we wanted to do nothing. I know me, so I know I must have guzzled water, then coffee, then more water to offset the diuresis of the coffee, because I medicate that way, dialectically, oppositely, like climbing a rope hand over hand.

The part clear in my memory is when I started sweating hard. It was around 11:00 AM when I started, and every movement caused me to burst with sweat, but the area is open, exposed as a skillet to the sun, and I lined up the vehicle, tied the rope on the shackle fittings, with a bowline, then a free length, then an extra bowline as a safety at the anchor point. By the time I finished the knots, I needed to drink a quart.

Skye was watching with the four FAd'H guys we had brought, in case there was anything to haul out of the well. Skye knew what I was doing, setting up a rappel rope to lock myself onto, so I could begin cutting the enmeshed, stringy, dry, thorny sisal out of the well. The FAd'H guys stood watching, dumbfounded at what foolishness we were involved in, mystified by all the rope work, curious about the purpose of the whole venture. The FAd'H guys were also amused by the way I sweat and the amount of water I drank. They had always been amused by that. They never indicated it, or said so, or even asked about it, but I know they were amused by it, because they needed something like that about us to be amused about. After all, we controlled them.

I stripped to my T-shirt and dropped my shirt on the pile I had made with my load carrying equipment (LCE) and rifle. I tied on a swiss seat, a diaper made with a rope to suspend oneself from a rope for a controlled descent, a rappel. Then I snapped into the rope that was anchored to the frame of the Hummer, slipped on a pair of heavy-duty leather work gloves, and plunged, ass first, into the well. I tied off only fractions of an inch from the tangle of sisal, and Skye handed down a machete. My attempts to extricate the sisal from the well went on with negligible result for over thirty minutes, before I had Skye and a FAd'H soldier snatch me out.

I drank about two quarts of water, and we all moved under a shade tree to get out of the midday sun. Rod and Mike showed up with the Toyota pickup, and told us they needed the Hummer to pick some people up at the helicopter landing zone in a few minutes. They promised to be back soon.

We had a few moments to shoot the shit, and as I was discussing the alternatives for searching the well, thinking out loud, as it were, I said what we needed was a small explosive charge to destroy the sisal. Then I happened to look at my LCE, sitting in the sun under my now dry shirt, with my rifle over the top of it.

I got up to move my gear under the shade, and when I placed my webgear on the ground, the four hand grenades were looking back at me. People were still talking, as I unsnapped a grenade. Then they quit talking.

"What are you doing?" asked Rod.

"I know what he's doing," said Skye.

I smiled at them, and flipped the safety clip off the grenade spoon. I walked over to the well, in a hurry because I did not want to debate this with Rod, pulled the pin and dropped the grenade into the well. I strolled away, plugging my ears with my fingers, whereupon everyone followed suit.

The resulting explosion was so attenuated by the walls of the well, that the ear plugging proved unnecessary. Just a short, sharp pop. While everyone else was standing around with their mouths open, I ambled back over to inspect the results. They ambled in behind me.

The well was releasing a lazy exhalation of white smoke that the breeze picked away as it trickled up out of the mouth of the well. We had to peer down for quite a while, waiting as we were for the smoke to dissipate. When we could see, I noticed that I had failed to remove the rope from the hole before summarily dropping the grenade in, and the rope was badly nicked by shrapnel in about a hundred places.

Oops.

The effect on the sisal was impressive, however. The heap of woven sisal had been pulverized down a full ten feet. The bottom of the dry well, however was not yet visible.

I fished the rope out and laid its remains in a heap by the front of the hummer, then retrieved another grenade from under the tree. Everyone moved aside, as I dropped the second one down the well.

Pop!

Again the smoke curled and cleared, and on our second viewing, we were rewarded with the flat, dust dry bottom, covered not in bones or fragmented weapons, but with the remains of exploded sisal plants. Search over.

We all loaded up on the hummer and went back.

While we had been hanging around the Colonial Well that day, Skye had confided in me. It was a weird interstice. I was on everyone's shit list, including his, and it was kind of frowned on to fraternize with me. He confided that he had spent some time when he was a civilian as a traveling meat salesman, a con man who went door to door claiming that he had some left over inventory in the truck—bulk meat—that he had to get rid of at below cost. In fact, when the arithmetic was done, which people seldom did, it was overpriced meat. He told me that he finally quit because the people who most often bought the meat were poor people and folks on Social Security, and his conscience had gotten the best of him.

Skye had a very mixed and unevenly developed consciousness of things. He was bright. He mastered a Creole phrasebook in no time, and seemed to enjoy using it. He was a veritable scholar on the subject of reggae music, but he seemed eager to start "the race war." He sympathized with Haitians one minute, and judged them the next. He thought of becoming a cop, but his conscience bothered him about overcharging old ladies for meat.

Skye and Rod would be out of Haiti when Mike and I fell, and shielded by fortune from the questions of team loyalty, from the peer pressure to participate in the little insurrection that was coming, and the accusations of "rat".

77 : MOTORCYCLE MADNESS

I bought a motorcycle right after I came back from Vietnam. A Suzuki 185 that I used around Fort Bragg while I was in the 82nd Airborne Division, and that I took back to Arkansas during my first break in service. I commuted in it, rode trails in it, learned to play little tricks with it. I taught it to leap off of ramps. I got run over by an Oldsmobile in 1972 on it, outside of Raeford, North Carolina.

The army put me back in the saddle of a motorcyle more than once.

When I was in Delta, this was around 1983, Marshall Brown and I were hotdogging on some Fort Bragg tank trails one day, when I came ripping around a corner only to find a four foot deep erosion ditch to my front. By the time I realized what it was, the bike was crunched into the ditch, and I was plowing a row in the clay across the ditch with my lower row of teeth. I came to, accompanied by the panicked pleading of Marshall wanting to know if I was okay. I have had trouble with neck spasms ever since. Marshall went on to lose his mind. For a while, he became a Christian fundamentalist, then he became a serial rapist and a jailbreaker who scared the law enforcement community shitless with his "Delta" training. Marshall was one of the most highly respected members of Delta. I never quite fit in, and was expelled from the unit in 1985 as a security risk, after it was rumored that I was having it on with a former FMLN *guerrillera* in El Salvador—which was true—and that I had had it on with her in the Ambassador's residence—which was not true. I was a security risk, and Marshall became a serial rapist. It seems our trails diverged quite a bit. He was always a super-patriot, and now I am a despised whistleblower.

Anyway, I was writing about motorcycles.

We decided to get motorcycles as added transportation sometime in mid-November. We went to Ouanaminthe to rent them, and took an entire day dickering and cajoling, until we had made what seemed a fair deal. As it turned out, we spent another three days buying parts at the bridge on the border with the Dominican Republic, and doing all kinds of repairs. The bikes were being run into the ground as taxis by people who obviously lacked either the skill or the resources to keep the bikes up.

Then the tire problems began. Dave Grau claimed to be an expert rider, but I could ride circles around him, and Skye could ride them like he was born at a motocross track. Dave insisted on trying them out overland on the third day, and proceeded to run over thorns and pop two tires on one motorcycle. He blamed it on bad tires, of course. Once those tires went, we seemed to have slow leaks that James worked on every day, patching and re-patching, pumping and re-pumping.

Ali proved to be thoroughly incompetent aboard the bikes. I suggested to him patiently that he take a long, slow trip with someone else on the next patrol, to get used to it. So he went to Terrier Rouge on patrol with Gonzo one day. He came back scratched, bruised, and angry. His handlebars were twisted off center, so the bike came limping in with one bar tilted forward, looking a bit like one of those dogs that runs cater-cornered.

Gonzo disappeared fearfully into the house, knowing the rage that we saw on Ali's face. Mike and I foolishly stayed outside to see what had happened.

Ali parked the motorcycle, spewing a steady stream of the vilest profanity he could think of, letting us know to give him his space. Silly me, I asked anyway.

"Motherfuck these motherfucking pigs!" he shouted and stalked into the house.

We assumed, naturally, that he was referring to the bike as a member of the porcine species. We iterrogated Gonzo behind the house, where, trying not to smile, Gonzo informed us that Ali was not talking about the bike at all.

Just outside Terrier Rouge, heading to the bridge under which the women did laundry, Ali decided to open up the bike. He had gained a measure of confidence after the ride out there. Ali hadn't even seen the pig until it was too late to stop. A big, black pig had scuttled out of the *raket* along the road and stepped directly in front of Ali's mount. The bike folded, of course, and Ali rolled and bounced down the road, and the pig screamed madly into the ville.

Ali never mounted one of the bikes for the rest of the time he was there.

78: TRAILS

Rod and James went out to see the guy. I lateraled to Rod out of sheer weariness with troubles. I didn't feel I could listen to another irresolvable conflict over a pig who ate a garden that was planted across the property line because someone had used magic to render the soil infertile as vengeance for spoiling a daughter. I just went into my room, flicked the mosquito net aside, and dropped down on the cot.

Rod was back in minutes. I needed to see this guy. He knew something about Ti Ben, the fugitive who had stolen FAd'H rifles and assaulted a woman at Trou du Nord.

I invited the guy into the shade and fetched him a chair. He was short, stocky by Haitian standards, weathered to an appearance of fifty or so, which meant he was probably in his thirties, African-black, with watery eyes. He had on a dirty blue short sleeve shirt, tattered trousers and no shoes. It was late, after 4:00 PM, and he was riper than even me at close range.

What was on his mind, I wanted to know, feeling for all the world like a thoroughly jaded beat cop, one who was in way over his head

He knew the whereabouts of Ti Ben, and could witness against the man for assault, robbery and vandalism. Ti Ben was in Sicar, with six to seven other *gonegs* (tough guys), terrorizing people.

Where in Sicar¿

Right there.

I could feel the bile rising. More of this unanswerable, open ended, universalized, Haitian bullshit! (I, too, had begun to transfer all my dilemmas and all my exhaustion onto Haitians.) Where exactly, in relation to the pump, the bakery, the well, the coffin builder¿ I queried patiently.

He was near the soccer field.

Can you show us¿

No, no, not now. Not in daylight.

Why not¿

People will see me with you.

So¿

Ti Ben is my brother.

Rod and I looked at each other through the silence, then back at our stool pigeon. I walked over to the railing on the porch, lit a cigarette, and leaned on the railing, hoping for a gust of wind to cool the little streams of sweat that ran out of my hair and over my face and neck.

Ti Ben's brother was looking back and forth between us. He seemed particularity uncomfortable with James, who's consumptive father lived in Sicar.

Okay, I said, hitting upon an idea. We'll put you in the front of the pickup, with the windows up, so the reflection will conceal you. We'll let you wear sunglasses and a ball cap.

I pulled the ball cap off James' head against a tiny move of protest. *Por favor, James. Solamente por un rato.*

This seemed agreeable to our informer. I grabbed Skye and Rod and James. The informer sat in front between Skye, on the passenger side, and me, driving. James and Rod rode in back. Having rolled up the windows on the cab, and turned on the air conditioner, we were confined with our collective stench, which was powerful. Skye started to get pretty vocal and obvious about it, and I told him to put a lid on it. Part of the job. The problem was, it was kicking my ass too. Furthermore, the three of us were overwhelming the air conditioner with our body heat, and the air was getting thick with warmth and humidity.

It became another standard goose chase. He led us all over Sicar, looking and pointing and sending us down dead end streets, where we were at point blank range with everyone on the street, who looked through the windows and past our half-assed disguise.

Our informant finally decided to start asking people, apparently losing interest in his anonymity. With a few queries, and a few more dead ends, just as I was down to my last abraded nerve, he indicated a house on a corner, south of the soccer field. It was no caille paille. This one was constructed with cinder blocks and cut lumber, with a coat of pale blue paint on it. When we knocked on the door, a sergeant from the garrison answered, seeming surprised to see us, but offering us his hand nonetheless.

Had he seen Ti Ben?

Why yes. Ti Ben had just come by. He was very excited.

How long ago?

Ten minutes. No more.

Where did he go?

Through there. The sergeant, standing in his khaki trousers and white tee shirt, pointed across the street, into an area of thick *raket* and thorn brush. That area extended into the mangrove Southeast of town and along the eastern borders of the neighborhoods. No fewer than ten well-worn goat trails entered the thickets.

We ordered James and the informant to stay with the Toyota, while Rod, Skye and I headed off into the thicket. By then it was past five, and dusk was beginning to dim the light. I chose a trail at random, slung my long gun, drew my pistol, and entered the thicket at a relaxed low ready.

Within moments, we were out of sight of the houses. Every twenty or thirty feet, we were presented with. . . choices, so completely crisscrossed were the trails. No trail was significantly different from any other. One to two feet wide. Fine, powdery dust. Footprints, shoeprints, goat tracks, pig tracks, goat turds. We were taking action, but did not know how that action might end. We were being decisive, but without any guide for making those decisions. Right. Left. Straight. Pick one. Inside of ten minutes, we did not know where we were. We were, however, absolutely sure that whatever we entered for, we were not going to get it done. Ti Ben had disappeared into Haiti, leaving us to find our way out of this little wilderness, chasing our compasses Northwest through the labyrinth of ruminants, and leaving his brother sitting in the FAd'H's old Toyota, suckling his poor and private grudge.

We had plenty of choices we could freely make. But without any information, every choice was pure chance, and no choice at all.

One of the clearest thoughts I would have came to me there. Rationalizations fell like scales from my eyes. We did not belong here. I did not belong here. We weren't part of any solution, and we had always been part of the problem.

79: Fatigue

So Titid was back for weeks now, and the anticlimax of it bore down on us, as scorchingly oppressive and empty as the glare on the midday street.

There's a trendy phrase making the rounds among intellectuals these days; compassion fatigue. We've just grown so tired of caring so much about the suffering of little black children in the Mississippi Delta, about the barbarism directed at gays and lesbians, about the murders of Salvadoran peasants, and the ferocious neo-colonial feuds in Central Africa, that we just really don't have the energy to give a fuck any more. Compassion fatigue, along with everything else, happened to my team in Haiti, and for the same reasons it "happens" to white liberals here. Compassion is a luxury of comfort, often paternalistic, frequently a thin veil over contempt. Solidarity is a much tougher proposition.

Liberals find it difficult to accept the elemental humanity of Haitians, because to do so is to acknowledge our national culpability, our own daily official collaboration in the Haitian (Vietnamese, Salvadoran, Guatemalan, Peruvian, Rwandan, Palestinian, Balkan, et al) situation. If they are human, and we recognize them as such, then they are entitled to the murderous rage seething under the veneer of temporary gratitude. So, they were not Dumas, or Etias, or Eaulin, or the school superintendent. They were "the Haitians," or more frequently, "the fuckin' Haitians." The troops' original "compassion" was something to get pumped up for a fight with, something to feel good about oneself, something basically arrogant and separated, a role. . . just like the bourgeois liberals for whom the guys declared their everlasting contempt. And so. . . "it". . . "fatigued."

There was real fatigue, muscular fatigue, to be sure. Physical exhaustion was sustained by doing everything the long way, pouring gas from a five gallon can by hand, bathing out of a bucket, flushing a toilet with a bucket, wringing out ones clothes by hand in a bucket, bouncing endlessly over the spine crunching potholes, sweating oneself to sleep at night, carrying weapons everywhere, pulling guard every night.

Psychic fatigue came from the distance to one's loved ones, the lack of structure in the days, the growing animosity between the command element and the rest of the team, the boredom.

For me it was responsibility fatigue. Every time someone came to the door, I had grown to expect a problem we would have to intervene in, delicately and diplomatically, or aggressively with an element of potential violence. In either case, it would be something where I was placed firmly in the middle. Collaborator in the betrayal of the Haitians. Collaborator against the never fully stated mission intent. So I was two half-assed collaborators, working in direct opposition to myself.

I had inoculated the locals as well as I could against the ever more compelling reality that the Task Force policies I was beholden to carry out were becoming more defined and antagonistic to the desires of the majority in our sector. My stock with mission commanders, never high, was slipping. Control was increasing over the hinterlands from Port-au-Prince, and I found myself under tremendous pressure from the team to back off my original alliances.

My team was tired, and I drove them through my agenda with the Haitians, so I was becoming "too pro-Haitian." When I reminded them how silly this sounded, being here in Haiti, they modified the charge. I had become "too pro-Lavalas." Certainly this was an indictment that could carry weight beyond the team house, that could be used against me in Cap Haitien at the AOB, or Gonaives at the FOB, or PAP at Task Force Headquarters. Everyone knew about Lavalas. For a force supposedly designed to put the legitimate president back in power, we had worked very hard to demonize his supporters. Schroer, who thirsted for my humiliation, would have a field day with that. More than once, I was sucked into the trap of defending, where I found myself lecturing about what we had been through, what we had seen, how wrong the propaganda and the intelligence summaries had been. By this alone, this open disdain for US Military Intelligence, my authority was thoroughly compromised. No amount of empirical data demonstrating the consistent inaccuracy of received intelligence would even be acknowledged if I were to be confronted by commanders above the level of Fort Liberte. The boys knew it. Mike knew it. I knew it.

And I was crazy. Ever since I'd snapped out the night the lights came on, that had become the theme for mutterings of mutiny. It was easy to support, if you just put the right twos with the right twos and came up with the crazy fours. Just think back. . . you remember how violent he got at the food riots. . . yeah, yeah, and he'll pull a gun in a heartbeat. . . and this obsession he has with Brunot Innocent. . . oh, don't forget the way he used to get when we fucked up our grouping on HALO jumps. . . and of course, there was the Gator incident. . . hey, he tells people that the United States is fucked up, that the CIA is fucked up, he tells Haitians and reporters. . . he wigged out on me for giving a spoonful of MRE to a fuckin' dog. . . oh, you shoulda been there when he went after Smith Edouard, man, he was possessed.

They had me by the nuts if they wanted me, and here I was becoming more autocratic by the day, the most immediate authority in sight. They were following orders only because they weren't sure who I would be traded for, and because they still maintained the vestiges of SF clan loyalty that said, what happens on the team stays on the team. Haiti had come between us, but they still lacked the catalyst for rebellion. I knew it, but whatever was happening *today* concentrated my attention, not the *potential* for this thing and that thing, tomorrow, next week. The future was as far away as Mars.

It was becoming apparent that, between the Task Force chain of command, above, and my detachment, below, my position would eventually become untenable as an advocate for any group of Haitians. More and more, I was losing any optimism I had left about the mission, and I wanted just to go home before I was forced into a choice between my career and my orders. Frankly, my career was so near complete, that I probably would have made some compromises if push came to shove. I had a family, I had worked long and hard for that retirement check, and I was not prepared for canonization. If I didn't do it, someone else would, right? I didn't know, and I didn't want to find out.

I now had something in common with my men. We all just wanted to get the hell out of Haiti.

So I told them I loved it there. I told them I never wanted to leave. I went on and on about how well I could live there on a military retirement, how wonderful the climate was, how many chickens I would keep, what I might like in my house, how the children would be schooled.

When they asked me if I thought we would be home by Christmas, I said we would be there through Easter. If they said they were tired, I told them to take a goddamn vitamin. It was my duty to them not to let them get focused on a false departure date instead of the job, and my duty to me to reciprocate their bile.

Ever since the incident with Gator, a door had closed between the boys and me. Besides Gator himself, who forgave the incident immediately and apologized for being offensive, Ali was the single exception who had accepted my apology and behaved as if he did. Mike told me to forget it, but it was apparent that my ability to direct their activity was no longer based on the confident loyalty I had from them at the beginning of the mission. All I had left was my naked tyranny.

Meanwhile, I confiscated time to disappear almost every day to Fort Dauphin, especially around sundown, where I would smoke and drink a Presidente and wish I could just turn into a Haitian for a while, so no one would interrupt my glorious sunset with a request for food or a crowd of stares. My white skin and my uniform had become a beggars' magnet.

Sometimes, I would be left alone to watch the swallows dive into the dry well in a whirlpool of wings and whistles, and the bellies of the clouds change from lavender to salmon to red. All these stolen pleasures were those of a foreigner, fed and fat in an impoverished land, taken next to a people who suffered under this beauty, who hadn't the energy nor the options to share these little raptures. I knew that. And I went there anyway.

I seldom stayed at Fort Dauphin after dark if I was alone. I do not believe in ghosts, nor am I a superstitious man. But I always felt surrounded by malevolence there after dark, like the long diffused battle blood and slave blood and murder and misery were being released from the ground by darkness. I loved that spot when I was alone at sunset. When night closed in, however, I was just a pale lunar face perched in the blackness atop a ruined French fortress, the latest in a line of invaders whom I wouldn't blame them for slaughtering.

After much thought, I am convinced that slaughter will provide the only avenue for Haitian liberation. The World Bank functionaries, the diplomats, the Haitian dealmakers, the fundamentalist missionaries, the petty bureaucrats, the families of the post-colonial oligarchy, the ubiquitous blancs (and this means white or foreign), the FRAPHists, the *macoutes*, all ought to give daily thanks for the continued domination of the Haitian peasant psyche by voudon. It is through this African religion that peasant rage is sublimated. The effete critics who put peasantry and its culture on a pedestal will have at me for this comment, but I stand by it.

Every night, near the river, near Sicar, I would listen·to the drums pulsing until two and three in the morning. Every day, the celebrants would step into the sun, sweep the packed earth in front of their *cailles-pailles*, then listlessly trudge the roads and paths in fatigued pursuit of the most elementary compulsions. . . water, food, wood. Were it not for killing white chickens and dancing to utter depletion in the darkness, white people and their colonial surrogates might be thrust across the altar of Haitian peasant emancipation. The emancipated might dance in victory at a river of blood.

In truth, and I will never say it more clearly in this account, this macabre scenario is what I concluded must happen in Haiti sooner or later. History leaves Haiti no options. There can be no question of reconciliation or reform or reconstruction. These have always been invitations into a chamber where the Haitian masses have been sacrificed, and they always will be. *Violence!* And the sooner the better, I mused. It is the only answer left to the violence that has subjugated the Haitian people since their ancestors were chained into the bottoms of boats to cross the Atlantic.

So there is another little editorial aside. These conclusions were conceived in darkness over a warm bottle of Dominican beer above the swish and splash of the Atlantic as it rubbed the bottom of the ruined Fort Dauphin.

80: The Visitors

The CIA agent had a Johnny Cash hairdo. He was of course ex-Special Forces, as was the Army spook that was with him from a secret outfit in Virginia.

I stepped on my aversion to them, more out of history than some moral repugnance, mainly because Mike and the rest of the boys were so awfully impressed by this brushing up against them. Everyone shook their hands and mutual introductions were made. The radio traffic announcing their arrival had simply said visitors and indicated that we were to cooperate with them.

Within the first few moments, I cynically established my credentials by dropping old Delta names they both knew, and in that way seized the representative role for the team. I spoke the lingo. They were on a "spotting" mission. Spotting is the initial process in constructing agent networks. Identifying likely candidates for the approach, the recruitment, the training, the employment, and the eventual decommissioning of local citizens who would work for U.S. intelligence. . . out of ideological affinity, out of revenge, out of some collaborative and self-interested motive, and most often out of greed.

When the small talk was being made, they connected with the boys through the most common anti-Haitian currency in circulation as the mission progressed.

"We've got to be careful. The way you can tell if a Haitian is lying is look and see if his lips are moving."

Nods around the room. Expressive mirth. Rod more emphatic than the rest.

I let it pass. I could have confronted it, but I sat stone-faced through it. I had to stay on the ground as long as possible, and this confrontation would have gained nothing. No minds would change. I would simply become a target, or should I say a bigger target. Mike was the only one who noticed my reaction.

At some point, the conversation turned to politics, and I couldn't resist.

"These folks don't feel they can trust the Agency. They all know it was y'all who started the story that Aristide was a psychopath, the story about secret Canadian psychiatrists and all that."

The young blue-eye from the Army agency became defensive.

"It was all true."

I let it go again.

Eventually we moved to the "ask." Who could we recommend. The request was directed at me. I waffled.

"Well, you know, these folks are still pretty emotional with everything that's happened. I'm not sure this would be a great region to recruit from. Everyone knows everyone's business, and it wouldn't win anyone a popularity contest to be associated with the CIA."

They became insistent. Just someone who might be interested in communicating regularly with us on general matters, economy, politics.

Then I fucked up. It was becoming almost a trademark. Out of some perverse sense of humor, I thought, I'll show them.

I gave them Vincent and Freddy. I knew that Vincent would manipulate them, and I figured Freddy would send them on some wild goose chase.

They left.

Rod received a radio message that day that his grandfather had died. He was sent out on a helicopter, and I never saw him again until I was back in Bragg facing charges.

The following year, when I returned to Haiti with my two young step-sons, I visited Ouanaminthe. Vincent—the "mayor"—had his name scrawled on the sides of buildings. . . "Namou—CIA." He's been discredited, and in his bunko-artist way, he fled, with over a million *gourds* of municipal funds. When I ran into my old Lavalas contact, he informed me that Freddy too had crawled directly into bed with them, in exchange for an ice making machine that he thought would give him a leg up against the competition that a Domnican-owned club across the plaza had created, which was ruining L'Escale. Freddy, my old contact assured me, was back on the straight and narrow now. "We helped him understand his error." I didn't pursue that.

81 : EAULIN

I'd plant the M&M's all around the house. The sundries we were being sent included hundreds of pounds of chocolate M&M's. We all consumed them until we couldn't stand the sight of them any more. So I started to plant them around the house like Easter eggs for Eaulin and her friends to hunt—which they did with a great deal of laughing and squealing.

Eaulin was eight, and was the size of an average four-year old in the States. She was related to Noogie, the woman Ali has dissed early in the mission, who lived behind us with her brothers. Sometimes Eaulin would stay with Noogie, sometimes with other relatives. She was coal black with just a touch of the red hair from nutritional deficiency, wiry and bright-eyed, and busy. I never saw Eaulin when she wasn't involved in some form of busy-ness. She worked, carrying water, washing clothes, even assisting with food preparation at Noogie's. And she constructed strange architectures with stones, searched the crannies of broken buildings and trash dumps for bits of food and treasure, or played "jacks" with small rocks. She was a natural leader, and she always seemed to be managing other children's mischievous plotting. Her hands were as callused as a farmer. Her clothes were changed each day and stayed clean for about one minute. She had a cherub face with a halo of wild pigtails that she somehow changed each day into a new arrangement.

We had made friends early on. I found her irresistible. She reciprocated by treating me like I was a long-standing and beloved relative.

She taught me how to play "jacks" with the stones, but I could never beat her at it. I found myself practicing when she wasn't around, but to no avail. Sometimes, when I was sitting out back, stealing some momentary respite from conflict and responsibility, she would pop through the back wall portal, as if by magic, and climb up into my lap. She'd lay her head against my shoulder for a bit, or smile and make faces—which I'd return—then like a cat, just as abruptly break the contact and resume her perpetual project.

She had a friend who begged—Eaulin never begged—who would show up with her sometimes. Her friend was from the edge of town toward Malfety, a very poor section in an already poor place. She went about shirtless and was just beginning to grow breasts. She had the typical ultra-prominent peasant navel, and the effect was that of three giant mosquito bites forming a triangle over her whole anterior surface. Her favorite greeting was "*Je fen*," I"m skinny. She was, but the meaning was that she wanted something to eat. She had just the beginnings of decay between her top front teeth, and you could see her future. Her body was beginning to ripen, even as it began to break down. She would be pregnant within two years, and by the time her third was born, at the ripe old age of nineteen or twenty, her teeth would already have begun to fall out. And here she was, bright and childlike, direct and smiling even as she begged. I remember her once emphasizing how hungry she was by wadding all the skin of her abdomen together in a wrinkled mass between her fists. She made it look like the skin on a hound—a very strange demonstration.

Against my better judgment, I would occasionally give her something to eat—on the sly. I knew the danger of this random reinforcement of her begging, and she did indeed continue to beg with even more intensity. But it wasn't pleading as much as friendly demanding, so I did it because I hated that she had so little time to still be this scintillating child. . . and because she was Eaulin's friend.

The hidden M&M's were a way to feed just Eaulin and her friends, that had a beginning and an end, and didn't look like *blan* charity so much as just playing.

One day we had bought a bucket of immature lobsters from a kid out front, and after we cooked them and ate the white flesh, I saw Eaulin looking at the scraps. I nodded for her to take what she wanted. She called for her friend, the one who did the wrinkled stomach trick, and they sat down and with their filthy fingers systematically scooped out everything soft that was left, eating it all with relish. Gray stuff, mushy white stuff, lungs, everything.

If any of us—the big Special Forces soldiers—had done the same thing, even with out laundry list of immunizations and our muscles and our years of "training", we would have become debilitated with illness.

I realized at that moment how weak we were.

Some day, when Haiti loses its fear of having nothing else to lose, there will be hell to pay.

82: The Nature of an Insurrection

By the 28th of October, the tension between the team and the command element had grown so tense, that Mike and I decided to call a meeting. We asked the boys if they wanted one, and they agreed one was needed, almost with a sense of relief. It was scheduled for that afternoon after we finished our chores and rounds.

We gathered in the operations room, planting ourselves in a circle, me in the fold-up field chair, the rest scattered on goatskin chairs and foot-lockers. No one was late. The boys all understood the rules laid out long ago on "these" meetings; all was permitted if done respectfully, and that there would be no retribution for honesty. By the same token, Mike had reminded me that it was our opportunity to get some things off our chest as well.

I lit the first in a chain of cigarettes.

Mike began. He said there were some misunderstandings and some animosity, and it was so thick it could no longer be ignored. He gave a bit of a pep speech about what a shame it would be if a team like ours was to let a mission tear them apart, how we were the best, et cetera. He said he was confused, because we weren't operating like the "old 354."

I was the most controlled I had been in a long time, and I let each man then go around and air his complaints and concerns, dutifully writing them all down. I would occasionally ask a short clarifying question, but I was scrupulous about not interjecting an opinion or a reaction.

Rod was still worried about how aggressive I was. He brought up the Smith Edouard incident, and the occasions when I had resorted to warning shots. He saw no reason to continually seek the capture and arrest of Brunot Innocent or Gabriel Dilorne or Ti Ben or Alexis Frandieu. We were not given any mission guidance to do these things, and we had been told not to "kick doors." He reiterated his mistrust of Adele, and said that my friendliness with her prevented us from giving a "balanced" appearance. He threw in that he didn't believe we should do anything on the word of a Haitian, because "they are all a bunch of goddamn liars." This remark started other heads nodding in agreement. He then sweetened his remarks by telling me that he still admired me and thought I was a great team sergeant, but that I had gone overboard in my sympathy for Haitians. More nods.

Kyle was as unintelligible as always. He wanted to know why I wasn't taking care of the team, giving them R&R (Rest and Relaxation), and why we didn't implement a leave policy. He said that we were going about our operations all wrong, because what we really needed to do was instill a work ethic in the Haitians by getting some money to pay them fifteen gourds a day to do the stuff we were having the team do. He complained about the uniform policy changes, which we had nothing to do with, but that was Kyle. . . the whining private at heart. He reiterated his complaint that we hadn't moved into the Hotel Bayara, and said that we had no business getting involved in Haitian politics. When I asked specifically what he meant, he said we were acting too anti-FAd'H and too pro-Aristide.

Skye said he had had trouble trusting me not to go off ever since the blow-up over Gator's "nigger-rigging" comment. He was not only afraid that I might punish someone for crossing me, but that I might actually provoke a fight. He said he felt that the team members didn't have enough input on operations, that I ran operations like a dictator, and that Mike was just rubber-stamping my decisions. He said it seemed like we were "taking sides", even when the commander's guidance sounded like it said not to take sides. I asked whose side he thought we were taking. He thought for a bit, then told me we were always siding with the poorest, regardless of what was going on. He said I seemed to have "a hard-on for every successful Haitian." It seemed, he explained, like I was pursuing some "liberal" political agenda. That didn't have any place on an A-Team, he said.

Gonzo was at his most childish and petulant. He refused to say anything, until Mike coaxed him along with all kinds of "we wanna hear your side" and "your opinion is important to us" crap. When he did talk, he was evasive and threatening. It wasn't the first time. He'd "seen a lot of stuff that ain't right", he reminded us. He told me that I had a lot of medals and badges (though we didn't wear our Class A uniforms in Haiti), that I may have done a lot of "stuff", but that he wasn't sure what I might have done or might not have done. He didn't think whatever I had done or not done was any reason for Mike to "do everything you say to do." He finished by reminding us how much work he did, and that he was doing his job, even though he didn't know what we were doing here in the first place. Like Kyle, Gonzo had the limited perspective of a private...everything was the fault of the most immediate supervisor in sight.

Then Ali had his turn.

Ali started with the soft soap. I had done wonders with the team. Mike and I were the best command element on any A-Team in 3rd Group. Blahzy-blahzy. But he felt like I singled him out for special treatment, for the severest criticism. He didn't think I should censor him so much with the Haitians, and he wanted me to take into account that he had "experience with Haitians" before any of us (in the camps at Guantanamo). He reiterated the value of his language capability, as if that were some bargaining chip. He told me that he had serious problems with the way I "trashed the United States to journalists and indij." I shouldn't tell them that the CIA has done fucked up things, or that the US bears some responsibility for the situation in Haiti, or that race was a factor in the immigration policies of the United States. Ali considered this disloyal. These were gross simplifications of things I had said to ground our own credibility with specific audiences. Ali was an immigrant, German and Iranian, and he was a hyperpatriot, more American than the Americans, out to prove that above all else, as well as a former Marine.

Mike and I listened patiently. Is everyone finished, Mike asked. They were. Would I like to say something, now? he wanted to know. No, sir, I indicated, he could go. I'd be happy to go last.

Mike finally let them have it. I had been fearful that he would go south as he had when we fired Vern, letting me be the lone heavy …that he would continue to give them the truth with a teaspoon of honey. But he let their asses have it, and I was proud of him.

A perfectly functional team, he told them, one that had the finest reputation in group, was what it was because of what we had done, the hard training, the discipline, the systematic development of skills, and the effective division of labor. Now they were talking and acting like a bunch of privates, pissing and moaning about how hard things were, that they didn't have relaxation time, and that they didn't get to dictate operations. He told them he was in fact the commander, and that he had not turned the team over to me, but that being the commander meant the interpretation of his mission, and part of executing that mission was having the sense to listen to his operations sergeant. He assured them that we disagreed, and that I was sometimes overruled, but that he had confidence in my judgment, because we had succeeded from day one in following that judgment. He said that he deeply resented the obligation they placed on him to be a tyrant (even though that task usually devolved on me) when they continually put their personal comfort and interests ahead of the mission and their job performance, as had been the case more and more since Aristide had returned. He told them that their performance of the mission for the first weeks had led him to begin doing the paperwork for across the board Meritorious Service Medals, but that the degradation of their performance recently, and the general immaturity and indiscipline was forcing him to reconsider. He cited how the street had not been fixed and how Kyle hadn't taken the least initiative to get it done. He cited how people were going on security patrols, then hanging out in the shade somewhere away from the house, and coming back before their shift was done. He cited how Ali had been AWOL more than once, because he was out getting his dick wet somewhere in the ville. He cited how no order was going unquestioned or at least un-commented upon.

He hit it right on the head. They were assholes.

Finally, it was my turn. I was determined to be tactful but honest, hard but fair.

I told them again that I was sorry to have lost my comportment on the night of the incident with Gator, and that I thought perhaps we had lost something then. But that said, I told them, I was the operations sergeant. I said that three times. "I am the *operations sergeant*. I am the operations sergeant. I am the operations sergeant. I am not the medic, and I have not tried to do the medic's job, even though I know how. I'm not the communicator, and I haven't tried to do the communicator's job. I haven't tried to tell Kyle how to engineer, and I haven't micromanaged Skye's responsibilities with the FAd'H and the weapons. I've only helped Rod out where he asked for it, and helped him integrate ops with intel. We can only have so many cooks in the kitchen, and in the operations kitchen, that would be Mike and me." This is roughly how I started.

Then I forgot my determination to be tactful. Did anyone there, I asked, really believe they had actively looked to see how he could exercise his role to the absolute best of his ability to support the command element's operational priorities? Had anyone taken the least initiative to carry out the mission objectives we had communicated? I didn't give a flying fuck, I told them, whether they disagreed or agreed with those objectives. Every one of us still had U. S. Army stitched over his right breast pocket, and that didn't translate into Burger King, and they weren't going to have it their way. I was aggressive, and I was going to remain aggressive. The army, I said, should get rid of the green berets we wore in garrison, because it seemed a lot of young men just wanted to punch a ticket to wear the beret and talk shit, and they had forgotten that it was supposed to represent—grown-ups who are willing to work hard and sacrifice their personal needs to the needs of the mission and the team—NCO's who didn't need to have discipline imposed on them, but who imposed it on themselves.

In Vietnam, I reminded them, our unit had gone sixty days once without a stand-down or a shower, slogging day-in and day-out over the mountains and carving out a path with a machete, exposed to the rain and sun, not to mention being in a real combat zone...and they had lived indoors most of this mission, which was just over a month old, and they were whining like toddlers.

My own impression was not that people agreed or disagreed with Mike's and my interpretation of mission guidance (which was pretty amorphous), but that they wanted us to interpret it to suit their personal comforts. I would not stay in a *macoute* hotel, and I would not alienate the civilian leadership that enjoyed the support of the majority of the population, and I would not assume that everyone who came to the door was a liar. All that had been explained. The response to Ali's assertions, however, were slightly more complex. I had to explain the value of our credibility, which they obviously didn't care about, and how that credibility was based on giving honest accounts to people who already knew things. If I told the Christian Peacemakers that the CIA and US foreign policy had been stirring the pot in Haiti for years, I wasn't giving them news. I was validating what they already knew and establishing myself as an honest broker. If I told journalists that Haitians still knew and cared about the racist Marine occupation of Haiti, I wasn't giving them a scoop. If I told Haitians in Ft. Liberte that they needed to organize now, because there was no guarantee that the FRAPH wouldn't be turned loose on them again, I wasn't creating some unique new expression of an unfounded paranoia. I was letting them know that we may not have been able to do what they liked, and that we may have ended up doing things they didn't approve of, but that we could at least continue to exchange one solid currency...our mutual honesty. Furthermore, if Adele was my friend, and if I liked a goodly number of Haitians, that was my own goddamn business. What the hell did "too pro-Haitian" mean anyway? Did they see the interests of the United States or of the Army or of Special Forces or of this team as antagonistic to the interests of Haitians? Was that it? "And Ali, when you are at your eighth conflict area and log in two decades of armed service, I will give you permission to question my loyalty." I was saying all of this very calmly.

"I know you're all tired. I'm tired. So what? So we're tired. I know you're all homesick. I'm homesick. So what? I know you're all frustrated because you don't know what we're doing here, and I have to admit, I get more confused every day. Big deal. You solve the problems of your job, and I'll solve operations. If I screw it up, I take the hit. Mike takes the hit. I've never not looked out for this team from day one, but I never quit making demands that are consistent with what this team is designed to do. You don't like the team? You don't like Special Forces? You can terminate as soon as we get back. I'll give you a hand with the paperwork. But if you act like children, don't get all pissy when I treat you like children. I never claimed to be perfect at this job, but when y'all have perfected your own job performance, give me a heads-up, and I'll let you come and do mine. No one gave you any guarantees about what this mission would or wouldn't be. You want to chase pussy in the Dominican Republic, you do that on your own time. You want a Hollywood production where you can be the hero and everything makes sense, I suggest you get a California phone directory and give Universal Studios a call. I don't do heroes. Wouldn't give a fuckin' dime for one. I want team members, not individuals."

Pretty tactful, huh?

Click. Click.

That night I spent a long time sitting alone on the crumbling coral and concrete wall in the empty lot across the street where we burned our trash. I was a real hard case. Tough guy. In the house. On the street. Here in the darkened lot, alone with a pack of *Comme il Faut Vert*, a stray chicken or two, and a sky distended inconceivably deep and thickly littered with particles of dead, burning gas ...I was empty.

Loneliness, isolation, and self-pity were kicking my ass. When times have been hopeful, I have been depressed and terrified by the inevitability of death. When times have seemed pointless, gratuitous, and even painful, death has been a hopeful thing ...the promise of respite. This is the demented paradox of human awareness. It's said the same way. "Some day, this will all be over." Whether that is pessimism or optimism depends totally on which syllables get the stress. It's the perfect expression of the relationship between objective reality and subjective reality. Either way you say it, it's true. Either way you mean it, it's true.

The next day, Kyle led a group into Cap Haitien, where they traded ten bottles of rum for enough concrete to fix the main street in Ft. Liberte.

A man came by who said he had been in the United States, and that he was the representative of EDH, the Haitian electricity company. He tried to tell us to go around town and remove all the "illegal" hookups, even though we were running the generator with US diesel and Gonzo was keeping the generator alive. He got loud, stood up and began shaking his finger in my face, so I had him put in jail.

Power.

That night, Skye gathered several dozen children around the front porch, while we nursed Presidentes, and hooked two chemlites (plastic chemical lights) to strings, then gave a very entertaining light show by creatively twirling and spinning them around, creating streaks and tracers and ovals and figure-eights. Kind of like the Fourth of July.

Mike went to the Citadel the next day, en route to Cap.

I recanted my arrest of the electric man, who apologized for becoming so agitated, then began to cry like a baby on the porch. I fixed him a cup of coffee, and told him to wait until we were gone to worry about the electricity here. He was concerned because his supervisors had given him the directive, and he wanted to ensure he got his old job back. I told him he could refer them to us, and we would explain the situation.

Mike picked up Pedro Munoz in Cap, so we now had both our communicators. Pedro came in boisterous and cocky, telling us that the word everywhere was that 354 was "kicking ass and taking names," which meant we were perceived to be doing very well. Mike was bouyed by that report.

When Pedro linked up with the team, and they began swapping stories, he related his exploits in the Dominican Republic, while they spoke in softer, more conspiratorial tones ...indicating to me that they were describing my madness to him.

That suspicion was confirmed when I walked Pedro around town to familiarize him with the area. He glared when I lit cigarettes. He seemed particularly disconcerted when I sat on the wall at Fort Dauphin and Eaulin came up and perched in my lap. She and another child, a little boy, held each of my hands as we walked back. This was pretty standard, but it seemed to concern Pedro a great deal, even though he said nothing about it. This was something that was merging with what he had been briefed by the other men, no doubt.

That evening, Pedro was still telling stories about DR, about what was happening in the States, all with a strong dose of his usual insecure macho bluster. He also went silent from time to time, cocking an ear to whatever was quietly being explained to him by the boys about their situation. Top was going native—Batman—I could picture the flat, red-eyed look of acknowledgment, the look of the stubbornly dim-witted when they think they understand.

On November 1st, the mayor of Fort Liberte returned from exile in Miami and Toronto. He sent an emissary to the house before our first get together to announce his intention of holding a meeting with us. Two hours later he arrived.

Exile had been good to Ferte. We never ascertained exactly what he did while he had been away, but he was thickly well-fed and bedecked in expensive jewelry and reeked of cologne. His English was quite good. He was a fast talker, who could shift gears from hauteur at one moment to obsequiousness the next. He reminded me of a con man or a high-pressure salesman, and I disliked him immediately. This, of course, meant that I had no objectivity with regard to Ferte Pierre. Combine that with the imperious stubbornness I was developing as I daily strengthened the walls between my commanders and myself, and my men and myself, and Ferte really never had a chance. It was totally unfair to him by any standard. He didn't know what he had walked back into.

Ferte Pierre, in fact, had been the mayor before the coup, and Adele had been the deputy mayor, but Ferte had packed up and left with no instructions and no forwarding address, and it had been assumed that he had dropped out of the picture to pursue different prospects. When he returned, he brought with him an entourage and a list of demands. He also began to strengthen the team's resolve to break the alliance between Adele and me.

He did that by spinning out a tale of woe about his "back pay" as mayor. Adele and her clique had conspired to take his money, and they owed him thousands of gourds. He was going down to the *Bibiolteque* the following day to audit the financial records of the Ft. Liberte Commune. The boys, especially Rod—who disliked Adele for his assumptions about her sexual orientation and his fundamental objection to women being in charge of anything—jumped on this "revelation" like a squad of hungry ducks on a wounded june bug. Damn it, they all knew something was wrong with her, and now was I going to quit listening to her and start listening to our own task force?

None to gently, I told them all to shut up, but even Mike had begun to waver as Ferte explained in his deeply wounded voice about the chicanery of the current "administration."

Who has the money now? I asked Ferte. He was convinced Adele had it hidden away. I see, I said, and how much a month was that and what was the total again? He repeated his figures, referring to a sheet of calculations he had prepared for just this meeting. And what exactly were we to do about this, given that we knew absolutely nothing about the administration of the commune's finances? Well, he explained, we were the only authority around, and thank God we had arrived to do such a superlative job of stopping these *macoute* police and all their minions, and since he was the rightful mayor, we were actually bound to help him seize the money from the commune's coffers and return it to him immediately.

I see, I said again, and how is it that Adele, of all people, was the only pro-Aristide civil servant who had received pay in the last three years? This puzzled him. What did we mean? What we meant, of course, was that our inquiries into the question of pay showed that no pro-Aristide civil servant had been paid since the coup, and even the pro-Cedras people had gone for the last several months without pay, because the central government was absolutely broke. This set Ferte to stuttering. He rose to leave, as he asked us to meet him in two days at the *Biblioteque*, so that he could prove his allegations to us.

On his way out, he became very chummy and conspiratorial. Don't listen to any of these people, he told us.

Who?

The people in Fort Liberte. They are very backward and very conniving, and they all use powders.

"Powders," I repeated. I hoped the rest of the team had heard this comment. I noted with some relief that Mike suddenly seemed to toss Ferte's credibility into the gutter.

"Don't even let them shake your hand, Sergeant Goff. They coat their own skin with an antidote, then press the powders into your hand. And they will blow it into your face through the windows as you sleep. I tell you this because I am so glad you are here, and for your own good."

I could have reminded him that we had been there for quite some time, shaking hands with reckless abandon and heedlessly leaving the windows open at night. It occurred to me that the last time anyone had tried to scare us away from the Haitian population with powder stories, it had been U. S. Military Intelligence and the Psychological Operations drudges. Now I was hearing it from a Haitian.

When he left, I heard Kyle making some comment to someone inside the house, that Stan will never believe anything bad about Adele. In his opinion—and this was loud enough that I believe it was for my benefit—none of these people was worth a shit, and they were all pathological liars.

I looked up at Mike, who had obviously heard, and he just shook his head slightly, signaling me to leave it alone.

He was tired. I was tired. It wasn't worth it.

On the morning of November 4th, I was leaning on the concrete porch banister with a canteen cup of thick chocolate coffee. James was raking up a pile of trash across the street and pouring gas on it to burn it. People were ambling down the street toward the market. A corporal from the caserne walked up and took a position at the bottom of the steps. He asked for Ali.

Ali was in back having his breakfast, so I called James over. Find out what he wants, I instructed James.

It turned out that Ferte had come by the FAd'H garrison the afternoon prior and indicated that when he was in charge again, something very serious and sinister was going to happen to all the soliders. Apparently, the soldiers, fearing that we would somehow back Ferte in whatever this threat implied, had taken it seriously, and there was a good deal of concern. What had they done wrong? he wanted to know. Hadn't they been behaving?

I had James tell him not to worry, that no one was going to do anything to them, least of all Ferte, and that I would talk with Ferte.

He seemed relieved, and left.

When I told Mike, he was as exasperated with Ferte's ham-handed stupidity as I was.

That day I had Ferte over. I sent James to tell him that he was to come to our house, that it was important.

I read him the riot act, complete with the threat to put him in jail if he or any of his people so much as lifted a finger against anyone while I was there. Did he want a full scale occupation of the place, with armored personnel carriers, barbed wire, machine guns on the street corners? Did he want our colonels there? I told him directly that most of them were probably sympathetic to the *attaches*, and they would be in bed with Calixte and Mozart in no time. Is that what he wanted? He began whining about his money again, and said he was preparing to take "legal actions." I got loud then, and said he was half a heartbeat from an MRE and a cell, with the same people he was threatening the day before left there to guard him.

The team had drifted into the front room to better hear what the commotion was about. Ferte left with the first glistening edges of tears in his eyes.

Kyle had an I-told-you-so look for the other boys. They hadn't heard about the threat. What they saw was me attacking an enemy of Adele. Ali's demeanor was becoming more and more distant. The boys perceived him to still be partly in "my camp," and I had to imagine the peer pressure was fierce.

That night a destabilization was begun. There were two beatings. Both were people who were with "Adele's group", one a teacher and one a school superintendent. They happened within minutes of each other. When Mike and I went to talk with the superintendent, who still had blood running into his eyes, another woman came running to us to say that her house was under attack by rock throwers. She lived by the market.

We responded by grabbing Ali and Kyle and beginning a patrol around the market. Then the rocks began to pelt the tin roof of the marketplace as they fell short of us. We were being barraged with stones from across the block-wide market building. I sent Ali and Kyle running one way, while Mike and I ran the other, to catch the culprits. Mike and I just got a glimpse of their heels as they dodged into an alley and disappeared. I knew I had lost them, but I didn't want to let it stand. So I fired two shots into the air.

We regrouped at the house, where Ali, Kyle, and I grabbed the night observation goggles. We then found a dark position overlooking the main thoroughfares going to and from the market, and laid down in the dark to observe. After one hour, everything was still quiet.

We went back to the house, and opened some cold Presidentes.

Mike and I agreed that we needed to talk to Ferte.

I knocked on Ferte's door the next morning before seven. He showed up bleary-eyed. Before he could say anything, I told him to keep quiet and listen. The next time there was an incident, I told him, I would assume he was responsible. He would be under arrest. I told him to tell his people I would shoot anyone who was caught in the act of an assault.

What the story was behind the beatings and the provocations I never fully understood. It was irrelevant. We were entering a time when we had less and less latitude to intervene on anyone's behalf, but I couldn't explain that—that the task force was extending its oversight, and that my own people were resisting my partisanship. That was irrelevant, too, except to me. My point, again and again, was that any overt actions, justified or not, would lead to the impression of instability. The task force would respond to "instability" the only way it knew how. It would send in the 10th Mountain Division, with their APC's, machine guns, fortifications, and their infinite reservoir of rules. They would re-arm the FAd'H, and prohibit us from interfering with them. It was a slope too slippery for us to step on.

Ali had been subject to intense pressure to back away from me by the others. It was obvious in his increasing discomfiture when we were together while the rest of the team was around.

Gonzo, Ali, and Kyle went to Acul Samedi on the 7th of

November responding to the claim that there was violence there. The last time we had been there, I had deposed several people who were witnesses to four house burnings during the coup period. The FRAPH had directed the arson, and they were carried out by FRAPHists and several *attaches*. While we had been there, I made it clear to everyone we spoke with that we would tolerate no FRAPH activity whatsoever. We had run into an obstacle with the court. Kenty, the judge, was still frightened and he manifested his fear through bureaucratic wrangling and stalling tactics.

That afternoon around 3:00 PM, the boys returned with an old man and a young man. Both were in flex cuffs.

"What happened?" I demanded.

The boys were very edgy, very alert. Ali explained. The other two watched his every move. As if they were grading him as a spokesperson. Something was very odd about this.

The detainees were both Lavalas. They were under arrest because they had dragged a FRAPH member out of his home and given him a beating, along with several others. He was identified as the person who gave the order for the house burnings. There had been no action taken with regard to the depositions we took about the burnings, and they grew tired of waiting. Justice had to be done. The beatings were a minor thing, according to the detainees.

The FRAPH member had lodged a complaint. That complaint had been heard by Ali the previous day. I had not been informed that it was a Lavalas beating of a FRAPH member. Ali had told me they were going to check on a beating incident. I had told them to go.

Now they were back, and Ali was very hyper, very aggressive.

"They are under arrest. Everybody gets treated the same. They will not be released until the judge sees them." He was telling me, almost commanding me.

I understood then. This was a test for me. They were challenging me with these Lavalas people. The whole trip had been concocted between them for that express purpose the previous day. Ali was proving to the others that he was not in my pocket. He, too, was being tested. And they had me.

I asked the detainees if they had beaten the man. They affirmed again that they had. I had Ali translate. I also had him tell them that we were sorry that justice as slow, but that we were required to treat everyone as if today were day one. I am sure that Ali altered the translation, because his tone was not consistent with what I was trying to communicate. No matter. My own little speech sounded sterile and stupid even as I said it.

Adele strolled up to the house. The detainees both greeted her, and she greeted them. They knew one another. Then she noticed the flex cuffs. The look she gave me made me feel about a foot tall.

I told Ali and Kyle to take them to the jail and give them both three MRE's apiece to eat for the next day. I called James out of the house to translate with Adele, and explained what had happened.

She said, in the most mechanical way imaginable, that they understood how important it was to avoid reprisals, and how that was the only way to move forward to reconciliation. It was a recital. Adele was now reshuffling her categories. She was part of an "us," and I had now joined with "them." Like the Haitian proverb said, your enemy may help you out of the well, but don't forget when you're out, he's still your enemy.

I asked what she had stopped by for. She said it wasn't important. I asked if she would like to share a bottle of water and a cigarette. She said she had to go. She wouldn't even look me in the eye.

I was still smarting the next day. I felt my control slipping, felt myself more and more becoming a cog again. That was what I was supposed to be, but I had grown accustomed to our relative autonomy, accustomed to defining our own situation. As I was being forced to confront the reality that I was again becoming just a soldier, I had to begin to recognize that what I had done and what I was continuing to do constituted a rebellion. The boys had been an instrument of that rebellion. Mike had been an instrument of my rebellion. Now the boys were like goldfish who saw me chipping away at their bowl, as poet Ken Cook would say, and exposing them to world upon breathless world.

For myself, I was beginning to recognize that I was not just involved in a rebellion against the Task Force, but against a whole foreign policy, a whole system. I was standing exposed like a fly, and a great storm was approaching.

The evening after the arrest of the two Lavalas from Acul Samedi, Gonzo and Ali were on their rotation of roving patrol. They were scheduled to patrol the sector from Malfety to Trou du Nord. I had been in Sicar, when I came back to the house and saw them sitting on the porch, over half an hour prior to the end of their shift.

"Just chillin' out?" I asked as I mounted the steps to the porch. I think I was smiling.

That's right. They were relaxing. It had been a hot drive.

"Your shift isn't over," I remarked.

Gonzo returned my matter-of-fact tone. "Nothin' goin' on." Ali nodded.

I didn't raise my voice. "But your shift is on for another half hour. So get your gear on, and get back in the vehicle, and drive in that direction for the next fifteen minutes, then you can come back."

They both looked at me incredulously.

"Do it now," I said. "Because I'm going inside to check the message log, and if you're here when I come back, I'll go back inside and prepare formal counseling statements against you both. And I caution you to remain at ease and not say a single word." I was still grimacing at them.

While I was reading the message log, I heard the hummer crank and drive away.

They got me yesterday, so I got them today. We were at war.

Click. Click. Click.

Dave Grau came back from his extended hiding out from Haiti on November 10th. Mike had seethed about Grau every day since he'd left "for his child's illness" from Gonaives. That illness had been wrangled into an extended vacation.

Mike had gone over his briefing for Grau with me the night prior. He wanted to set everything straight, to lay it out exactly right.

When Dave came in on the vehicle from Cap Haitien with supplies, there was a general good-natured welcome, a cacophony of exchanges about what was going on in Bragg, what Port-au-Prince was like now, the bustle of putting up supplies.

But when the dust settled, and when the Cap crew had gone, Mike invited Dave into his room alone for the briefing. Only Mike and I knew what that briefing consisted of. That his delays in returning were unprofessional, that he had deliberately sought his own convenience and comfort ahead of the mission and his team, that his performance while in Gonaives was often whining and immature and inconsistent with what was expected of a warrant officer, and that he was on a form of probation until further notice. Mike told him that he was being granted an opportunity to overcome his past shortcomings, but only if he worked hard and diligently at it for the remainder of the mission.

When Grau emerged from the briefing, I was the only one that understood his look of quiet consternation. Grau was a cornered rat. His career was on the line.

That evening, while Mike was recording entries in his journal and writing a letter to his wife, and I was having a beer on the front porch, I drifted back through the house to see what people were up to. Dave and the rest of the team were huddled on the back porch. When I stepped out on the back porch, they all became completely silent, and every eye was averted.

The next day, while I was tidying up my room, I heard Gonzo saying, loudly enough so everyone would have a taste of his frustration at being in Haiti, "I seen a lot of stuff around here that just ain't right. I bet other people would say it ain't right either."

It was the kind of veiled threat cocky privates make when they've been pushed just to the edge of their tolerance. The difference was, I knew he was right about the last part. I was further outside the fence than ever.

November 12th, I became 43 years old. By pure coincidence, that was my down day, and I was allowed to roam and loaf.

It was a policy we had recently implemented, and most of the guys used it to swim and lounge down by Calixte's hotel. They had also scrounged a variety of pipes and giant sprockets from the ruins of the sisal plant by Phaeton, and made a set of weights. Kyle had constructed a weight bench. They could show the most remarkable energy, initiative, and resourcefulness, when it was for something they wanted. There had been a time at the beginning of the mission, where they would have exercised those qualities for me—but that was a fading memory.

I had decided to go to Ouanaminthe and write. The urge to begin putting some of my thoughts down about the mission had begun to preoccupy me. Partly it was my growing sense of isolation, and the need to talk to someone who wasn't there. I couldn't share my thoughts with any of the boys. I could only find limited common ground with Mike with regard to the team clique of resistance. I surely wasn't about to write Sherry and worry her when she was in no position to do anything but worry. So I settled on the idea of writing things down. This book was conceived on my 43rd birthday.

I left on one of the Yamahas at around ten that morning. At Ouanaminthe, I dropped by L'Escale. Freddy wasn't there. He'd gone to Port-au-Prince for two days. The place was empty except for a few folks who meandered in and out, so I put a pack of cigarettes on the table, ordered a soda, and opened my notebook.

I would wait for some resentment to build, dwell on it as I filled my lungs with toxins, then scribble my reactions. I wrote notes describing L'Escale. I wrote notes recalling the day the Chinooks dropped the walls on top of the citizens of Ouanaminthe. I wrote nasty caricatures of the boys. I thought of at least ten different poisonously funny descriptions of Schroer. I was so wired on Pepsis and nicotine by four o'clock, that I decided it was time to head back.

At the end of it all, I had expected some kind of therapeutic result, but the whole exercise actually increased my sense of isolation and made me so homesick I could have died.

The road between Fort Liberte and Ouanaminthe is a treacherous, spine-bashing gauntlet of potholes and stones and loose patches of gravel, with a perpetual cloud of lingering dust suspended over it from the trucks' passing. The ride over on the Yamaha had taken over half an hour, and the ride back took the same. It was physically and psychically exhausting. I had no helmet, no goggles, no sunglasses. By the time I approached Fort Liberte, I was a powdered apparition with my dusty woodland camouflage and daypack, and my wild, dust-stiffened, windblown hair.

As I passed the *carrefour* that led four ways to Ferrier, Malfety, Ouanaminthe, and Fort Liberte, I glanced left and caught sight of a Hummer rounding the bend from Chivry, headed my way. Adrenaline spread through me like a tidal wave.

My first thought was that it was Schroer on a surprise visit. And I was on a motorcycle with no helmet, in violation of directives, traveling alone, in violation of directives, having come from another team's sector, in violation of directives, carrying only a pistol, in violation of directives, without my LCE, in violation of directives, and worst of all, with my sleeves worn in a three-quarter roll.

I had just over a mile to go, with the Hummer less than a quarter mile off my tail. I couldn't tell whether they'd spotted the uniform on the bike or not. I rolled the throttle back and began deliberately cutting fishtails in the dust to put a smoke screen of dust between me and the Hummer. Sitting well back on the seat and pulling rearward on the handlebars, I skipped through and around the potholes bouncing like a motocrosser. When I checked the rear view mirror, the Hummer was gaining on me. They were going to catch me in spite of my reckless attempt to escape.

Just as I got to Sicar, I could make out three bodies in the Hummer, and they didn't look like my team. In a final, desperate maneuver, I geared down suddenly, then throttled into a crazy swimming right turn, hopped into and out of a ditch, completely lost control of the bike, and crashed into the raket hedge in front of a little caille paille. I didn't even lay still to inventory my body for injuries. I rolled back onto my feet and ran around to the back of the caille paille like a flee-ing felon, then squatted behind the house like a frightened child hop-ing they would drive past. The bike was still laying over in front of the caille paille, propped ridiculously on a peg, with the front wheel spin-ning at an nutty angle.

Three Haitian men and one woman in an adjacent lot were sitting where they had been swapping gossip. The didn't get up, but they quit talking. They just sat and stared at me, peering around the back corner of the house at the passing vehicle. When it passed, I looked sheepish-ly over at them and smiled, putting a finger to my lips to indicate we were sharing a secret. One of them said something, and they all laughed.

I checked to make sure I had everything, daypack, weapon, an intact skeletal system, then recovered the bike. It had leaked some gas, but the only damage was a twisted clutch handle that still worked. It started right up, and I zipped away around the back of Sicar.

My route circled near the salt marsh and brought me to the mar-ket two blocks from the house. I parked behind the market warehouse and sidled up to the corner to get a peek at who was in the house.

Ali and Mike were in front talking to them. Ali was in his t-shirt with a cup in his hand, so I knew it wasn't anyone from either the AOB or the FOB. They were neutrals. I had nearly killed myself hiding from someone who didn't give a damn.

When I parked the bike in front of the house, it was Captain White with two companions. They had dropped by to say hi on the way to Belladere or someplace.

We had a very pleasant chat.

Every time I rounded a corner, it seemed, I'd find the boys in hushed conversations. Neither Kyle nor Dave would even look me in the eye any more.

While I was in the operations shop one day, mid-November, Kyle and Pedro and Dave were talking loudly for my benefit on the back porch. They were talking about how "higher" had begun saying that we had to begin "turning it over to the Haitians." That meant to let the FAd'H begin policing again. I bit off the urge to say they'd never police this town as long as we were there.

"They can take care of their own shit, 'cause this is their own shit-hole," said Kyle.

"It don't matter if they're real police," said Pedro. "'Cause this ain't a real fuckin' place."

I glanced out to see Grau cracking up over this one, as he looked directly in at me. It was his little challenge from the comfort of his little group.

The clique I had intended to dismantle when I had taken the team was rising like a phoenix. The formerly excluded were being included. I had finally accomplished my first team sergeant's mission. I had built a team that was focused on a common task. And the object of that task was—me.

83: The International Police Monitors

We were all waiting breathlessly for the Bolivians. It was our understanding that they would take over all supervision of the FAd'H, relieving us of the same. The Bolivian International Police Monitors were our preferred nationality, because we had heard that it was between them and the Argentines. And the Argentines had already established their reputation in Cap Haitien—as pigs. They were reported to be brutalizing Haitians, including committing a fair number of sexual assaults. They were racist and colonial in their outlook, and in their wake the camp follower culture had grown up—flim-flam men, prostitution, petty-theft and fencing rings.

They showed up on November 19th. Mike and I had to find them "quarters", and the only place that could accommodate them was Calixte's Hotel. So now the invasion had become a windfall for Nyll Calixte, financier for the FRAPH, unrepentant Duvalierist, the protectee of the US military Task Force by order of the National Command Authority.

Mike fell in love with them. They were friendly. Dave Grau, who had returned, was on hand to interpret. They talked like mid-level officers everywhere, and they listened appreciatively to Mike's briefings. Mike couldn't shut up about how professional they were, about how they impressed him with all the right answers—whatever that meant. And of course they invited him to sit down dinners at the Hotel Bayara, where they would break out the Scotch and order cold Presidentes.

The boys ended up taking a shine to them too. They had a television and a VCR and a whole collection of movies in English with Spanish subtitles. We received an open invitation to go there any time to relax. So the boys finally got what they'd demanded in the beginning—access to this island of opulence overlooking the bay. Every moment they had free was spent there. Much as I resented it, there was a windfall for me too. When the boys weren't doing anything, they were no longer hanging around the house sulking and feeling sorry for themselves.

The night our IPMs arrived, we were listening to Colonel Boyatt's now familiar briefings on the radio—what he called his fireside chats. Boyatt had a grandiose streak that we all knew well, but that night we were treated to one of the strangest radio transmissions of my entire military career.

He came on with his usual checklist of gossip and veiled warnings on how to stay out of trouble with the Task Force authorities. But when that was out of the way, he launched into a weird homily.

"This is the greatest opportunity of your lives. You are making history." So far so good. Typical Boyatt. "You are in charge. You are in a vast laboratory." We suddenly began to pay attention. This was sounding very Kurtz-like. "This is your kingdom. Mold it. The entire population is at your beck and call, waiting for your directing hand. You have now entered into the perfect Unconventional Warfare environment. The population is the G-Force. Your local governments are the auxiliary. You can build networks of agents to act as your underground. . ." This rant went on, becoming more detached from reality by the minute, for over an hour. After ten minutes, Mike ordered Pedro to grab a tape player and record it. When it was done, we were all left sitting in a circle in the Operations room, staring silently at the radio speaker, perfectly dumbfounded by the scope of Boyatt's apparent psychotic episode.

The following day when we went to Cap Haitien to pick up supplies, we ran into another team from Grand Riviere du Nord. We asked them if they listened last night. The said they had. The team sergeant looked at me and asked, "Which one of us is going to be assigned to go get him?"

The following day, I took some cement we had raided from Cap, some steel bars, and some 4x4s, and build an exercise station with dip bars and a chinning bar. The rest of our cement I was stockpiling to repair the huge erosion ditch on the main drag through the middle of Fort Liberte.

Schroer came by unannounced, and we received an ass-chewing because our sleeves were up. We attempted to explain what had been going on in our sector, but he wasn't the least bit interested. Schroer did not care about what anyone did. His concern was that we have our sleeves down in the 95-degree heat.

The other thing Schroer said was that we were now responsible for the actions and operations of the Bolivians! Mike and I were bowled over by the stupidity of this directive. How, we asked him, were we to control the actions of a foreign army that was not in our chain of command? Schroer went into his Napoleonic act, geting loud and looking silly, and told us that he was the "ground commander" and that we would be held responsible for the Bolivians.

When Schroer left, Mike commented that he should probably just go ahead and declare himself the president.

The next day the Bolivians spent three hours trying to teach the FAd'H how to get into formation.

The 22nd was Mike's birthday. We arranged to give him a down day, where he went to the Bayara (about which I kept my mouth shut), and Rod and I went to Ferrier.

We were hearing a lot of rumors that there were guns being shipped across the Dominican border there, and we wanted to look over the terrain. While we were there, squeezing the hummer between the *raket* and brush along the trail to the border, we passed a group of people standing around a mare who was laying on the ground.

"*Ki moun pale espanol?*" I asked. Two raised their hands. Ferrier was on the border and Spanish, at least the rudiments, were very common there. We asked what had happened. She's dying, they told us. The mare was hugely round, gasping for breath, and her eyes were already dead looking. She's not pregnant, I asked? No, no. Fingers wagged the negative. They all seemed to know what was killing her. I reached down and thumped the round belly of the horse. It echoed like a drum. I'd seen it again and again at the goat lab in Ft. Bragg when I underwent medical training there. Bloat.

I looked around. Ferrier is in a richly vegetated area, with acre after acre of tall, bright green grass. Too much of it will cause ruminants to bloat, which I knew for goats could be lethal. I'd never thought about it with horses, but here one was.

"Rod," I called. "Get me the medical kit."

"What the fuck are you doing *now*" he asked. "Just leave that motherfucker to die."

"Just wanna try somethin'"

He carried the kit to me, exasperation all over his face. Rod really disliked having to deal with Haitians, and there was already a small crowd beginning to form around the *blancs*.

I pulled out a 14-guage Angiocath Intravenous needle and catheter assembly. I was going to try something desperate, whether it worked or not, just to satisfy my own curiosity about whether my diagnosis was correct. A few more thumps around the abdomen to find the greatest timpani, and I pulled the plastic protective case off the needle-catheter assembly and plunged the needle into the mare's abdomen. I withdrew the needle and put my ear to the catheter hub to listen for a stream of gas. Nothing. The Haitians were becoming intensely curious and had started quite a chatter. I re-inserted the needle into the catheter, withdrew the whole thing, then drove it back into a spot less than three inches from my first penetration. When I withdrew the needle this time, I didn't even have to put my ear by it. It started whistling and hissing away. Paydirt.

The gas hissed out for over five minutes when it was suddenly occluded by a frothy green head of chyme. I wiped a finger over the green foam, leaned over, sealed my pursed lips around the hub of the catheter, and gave a vigorous blow. I could feel the catheter clear. I spit, and withdrew the catheter around half an inch to keep it clear, and the hissing started again. When I looked up, Rod looked sick. He was staring back at me like I'd just eaten a turd.

When the hissing stopped without occlusion, I removed the catheter. I looked at the mare's eyes, and they actually looked awake and alive again. A minute later she raised her head. A murmur of voices swept through our Ferrier audience. Within ten minutes, she was on her feet, albeit a bit unsteady, shaking her head and snorting, and even rewarded us with a short, sharp fart. My hand was being siezed by a score of people. I told Rod to crank the Hummer and get us out of there.

Half an hour later, driving out of Ferrier toward Ft. Liberte, no fewer than three people shouted at us as we passed. They had sick animals. Could I come have a look? A new query began to show up at the door from time to time after that. People would come by the house and ask for the animal doctor. We had to explain that there was none.

That night we went to the IPM's dinner at Bayara for Mike's birthday party. Rod told the horse story, which everyone enjoyed, especially the look on Rod's face when he described me clearing the catheter.

When dinner was finished, the Bolivians broke out a bottle of Johnny Walker Black Label and offered a drink to all of us. Mike and I took a shot. I found it odd that absolutely not one other member of the team accepted. Rod was the only teetotaler on the team, and the boys had never before seemed reluctant to have a drink.

The 24th of November was Thanksgiving. Ronnie and Freddy came by. Ronnie had been to the States, and he picked up two big cans of cranberry sauce. They also brought by a bottle of Barbancourt Rum and a case of Presidentes. A chopper had dropped mermite cans with turkey and dressing and green beans, so we sat down on the back porch under the acacia tree and pigged out. Mike and I, along with Freddy and Ronnie, were again the only ones who had a couple of Presidentes. We stashed the rest in the refrigerator, along with the rum. I took the abstinence, again, as a little dig—refusal to share in anything social or festive. For about the 100th time, I was clueless.

The boys were unusually rude, talking among themselves, and essentially ignoring Freddy and Ronnie. Mike and I, however, had a good talk with them, catching up on gossip from Ouanaminthe and catching them up on the ups and downs of our work. The boys, since Grau had returned, had almost refused anything but the most absolutely necessary contact with Haitians, and that included our guests.

The minute the Thanksgiving food was eaten, everyone but Kyle, who was on house detail that day, headed over to the *macoute* hotel to watch television with the Bolivians. I had given them a down day for Thanksgiving, and they used it to give us this last little snub.

I retaliated the following day. I put the whole team to the task of fixing the street. I also forced the FAd'H members to help out—removing the paving stones, cutting out the erosion ditch, emplacing and padding the pipe we'd scavenged from Phaeton, leveling the pipe padding and replacing the paving stones, then locking them all together with a large cement patch at the downhill end of the new culvert. The people in town were extremely pleased with the whole operation. Many of them pitched in with the work. It was a nice piece of civil action, and the boys were fuming the whole time. The worst malcontent among them, and the one whose anger they seemed to drink from, was Dave Grau.

The Bolivians had come by and remarked on what a good job we were doing, but they were clean and pressed. They didn't offer to help.

Days later, in a conversation with the Bolivian commander, he asked, as Latin American officers are wont to do, about the combat experience of my team. Rod and Mike had Combat Infantry Badges from Desert Storm, where neither of them saw a shot fired in anger. The rest had never seen a combat zone. I told him that the only thing any of them except me had shot were targets. In Spanish, the word for targets is blancos. Whites.

"*Solamente han disparado blancos.*"

His reply, an attempt at punning: "*Nosotros disparamos negros.*" We shoot blacks.

Here it was again. That casual racism that assumed my complicity because of my white skin.

I walked away, feeling yet more alone.

Etias in Trou du Nord had been asking for assistance we didn't have the wherewithal to provide for weeks. The level of insecurity was becoming insupportable. Criminals were taking maximum advantage of the lack of any police force and the distance we—the only security force with any credibility—would have to travel to respond. The Bolivians, he told us, only drove through town to shop and drink. They were curt with the population. I told him to take whatever means necessary to establish a popular constabulary. He felt he needed our permission.

He organized 70 young men from the host of popular organizations, and every seventh day, ten of them would take a turn responding to incidents in the day, and patrolling on foot about town at night. They were armed with clubs and machetes, and Etias reported that it had worked. . . in town.

Around the 1st of December, there were two murders within three days, one in Caracol, and one in the hills South of Trou. Both were committed with machetes. The first was particularly savage. We dispatched the Bolivians to investigate, and they came back claiming there was no way to ascertain what was happening—that it seemed like some kind of feud.

When Ali and I went down to investigate on the 6th of December, Etias was livid with the Bolivians. I had never seen Etias openly frustrated before. He was usually the picture of calm. They had done nothing, he said. When people explained that the murders were not in Trou, they flatly refused to travel anywhere to check it out.

We had been directed to take along a Psychological Operations Team as part of the latest push to ram the "reconciliation" message down the Haitian's throats. There was a buck sergeant and a Private First Class. The had a loudspeaker with a bunch of prefabricated Creole tapes with the propaganda speeches. Ali and I decided to stop at a restaurant we knew there and get a bite of *kabrit* and rice. Etias sat down with us and explained where we were going afterwards to ask questions of the people who lived near the place where the latest murder had taken place.

We had taken a trip to the morgue to look at the body, so we could describe the wounds. It was un-refrigerated. The cadaver had one machete slash across the shoulder and one across the forehead that went clear through the skull—the fatal wound we assumed. The body had bloated with the heat, and the man's penis was filling with fluid, so it stood up like a giant purple water balloon. Ali seemed a bit unsettled by the whole thing, but said he still could muster an appetite for lunch.

As our food was being brought out to us, we were suddenly scared out of our wits by the loudspeaker. The Psyops Team had taken it upon themselves to begin blaring their obnoxious propaganda in the crowded street right outside the restaurant. I went nuts.

"Turn that shit off, now!" I burst out the door yelling.

The psyopers looked at me.

"Fuckin' cut that shit off right now!" I screamed again.

They killed the tape.

"What in the hell was that all about?"

"Sergeant," the buck sergeant pleaded, "We were told that this is our mission."

"Not here," I scolded. "Not now."

He tried to argue with me that we weren't letting him do his mission.

"Look!" I said. "We were saddled with you with no prior coordination, and told to take you along on our patrols. This is it. This is the only thing going out today. But we are conducting a murder investigation. Take fuckin' notes. You will not blare that horseshit propaganda around the place we are working, and you will not mix that bullshit in with the business we're trying to conduct."

The psyopers went sullen for the rest of the trip, which lasted most of the day.

We went about fifteen kilometers South on a treacherous muddy road to the site of the crime. We asked about twenty people questions, and there were half as many witnesses available. They knew who did it, a local thug who was paid 700 gourd (less than $47 US), and who had it done—the victim's brother-in-law. It was a land dispute that had been festering for several years. We hiked about two miles up a mountain, leaving the psyopers to guard the Hummer, and collected the father-son team who allegedly hired the murderer. Etias asked them if they did it, and they readily admitted they did. Their justification was that the victim had been using magic against them. Etias gave them some kind of lecture in Creole. We flex cuffed the two of them, and escorted them down the hill to the Hummer. One woman and three children watched blankly as we left their caille paille.

On the way back, we queried ourselves to the house of the alleged contract killer. He was gone. The neighbors said he had heard the Americans might come and escaped to Santo Domingo.

We jailed the two suspects and notified Kenty that he was going to have to try them. The psyopers stayed the night and caught a helicopter out the next day. I told Mike about the Bolivians failure to do anything. He made some lame excuses for them, and said we should go out again the following day and check on the other murder.

The next day, Ali and I paid a visit to the cemetery where the first victim had been interred. He was from Caracol, and people suspected it was a political killing. I was going to go through the same routine, checking the body and describing the wounds for the report to Kenty. But the cemetery attendant who was standing by a little brush fire in the paupers section told us the body was so slashed up that he had buried it in a gunny sack.

He showed us the fresh grave. He said it was only abut a meter deep, and from the surface we could see that it was also only about a meter long. Ali absent-mindedly kicked at something that looked like a smoldering gourd and it cracked into several pieces. Then I recognized the structure of a maxilla.

"That's someone's head you just kicked, Ali."

He started. "oh. . . sorry. . ." He almost seemed to say it to the skull. The attendant took no note. He was burning bones around the cemetery. We asked him why he did that, and he said the place got full. So ever so often they would just clear off the vines, plow up a piece of ground to stir the bones to the surface, and burn what came to the top. The wealthier Haitians got above ground tombs, which were brightly painted and next to the road.

We decided against disinterring the victim. Our inquires that day came to a dead end, no pun intended. There were no witnesses, and the man's body had just shown up in the street one morning. He was a Lavalas activist, we were told, but his potential enemies were too numerous to count.

When we got back to Fort Liberte, Mike was stirred up. The psyopers had caught a bird out that morning and dropped a dime on us as soon as they disembarked. We were being chastised by someone at task force headquarters for not letting the psyopers "do their job." It was a bit worse, because three days prior to this incident, I had waved off a psyops helicopter who was blaring unintelligible recordings at the town and stirring up a crowd scene to no purpose whatsoever. So now we were being perceived as trying to block Psyop's "mission." In fact, there was nothing I wanted to do more than block their mission, because it stood to destroy my credibility with the local population.

On the 8th of December, we were sent a huge banner to stretch across the street, with direct orders to display it in the main street near the caserne. I said some shit about democracy and *reconciliation*.

The Bolivians told us on the 8th that they were leaving. Their mission was done. I was confused. What was their mission? We were told they would take care of administering the FAd'H and doing police stuff, neither of which they had done worth a tinker's damn.

84: WOMEN

Gigash was the sixteen-year-old girl who lived next door with her mother, who was a nurse at the regional hospital where Max Mondestin worked. They were nice enough people, comparatively well to do—that is, they had a concrete home with decent furniture, running water, and electricity. . . when it worked. Gigash had aquiline features—white features some would say—she was pretty, slender, and like many sixteen year-olds, she was coquettish. Ali and Skye took on a predatory aspect around her, which worried me. She sat on her roof in the evenings and recited her lessons, as Haitian school kids are wont to do, over and over and over, learning them by rote. I occasionally shared a beer with her mom, blundering at Creole while she attempted to blunder at English. I never felt I had much in common with her, but as neighbors we were always cordial and exchanged greetings. The boys seemed to be put off by even that, toward the end.

It was a male thing. Relations with women that did not exist on an axis of domination and obsequiousness were out of the box. Simple mutual respect, or friendship—like Adele and me—were some kind of betrayal.

My consciousness of gender as a social and political issue had been influenced heavily by early association with Chris Platt, a woman who shared a few teenage years with me, who became an on-again, off-again lover, and who embraced feminism when she was at Case Western Reserve University, where she studied physics. My psychotic relationship with my first wife had truncated that association, but the seed was planted, and I have remained aware of male supremacy at some level ever since. Chris—as I last heard—is a high-powered physicist with the superconducter project at the Department of Energy. When my first marriage dissolved, I re-established a close relationship with my sister, Celia Wildroot, who is an out lesbian and a feminist. Our dialogues led me back to the question of gender again, and were largely responsible for breaking up the logjam in my consciousness about many of the dominant categories through which I viewed life. My spouse now—Sherry Long—is the embodiment of working class strength in a woman. She had done the single mom thing, often working three jobs to make ends meet, taking no shit, and emotionally resilient as women are not "supposed" to be. And she has held me accountable when my pronouncements failed to match my behavior. Every straight male should be so lucky. Since then, strong political women have played a dominant role in my post-military experience. I can say that I have been fortunate. Powerful women have had a profound formative influence on me, and it's been instrumental in helping me to shed many of the "male" expectations that bound my work, my relationships, and my psyche.

In Haiti, I watched the women. I watched them work their asses off in the midst of "70 percent unemployment." They slave away in the sweatshops of Port-au-Prince, they carry the water back and forth that keeps the whole struggling society alive, they bear the products of the country from one place to another on their heads, they wash the clothes on the river banks, shoo the animals out of the gardens, sweep the packed dirt floors of the huts, care for the children—and many of the men stand by.

In Ferrier, I was talking to three nuns who had a mission there. I mentioned that the women were doing the lion's share of the work. They enthusiastically assented. They told me that when the pump was broken in town, the parts were delivered. A fair number of men knew how to fix the pump, but the men did not carry water. So they didn't bother for months. Meanwhile, the women were walking two kilometers one-way and back to bring water into town to drink, cook, bathe, and wash. It simply didn't occur to the men to fix the pump, because it didn't affect them in their agitated discourses about unemployment, or in the domino games they occupied themselves with while they waited for something to come along. In fairness, this is not the case with the rural peasants. Male and female, they work from sun-up to sundown, with little food or water, to merely survive.

Magda, our original housekeeper and cook, was hired by Ali. He was appointed our one-man committee for this because his French was so good. Magda had two children. And she was a little bent. She was contentious, reputed to be a thief, and she was not popular around Fort Liberte. But she displayed a fierceness that I liked, and there was no doubt that Magda would survive, whatever the circumstances. She had a bit of the fighter in her, and a bit of the crook, and left the impression that she might strike back if she were offended. She argued with Ali about purchases at the market. She huffed off dramatically when the boys told her they didn't like the food. In fact her food was mediocre, and she was liberal with the grease, but it was a damn sight better than MRE's.

Skye began watching her closely when James told us she was a thief. He constantly inventoried the huge surplus of milk, M&M's, cheese crackers, MRE's, and bottled water. He didn't bother to conceal his distaste for her from the beginning, and he slighted her every chance he got.

I suspect Magda was stealing bits and pieces here and there, but she never bothered anything in the operations room, and I didn't believe she would take personal items that would be missed. We were paying her 25 *gourdes* a day—less than two dollars—and we had plenty of the stuff in question. I left a ten-gourd note on an MRE box in my room one day to test my hypothesis, and it did indeed disappear. But she obeyed the rules about operations, we had gotten to know her, she struck good bargains for us with street sellers, the work was always done according to guidance and on time, so I didn't give a shit.

She started coming to me on the sly and asking if she could have a carton of milk—the "nuclear milk" we called it, that came in sealed one-serving boxes you could leave on the shelf unrefrigerated for two centuries—and I found myself reluctant to give it to her. If I gave in once, she would came back again and again, making a pest of herself, and the boys would object that I was giving their stuff away. When the relationship between the boys and me began to seriously sour, however, I slipped her a milk and a package of cheese crackers, pretty much every day.

Then, in mid-November I overheard Ali telling Skye that he had paid Magda to give him a blowjob. They were giggling about it.

That afternoon, I conspicuously asked Gonzo if he had any oral anti-mycotics. When he asked me why, with Ali arranging his gear in the corner of the room, I told him Magda had complained to me about a mouth infection. I told Gonzo that when I examined her, she seemed to have thrush and a pretty advanced case of "bacterial gingivitis." Ali alerted.

"What's that?" he wanted to know. He was very attentive.

"Oh, just some pretty common problems when people can't practice good oral hygiene," I told him. "Though thrush among adults can be a sign of HIV."

Ali seemed preoccupied for the rest of the day. It was mean, but he had no business tricking with Magda like that. It was colonial bullshit.

A week later, Skye finally caught Magda. He stopped her as she left the house, and found four packets of cheese crackers stashed in her shirt. Mike gave them permission to fire her and hire a new person. I stayed out of it.

Two days later, Ali hired a married woman from Ft. St. Joseph. She asked us to just call her Jessi. She was a Protestant, very devout, and well respected about town. She worked well and almost too hard, but refused to heed my own advice for her to slow down a bit. Within a week, I saw the look on Ali's face. His eyes were beginning to fix on the curvature of Jessi's hips when she bent to stir her pots and squatted to wring out wet clothes. I confronted him straight out.

"You are not to make any moves on Jessi," I said.

"What the fuck are you talking about, Stan?" His denial was predictable as it was false. But it worked.

Jessi was still working at that house a year later, when I visited. There were Ghanian soldiers there by then—part of the UN group— and Jessi had cobbled together enough savings from her work at that house to begin building her own new house in Ft. St. Joseph—cinder blocks with a finished concrete floor. The occupation economy was beginning to pay off—for a very few.

85: GREEN SLEEVES

On November 20th, Schroer met us a Cap Haitien. He ordered us to roll our sleeves down. He also chewed my ass, because he was "under the impression" that I was not allowing the FAd'H to function.

On December 2nd, Col. Boyatt announced in his fireside chat that the uniform was "sleeves up."

On December 3rd, some of the team went to Cap for supplies. Major Fox told them that LTC Schroer had ordered that all sleeves would be down.

Ah, the weighty preoccupations of command!

86: ENDGAME

I thought the mail incident in Cap Haitien on the 26th of November was some kind of stress-related anomaly from the AOB. But it was foreshadowing.

Mike and I had gone into Cap to pick up the mail and some supplies. Mail was being run by some support outfit at the airport. When I went in to get our team mail, I was met by a surly PFC. He said he didn't know anything about our mail, and he made no effort to get off his ass and find out. This is not behavior that is tolerated by any NCO in the army, and I wasn't going to tolerate it either.

"Would you mind very much finding out where our mail is?" I said, dripping sarcasm. I was interrupting a movie he was watching on the VCR in his tent.

When he groaned to his feet and shut off the VCR, he said to no one in particular, "Man, fuck!"

"Hold on," I said. "Don't get me my mail. Just go ahead and get me your first line supervisor and come back here with him."

"Whatcha need him for, man?"

"Do you see my collar?" I asked, holding a corner of it out between thumb and forefinger. "I'm a Master Sergeant. I'm not your buddy. I'm not your daddy. And I'm not your man. If you fail to address me in accordance with military policy one more time, and if you display so much as a hint of further disrespect, I will bring your ass up on charges so fast it will make your head swim. Now come to the position of parade rest, and answer me in the affirmative or the negative whether you understand what I just said."

It killed him, but he complied.

"Now go get me your supervisor, and don't make me wait."

He came back in around five minutes with a Specialist 4, who I assumed was his supervisor. I was prepared to let the Specialist understand what was happening and to allow him to take corrective action, collect my mail and be on my way.

But the Specialist 4 decided to come in and be his buddy's shit house lawyer.

"Why you cursin' my man?" he demanded.

"Whoa!" I responded. "When did you forget military courtesy and the entire Uniform Code of Military Justice?"

"Why did you curse my soldier, Master Sergeant?"

"I didn't curse your soldier, Specialist. I told him to get off his ass, which he showed no inclination to do, and get my mail. And I'm not here to defend my prerogative as a non-commissioned officer to a Specialist 4 either. If you don't assure me that you will take corrective action, and get my team's mail within the next few minutes, then my next stop will be at your Sergeant Major's tent, where I will inform him that I am about to write a formal counseling statement against you both for disrespect, insubordination, and failure to repair."

Off they both went in a huff, but I did get my team's mail in the next five minutes.

It was not an unusual scene in the army. It was an NCO behaving pretty much as any NCO does when privates try to front them off.

So when I left, I forgot about it.

The next day, Ali took down a long message from the AOB, chastising me and by extension Mike, for "starting trouble" with the support people at Cap Haitien airport. They said that they had had trouble for quite some time with the mail, and this unit finally sorted it out, and that I had "jeapordized the AOB's relationship" with them.

I was stunned, and so was Mike. "Relationship?" They were a support unit. Getting us our mail was their job! The incident had started and finished with a pretty standard bit of military business. In fact, had I not corrected the troops at that unit, and any other NCO had seen it,

I would have been subject to disciplinary action myself for not carrying out my responsibilities as an NCO. This screed from the AOB was horseshit.

Mike wrote the whole incident and the AOB response off to the AOB being a bunch of bureaucratic pushovers who'd forgotten they were in the army. I took it as evidence of the frustration of the AOB at our foot-dragging with regard to the FAd'H and other resistance.

But it was more. We were now being placed under a microscope, but we didn't know it yet.

Major Fox started dropping by almost every day. He came on the 7th, and the 8th, of December. All my uneasiness about the ever-tightening control from the "center" was being confirmed. The original element of autonomy we had enjoyed was now being systematically squeezed out. If I had thought about it at the time, I would have realized that given the number of sites under the Cap Haitien AOB, two visits in two days to us didn't make mathematical sense. We were receiving special attention. The clammy hands of Bonaparte Schroer were busy, busy, busy behind the scenes.

When Fox came by on the 7th, he had changed. Always a man with a little too much starch in his shorts, he was now coldly detached. I gave him the news that Kenty had finally signed a warrant for the arrest of Brunot Innocent, and that the warrant was now the hopeful talk of the whole sector. He was absolutely unaffected. He was somewhere else altogether.

To this day, no one has begun the systematic prosecution of the *de facto* regime criminals. Many are being sheltered by the United States government, including Toto Constant, head of the FRAPH.

When Fox came by on the 8th, we became privy to at least one of his preoccupations. The whole task force was being "realigned." We were to prepared to leave Fort Liberte within the week, and be re-stationed at Petit Goave.

Kyle was delighted.

"Finally!" he said. "We're gonna leave this shit hole. And when we get there, we are gonna do whatever they've been doing. . . not make anything up!"

"You been promoted?" I asked. "When we get to Ti Goave, are you gonna be the team sergeant? Or have you been commissioned? Maybe you're gonna be a captain."

My sarcasm was met by dead stares all around, except from Mike, who shifted around uncomfortably with the tension surfacing again.

On December 9th, Kyle and Dave Grau took their down day in Cap Haitien. They left at nine in the morning, and didn't get back until almost dark. Both of them went to their sleeping quarters, where they diddled with equipment, paged through smut, and generally avoided company.

87 : Fifteen Dash Six

December 10th. The anniversary of something, somewhere.

Mike and I rose early. We woke the team early. Activities were scheduled to avalanche us that day, so we started quickly, folks bursting into the bathroom behind the last occupant, tugging on uniforms. We had to send a vehicle to Cap Haitien with Ali and Kyle. An IPM bird was due in at nine to carry off our Bolivian colleagues. Admiral Richards was due in at eight for a visit. The exchange team was due in at an unannounced time to begin the tedious and (for me) sad business of transition.

Water pots were dropped into the glowing charcoal to make instant coffee. The Dutch oven lid was jammed between them, full of hot oil that exploded around frying eggs. James had picked up bread that was still warm from the oven. I ate oatmeal only, gazing with some consternation at the little boa of fat that had begin to nest around my navel. Gonzo was on radio watch, contented to have a responsibility wherein he could avoid human interaction. Mike and I were fully outfitted, prepared to dash out to the LZ and meet Richards and company. Dave was in his room, looking even more strangely agitated and evasive that had become the norm. He was busily shuffling papers, preparing we assumed to link up with the new IPM representatives, since he was our designated liaison.

Admiral Richards was on time. We picked him up with his ever-present, stone faced female captain in the Oakleys, his SEAL team and Delta bodyguards, and a lieutenant colonel who wore that "I'm really a civilian" apologetic look. The four-seated Hummer had been deemed unsafe for the trip to Cap, so we used it to pick up the Task Force commanders entourage. Besides it had more seating. Arriving at Fort Dauphin just as the dust drifted off the Blackhawk in the breeze, I drove back, while Mike chatted up the visitors. The Admiral rode in the right front seat, a position reserved for the highest ranking person, if you go for that kind of convention.

The visit went as always, routine now, until we dropped off the group at the LZ for their departure. Mike returned from a short conversation with Admiral Richards looking shaken. The admiral had made some pointed but obscure comment about watching our security. Mike, ever sensitive to these coded communications among officers, was visibly upset. He had come to hate any indication that anyone was in any way dissatisfied with our work here.

Mike speculated frantically about what the comment meant on the way back to the house. Did it pertain to Boyatt's visit days earlier, when the chopper landed without warning, and Boyatt had traipsed into the house before we could scramble his vehicle? Had Boyatt been poisoned at last by Schroer? What kind of "security" had he referred to?

We were in the house for only a few moments, me trying to calm Mike in spite of my own grave misgivings about what it might mean, when Gonzo called into the foxmike, "Army aviation, Army aviation, this is Delta Six Tango, over." The other bird was inbound.

Pedro and Dave had apparently already departed to the Bayara Hotel, so Mike and I re-scrambled, snatching rifles and web gear, and tached over to the LZ on the weak clunking springs of the four seater over the pitted causeway.

The entire party, I have forgotten the nationality now, needed only a ride to the hotel. We accommodated them. On the way, we passed Major Fox (Wherethefuckdidhecomefrom?) in a Hummer with some young major we did not know. He signalled to meet us at the house. We acknowledged.

At the hotel, the original Bolivians were hauling equipment onto a five-ton truck. We were shocked, again. No one had mentioned (that is, Dave hadn't mentioned) that the IPMs would be leaving today. Too quickly we exchanged a mushy *despidida* with our Bolivian counterparts, Mike becoming upset at the rush. He had been moved by the birthday party they had thrown him, and was looking forward to the opportunity to reciprocate.

"This is so fucked up," he lamented in the Hummer on the way to the team house. "They're takin' our town and givin' it to someone else. Richards thinks were soup. Can't say goodbye the right way. And now fuckin' Fox shows up. What's he doing? What else can go wrong? This is just fuckin' depressing." He slowly shook his head. "Remind me to put this one in my journal."

A person who gets run over by a bus does not think five seconds before it happens about the possibility of it happening, or it wouldn't happen. He reviews his "to do" list for the day, recalls last night's sex act, reminds himself that Grandma's birthday is coming, calculates how he will find the money to replace the water pump on the car, worries that Junior will be forced to repeat the third grade, all stuff Sartre called writing blank checks on eternity. Crossing the street is just one of those mindless instrumental activities. We all live a good part of the time in denial of the abrupt, messy, careless nature of Fate's little confrontations. Just when our hero decides how to pay for the pump, the solution suddenly clear, he congratulates himself, forgets for an instant to look away from the stiff breeze that covers the noise of the bus engine, and his life changes irrevocably.

Major Fox and Major McCoart, the latter of whom we did not know, were standing stiffly on the porch when we set the brake on the hummer, killed the engine, and stepped out. We both tried on the phony smiles of subordinates as we pulled our rifles out and mounted the steps. The smiles were not returned. Something gripped by stomach, and danger signals began to explode all over my skin. I became very, very alert.

"This is Major McCoart," he announced flatly. Mike and I took turns shaking his hand, though I must have regarded him like a viper. He had that legal, bloodless, executioner's look. "He is here to conduct an Article fifteen dash six investigation of misconduct by this team."

Mike and I exchanged a confused, beseeching glance.

"Before I begin," said Fox, flipping to the right reference on his clipboard (one I had just noticed), "I need to advise you both of your rights under Article 31 of the Uniform Code of Military Justice." This was the military equivalent of Miranda. This was serious. He read the text of Article 31. I had heard it before. I had read it to others.

Then the charges began. There was a discrepancy in our ammunition status report, and a reference to the firepower demonstration of October 14th.

I relaxed a bit. This was going to be easy to explain, all perfectly legal and authorized.

"That's easy," I explained. McCoart held his hand up for me to be silent. I obeyed.

Fox continued. It was alleged that we had operated in contravention to General Order 1, with regard to the alcohol prohibition. I was suddenly glad McCoart had shut me up. We had consumed alcohol, permitted the team to consume alcohol, and displayed unprofessional behavior while under the influence of alcohol.

Who? rang in my head, Who? Who? Who? What motherfucker was diming out this team? This was chickenshit. The whole fucking task force was drinking outside of PAP and Cap, and everyone knew it. Was it the Tactical Psyops Team, upset that I wouldn't let them broadcast their prevarications to our sector? Had some born-again visitor seen an empty Presidente bottle? Were the boys talking too freely at Cap on their visits? Was this a fishing expedition by the FOB to gain a confession to punish us for some attitude offense?

The ammunition issue was pure horse shit, and I had not a shred of a doubt that I could justify it to anyone. But the alcohol was a perfect legal weapon in the hands of someone like Schroer, whom Mike and I both immediately suspected of being behind this fishy-eyed treatment. My future, like that of the bus victim, suddenly had a gaping void in it.

We were guarded and searched. Our footlockers were searched. Our bags were searched. Our rucksacks were searched. Our things were pulled out, opened, peered into, and discarded on the floor like trash. Our magazines were emptied. Our weapons were cleared. Major McCoart sternly noted that my 9mm was off safe, which is how I always carried it, hammer down, making it no different than any double action police revolver. Mike and I were segregated for the search— so we couldn't signal to one another I suppose. Socks were unrolled. Caps popped off shaving cream cans were tossed carelessly aside. My gas mask was disassembled, every snap and band. My belongings were spread, like my dignity, on the floor.

Self-recrimination, a most pointless and irresistible creature, emerged and filled my consciousness. We should have been more humble, I thought. We could have chosen different battles. . . not the hair and the sleeves and the anal uniform policies. The value of accommodation is never more apparent that when defeat is suddenly imminent. My self-flagellation was interrupted by a flash of insight.

Dave!

For a fleeting moment I thought of our own team tech. Dave might have been the stool pigeon. Hadn't he just been to Cap Haitien the day before? Wasn't his loathing for Mike and me more tangible by the day? Hadn't I been warning Mike that he appeared to be subverting the command element? Was I being paranoid?

In the interest of paying attention to the concrete facts of our new-found situation, I filed the suspicion away with a host of others.

1985 again. I had had a similar experience in conjunction with a massive investigation involving a former unit I had belonged to that year. A trap that closed silently and inexorably. I knew, from 1985, that until I better understood what was happening, silence was my only defense. When you are massively outgunned, you do not fire and give away your position.

In a moment we had to confer beside the majors' Hummer, I whispered to Mike that we needed to say nothing until we saw a lawyer. Stonefaced, he assented with a nod.

We loaded the Hummer with our clumsily repacked equipment, having been told that we were summarily suspended from our duties as team leader and team sergeant of Special Forces Operational Detachment 354. We were being transported to Cap Haitien, where we would be kept pending the outcome of the investigation.

There were no handcuffs. In the strictest definition of the law, we were not. . . but we were. . . under arrest.

88: Goodbye Fort Liberte

As comfortably as I could, I settled in the back seat of the Hummer next to Mike. The confusion, anger, fear, and depression that took turns dominating my consciousness would stay with me for longer than I could realize at that moment.

While we had been packing and loading our gear, Major McCoart disappeared into the back of the house, from whence neither Gonzo, Pedro, nor Dave, all back at the house now, came out. Everyone was being searched and, we assumed, questioned.

I feared one loose Presidente cap kicked carelessly under some-one's clothes. I feared the animosity of my men. I tried vainly to reas-sure myself that none of them would rat out members of their own team, even with our differences. That was an unspoken law in SF. All of them, after all, had enjoyed the relaxation of policy. All of them had laughed at the General Order as they signed it, with its preposterous prohibitions against local food, pets, and the like, in Guantanamo Bay.

Gigash's mother walked past and waved, decelerating as she noticed the gear loaded on the hummer and the stony looks worn by Mike and me. Her smile twisted into confusion, and her palms went skyward in a question.

"*Nous allons*," I said. She responded in Creole, in words I didn't know, but in a tone I understood.

"*Oui,*" I told her. For good. I held out my hand, and she took it. "*Au revoir. Explique tout moun pour moi sak pase,*" I told here, hoping my maimed French and Creole made some sense.

"*Oui,*" she answered. I hoped she understood. Explain what happened to everyone. It had just occurred to me that I was not going to have the opportunity to say goodbye to my friends.

Jessi walked up, having just returned from the market. She had the same astonished look. I stepped out of the Hummer, gave her a quick hug around the shoulders, careful not to upset her basket of groceries, and told her, "*Bon chance.*" Looking at the ground, I dropped back into the seat of the vehicle. Jessi went into the house. I thought of Adele, her brother, Dumas the mad fisherman, Eaulin, the orphan, Noogie, Freddy, Ronnie, Etias. . .

When we pulled out, I was unabashedly in tears.

The ride to Cap was excruciatingly slow. We passed under the arch, through Sicar, the thorny pastures on the way to Carrefour Chivry, Savanne Carrie, Malfety, Terrier Rouge, past the sisal fields with their endless acres of dead porcupines, the rivers, the stubbornly green valleys, the endless lines of women carrying Haiti on their heads, the donkeys, the pigs, the goats with triangles lashed to their necks, the skinny horses carrying skinny men, the dusty naked children squealing and waving, the loafers and gamblers, the marketeers, all of them, everyone. They still waved.

It was an effort, but I followed my own now antiquated directive, and I waved back. It was the only defiance I could allow myself, so I forced a smile for the wild children charging the road to wave, giving them what I could not give my own countrymen. Besides, I really was pro-Haitian.

When we passed the fording site at Trou du Nord, Kyle, Ali, and Fritz drove past us, going the other way. They were returning from Cap. We waved weakly, and they reciprocated weakly. I grew a little restive at the lack of surprise they exhibited.

Mike and I exchanged a few quiet comments, but remained mostly silent. Across from the plantation headquarters, where Gonzo and I had explored the equipment graveyard, we pulled off the road and took a collective piss.

I smoked pretty constantly as we rode. As the familiar scenery rolled past, I tried to boost my psyche into it. . . out of myself. . . but there was no way. The bus had hit. I would reassure Mike that it was all a fishing expedition organized by our enemies at the FOB, but my bowels knew. All that remained was to sort out the injuries, to see what was left us when the dust cleared.

We passed the familiar landmarks, cane fields, mills, gas markets, shops, the bridge over the filthy river full of patchwork boats, the hole in the road in front of the port with the bush sticking out to mark it for vehicles. We finally passed the rows of tents on the right, the aligned vehicle park on the left. Everything familiar. Everything devoid of significance. Only an uncomfortable suspense was left me. I knew that Mike felt the same way.

We were put up with our gear in a supply tent at the north end of the point, where the FOB was concentrated. Tents clustered there. Generators growled. Televisions played VCR tapes. Camouflage nets were strung everywhere to provide shade. Men wore a combination of PT clothes or partial uniforms. Under the nets was the safe area, uniform relaxation. Two guys played poor chess with bored expressions.

It felt like we were members of a tribe of wild people who had been captured and brought back to a fortress of curiously inhibited, tight-assed people. It felt like a scene from *Dances with Wolves*, like we were the white men who had "turned injun."

People treat you funny when you're about to be excommunicated. They still greet you and exchange amenities. But they don't want to get too close. It's like you have a communicable disease.

Mike and I had agreed to talk to no one except one another, and to tell one another everything. We weren't sure why, but we sensed that our absolute solidarity was necessary to survive in our newfound wilderness. We agreed that they would probably try to drive some wedge between us. . . to get us to turn on one another so we would each support the attempt to press some kind of charges against the other.

The first day in Cap Haitien was interminable. Our first interrogations—investigative interviews—were to be tomorrow. We had to start writing statements that day. So we collaborated on our stories for those statements, carefully synchronizing our stories, and tweaking one another's statements to ensure that we knew exactly where to stop, exactly when to say that we would say no more without a lawyer, and filling our account with anecdotes of our successes.

89: INVESTIGATION

Mike was the first interrogated by Major McCoart, the investigating officer. When he came back from the "interview," he was pale.

"They fuckin' rolled on us."

"Who, Mike?"

"All of them. The boys. Every one of them wrote statements against us, telling everything and even making a bunch of shit up."

"Like what?"

"The beer. The comments you made about intel being fucked up. They're claiming that I had lost control of the team to you. They got the batman shit in there. They even got the stuff we said about Schroer in there. They came down real hard on you, Stan."

"How?"

"Saying you're a commie. Saying you took sides with Haitians against the team. Shit like that."

"It's Grau, Mike. Grau set this shit up."

"He may have," said Mike. He was still skeptical. "But it could have been one of the visiting officers, or someone else we pissed off, or whatever."

"It's Grau, Mike. Grau was down here with Barrington yesterday. He's been organizing little meetings with the boys since he got back.

Grau wants your job. He wants to be the team leader."

That turned the light on.

"That motherfucker! He was down here yesterday!"

We would eventually find out that not only was it true, but Grau had been writing things down ever since he returned to Haiti. He had turned over a deep pile of paper to the AOB in Cap Haitien. Major Fox had asked him twice if he was sure he wanted to do this. Dave insisted. I would find in the course of the investigation that Fox's reluctance to accept Grau's indictments was based on his foreknowledge that we were probably facing relief in the near future on the grounds that we had refused to let the psyopers "do their jobs" and other "infractions." Grau's introduction of alcohol, an issue the SF folks wanted kept separate from anything involving conventional commanders, would force the SF commanders to crack down in an area where they didn't really want to crack down.

But alcohol was the last thing on Major McCoart's mind when he talked to me. We dismissed the subject out of hand. He asked if we had used it, and I said I would address that in the presence of a lawyer. He was satisfied with that, and moved on.

His real emphasis began with the question of why I had not allowed the psyopers to broadcast their messages. I told him that we had spent weeks and weeks establishing ourselves on our credibility, that we dealt straight with the Haitians and they dealt straight with us. I told him that these recorded messages were scoffed at by the population, that they were considered to be bald propaganda for ulterior purposes, and I didn't want them associated with us.

He responded by asking if I thought a soldier had a right to select which orders he followed. I told him that I when I stopped the broadcast, I had not been ordered to allow it.

He asked what about the messages I objected to. I told him that Haitians objected to them. I was being very cagey. I felt a trap about to be sprung.

He changed course. Did I in fact tell foreign and US journalists that the CIA was fucked up, and that it was probably part of the coup?

I told anyone who asked what everyone knows about Haiti and about the CIA. I didn't say anything that was classified. I didn't tell anyone that the CIA had been involved in the coup. I told them that there were connections between the CIA and the FRAPH. It was in the newspapers. Everyone already knew it. If I sugar-coated it, I would lose credibility.

Don't you think this borders on sedition¿

Only if honesty is tantamount to sedition.

This kind of sparring went on for over two hours.

What about my relationship with Lavalas¿

What about it¿

Do you think you are pro-Lavalas¿

What does that mean¿

Do you think you favored Lavalas over other groups¿

What other groups¿

Groups other than Lavalas¿

I don't know of any other popular groups besides Lavalas¿

Do you think you are anti-FAd'H¿

Yes.

Why are you against the FAd'H¿

Have you talked to Haitians about what all they did¿ They're criminals.

But we were told to work with them.

I did. I worked with them every day.

Your team members said you showed unremitting hostility to them.

I was ordered to work with them, not like them.

Are you anti-FRAPH¿

Yes.

Why¿

They're a death squad network.

According to the task force command, they are to be treated as the legitimate political opposition.

They're still death squads. Were we ordered to work with them, too¿

No, you weren't ordered to work with them. But it sounds like you harassed them.

I arrested them when I had permission.

You arrested a man with diplomatic immunity, too.

How can someone have diplomatic immunity in his own country when he's not an ambassador any more¿

Didn't your own team warn you that you shouldn't arrest Nyll Calixte¿

My team also wanted to move into his hotel. I ran the team.

Have you read the intelligence reports on the activities of Lavalas¿

Sure.

Have you seen how much violence they are responsible for¿

I dismissed the intelligence reports.

You did what¿

I dismissed them. They were never accurate when I had anything to test them against.

Don't you think that endangered your team?

No. The intelligence reports read more like anti-Aristide propaganda than they do as information summaries.

Do you think your government is engaging in propaganda?

Certainly. They always have. You know they do.

Did you take sides with Haitians against your own team?

That's absurd. How could I do that?

Did you take the word of Haitians ahead of your team?

If something had to do with our sector or with the business of Haitians, of course, I relied on the Haitians before my team. They don't know any more about Haiti than I do.

Did you tell a member of your team that Vietnam was a race war?

Yes.

You don't think that's seditious?

Where did this word "sedition" come from? I am still entitled to my own beliefs, am I not?

Of course, of course you are. But "race war?"

Were you in Vietnam?

No, I'm afraid that was before my time.

It wasn't before my time. I was there. In my opinion, regardless of what the national objectives might have been, on the ground it played out as a race war.

It seems you are awfully sensitive about the subject of race.

I wasn't as cool inside as I was out. I was terrified. I was due to retire soon, and I didn't know whether there was enough to prosecute me or not.

McCoart got on the issue of race, and he described the incident with Gator the night I went off on him. He asked me if I had lost my comportment, and I admitted that I had. He checked his notes and referred to my reported comments from the incident that Special Forces was a racist organization. Had I meant that?

Here we were. We were on the subject of the "dirty little secret."

I told him I found a lot of racism in Special Forces, that I had seen racism in the Q-Course, that racism was openly tolerated on the teams and overlooked by the commanders. I didn't realize it at the time, but I may have been saving myself.

He wanted to know how I defined racism.

Disparate treatment of people by other people and institutions based on skin color. (It was a half-assed definition, but it sufficed for the moment.)

Do you consider members of your team racist?

Yes.

Do you know of any racist commanders in Special Forces?

Yes.

How come you haven't reported them?

Because being a racist is not against the law in the army. The threshold for proving racism is very high.

Don't you think, he asked, don't you think that sometimes you might be a little oversensitive?

No.

But don't you think, I mean, can you call it racist, I mean, no one should tolerate the "N" word (Thespian expression of pain and distaste here), but do you think it's racist when the troops get frustrated with Haitians and just refer to them as "the fucking Haitians?"

He was miserable. He had painted himself into his own corner. So I asked him what he thought.

He bantered on for about four paragraphs, torturing his explanation with stops and restarts, contradicting himself, adding explanations to support his explanations. . . For that moment, I had become the skilled interrogator.

We went over my "obsession" with Brunot Innocent, my Lavalas "contacts," my relationship with Adele, my threats to the FAd'H, and on and on. For an investigation that ostensibly was focused on ammunition expenditures and beer drinking, we spent an inordinate amount of time discussing my "too cozy" relationship with Lavalas.

We were busted on the beer.

I knew it and Mike knew it. Mike began spinning out strategies to show how widespread violations of General Order One were. I had a different agenda. I had to retire.

I got a call through to Sherry. I was very nervous about laying the whole mess on her, but she had to be in the loop. I was in trouble again, the year after I had been in trouble with Somalia, and now it was our retirement—the centerpiece of our immediate plans to start fresh—that was in jeopardy. She had nothing to do with this mess, and here I was, dragging her into another crisis. I was prepared to accept and bear the burden of any and all recriminations.

When I got her on the phone, I explained the situation. Without the least hesitation, the first question she asked me was "Are you all right?"

I shall never forget that. My friend, my lover, my comrade, my co-parent, and my partner—she asked me if I was all right. I was suddenly no longer isolated. I looked out over the ocean to the north, and knew that somewhere on another patch of this planet, standing at the phone in the house where I'd left her behind three months earlier, someone loved me. She'll never know how that simple question put the floor back under my feet.

I had seen what happened to other exiles. They were sent back to become slaves for the Operations office at Group headquarters in Fort Bragg. The thought of ever donning a uniform again, of ever contributing another ounce of energy to the Army, made my stomach turn. I wanted to drink.

Knowing that I couldn't handle what was coming, I decided to do something I had been considering for several years. I wrote a statement declaring my intention upon returning to Fort Bragg to enroll in an alcohol recovery program. I needed some space and time to reorganize the chaos in my head.

Two days later, in Gonaives, Mike and I stood before Lieutenant Colonel Schroer. He read and signed our official orders relieving us of our positions as Team Leader and Team Sergeant. His face was a mask of petty triumph. It was the first time I saw a smile cross his lips—if that's what you could call the sickly grimace. Lieutenant Colonel Schroer's sleeves were perfectly pressed and neatly buttoned at the wrist.

90: ESCAPE

When we went before our real Battalion Commander and his Sergeant Major, they seemed sad. LTC Jones liked us. He said we had the best combat focus of any team he'd ever seen in Group. Command Sergeant Major Gordon Smith, whom I had served with in 7th Group a few years earlier, sat us down and got our side of the story.

Gordon Smith called Gary Jones back in and said that it was obvious to him that 354 had developed a clique. Smith and Jones were professionals—real professionals—and they hated cliques. Jones made the decision then and there to break up ODA 354. Within two days, the team we had trained and deployed to Haiti no longer existed.

Jones told us to lay low. He feared that he couldn't protect us from the draconian actions that might be meted out by 10th Mountain Division, whose overall command we were still under.

So we hid out in the Mev complex at Port-au-Prince for four more days, then two days at the airfield, and somehow Jones got us on a plane and sent us home.

On December 23rd, I was with my spouse and children again in Fayetteville, North Carolina.

91 : Negotiations

Gary Jones and Gordon Smith were not typical of the whole Army. Their co-assignment was one of those—for the troops—happy coincidences.

When I got back to Bragg, the reactionaries, careerists, and bureaucrats were sharpening their knives. I was called into the office of the Group Sergeant Major the day after the holiday break, and informed that the Army was considering the preparation of a court-martial.

I asked what the charges would be, and I got a lecture on insubordination, violation of orders, unprofessional conduct, the whole list.

So I told the Sergeant Major that even if the Army chose to offer me non-judicial punishment—which is less than a court-martial—that I would turn it down and demand a court-martial. But when it happened, I said, I intended to talk about a lot of things. I intended to talk about racist propaganda passed off as intelligence summaries, about the incident at Belladere, which I considered a gross cover-up, and about violations of General Order One I had observed at every level of command at every site I had seen. Yes, I wanted a court-martial. I was fighting for my life here, I told him, and I would take off the gloves. I would make a court-martial into a mud wrestling show, and I didn't give a shit who got splattered.

The next day he called me back to his office. He addressed me by my first name.

"Stan," he said. "You've actually had a pretty distinguished career in the Army. But these things've come to a head, and I'm not sure you'd ever be happy in the Special Forces community again. We think it might be in your best interest to retire."

I agreed. And the following year, that's exactly what I did.

Between then and now, I've been back to Haiti eight times. The first time I took two of my kids. I wanted them to see the real world.

I went back and saw some old friends, but I've made new ones. Political people. In that time, I have studied history, sociology, and political economy—not formally—on my own. A lot. Right now I'm delving into *The Attitude of the Worker's Party Towards Religion*, by Lenin. The information I needed, and the basis I needed to organize my own experience, I've found in the forbidden texts.

Haiti taught me what I was and showed me what I must become.

92: No Apologies

I can't count the mistakes. They are too numerous. My whole belief in the mission at first was just the beginning. Ignorance and miscalculation were my truest and most constant companions. I was often a fool, blinded by my socialization, bewildered by circumstances, manipulated by opportunists, and trapped by scoundrels. My best intentions could not have made anything right on this mission, because the mission was simply a clumsy but logical extension of my government's long standing approach toward Haiti. I was a reluctant tool, then a rebellious one. But I was still a tool, and when I became dull and dangerous, I was removed. This book may finally be the good that I can bring out of the whole operation... even out of a whole career. I know that when I left, I was resolved to learn. Nothing more, at first. Just learn. Having worked at that for some time now, I can recommend it to anyone. I always said that sound intelligence drives sound operations.

Some will claim that with this book I have bitten the hand that fed me. The Army. That's bullshit. I worked for the government of the United States of America, and had only sworn to protect the Constitution of that entity. I never took an oath to conceal stupidity, nor to ignore perfidy. This nation is composed of some 270,000,000 people. Most of them are not really represented by their government. I never took an oath to defend the consolidations of monetary power that pilot the ship of state for their own narrow purposes. I resented the fact that the armed services have been employed to protect the financial interests of the powerful few abroad, and I emphatically resented the way we have had sunshine pumped right up our asses in lieu of the truth. I shall never forget nor forgive the propagandists who talked me into Vietnam. They lied. They lied about El Salvador, and Nicaragua, and Panama, and Grenada, and about the so-called War on Drugs. They had the nerve to talk of a war to "liberate" Kuwait. And the NATO aggression in the Balkans combined brutality with stupidity in the most stunning way. As I write this, the baleful eye of capital is turning on Colombia. I believe that keeping silence is the antithesis of loyalty to one's nation, because it assumes one's nation is embodied in its rich and influential, and not in the masses of its deceived and sweating citizens.

The power elite of this nation did not pay me. Citizen taxpayers did, and to them I say thank you. I owe them my livelihood for twenty plus years, and I owe them an honest account, at least as honest as I can give them. The honest assessment I have of Haiti is that I don't honestly know how it will turn out. A nation with nothing has little to lose, but I am unhappy at how much the US did to bring Haiti to the state in which it finds itself. I am determined to continue to tell people about CIA ties with Emmanuel Constant, the military theft of Haitian documents to cover up our government's crimes there, about the ties with the power elite in Haiti that were being forged by the US military. I was an instrument of imperialism for quite a long time before I realized what I had become. I learned what I was, and began learning who I must become in Ayiti.

Ayiti grinds abstractions down, one bare foot at a time, not with a killing twist, but with a light and passing tread, the way rocks are smoothed by the sea, in an amplitude of days. In *Ayiti*, those days are long with children. The sky there paints your retinas with the coming and going of the sun. That sun is luminous and liquid and confronts containment. *Ayiti* is the girl with buds for breasts, and the first black spots of decay between her incisors, crushing the skin of her abdomen in her fists, like a dish rag, to show you there's no food in there, all the while smiling and looking you smack in the eye.

Ayiti is the bubble and bump of Creole drifting up from the dust cloud in a schoolyard. It's sharing a metal cup of syrupy coffee—hot as the rocks—with bees on the roadside, and paying for it with money that's crumbled nearly to ashes; the plaintive grip of *ti enfant* on your startled finger; the clear wind on the clear water around Fort Dauphin, and the bicycle hordes that clutter the wharf when a ship comes in.

Ayiti is mountains and murder and resistance, all covered in paths that lead always back to the beginning, forming a serpentine perimeter against the Northern weapons of inquiry. *Ayiti* is the insane majesty of The Citadel next to the insane necessity of the *caille paille*. It is the straight strong necks of women bearing baskets—bearing *Ayiti* on their heads. It is the shining black backs of women bent over rivers full of cloth, and the scaly-bark hands of old men with machetes and pink gums abandoned by all but a tooth.

Ayiti is the sum of the ribs and sores of dismayed horses. It is the cemetery full of stirred bones and flowering vines, reminding me that I, too, am an island, and like Fort Liberte, on the Eastern frontier of my Western years. *Ayiti* is the sum of day-to-day insurgency and adaptation in the face of western capitalism that chose this Republic of the Slave Rebellion with which to make an example—the ongoing lynching of a society—and as an overflow valve for the subordinated misery of a hemisphere under the heel of profiteers.

Every Haitian knows the meaning of 1804. Now I do too. To the *blan* still occupying with his armed surrogates and his banks, I ask, who knows what the revolutionary bicentennial might bring?

93: No Conspiracies

It's essential to connect the specific with the general.

I wasn't expelled from Haiti as part of some grand conspiracy. A group of florid, cigar-smoking master planners did not get together in a little room and say, let's take care of this problem with the little pinko in Fort Liberte. Things don't work that way.

As Smedley Butler, a former Marine Corps Medal of Honor winner turned critic of capitalism, once said: "The flag follows the money, and the troops follow the flag." That's about as nice a summation of the general situation as anyone could come up with. People specifically satisfy their needs and interests. The banker follows his interests, and provides money to the politician, who follows his own interests, interest which are now in concert with the banker's interests. The reporter with the corporate press knows what does and doesn't please the boss, and she follows her interests—that often being not to offend the editor, who doesn't want to offend the owners: The reporter also doesn't want to jeopardize her access to "official sources" at the embassy. The General doesn't want to risk his career around the reporters, nor does he want to buck the directives of the foreign policy hack or the defense contractor who is holding his post-retirement position. The mid-level officers read into the problem, so when they see what the real tenor of their mission is, they bend their subordinates to the task. The soldier wants to stay out of trouble, maybe has some ambitions, and can't live with the idea that what he does might be fundamentally wicked, so he seeks the rationalizations they need. The sergeant has to make the soldier fight, if necessary, so he has to instill contempt for the value of the people who the soldier may be called upon to kill. So it goes.

So there was no conspiracy. The system simply exercised its logic on me. That logic played out in the innumerable little dramas described in this book. I stepped out of my line, and they rest of them just walked over me. So while I can say categorically that there was no conspiracy, I can say just as categorically that I was ejected from Haiti because of the direction my politics took me. To call it a conspiracy would be like calling the action of a phagocyte a conspiracy. It's a system.

I wish more so-called progressives understood this. Vietnam and Nicaragua and the Gulf War and Haiti and the NATO attack on Yugoslavia and the deepening involvement in Colombia, these are not screw-ups in the system. They are an integral facet of the system. To stop this insanity, there is no choice but to replace the system. There's no doubt that the system uses conspiracies as a tool, but they are not the essence of the system. The essence of the system is profit.

Racism—if you look closely—is about profit. The whole system was built on it. War—if you look closely—is about profit. Poverty, which is not, and never has been, an accident—if you look closely—is about profit.

EPILOGUE

I feel like I have aged decades since I was expelled from Haiti, retired from the army, and began writing this account. Certainly I have become much clearer. I'm only supposed to relate—to be evocative—because I'm a soldier, and if I begin to tread in the realm of theory, if I begin to form conclusions, I become threatening, and I lose my charm. But I've already broken a whole jar full of taboos, so fuck it.

Annie Dillard once wrote, "Evolution loves death more than it loves you and me." Nature is based on real choices that conform only to laws of nature—amoral and ruthlessly impartial. No one intervenes when you miss the turn on a mountain pass, and no one intervenes when a bunch of drugged-up teenagers slaughter an old woman hoeing her potato patch.

Average Americans, part of a TV culture raised on a steady diet of neat, moral resolutions, with a conditioned attention span of one to two hours, are often incapable of grasping this kind of reality. Trapped in our individualism, cut off from community and its identification with the collective and with history, anesthetized by bread and circuses, many sharing in the loot of our world domination, we are left with only our self-absorbed vanity. Not the vanity of the mirrors in chic gymnasiums (though that's part of our pathology for those who have the privileges of money and time), but the vain pursuit of compulsive sensual gratification and status through acquisition.

The subjective reality of late capitalism has become a journey alone, with every other an instrument, in a desert where one clothes oneself against the stark glare of mortality in the robes of denial of death. Comfortable American white folks are soft in this interior reality. They can not sit with the hard reality that there is no happily ever after. So the interior "reality" is forever divided from the exterior one of necessity. We acknowledge necessity only through our actions, working, sleeping, eating and excreting, absolutely inseparable from the concrete, with only our consciousness divorced from material reality. I can't forget Ronnie chiding me that Haitians are ever aware of their mortality.

Values are socially transmitted, and the paradox of this society, the paradox that secures the door of society's rulers—who manufacture those values—against resistance, is that our core social value is individualism. And so we seek individual gratification, individual meaning, and individual salvation. Solidarity is subverted, and the majority-obsessed is neutralized from intervention in its own history. Individualism is a bourgeois ideology, deployed in the service of the bourgeoisie, and as such antagonistic to the aspirations of everyone else—but the domination of society's economic life becomes domination of its ideas, and we are all contaminated with it.

I call the bourgeoisie that now, because that is the correct word. I have become a devotee of precision of terms. "Some people think we can make the revolution while the bourgeoisie is asleep," said a Haitian friend. "But the bourgeoisie never sleeps, and we must make the revolution right in front of them."

A disclaimer. Before I say what is on my mind with regard to religion, I want to acknowledge that there are impulses in religion that are becoming revolutionary, because they validate material reality and community, and accept necessity. I have no fight with these theologies of liberation. We are often in community in practice. The *Ti Eglis* used to be an example of this.

Religion is a persistent force not because human beings are spiritual, but because they are material. They fear individual extinction. Spirituality is the tough brown skin of the onion, but under that is layer upon naked layer of denial—denial of the evidence of the senses, denial of the evidence of science, denial of the evidence of history—and at the center is pure, unadulterated dread of the inevitable. Each and all of us shall become corpses. Our response to this realization comes directly from the adrenal cortex. Pure epinephrine. Fight or flight. It's the most natural response in the world; a primitive purely physiological evolutionary defense mechanism in response to an awareness so evolved it sees the one sure future. The universe is a dead thing, and in the end it will swallow us each back up into all that deadness... forever. You will not be back. I will not be back. We shall disappear.

When religion is no longer tenable, when learning and science has swept it into space and into utter diffusion, individualists often seek surrogate religions. "Nature" personified undergoes an apotheosis. The reactionary impulse, flowering out of the parched earth of isolation and dread, sends us running backward, where we seek to become Druids, astrology-buffs, pagans, nature-worshippers, new-agers, or fascists.

For some the contradiction is overwhelming, the alienation complete, and they embrace nihilism. We wonder about Colombine High School? For those without learning and science, there is fundamentalism—that hard-shelled orthodoxy built like a sandbag bunker against the inevitable, and against change itself—emblematic of our personal transience. *Leviticus* and *Deuteronomy* instead of *Origin of the Species* and *Capital*, or Khalil Gibran instead of Franz Fanon. Individual salvation and individual awareness in place of species, society, class, none of which can go away. Individualism is denial.

This is not all that religion is, but it is certainly what accounts for the persistence of the religious impulse. This thesis will touch some raw nerves, but it can't be helped. These things need to be said, because we are aiming for the extinction of our species until we come to grips with what we won't say. I've seen our future in the deforested and sterile stretches of Haiti and in the staggering misery there. I may also have seen our collective salvation in the indomitable will to resist. . . collectively.

Religion helps us deny death, and in that I stand opposed to religion. This central denial allows us all the other ones, and especially the denial of necessity.

Society is a superstructure of culture and art and religion and politics, but it is also its material foundation—its instruments and means of survival through production, exchange, and distribution, with all the attendant social relations. Marx was absolutely right. The fact that we can not live apart from society, that we are thoroughly interdependent, is—like all facts—deniable, but inescapable. Human beings evolved into our present form and status as social creatures, not as individualists, because this was the choice made by natural law. Natural law does not care one whit for the individual, who it lashes forward in search of food and shelter and copulation. Nature sets its judgment on the species. It's a simple formula of the capacity to reproduce as fast or faster than the multitude of accidents that whiz around it or inside its genetic code can kill it off. I didn't need a college course to learn that Marx was right. The army sent me out to learn how right he was. Every student of Sociology and Economics and Political Science needs to be dropped into Derac and forced to spend a week there.

Human beings have evolved the capacity to "take over" from evolution. We have come to direct our own future. But we do that collectively, not individually. We can not find solutions to the threat of global anarchy, to nuclear winter, to global climate change, to the loss of arable land, to the elite hoarding of global resources except as a collective, and these are real threats to our species. They are created and perpetuated by a system that exalts the competitive individual, and that develops with no coordination between its parts. The penalty for individual mistakes in nature is death, and as we have come to insulate ourselves from the consequences of our own mistakes in the short run, nature will surely exact its price collectively and over the long run. If you want to see our ultimate future under capitalism, look at Haiti.

If we are to conform to necessity and survive, our species must shed the doctrine of individualism that cuts us off from one another and from community. As an interior reality, this means identification not with the self, but of the self with the community. It is a total reorientation of values, and one that renders moot the question of individual death. It does not nullify the adrenal cortex, but it neutralizes the preoccupation with mortality and thus the need for layer upon layer of denial and subterfuge. The exterior and interior substance is reconciled. Only the community can provide the context for meaningful individuality.

We love to talk about rights and choices. We all value our "entitlement" to an opinion, no matter how uninformed or destructive or bigoted or backward. This is part of our preoccupation with individualism. We have learned to ignore those rights to which the collective might be entitled, and we have failed to examine what makes a choice meaningful. A choice is only as meaningful as it is informed. When

Rod and Skye and I pursued Ti Ben into the thickets outside of Sicar, we chose freely at every trail junction. But not knowing anything about where Ti Ben might go or about what lay at the end of each section of trail, our freedom to chose was an empty abstraction.

In Haiti it's said that a voudon spirit is more real than a space capsule. A Haitian peasant knows the world through her pantheon, just as we know it through physics. How is it, then, that the average peasant from Terrier Rouge is more capable and prepared for what must be done to transform society than the average academic of Chapel Hill, who is probably college educated, probably understands something about how a space capsule works? The answer has something to do with self-interest, a characteristic the peasant and the academic share, and a real sense of community, something they do not. The academic is sharing in the bourgeois' loot, in a hundred little ways. And the peasant understands necessity as something that transcends morality. To be in community with that peasant, the Chapel Hill academic will have to commit class suicide. In community with one another, the peasant and the scholar, the worker and the doctor, the African with the Palestinian with the Colombian with the Filipino, the American with the Haitian, they might intervene in history and be the salvation of a species. If they can do what is necessary.

There are choices to be made. Nature is waiting with consequences and no bias about outcomes.

Disagree if you wish. You are certainly entitled to your opinion.

finis

INDEX